P9-BZS-637

BEETHOVEN'S MASK

Beethoven's Mask

Notes on My Life and Times

George Jonas

KEY PORTER BOOKS

Copyright © 2005 by George Jonas

All rights reserved. No part of this work covered by the copyrights hereon may be repro-
duced or used in any form or by any means—graphic, electronic, or mechanical, including
photocopying, recording, taping or information storage and retrieval systems—without the
prior written permission of the publisher, or, in case of photocopying or other reprographic
copying, a licence from Access Copyright, the Canadian Copyright Licensing Agency, One
Yonge Street, Suite 1900, Toronto, Ontario, M6B 3A9.

Library and Archives Canada Cataloguing in Publication

Jonas, George, 1935-
    Beethoven's mask : notes on my life and times / George Jonas.

Includes index.

ISBN 1-55263-710-7

    1. Jonas, George, 1935-. 2. Authors, Canadian (English)—20th century—Biography. 3.
Journalists—Canada—Biography. 4. Radio producers and directors—Canada—Biography.
5. Television producers
and directors—Canada—Biography. 6. Canadian Broadcasting Corporation—Officials and
employees—Biography. I. Title.

PS8519.O5Z46 2005   C818'.5409   C2005 902745-2

The publisher gratefully acknowledges the support of the Canada Council for the Arts and
the Ontario Arts Council for its publishing program. We acknowledge the support of the
Government of Ontario through the Ontario Media Development Corporation's Ontario
Book Initiative.

We acknowledge the financial support of the Government of Canada through the Book
Publishing Industry Development Program (BPIDP) for our publishing activities.

Picture Credits
Page 13:TL036588—© Peter Turnley/CORBIS; Page 89:BE080879—© Bettmann/CORBIS;
Page 147:HU056289—© Hulton-Deutsch Collection/CORBIS; Page 203:U1831240—©
Bettmann/CORBIS; Page 255:BE020394—© Bettmann/CORBIS; Page 275:HU006629—
© Hulton-Deutsch Collection/CORBIS; Page 299:BE085900—© Bettmann/CORBIS; Page
331:RE002238.—© Ric Ergenbright/CORBIS; Page 361:UT0093891—© Reuters/COR-
BIS. All other photographs are the property of the author.

Key Porter Books Limited
Six Adelaide Street East, Tenth Floor
Toronto, Ontario
Canada M5C 1H6

www.keyporter.com

Text design: Peter Maher
Electronic formatting: Jean Lightfoot Peters

Printed and bound in Canada

05 06 07 08 09 5 4 3 2 1

Past things shed light on future ones;
the world was always of a kind; what is and will be
was at some other time; the same things come back,
but under different names and colours;
not everybody recognizes them,
but only he who is wise and considers
them diligently.

FRANCESCO GUICCIARDINI, 1483–1540,

Storia d'Italia.

Contents

PART 3. TWELVE GOLDEN MULLETS

PART 4. ON BEING A MARTIAN

PART 8. IN PRAISE OF GOOD FENCES

PART 9. SHEEP YEARS AND TIGER DAYS

PREFACE

My father debuted as a soloist with the Viennese State Opera in the role of Renato, the betrayed husband in *Un Ballo In Maschera*. As he explained it later, his feelings were divided between delight and dismay. He was delighted by Verdi's music and dismayed by Antonio Somma's libretto, which was incongruous even by operatic standards. It was not entirely the librettist's fault, for 1859, when the opera was first performed, had been a volatile year. The crowned heads of Europe tossed and turned in their uneasy beds, and their subjects were equally restless. *Un Ballo In Maschera*, based on Scribe's play *Gustave III*, was originally set in the royal court of Sweden. In the Swedish version a prince masquerading as a blue domino wearing a red sash was cut down during a masked ball. This upset the censor. In Italy under the Bourbons the idea of assassinating a prince was too close for comfort. Felice Orsini had just missed blowing up Napoleon III the year before. The plot needed to be ethnically, geographically, and socially cleansed, so the censor deported it to the governor's mansion in colonial Boston. Without shifting its locale to America, Verdi's opera could not have premiered in Rome.

Father found it amusing, in a grim sort of way, that his breakthrough as a singer should come in an opera designed by a censor. The masked ball of Boston stayed on his mind long after his career as a baritone had ended. Reading in the 1950s that Milan's La Scala was going to give Verdi's opera again, with Maria Callas and Giuseppe di Stefano in the lead roles, supported by Tito Gobbi as Renato, my father exclaimed that the whole world reminded him of a masked ball.

"Europe is a carnival in Venice," he offered, "with assassins dressed up as lyric poets. Butchers lurk in ducal palaces wearing Beethoven's mask. The voice is Beethoven's, but the hand is Beria's."

Beria was the chief of Stalin's secret police.

As I was jotting down these notes about my life and times, my father's remark came back to me. As a soloist in my own beggar's opera, I have shared his dismay with the text and his delight with the tunes. Nothing has changed since 1859 except the cast. The Old World is still a carnival with Milosevic's hand reaching out from Beethoven's shirtsleeves. The New World is *un ballo in maschera* exiled to Boston, with officials superimposing European (and Middle Eastern) plots on Yankee landscapes. The curtain rises on assassins disguised as violins chasing blue dominos wearing red sashes to avenge "America's grief." *Sconterà dell'America il pianto.* Waiting in the wings is a muezzin with a loudspeaker, calling suicide bombers to prayer. Life continues to be an Italian opera, adjusted by the censor. The story is absurd, the music irresistible.

TORONTO, 2005

GJ

1

YESTERDAY'S
TOMORROW

1

EUROPE

BEFORE AND AFTER

The sun of Rome is set. Our day is gone.
Clouds, dews, and dangers come;
our deeds are done.
—SHAKESPEARE: *Julius Caesar*

IN 1935, WHEN I WAS BORN, the word "European" was still a synonym for "civilized" in popular parlance. Minimally, it was an antonym of "feral." Many people took it for granted that Europe was the pinnacle of human achievement, in matters spiritual as well as temporal. "European" was not only a word for a geographic location, but for a particular style and a set of values.

The Eurocentrism of the period was frank and unapologetic. It was also unselfconscious. Europe's superiority—moral, cultural, stylistic, even technological—seemed manifest. Did other civilizations of note exist on the planet? Yes, but only as history or myth. Mid-twentieth century Asia was nothing but Oriental despotism, chaos, and famine. Its legends of grandeur were lost in the mists of fable or antiquity. Lands of former greatness or self-containment, such as Turkey or Japan, seemed to be at war with their own cultures. In Turkey—portrayed in Edwardian English cartoons as "the sick man of Europe"—Westernizers of Kemal Atatürk's ilk were prodding their reluctant compatriots to emerge from under the wreckage of the Ottoman Empire. A similar process had been set in motion in Japan fifty years earlier, when after the Meiji Restoration of 1868, Japan's "young Turks" began dragging their compatriots from under the shadow of the old

Tokugawa shogunate. Though the worlds of the samurai and the Janissaries were no longer competitive, at least they still existed. In contrast, many South Asian civilizations had been altogether reclaimed by the jungle. The Khmer empire's Angkor Wat might have vanished without French explorers stumbling upon it in 1861. Africa, barely on the map, was noticeable only as Evelyn Waugh's *Black Mischief*: a place whose naked savagery, at once fearful and ridiculous, was put into even sharper (and more comic) relief by the British public school education of some of its leaders. Australia, Canada, and Latin America were largely beneath Europe's notice, except as dreary places of exile, or exotic, sometimes fabulous but often ill-starred adventures. The United States was thought to have been aptly described by Oscar Wilde, who called it a country that passed from barbarism to decadence without the intervening stage of civilization. It was a description that many Europeans, and more than a few Americans, viewed as not only amusing but accurate.

Initially, the rise of fascism only heightened the sense of Europe as an ideal. Those who supported fascism in its various guises routinely justified their support in terms of safeguarding European values against the savage influences and barbaric hordes at the gates. But those who opposed fascism often did so in the name of Europe as well. They abhorred Mussolini and Hitler because they considered them insufficiently civilized and consequently "un-European." Anti-fascist intellectuals joined the battle against the Führer's brownshirts in the name of European culture. In 1937 the Hungarian poet Attila József welcomed the German novelist Thomas Mann to Budapest with these lines: *"We will just look at you, happy that we might / See someone who is European, and not merely white."*

People did understand that "Europe" used in this sense denoted an idea, not a postal code. Still, it was taken for granted that there would be a high degree of coincidence between the idea and the address. Ideal Europe resided in geographic Europe, and it seemed to be a permanent residence.

The idea persisted for the first part of the twentieth century. "It seems the natural thing for us to listen whilst the Europeans talk," wrote the American philosopher William James in 1902.[1] Thomas L. Friedman notes in his *The Lexus and the Olive Tree* that the first foreign affairs column of the *New York Times* when it appeared in 1937 was called "In Europe." As Friedman writes, "It seemed perfectly natural that the paper's one overseas columnist would be located on the European continent."

Europeans were aware of the existence and achievement of other civilizations. They employed Arab numerals and used (only too liberally) the Chinese invention of gunpowder. But non-European cultures were viewed partly as oddities, exceptions that proved the rule, and partly, after the ideas of Oswald Spengler came into fashion around the turn of the century, as illustrations of how once great civilizations can go into decline. There was an awareness that in previous times the civilization currently called "European" would more likely have been referred to as "Christendom." Many also realized that by the eighteenth century "Western civilization" was a more accurate description of an entity that did not merely extend from its Mediterranean cradle to its peninsular edge at the narrow channel the French called la Manche, but included the British Isles and Ireland as well as the continents of North America, Australia, and New Zealand. Nevertheless, the Eurocentric perception prevailed. In 1935 "European" was still entrenched to mean "civilized" in common parlance, not only in Europe, but in most regions of the world.

It goes without saying that this was an illusion. But the more interesting point is that only ten years later the illusion was dead. It is possible to pinpoint the date and location of its demise. I believe it happened between April 11 and 24, 1945, as the Allies were liberating the concentration camps of Germany.

Before the concentration camps were filmed and photographed, Europeans had a certain view of themselves. It was a view shared by the rest of the world. It seemed obvious that the people who created the Acropolis of Athens, the sculptures of Michelangelo, the paintings of Tintoretto, the printing press of Gutenberg, the cantatas of Bach, the plays of Molière, the operas of Verdi, the artifacts of Cellini, the reasoning of Erasmus, the calculations of Galileo, the insights of Kant, the enlightenment of Diderot, the strategy of von Clausewitz, the inventions of Marconi, the vaccines of Pasteur, or the theories of Einstein, were occupying a higher plane. Like the legendary princess Europa, Europeans had all but exempted themselves from the human condition. Zeus came to the Phoenician king's daughter in the shape of a white bull, and she ended up bearing his children. The divine will had its way with the continent in a similar way. The assumption, to slightly misquote Congreve, was that Europe, like music, possessed "charms to soothe the savage breast."

It was this assumption that cracked during the spring of 1945. The film footage of bulldozers pushing skeletal corpses into mass graves at death camps swept away the myths of an entire civilization. In 1945 images still had a power to shock. They made the world realize that

"Europeans had a certain view of themselves." Shopping street in Budapest, 1933. The young woman on the right is my mother.

Thomas Mann was not representative of Europe. Most people living between the Ural Mountains and the French port of Calais were merely white, not European.

The effect was shattering. As the American historian Barbara Tuchman wrote later, seeing six million people being deliberately killed in the space of five years may have inflicted a moral damage upon mankind. "It may be," she observed, "that the offense against humanity committed by the Germans and permitted by the rest of the world was such that a moral barrier like the sound barrier was broken through, with the result that man, at this moment in history, may no longer believe in his capacity to be good or in the social pattern that once contained him."[2]

For many it was a shock to discover that the "heart of darkness" of which Joseph Conrad spoke in 1902 might be located in Europe rather than in Africa. (Conrad himself might have suspected it, but that was a different matter. Other writers—Franz Kafka, for example, or James Joyce—also considered Europe in a similar light.) The illusion that the accoutrements of European civilization—art, science, and technology—were the essence of Europe was not a universal error, only a popular one. Still, it was a deeply ingrained error. It persisted until the first camera crew passed through the gates of Bergen-Belsen.

The next thing that happened was predictable. No sooner did the old illusion vanish than another illusion took its place. It resembled the first one in that it was equally specious. This new illusion held that European civilization had been nothing but a myth all along. It was fitting for Dachau to be in the heart of Europe, as Europe was nothing but a force for evil. Europhilia, the norm as the twentieth century began, metamorphosed to Europhobia by its end.

Universities were in the vanguard of the new error, as they had been of most previous ones. The academic elite's Europhobia was not limited to geographic Europe: many students and their professors extended it to the civilization of the West. "Hey, hey, ho, ho, Western culture's got to go," became the chant of the new barbarians. It proved once again that seats of higher learning, whatever they may do for enlightenment and knowledge, are ever-reliable instruments for spreading darkness and ignorance.

2

THE YEAR 1935

The only living works are
those which have drained much of the
author's own life into them.
—SAMUEL BUTLER

EVENTS IN THE YEAR OF MY BIRTH forecast rather clearly the kind of world in which I was going to grow up. In Germany, Adolf Hitler denounced all clauses of the Versailles Treaty that provided for German disarmament. In Britain, Prime Minister Stanley Baldwin's cabinet responded by offering an agreement, widely seen as firm but conciliatory, that limited the size of the German fleet to thirty-five percent of the Royal Navy. The Anglo-German naval pact, an early attempt at appeasement, was signed on June 18, three days after I was born.

The same month saw the Comintern, the Kremlin's long arm abroad, introduce the idea of the so-called Popular Front. Joseph Stalin would permit Communists to participate in non-Communist but "progressive"—i.e., socialist or socialist-influenced—coalition governments as a counterbalance against the growth of competing totalitarian systems. Liberals saw this, mistakenly, as Stalin's compromise with Marxist-Leninist ideological purity for a good cause, the cause of anti-fascism. The Kremlin saw it, accurately, as a window of opportunity to infiltrate and subvert liberal democracies.

The rise of the swastika continued. A plebiscite in the Saar Basin conducted by the League of Nations at the beginning of the year showed nine out of ten voters preferring reunion with Germany over union with France or continued rule by the league, which had been administering the region since the end of World War I. The league duly returned the Saar to Germany on March 1—which did not prevent Germany from announcing seven months later, on October 14, that it was withdrawing from the league. Japan also withdrew, having already announced two years earlier that it would. Italy made no announcement, but on October 3 it invaded Abyssinia (now Ethiopia). Mussolini's troops reached and occupied one of Emperor Haile Selassie's provincial capitals, Makale, on November 8, to which the bureaucrats of the league responded by imposing economic sanctions on Italy ten days later, on November 18.

Before the first snows fell on the soil of Europe in 1935, one side of the world's future combatants, the Axis powers, had in effect declared the League of Nations, along with its Wilsonian ideals, null and void. The institution continued its slide into irrelevance. With unerring instincts, the league's bureaucrats chose this moment to move into their splendid new headquarters, a gleaming white palace constructed for them in Geneva at the cost of six million dollars.

"Mother decided that it was time to start weaning me." At meal time with mother in the fall of 1935.

Meanwhile in France, Pierre Laval, then fifty-one, formed a new cabinet. Laval had been a lawyer, a defender of left-wing causes, a pacifist, an ex-socialist deputy. The thought that ten years later his countrymen would execute him for collaborating with the Nazis would not have crossed his mind; in fact, the thought that he *would* collaborate with the Nazis would probably not have crossed his mind. In line with Stalin's new policy, French Communists merged with socialists in an up-to-date "Popular Front" to combat fascism and liberal democracy: the first with much fanfare, the second without. The merger happened in November, the month in which about one thousand kilometres east of Paris my mother decided that it was time to start weaning me.

Meeting in Nuremberg on September 15, the Nazi Party Congress enacted the Nuremberg Laws. The edicts deprived Jews of German citizenship, prohibited intermarriage with Jews, and made sexual intercourse between "Aryans" and Jews punishable by death, introducing the new crime of "racial pollution." Definitions of Jewish descent, published two months later, established the categories of mixed offspring, or *mischlinge*. The first degree included anyone with two Jewish grandparents, the second degree anyone with one Jewish grandparent. I had four Jewish grandparents myself.

On the other side of the Atlantic, European events still seemed far away. Two strands of modernity converged in January when Amelia Earhart became the first woman to fly solo from Oahu, Hawaii, to Oakland, California. A contemporary snapshot shows her at Wheeler Field, sitting on the running board of a Standard Oil fuel truck, wearing a brown jacket, a print scarf, and a pensive expression on her face. On May 14 Americans played their first major league night baseball game at Cincinnati's Crosley Field. The game was started by President Franklin Delano Roosevelt pressing a button in Washington, D.C., which turned on 363 lights of 1,000 kilowatts each mounted on eight giant towers to illuminate the field. The top news featured the trial of Bruno Richard Hauptmann for kidnapping the Lindbergh baby (January 3); a tragic plane crash that took the lives of comedian Will Rogers and aviator Wiley Post (August 15); and the assassination of Louisiana senator Huey Long (September 8).

Though removed from the concerns of Europe, America did not remain untouched by the times. On August 14, exactly three months after the night baseball game in Cincinnati, the U.S. Congress passed the Social Security Act. Two weeks later, on August 30, a revenue act passed by Congress provided for inheritance and gift taxes, over the bitter protestation of critics who said, accurately enough, that the new law meant double taxation. On November 9 the predecessor of the AFL-CIO, called Committee for Industrial Organization (later Congress of Industrial Organizations, or CIO for short), was formed to expand unionism in industry. "The President Wants You To Join The Union," proclaimed the leaflets distributed by John L. Lewis, head of the United Mine Workers.[3] The era of the New Deal was in full swing.

Meanwhile in the north, Canada not only followed but extended the interventionist trend. Parliament established a Wheat Board with headquarters at Winnipeg, Manitoba, to handle barley, oat, and wheat exports. The board would tell farmers how much they could plant each year with a guarantee that the government would buy what they had planted.

The rest of the world was seething, though perhaps no more than usual. It was the year in which Persia became Iran by order of Reza Shah Pahlevi, who by then had been controlling the country for ten years. China was just emerging from the latest conflict with its own Muslim population, the "Turki" Rebellion of 1932–1934. Chiang Kai-shek's Kuomintang had its foothold in Nanking; Mao Tse-Tung had just embarked with his ragtag Communist forces on the Long March. Merchants along Marco Polo's old trade route knew that times would be ominous when the price of dried dragon's eye rose to one Chinese dollar and twenty cents for half a catty.

The newly created Czechoslovakia's first president, Thomas Masaryk, resigned at the age of eighty-five, handing the succession to his foreign minister, Eduard Benes.[4] Belfast saw anti-Catholic riots in July, followed by an early example of ethnic (or at least religious) cleansing, in which Northern Ireland expelled Catholic families, while Catholics in the Irish Free State retaliated in kind. Siam's King Rama VII, originally named Prajadhipok, abdicated after a ten-year reign in favour of his ten-year-old nephew, Ananda Mahidol. By the time the boy began his reign as Rama VIII, the Siamese had abolished absolute royal power. In England, Lawrence of Arabia died in a motorcycle crash. Shortly before his death he wrote, "To have news value is to have a tin can tied to one's tail."[5]

Moscow's Metropol subway opened in May with 5.5 miles of track that would eventually grow to become a 105-mile system with more than ninety stations. Some stations were modelled after the great nineteenth-century U.S. railroad terminals with marble, magnificent murals, and chandeliers. This was duly noted by Europe's chattering classes. They failed to note Stalin decreeing the same year that Soviet children above age twelve would be subject to the same punitive laws that applied to adults—eight years in a labour camp for stealing corn or potatoes, for instance, or five years for stealing cucumbers. Though the famine in the Ukraine had eased, scientific socialism still found it easier to build showcases in Moscow or labour camps in Siberia than to feed children in the countryside.

Several events in science and technology foreshadowed why the West would eventually triumph and the Soviet system eventually collapse. On the British coast a Scottish physicist named Robert Alexander Watson-Watt set up the first radio detecting and ranging (radar) systems on behalf of Britain's Government Radio Research Station. In America, Pan Am Clipper flights provided the first hot meals to be served in the air. Alkali Division of Britain's Imperial Chemical Industries developed polyethylene, the first true plastic, signalling the dawn of the age of composite materials. Meanwhile in the Soviet Union agronomist T.D. Lysenko called his scientific critics "Trotskyite bandits" to the applause of Stalin. "Bravo, comrade Lysenko, bravo," the Great Leader said, making Lysenkoism the agricultural gospel of the Soviet Union. The agronomist, who thought that acquired characteristics could be inherited, offered Stalin a thesis that expressed the ultimate superiority of nurture over nature, planning over evolution, the iron fist of the commissar over the invisible hand of the market. Lysenko's theory implied that social engineering could not only alter human traits, but that the changes would become part of the genetic makeup of the newly engineered citizen. Once people were brainwashed into worshipping the state, their children would be born as state worshippers, elevating Marxism-Leninism from a creed to a genetic trait. No wonder Stalin admired Lysenko.

Seventy-three years earlier, Prince Otto von Bismarck remarked that the great questions of the day would not be settled by speeches and majority decisions but by iron and blood. In Germany, Hitler created the Luftwaffe, appointing World War I ace Hermann Göring as Reich Minister for Germany's air forces. In the United States, President Roosevelt set up America's first independent strategic air force under the command of Brig. Gen. Frank Maxwell Andrews. Four years later World War II would begin by the Luftwaffe's Junkers Ju 87 Stuka dive-bombers screaming across the Polish frontier. Seven years later the tide would turn as Boeing's B-17 and then B-29 "Flying Fortresses" began to deliver their payloads over Germany and Japan.

Someone suggested to my father that this was not a particularly auspicious time for a European, especially for a Jew, to bring children into the world. My father replied that there would never be a more auspicious time for him, considering that he was already fifty-two. "Hitler, I might survive," he said. "But how can I survive my own body?" He followed his remark, as he often did, with his favourite anecdote. It concerned a Jew who under Béla Kun's short-lived Communist regime in 1919 was sentenced to life imprisonment for some political offence.

"Any questions?" the Communist judge asked him.

"Only one," said the Jew. "Whose life?"

Kun's Budapest Commune lasted three months.[6] Hitler's Reich was designed to last a thousand years. Father doubted it. He felt that Hitler might outperform Kun, slightly. In this he turned out to be both right and wrong. As history is measured, Hitler did not last much longer than Kun, but outperformed him by a factor of six million.

The first six years of my life in Europe were sheltered from history. The next fifteen became very much exposed to it. Naturally I had no inkling of what was to come. I knew nothing, not even that I was unusually long and red at birth, prompting my mother to remark that I looked like an earthworm.

3

OPERA

L'autore ha cercato invece
di dipingervi uno squarcio di vita.
—FROM THE PROLOGUE TO LEONCAVALLO'S *I PAGLIACCI*

I CAN TRACE MY FASCINATION with opera to a Turkish lady named Fatime. More precisely, I can trace it to a contest between my uncle's sense of balance and Fatime's abdominal muscle.

My parents had asked me to join them at a dinner party for Fatime, a retired diva, who was visiting us with her husband, whose name I no longer recall. We often had operatic visitors, but Fatime's party was the first I was invited to attend.

As I recall the events (later my mother and father were to dispute some details) it began with Fatime standing against the wall in the blue salon. As a rule, my parents entertained only cultural guests in the blue salon. Business guests were usually herded into the dining hall, underneath Beethoven's death mask, where the seating arrangements were more formal. But that night it was only Fatime with her husband, along with my uncle and my aunt, and maybe two or three other people. This was probably why I was allowed to take my meal with the guests (served at a separate table, of course.)

Fatime spoke German fearlessly, albeit with an intriguing Turkish flavour. Her rich alto was booming across the room. "Belly is rock, rock is belly," she declared. "The voice is all belly. You say to me, a singer has the voice by the throat? I reply: ha-ha! I show you."

Fatime paused. "Who big here, to try?"

Her glance fell on my unfortunate uncle. "I want that you push me!" she commanded. "Not where you sit like mushroom, but standing on legs like real man."

I looked up from my plate. Clearly, the conversation was taking an interesting turn. Fatime, her splendid abdominal muscle wrapped in a minimum of silk, was resting her back against the wall. "In belly," she instructed my uncle. "Not poke-poke-poke like chicken, but push like a man! Make a ball with your how-you-call-them, fingers."

My uncle certainly had the bulk to push like a man; what he may have lacked was the heart. He was a manufacturer of red and yellow bricks, born as one Géza Stiglitz, but by then the possessor of a much more melodious name. My father, a man with some capacity for mental cruelty, had nicknamed him "Stiglitz the Nimrod" many years earlier, after learning that uncle had joined a rather exclusive hunting club.

Uncle Nimrod hesitated for a second, then essayed a tentative push against the undulating silk.

"Ha!" said Fatime, derisively. "My nanny goat push more, when little girl in Anatolia. Push like you give birth to locomotive."

A suggestible man, my uncle paled. "Please, dear lady," he whispered, "I'm quite heavy, I could hurt you by accident."

"Push!"

My uncle closed his eyes and began to push. He was pushing, still cautiously at first, then in earnest. Finally he was driving his fist into Fatime's abdomen hard enough for the carpet to begin sliding under his feet.

"Good, just hold table with free hand," Fatime advised him contemptuously. "Now I will sing you."

My father, who must have known what was coming, had already seated himself at the piano. The black Bechstein roared to life, and so did Fatime's abdominal muscle. *"Stride la vampa!"* she began ominously, in the accents

25

of Verdi's gypsy lady, her famous role in Vienna and Milan. Frightened and hopelessly off balance, with the rug slowly slipping out from under his feet, my uncle was no longer in a position to withdraw his fist. *"Sinistra splende sui volti orribili,"* Fatime insisted, staring into the middle distance. *"La tetra fiamma che s'alza al ciel!"*

Picture, if you will, the situation from my point of view. I was not particularly backward for my age, but until then I had led a rather sheltered life. It was my first operatic dinner party and I was anxious to make a good impression, but it was a challenging spectacle for a six-year-old. There was my uncle, as red in the face as any of his bricks, balancing his entire bulk upon the belly of a Turkish lady, who by then was screaming *"Grido feroce di morte levasi!"* at the top of her lungs.

Any healthy boy could see that it was to be a race between the aria and the heavy Persian rug, sliding as slowly but as inexorably as a glacier from under my uncle's feet. A brick manufacturer leaning at a 45-degree angle is not a dignified sight, and it does not help matters when he appears to be coaxing dark and powerful musical notes from the belly of a fat lady in silk. My behaviour did not help, either. I pointed my finger at them and began turning purple.

Later my father called me an annoying child. It was not a supportive comment but it was not inaccurate, because to say that I laughed would not begin to describe my reaction at the end of Azucena's lament. I howled. I hooted. I am afraid I actually stomped my feet, while my poor uncle slid slowly to the floor, still hinged, as it were, to Fatime's belly by one fist.

Perhaps it should be noted that this phase in my life occurred in the spring of 1941. Though Hitler was already preparing for Operation Barbarossa, the Molotov-Ribbentrop pact still held. Initially, the pact had deeply disturbed everyone in our liberal circles, except my father, who thought that it was a perfect treaty between two identical systems. "Isn't it logical for the Nazis to be allied with the Communists?" he kept consoling his suicidal friends. "Isn't it natural? The unnatural thing would be for the great democracies to be allied with either one of them."

As it turned out, my operatic education continued against the backdrop of precisely such an unnatural development. "So, Stalin is now a friend of

Roosevelt's," my father offered, "yet some people find it incredible that Azucena should throw her own baby into the fire instead of the old Count di Luna's. Well, Azucena was quite upset at the time—as we know, her mother had just been burned at the stake—and it is also a fact that one baby looks very much like another. Also, Azucena was a simple gypsy, while Roosevelt, for instance, is a man of education. He is Felix Frankfurter's buddy. Yet, if you ask me, if Roosevelt doesn't watch out he could end up throwing his baby into the fire by mistake as easily as Azucena."

"Operas were absurd but at least they were majestic." Father on stage, at the Viennese Opera in 1901.

Opera does arouse a certain kind of enthusiasm in people, my father explained, as shown by an incident at the Budapest Opera when Anna Medek performed there shortly after the turn of the century. The cast included the famous Italian tenor Giuseppe Taccani and at the end of the first act a gentleman set up a rhythmic chant, shouting "Medek! Taccani!" over and over again. He obviously liked the performance, and he may have forgotten that in Hungarian the words he kept yelling amounted to a statement of his intention to defecate without delay. "Go, by all means," someone said to him finally, "but why must you announce it?"

My father likened the incident to the Nuremberg rallies. "You shouldn't stretch the parallel too far, of course," he cautioned, "but it's a fact that many people don't know what they are shouting when they get carried away."

Operas were absurd but at least they were majestic. It was silly for people to criticize them in the name of reality, my father suggested, when reality was just as absurd and often devoid of any majesty. "I've known some modern realists," he mused, "who walked out of Tosca because of Scarpia's behaviour in the second act. Well, perhaps Scarpia does act a little melodramatically—but then I've watched the self-same realists sitting glued to the radio, listening to Mussolini speak."

Some years later—this is an aside—my father and I were watching a newsreel showing the bodies of Mussolini and his mistress hanging by the heels from a pole outside an Italian gas station. "Scarpia?" I asked him. Sotto voce, but with the wicked smile of someone proved correct by history itself, my father sang his reply: *E avanti a lui tremava tutta Roma!*"

One could sympathize with Madame Tosca's curtain line: by 1945, indeed, it was hard to imagine all of Rome trembling before a charred side of beef, in trousers, hanging from a pole. However, in 1941 the curtain was still a long way from falling.

I continued my operatic education while the fall of Moscow seemed imminent to many realists who considered operas absurd. My father was virtually alone in the view that Hitler would have had second thoughts about invading Russia if, in addition to his favourite composer, Wagner, he had also been acquainted with Borodin's operas. The German high command should especially have listened to Prince Igor's great baritone air, *"Oh dahtye, dahtye mnye svobodu,"* which gave some indication of how Russians might react to the idea of foreign, as opposed to domestic, servitude. My father immediately sang Igor's aria for me, in a comic version of course, accompanying himself on the black Bechstein and roaring with laughter, until my mother bade him stop.

Soon after our musical soiree my socially ambitious uncle Nimrod was taken to a labour camp named Bor, quite famous in its time, in Nazi-occupied Serbia. Fatime and her husband began holding seances as the best means of communicating with their only son, Martin, who had disappeared on the Russian front. Except for the *Götterdämmerung*, I don't remember hearing any opera. The music on the radio was mainly brass in those years. The Gestapo had discovered other uses for piano wire.

4

THE GRADUALISM OF EVIL

THE DIARIST VICTOR KLEMPERER'S entry for December 30, 1934, quotes some German Jews saying "rather Hitler than someone worse!" In hindsight this sounds like a grim joke, but it reflects an attitude that would be just as common today. Klemperer calls it the "ghetto spirit." In my view, it goes much beyond that.

There are two observations to be made about this state of mind. The first is that "rather so-and-so than someone worse!" describes a prevalent disposition within the chattering classes. In the 1960s there were appeasers in the West who regarded themselves as realistic or sophisticated for advocating a modus vivendi with demented tyrants like Pol Pot, in order to preempt the emergence of something "worse"—as if anything could be worse than Pol Pot, or as if it mattered if something was.

But the remark also illustrates the gradualism of evil. Like many other despotic movements, Nazism invaded the body politic gradually: in the manner of a cancer rather than that of a stroke. It spread much more slowly than Communism did in Eastern Europe after the war (and even Communism usually took about three years after a country's occupation by the Red Army before it blossomed into totalitarianism).

Hitler took his time in taking over the German state. True, the signs were all there. Exclusionary Nazi ideals of "blood and soil" *(Blut und Boden)* were rapidly acquiring official status by the early 1930s. By 1934 Germany was already a mixture between a political cabaret and an insane asylum (for instance, as Klemperer notes, a periodical for pet fanciers called its cover story "The Care of the German Cat"). But many murderous Nazi edicts and practices that became commonplace by 1941 were still unthinkable. In 1934 it was not yet ludicrous to speak of someone "worse" than Hitler, even from a Jewish point of view.

Stefan Zweig writes in *The World of Yesterday* that Nazism "was wary about disclosing the full extent of its aims." The Nazis "practiced their method carefully," Zweig writes. "Only a small dose to begin with, then a brief pause." Zweig recounts warning his publisher after the Reichstag fire that, as a Jew, the end of his books being published in Germany was in sight. "I shall not forget his astonishment. 'Who is there to forbid your books?' he said then, in 1933, still nonplussed."[7]

In May 1935, Victor Klemperer received a letter from his brother, Dr. Georg Klemperer, expressing astonishment that despite the rise of Nazism, Victor would still "cling to [his] house and Germany." Georg, who had left the country by then, wrote that he would "rather starve [abroad] than live in comfort and dishonour here in Germany."

Today we know that what awaited Germany's Jews under Hitler was not merely "dishonour" but the death camps. But even Georg could not think of gas chambers in 1935. He knew that Hitler and his followers were exposing Jews to hatred and were ready to strip them of civil rights, but pogroms and murder still belonged to other ages and other continents.

Georg did not advise his brother to flee for his life, because he never dreamt that Victor's life (or perhaps even his "comfort"—i.e., his pension, property, etc.) were in danger from the Nazis. He would have worried about sounding distastefully alarmist, even hysterical, had he called fleeing Germany a matter of life and death. In 1935 Germany was still part of "civilized" Europe. In spite of everything, certain horrors remained unthinkable for a few more years.

There is another matter worth noting. Georg happened to be a wealthy man. Though by then he was seventy years old, as a medical specialist he had some ability to continue earning an income abroad. He could easily say that he'd rather "starve" than live in dishonour as he was not, in fact, in any danger of starving outside Germany.

His brother, Victor, fifty-four, was facing a harder choice. Victor was practically penniless, could only teach in German, and as a professor of humanities had next to no marketable skills outside his own cultural milieu. Victor and his wife might have faced *actual* starvation had they left Germany, or they would have been reduced to accepting handouts from Georg.[8] But this is another subject.

5

THE HOLOCAUST

Nothing becomes so offensive so
quickly as grief. When fresh it finds someone to
console it, but when it becomes chronic,
it is ridiculed, and rightly.

—SENECA

WHEN I WAS NINE, I TENDED to believe adults. That's why when Mr. Gervay made a remark from which I concluded that Gentiles looked like heifers, I believed him. Mr. Gervay, himself a Gentile, was commenting on my looks at the time. We were standing in his darkened living room, father and I, near the heavily shaded light. Mr. Gervay was scrutinizing my features, touching my nose, and turning my chin left and right.

"You don't have to worry about the boy," he said to my father. "Nobody would take him for a Jew. He looks like a heifer."

My father seemed pleased. I was not, because I thought that heifers looked stupid. Still, I was proud because my father patted my head approvingly. He usually patted my head in this fashion when I achieved something, from which it followed that looking like a heifer was an achievement, or at least not looking like a Jew was. I was happy to have pleased my father and tried to force a modest expression on my face.

Then Mr. Gervay picked up our new identity cards.

A week earlier I had seen my cousin from Prague prepare the same cards at our kitchen table, fussing with egg yolk, fine pens, and blotting paper, all the while hissing like a snake. Pali, my Prague cousin, had a habit of hissing when he concentrated on something, such as transferring official stamps from one piece of paper to another. I remember that he looked pleased with himself when he was finished. "There!" he had said to my father, wiping his hands.[9]

Now Mr. Gervay was looking at these documents, sniffing them, feeling the texture of the cardboard covers between his fingers, and holding the thin pages against the light to inspect the watermark. It was only when he put them back on the table that he spoke.

"Not bad," he said to my father. "Not bad at all."

I knew who I was, and recited it for Mr. Gervay's benefit. My name was Szabó, according to Cousin Pali's documents, and I was a refugee from Transylvania. My mother was my mother and her name was Magda Szabó, the "Magda" part being real. My father was not my father, however, and he had some other name. (I can no longer remember what his name was, though I memorized it at the time. I asked my mother before she died in 1997 at ninety-two, but she could no longer remember it either. My father, who stayed in Budapest, died in 1972 in his eighty-ninth year, easily achieving his ambition to survive both Hitler and Stalin. "Look at those two powerful goyim, hell bent on killing us," he explained to me in 1950 when he was only sixty-six. "Well, we've already survived one and we'll survive the other. You will for sure, anyway, and I'll try my best.")

Father could crow a bit by 1950, but six years earlier, at the time Mr. Gervay was fingering my chin, it was not such a safe bet. It was clear enough that Hitler would be whipped, Mr. Gervay said so himself, and never mind all this nattering about *Wunderwaffen* or miracle weapons, but it was not so clear that he would be whipped before he managed to kill father, mother, and me.

Hitler was not doing the killing himself in Budapest. He used proxies, and they were not his own soldiers as a rule, though the city was crawling with Wehrmacht and SS, and even the Gestapo had rented a villa somewhere for its headquarters. The Germans had marched into Hungary in the early spring of 1944, having no confidence in the loyalty of their ally, the regent Admiral Horthy, nicknamed "the mounted sailor" from his habit of sitting in the saddle of his white horse on all imaginable occasions, but always wearing a naval dress uniform. The Germans had assessed the admiral as a rat, according to what I had overheard father say to one of his friends, because rats have a marked tendency to desert a sinking ship. (In fairness, the old-fashioned naval gentleman might have been ready to go down with his own ship, but he was damned if he was going down with Hitler's.)[10]

Getting back to who was doing the killing in Budapest in the fall of 1944, it was mainly the greenshirts, the Arrow Cross people. When Hungary's ratty old admiral did try to desert the sinking ship in October 1944, just a tad too late, the Germans called on the greenshirts to replace Horthy's government of doddering old anti-Semites with a bunch of ragtag thugs equipped with Männlicher rifles. The ancient sword-buckle crowd were only fascists, Hungarian-style; the scruffy thugs were Nazis. Today people may think that there was little to choose between them, but that is not true. The difference, as my father pointed out at the time, could be the difference between life and death.

In practical terms, the difference was that Horthy's old-fashioned anti-Semites would never have come up with the idea of shipping Hungary's Jews to camps like Birkenau to be gassed and incinerated. To begin with, gassing Jews was an *idea,* and Horthy's redpants were quite bereft of ideas. But even if Adolf Eichmann's office had submitted it to them as a proposal complete with blueprints and train schedules, they would have been uncomfortable with it. In fact, they would have opposed it. Minimally, they would not have wanted to know the details.

What Horthy and his friends found acceptable for Jewish men between the ages of eighteen and fifty-five was a stint at the Don River in Russia. With yellow armbands for practising Jews and white armbands for those merely of Jewish descent, they would be building roads and clearing mine-fields for the 2nd Hungarian Army. Some individual sadists among the admiral's officers might complement this plan with private entertainments such as hog-tying Jews under their command or chasing them naked to the top of trees and making them crow like roosters, but that was about as far as they were prepared to go. (It was enough to cause the death of thousands in the forced labour squads.)

The Arrow Cross had no patience with such mild measures. Their idea was to line up all people of Jewish descent on the banks of the Danube, regardless of age, gender, or current religion, and shoot them on the spot. It was a low-tech and inefficient plan, confirming German beliefs that

Hungarians were a hopelessly backward people, but at least it showed that the greenshirts had their hearts in the right place.

Hungary's Nazis were dressed in green shirts, and their emblem was four arrowheads arranged in the shape of a cross, denoting, presumably, their origins as pure-bred Aryan horsemen, albeit influenced by Christianity. Whether it was the Aryan or the Christian part of their heritage that inspired them to mass murder was never adequately explored.

These were unsettled times, to quote my father, who was given to understatements. Smart people did their best to lie low until they passed, as all unsettled times were bound to pass sooner or later. Lying low meant unstitching one's yellow star from one's topcoat, thereby becoming indistinguishable from the Gentiles, unless of course one was betrayed by one's neighbours or one's own Semitic features. Or, in the case of men, by one's penis. "Your penis is your worst enemy," my father explained to me. "It can hurt you at the best of times, but in times such as ours you must be especially careful to keep it firmly inside your pants." Virtually no boy was circumcised in Eastern Europe at the time unless he was Jewish.

Father planned to get through Hitler's unsettled times by having mother and me call ourselves Szabó and himself some other Gentile name, bolstering our change of identity by Cousin Pali's concoction of egg yolk and blotting paper. The documents yielded by Pali's artistic pen might not have deceived the counterintelligence of the German Abwehr or the Russian NKDV, but they carried enough weight for most greenshirts, who tended to be moronic as well as illiterate.

All the same, one greenshirt we encountered had a fair hunch. When he saw me in a restaurant greedily demanding a jellied salmon sandwich from my mother, he asked to see our documents. This showed good instincts, for Gentile children in Hungary rarely whined at their parents. It was a tense moment, but perhaps because the greenshirt happened to be drunk in addition to being illiterate, the official appearance of Pali's egg-yolk stamps satisfied him. The episode proved that life hung on a rather thin thread in those days because in Jewish matters the law allowed individual greenshirts considerable latitude. For instance, had our greenshirt not been satisfied, he could have marched us to the Danube. Jews carrying false

identities in Budapest faced summary
execution in the late fall of 1944—an
unreasonable penalty, as my father
was moved to remark later, for a jellied salmon sandwich.

Getting back to Mr. Gervay, who
was a large man with a florid face, he
puffed up his cheeks for a moment
after inspecting Cousin Pali's documents and my heifer-like features,
then instructed his wife to make up
beds for the three of us in the living

*"Looking like a heifer was an
achievement." With mother in
Budapest, circa 1944.*

room. His wife obeyed him with quick and nervous movements. Her ner-
vousness made sense. "Jew hirelings," as Gentiles who aided Jews in
evading greenshirts were described on posters pasted all over Budapest,
were threatened with execution. The greenshirts expressed their threat
through the quaint and ancient Hungarian word *felkoncolás,* akin to the
American word "chumming," which means chopping up fish or meat for
groundbait. The Arrow Cross posters, signed by the National Leader, an
ex-schoolteacher named Ferenc Szálasi, always proclaimed his threat in the
first person: "I hereby order all Jew hirelings to be chummed." It was all
talk because in practice the greenshirts never bothered chopping up people
into pieces; they simply shot them or, if time permitted, strangled them in
a noose. This last method was not the Arrow Cross's invention, but a common way of execution in Europe from the Pyrenees to the Urals, usually
modified by breaking the prisoner's neck with a humane twist of the hangman's knot. This was how Szálasi himself ended his life after the war inside
the prison yard of the Markó Street jail. His executioner let him go the easy
way, allowing everyone to see the clonic shiver of a severed spinal chord on
the National Leader's face before the hangman's chief assistant kicked out
a stool from under Szálasi's feet and covered his head with a black hood.

Spending a night at Mr. Gervay's home was vital for us because of the
following circumstances. Three days earlier we had unstitched our yellow
stars and walked out of the ghetto district of Lipótváros, where the Jews

were being rounded up street by street. We did not know where the Jews were to be taken—no one could be sure at the time—but, as my father put it, there would be ample time to satisfy our curiosity after the war. We had already obtained our false papers, identifying us as refugees from Erdély, i.e., Transylvania, but Cousin Pali had not yet managed to steal one essential stamp from the Transylvanian Refugee Commission. During the day it was possible to move around the city without that last piece of paper, which was required only for renting an apartment or booking into a hotel, but we could not stay out of doors after the curfew. After 10 p.m. only the Arrow Cross patrols roamed the blacked-out streets of Budapest. All citizens, Jewish or not, were supposed to be in their homes.

While waiting for the last stamp, my father's plan was to seek shelter with Gentile friends of personal courage and liberal views. Mother offered the opinion that such people might be in short supply, but father replied that we only needed three, one for each of three nights. Cousin Pali was sure to steal the last stamp by the end of the week, and then we could move into an apartment. "I know dozens of people in this city," my father explained. "I've done business with them. I served with some in the army, I was a guest at their clubs, and I hosted dinner parties for them in my home. They're not all anti-Semites, you know."

"Maybe not," my mother said thoughtfully, "but they're all cowards."

Mother had a point, for while Gentiles of liberal views were not such a rarity even in Hungary, especially by the late fall of 1944, liberal views were only an abstraction, whereas the greenshirt patrols with their Männlicher rifles were a reality. In the tense days that followed, my father had less reason to be disappointed in the liberalism of his Gentile friends than in their guts. Most wished him luck and expressed the hope that we would survive despite the fact that they could not put us up for a night. After all, they explained, the war cannot last forever and Germany was sure to be defeated. But meanwhile they had nine-year-olds themselves, or maybe untrustworthy neighbours who'd be sure to report the sudden appearance of three strangers to the Arrow Cross.

"Well, you can't expect people to relish the idea of being chopped up for groundbait," my father would say to my mother from time to time, as he emerged from the phone booths where he had been making his calls. "Would you like to be chopped into groundbait for them?"

"I don't know," replied my mother. "All I know is we *will* be groundbait if we're not off the street within the next hour. Do you need another coin for the phone?"

In those days, Budapest phones ran on coins called *tantusz*. For some reason it was always father's last *tantusz* that did the trick. We spent the first night at the place of a widowed lady named Mrs. Rózsa, who had a son my age, and who simply said, "Come!" when my father explained our predicament to her. Supper was waiting for us when we arrived. She would have put us up for a second night, but father considered two nights in the same place too risky, so the next evening we ended up at Cousin Pali's. We went there reluctantly for we did not want to draw attention to the little forgery workshop Pali had set up in his illegal apartment, but we had no other choice. The third night we spent at Mr. Gervay's.

I don't know if Mr. Gervay would have described himself as a liberal. He was a civil servant in the Agricultural Ministry. He had two children of his own, a slim wife, and a small apartment in the classier part of old Buda. He was a man of about forty-five at the time, with no possessions in the world except his salary, a crested ring, and the ancestral furniture he inherited from his family of small Hungarian nobility.

Mr. Gervay had been a casual business acquaintance of my father's. I think my father phoned him after he had run out of liberal friends to call. My mother had never met him before. "Who exactly is he?" she asked.

I still remember father's reply. "An anti-Semite, believe it or not," he said.

As father explained it, the man who would help save our lives at some risk to his had the traditional prejudices many Gentiles have about Jews, but he also had certain standards. He drew the line at the Ten Commandments. As a Christian and a man of conscience, standing by while thugs in green shirts chummed up women and children for groundbait made him feel uncomfortable.

That's how it happened that we spent the third night on Mr. Gervay's baroque sofa—at least mother and I did, because father stayed up all night in the armchair. The next morning we shook hands with Mr. Gervay, who first patted me on the head, then called his slim wife, who nervously handed us a basket of food. We took the bus to the east side of the city, picked up the final forged document from Cousin Pali, and then moved into our own apartment.

The next two and a half months were uneventful, except for the time I pulled a chair out from under an insufferable little girl, who of course went whining to her parents, our neighbours, who in turn complained to my mother, whereupon my father took me aside to explain that I was not to pull out chairs from under insufferable little girls for the duration of the war. "I can't say I blame you," my father said, "because Pimpell is a little beast. In due course you may pull the chair out from under little beasts whenever you like. However, right now I want you to remember that you are a Jew in hiding." The only other event I recall was the siege of Budapest, a noisy affair, during which we lived on dried beans and peas in the air-raid shelter like everybody else, and I dreamt mainly of meat.

I do not want to create the impression that I overrate guts, so I will recount one more incident. On the last morning of the siege my father, carrying his alpine stick, clambered over some bomb craters to the dugout of a German lieutenant. The lieutenant commanded a Wehrmacht platoon that held one of the last blocks of houses that the Red Army had not yet occupied on the east side of the Danube. It happened to be our block, and by then it was surrounded by rubble, live Russians, and dead horses.

"As an artillery officer from the First War," my father said to the young German, "I recommend that you surrender. There are women and children in these blocks of flats. You have done your duty. You can accomplish nothing more."

"This is typical Hungarian thinking," the lieutenant replied. "We have a different attitude." (The lieutenant spoke in German, of course, so what he actually said was *Wir sind anderst eingestellt*," or "We're dialled in differently," which sounds even better.)

My father shrugged and made his way back to our air-raid shelter. The shooting continued until the evening, when a direct hit scattered bits and pieces of bloodied Wehrmacht uniforms into our courtyard. The German lieutenant and his men had guts, and some of them ended up in front of our shelter. This was the last incoming shell, after which the Wehrmacht platoon was gone, and so was the Nazi era. It was the eighteenth of January, 1945.

My reason for recounting this episode is to put human courage into context. Mr. Gervay was a courageous man. So was Mrs. Rózsa. So was the young Wehrmacht lieutenant. It goes to show that you cannot tell much about a person by noting that he or she is courageous. Nor can you tell much about a person by noting that he or she is a liberal. It seems that you cannot tell much about people, period, just by noting one or another of their attributes. Good people and bad people attend the same schools, subscribe to the same magazines, and pray in the same church.

Many years later, in the 1990s, a Canadian Liberal senator, the Hon. Jerry Grafstein, wanted to know how I first became aware of the Holocaust.[11] The truth is, I first became aware of the Holocaust after I came to Canada in 1956. In Budapest I had no idea that I was witnessing the Holocaust: I thought that it was just Gentiles killing Jews, as they often do. Except, clearly, sometimes it was also Gentiles risking their lives to save Jews. Why Gentiles kill Jews or why Gentiles risk their lives to save Jews is still a mystery to me.

I wish I could explain why Mr. Gervay took us into his small, elegant apartment, turning his slim wife into a nervous wreck. I wish I could explain why Mrs. Rózsa was not afraid of being chopped up into groundbait. She was a Catholic, but not very religious, according to my mother. A hard-working widow, she had no interest in ideas or politics. Her hobbies were sewing and knitting. I wish I could say I understood what she was doing for us at the time, but the fact is I did not. I wish I could at least recall her features so that I could describe her, but I cannot even do that. I remember nothing about Mrs. Rózsa, except that she had supper waiting for us one night in 1944. Many years later when I visited Budapest I wanted to look her up, but my mother told me that she had committed suicide sometime during the 1950s. My mother could not tell me why.

POSTSCRIPT

In 2004 the American columnist Charles Krauthammer suggested that "anti-Semitism, once just a European disease, has gone global." My father would have smiled at this because he viewed anti-Semitism as something eternal and universal. He felt no Gentile was ever neutral about Jews, anywhere, at any time. Non-Jews were either anti-Semitic or philo-Semitic, with the former vastly outnumbering the latter. There was essentially nothing in between. This was simply a fact of life—an unfortunate but inescapable fact, not only in relation to Jews and Gentiles, but to ethnicity and race in general. People were anything but "colourblind" by nature. Each group had a view of all others—usually a dim view, though sometimes it could be unrealistically rosy. It was almost never unbiased.

This dark cloud had a silver lining. Most people were not defined solely by their prejudices. They were defined by other qualities even more. In their actions human beings were guided less by their ideas and more by their nature and their moral standards. Their ethical bias would be more reliable than their ethnic bias in predicting how they might behave in a given situation. This was why an anti-Semite with conscience and courage—as I discovered at the age of nine—might risk his life for a Jew.

Many years later an English journalist told me that her mother was, as she put it, "probably" an anti-Semite. She had all kinds of notions about what she regarded as Jewish pushiness and avarice. But—and this was the journalist's point—her mother would have been absolutely aghast at the suggestion that Jews should be rounded up and put into death camps. "I expect this is the difference between us and the Germans," the journalist concluded in a neat exhibition of British smugness.

My father would have smiled at this, too. True, a genteel anti-Semite like the journalist's mother *would* have been aghast at the idea of rounding up Jews—not necessarily because she was British but because she was genteel. The journalist's mother might have agreed with Third Reich shibboleths about "Jewish pushiness and avarice," but not with what Hitler proposed to do about it. Considering that it was what the Nazis did that eventually translated into Auschwitz, her disagreement with the second proposition was more important than her agreement with the first.

Well-meaning efforts to stamp out anti-Semitism, along with other forms of ethnic and racial prejudice, might be misplaced. By targeting prejudice, perhaps we have got hold of the wrong end of the stick. It is not by making a crude prejudice—say, that Jews are avaricious—unthinkable that we avoid the next Holocaust. We avoid holocausts by making it unthinkable to murder people, whether we think they are avaricious or not.

It seems impossible to teach people not to be prejudiced, but it is possible to teach them not to murder (most are not too keen on murdering, anyway). Most societies have refrained from slaughtering Jews, and most individuals have refused to participate in pogroms or lynchings even in societies that sponsored them. It seems that "thou shalt not kill" is easier to get across than "Jews are like everybody else."

Genuine indifference to Jews is hard to come by, except in places where there are almost no Jews, like Norway. Proposing that "Jews are better than everybody else" is actually easier. Philo-Semites may be few in number, especially compared to anti-Semites, but they almost make up for it in exuberance. Some look upon Jews with the kind of inter-specific adoration the late Dian Fossey reserved for gorillas. (I don't know how gorillas felt about Fossey, but I find the ebullience of some philo-Semites hard to take.)

None of this is to defend anti-Semitism, obviously, let alone to praise it, only to put it into context. People who dislike Jews are not the big problem. The big problem is people who think it is all right to blow up people they dislike. Mr. Gervay, who gave us shelter in 1944, may have been an anti-Semite, but he also thought that children should not be murdered. If all anti-Semites shared his view, anti-Semitism would be significantly less poisonous. Perhaps governments, instead of trying to root out prejudice, should concentrate on promoting the Ten Commandments.

6

COUNTERFACTUALS

COUNTERFACTUALS ARE POPULAR these days. The question is raised from time to time whether history might have taken a different turn if the Nazis had behaved differently in German-occupied territories, especially in the East. What would have happened if, say, Gauleiter Erich Koch, Hitler's man in the Ukraine, instead of referring to the Ukrainians as "niggers," had given them fair governance, security, market opportunities, and a measure of autonomy? The historian Mark Mazower calls it "one of the great might-have-beens of the war."[12]

I am more inclined to be puzzled by the question itself. Frankly, it strikes me as nonsensical. If the Nazis had behaved differently, they would not have been Nazis.

True, people in many regions were ready to collaborate with Hitler's New Order—not just in the East, against Stalin's hated commissars, but even in the West. "Collaboration" was not the dirty word in 1940 it became after the war. In 1940 the ancient regimes seemed bankrupt. The Nazis heralded economic renewal coupled with military triumphs in blitzkrieg-ridden Europe. The autobahn came before Auschwitz—not in significance, obviously, but in point of time. Hitler's legacy turned out to be his death camps, but he built his superhighways first. In this ambiance, collaborating with what to many looked like the shining face of the future appeared logical—not only in defeated France or occupied Soviet Ukraine, but to some extent even in distant America and not-yet-defeated Britain.

But the Nazis, being what they were, behaved as they behaved. Sooner or later they alienated many of their would-be collaborators. What if they had behaved differently? A nugatory question. If one's grandmother had three black legs she might be a piano, but it makes little sense to inquire into the consequences of such a conjecture.

If the Nazis had not been Nazis, collaborating with them might have been fine. But if the Nazis had not been Nazis, they would hardly have been in a position to be collaborated with in the first place. If the Germans of the Hitler period had not been exactly as they were between 1935 and 1945, they would not have set foot inside France or the Soviet Union.

Counterfactuals amount to trying to pull a thread out of the fabric of history without unravelling the whole cloth: an exercise as futile as it is irresistible. Take Franklin Delano Roosevelt, who had no illusions about Hitler but did (at least arguably) have certain illusions about Stalin. Roosevelt was first elected president of the United States in 1932 and served until his death in 1945, being re-elected in 1936, 1940, and 1944. It could be postulated that if FDR had not been in office during this period, Hitler would have triumphed—and if FDR had remained in office after this period, Stalin would have triumphed.

Had Roosevelt lived for even a few more months, he might have turned the Potsdam Conference into another Yalta. He might, for instance, have given the atomic bomb to Stalin at Potsdam, instead of just telling the Soviet dictator, as Harry Truman did, that the United States possessed "a new weapon of unusual destructive force." It would have been even worse had FDR died a year *earlier*, because then, instead of the staunch and sceptical Truman, the vice-president inheriting Roosevelt's office would have been the proto-communist Henry Wallace, who might have given away the entire store to Stalin. (This is a hair-raising possibility. As George F. Will pointed out in a 1984 essay, considering Roosevelt's condition it is a wonder that he did not die in 1944, and if he had, Wallace "would have become President as the Red Army poured into Europe." The consequences might have included the Iron Curtain extending all the way to the English Channel.)

In this sense it was providential that FDR lived exactly when he lived and died exactly when he died. Before one gets carried away by the workings of Providence, though, it is useful to remember that Providence need not have troubled to save the world from Hitler and Stalin if it had not created them in the first place.

Talking of counterfactuals, it would be intriguing to consider what would have happened if the physicist Enrico Fermi, working in his laboratory at the University of Rome in 1934, had realized that when he irradiated uranium with neutrons he actually split the atom. As it happened, Fermi had no idea at the time that he induced a fission reaction; he just believed that he had produced the first transuranic element. Even Otto Hahn and Fritz Strassman did not understand four years later, when they split the uranium atom in Germany and formed the elements barium and krypton, that they had achieved nuclear fission.

It was perhaps fortunate that Hahn and Strassman did not realize that they had cracked the door to unleashing the awesome energy that becomes available when the nucleus of a heavy element splits into the nuclei of lighter elements. By 1938 Germany was ruled by Hitler. After Hahn and Strassman's experiment the Führer had the atomic bomb in his hand— luckily, without knowing it. If he had known it, the consequences for the world would have been disastrous. But what might have happened if the realization had dawned on Fermi four years earlier?

The discovery of the atomic bomb in Mussolini's Italy, which would very likely have come about if Fermi had realized what he had done, might have had salutary consequences. By 1934 Mussolini's affection for his one-time admirer in Germany had become depleted. Il Duce considered Hitler an upstart and a rival. With the ultimate weapon in hand, he might well have regarded it more prudent to seek an alliance with the West to contain his Teutonic ex-disciple, who was getting too big for his britches. A Franco-British-Italian alliance would have pitted the ancient civilization of maritime Europe against the continental Germanic-Slavic barbarians from the East. In the face of a nuclear West, the most nightmarish systems of the twentieth century, Nazism and Communism, would likely have crumbled. The Holocaust and the worst of the Gulag might never have come to pass.

But history followed its own script. In 1934 all Fermi did was to write a paper about his experiment, modestly entitled *"Tentativo di una teoria dell'emissione di raggi beta."* It was rejected by the journal *Nature* because the editors thought that "it contained speculations too remote from reality to be of interest to the reader." One of Fermi's assistants later remarked

that "God, for His own inscrutable ends, made everyone blind to the phenomenon of atomic fission." One wonders why God changed his mind.

7

MY ZIONIST UNCLE

*It was not reason that besieged Troy; it was not reason that sent forth the Saracen
from the desert to conquer the world. . . . Man is only great when he acts from the
passions; never irresistible but when he appeals to the imagination.*
—BENJAMIN DISRAELI

THE GENTLEMAN MY FATHER called "your Zionist uncle" lived in a block of
apartments in the Lipótváros (Leopoldtown) district of Budapest, designated as a ghetto after the German occupation in March 1944. Uncle
Árpád was my father's brother-in-law, at least technically. He had spent one
night with my aunt Amelia following their wedding in Vienna shortly
before the turn of the twentieth century.

The story was that after the first night of her honeymoon, my aunt took
the train home, startling her widowed mother, my grandmother Hermina,
who lived in a manor house people nicknamed "The Plantation" at the
edge of a village high in the Slovakian hills.

"I'm not going to go back to that man," my aunt announced. "As soon
as we were alone, he tried to do something awful to me."

"What, for heaven's sake?" my grandmother asked her.

"I absolutely refuse to tell you," Amelia replied, then instructed the
coachman to take her suitcase upstairs. For the next forty-four years she
stayed in her room, never mentioning her husband's name again, until the
Germans marched into Czechoslovakia, reached "The Plantation" in the
hills, and took Aunt Amelia, along with my grandmother and my other
aunt, Dorothea, via Terezin, to Auschwitz.

The mystery of what Uncle Árpád wanted to do with Aunt Amelia in a Viennese hotel suite in 1895 perished, along with more important lore, in the flames of the Holocaust. My father always remained noncommittal about it, and proceeded to maintain a cordial relationship with his brother-in-law. In his view the problem had been Amelia's innocence. While most women could cope with the sheltered upbringing customary in the Victorian era, his sister happened to be one who could not.

"I suspect your uncle attempted sexual congress," Father told me once when I pressed him. "I could see how it might have upset poor Amelia."

Uncle Árpád formed no further romantic attachments and continued to live with his unmarried sister, Jeanette, who had a heavy limp. He was well over eighty by the time I met him, and a little hard of hearing. He usually received us in bed, wearing a yellowing nightcap with a pompon of tufted wool dangling from its peak. Until then I had only seen such headgear on the frontispieces of old editions of Dickens, and it fascinated me. "Ask him how he is," my father advised me, "and speak clearly. It irritates him when people mumble."

"How are you, Uncle?" I shouted at the red nose sticking out from under the nightcap.

My Zionist uncle liked the question. "I will answer you with two proverbs," he said to me. "One is from the Bible. It tells us that human life is three-score years and ten, and whatever comes after that is a gift from God.

"The other is an old English proverb: You don't look a gift horse in the mouth."

Uncle Árpád often spoke English to me, a language he learned in the 1870s during Queen Victoria's reign when his anglophile parents sent him to a minor boarding school in Kent. My parents encouraged it because English was supposed to be what people spoke "in the world," wherever that place might be, but Uncle Árpád was urging English on me for a different reason.

"It's important to speak the language of the enemy," he explained, "and of course the British are our enemies in Palestine."

"Why don't we speak German, then, Uncle?" I asked. "The Germans are our enemies here in Budapest."

The old gentleman snorted derisively. "One has to draw the line
somewhere," he replied.

Uncle Árpád started out as a
lawyer and a scholar in Vienna, but in
the late 1890s he became active in
Theodor Herzl's Zionist movement.
Like Herzl, with whom he was
acquainted, it was the trial of Captain
Alfred Dreyfus in France that dramatized for him the necessity of
establishing a Jewish homeland. This
put him at odds with my father, whose
answer to "the Jewish question," as it
was then called, had always been
more emancipation, liberalism, and
assimilation in Europe, which he considered the only place fit for human
habitation in the world. His weightier
objections to Zionism aside, Father
found it ludicrous that civilized people

"Via Terezin, to Auschwitz." Father
with my paternal grandmother in
1937, near "The Plantation," high in
the Slovakian hills. A year later the
Germans marched into
Czechoslovakia.

from a temperate climate should try to settle in the Wilderness of Judah.
Another problem was that as a young man my father had heard Herzl
speak, and took an instant dislike to him. He thought that the public relations genius, the son of a Budapest merchant, was a shallow egotist.

Uncle Árpád's impressions of Herzl were different. He first met the
Austrian journalist on a trip to Paris, where Herzl was doing a stint as correspondent for the Viennese *Neue Freie Presse.* Uncle Árpád devoured *The
Jewish State* in 1895 when his friend's book was still in manuscript. Seven
years later, as Herzl published his Utopian novel, *Altneuland,* shortly
before his death, Uncle Árpád discovered in its pages, set in the then distant future of 1923, his ideal society.

Altneuland affected my father in exactly the opposite way. "A Venice in
the desert, under Herzl as the Doge?" he kept asking my Zionist uncle. "An

aristocracy of Galician Jews dressed up as benevolent despots? Is *that* supposed to be my future? It's a nightmare."

The two of them went on disputing the subject even in the Leopoldtown ghetto. They banished me to the kitchen but their voices filtered through the walls, attracting me to Uncle Árpád's side of the argument. I could see why he was frustrated by my father's refusal to admit the Zionist point.

"My dear Mutzi," uncle said once, "when you and I were young, it may have been possible to dream about the coming of liberalism in Europe. But in 1944, with the man Schicklgruber"—uncle refused to call Hitler by any other name—"breaking down your door, wouldn't you finally admit that history has proven us right?"

Father remained undaunted. "Hitler is an aberration," he replied, "soon to be remedied by Churchill and Roosevelt."

"You suffer from the illusion that Europe is Churchill," uncle said. "I'm not so sure that it would be a good thing even if you were right, but in any event, you're wrong. Europe is Schicklgruber."

"Europe, Schicklgruber?" My father sounded astonished. "Schicklgruber is a housepainter from Linz. We all know that tradespeople from small Austrian towns have peculiar ideas. They have to be put in their places from time to time when they get out of hand. Europe isn't Schicklgruber. Europe, for your information, is Goethe, and Schopenhauer, and Mozart. Schicklgruber's charade will be over in a few months, but you and your Zionists will still be pursued by Arabs on camels fifty years from now."

"Maybe, maybe not," said my uncle. "You and I will never find out because an aberrant housepainter from Linz will have murdered us before your friends Churchill and Roosevelt have had a chance to put him in his place."

Uncle Árpád had never been to Palestine, or *be-Tugarma* (The Land of the Turk) as he sometimes referred to it, borrowing Ben-Gurion's Hebrew phrase. Unlike many others in the Zionist labour movement who joined the three great *aliyas*, or waves of emigration, and often ended up planting trees in the desert, Uncle Árpád's job was to do brainy things for the movement in Europe. The word "Mossad" did not exist back in the 1920s, but uncle's work amounted to a bit of the same thing, so he kept the details to himself. "That's how I got stuck with Schicklgruber," he once said bitterly.

Occasionally my father shifted ground. "Analogies are always imprecise," he would say, "but I will risk one. If humanity is a body, we Jews are the blood. We don't congeal in one place, like other tissues. We circulate.

"Blood exists in all organs, from brain to heart, from head to toe. But while our cells are at home in all parts of the body, we aren't any of those parts. We live in lungs and kidneys, but we aren't lungs and kidneys. We're blood.

"We live in other organs and we nourish them. That's our function," Father concluded. "Without us they would wither and die."

Uncle Árpád emitted a staccato series of guffaws.

"Why does humanity consistently reject us, then? Tissues don't reject blood."

"Because," my father said, "things are never so simple. Yes, we carry oxygen to tissues, but sometimes we also carry disease. We carry cancer cells. We carry bacteria. During the 1919 Commune in Budapest half the commissars were Jews. Béla Kun himself was a Jew. Just think of it. Ten percent of the population making up fifty percent of the organizers of a criminal madness. We Jews are usually the first to absorb and distribute things throughout the body politic, whether they're medicine or poison."

My father chose the wrong example. Uncle Árpád, like other *Bundists* in the Zionist labour movement, was soft on Communism. Though reluctant to admit it, he looked at the Bolsheviks as the black sheep of his own socialist family.

"Ah, we carry poison," he replied sarcastically. "Great. You seem to understand why Schicklgruber, the old-fashioned physician, is now trying to indulge in a little blood-letting."

"I do not confuse murderers with physicians because they both indulge in blood-letting," Father said coldly. "I leave such errors to others. All I'm saying is that nationalism is an infectious disease, and Zionists are carriers."

Whatever circuitous route the argument might take, it would reach this junction as predictably as a train. "Nationalism" was the magic word.

Father would utter it like a hex, and it would set off a chemical reaction in uncle. Agitating a tube of nitroglycerin could not have produced a more explosive result.

"Here we are!" he would exclaim, pulling off his pompon and disclosing a remarkable expanse of ivory-coloured skin under his nightcap. "For Jews, nationalism is a disease. It's heinous and unnatural. Mind you, it's very natural for other people, for Englishmen, say, or for Germans. We all know that there will always be an England, not to mention *Deutschland über Alles*. That's normal, healthy, and civilized. Just look at the globe: here's France, there's Denmark, there are the Netherlands. It's the way it is. But Jews? If a cartographer printed 'Israel' on a map they'd lock him up in an asylum."

At this stage Uncle Árpád might be sufficiently exasperated to swing his spidery legs over to one side of his bed, as if ready to get up.

"Explain to me why," he demanded, "why is it a disease for Frenchmen to live together in a country called France? Why is it a disease for the Dutch to live together in a country called Holland? And if it's not a disease for them, why is it a disease for Jews to live together in a country called Israel?"

"It's not for me to explain it," my father replied. "You should explain it to the mufti of Jerusalem. It ought to be easy because the venerable Haj Amin el-Husseini thinks like you do. He thinks that it isn't a disease for Arabs to live together in a country called—whatever, Greater Syria maybe, or the Emirate of Transjordan. Not Israel, for sure."

"But there *is* no Greater Syria, for heaven's sake," shouted Uncle Árpád. "There's a strip of desert between a sea and a river, administered as a mandate by the British. Before that it was a province administered by the Turks. And long, long before that, it was a land called Israel. Why shouldn't it be a land called Israel again?"

"Why shouldn't it be a land called Arabia?" my father replied. "You see nothing wrong with nationalism; why should the mufti? Arabs also think it's natural for them to live together in a country called Arabia. Haj Amin el-Husseini is your doppelgänger. He doesn't see why he should be content to live in *your* country any more than you see why you should be content to live in *his* country. Oh yes, I know: because if it's his country, he might not treat you well. He might turn out to be another Schicklgruber. Well, el-Husseini worries that if it's your country, *you* might not treat *him* well.

"That's why nationalism isn't the route to a homeland of milk and honey. It's the route to an impasse."

"Impasse" may have been the word, because the argument would usually bog down at this point. Uncle and Father might go on hurling phrases at each other for a while, but only in sporadic flashes, the way disengaging armies skirmish after a battle.

"Do you think Herzl invented nationalism?" uncle would often ask. "I'd say it was Garibaldi, Kossuth, and Bismarck."

"Herzl invented nothing, that's for sure," my father would reply, "except maybe self-promotion. Yes, it may have been Garibaldi, or that ecstatic bovine, Joan of Arc. All dazzling Gentiles. They discovered nationalism. The Zionists only made sure it infected the Middle East."

My father would look for any excuse to bring Joan of Arc into the conversation because he had a particular loathing for the Maid of Orleans. Also for bovines. I could never discover the origin of his distaste. "When you bump into a mad cow," he would often say, "you don't argue. You just get out of her way." Once I asked him: "Daddy, how often did you bump into mad cows in downtown Budapest?" He grinned. "More often than you'd think, dear boy," he answered.

Other key points in the argument were electricity and irrigation. "Why should the Arabs resent us?" uncle would demand. "Because we bring them electricity and irrigation? Because we're planting trees? Because we're making the desert bloom? Because we've reduced infant mortality in the entire region?

"Education, patience, and time. That's all it takes. When the Arabs realize that we mean them no harm; that we're delivering them from the Middle Ages; that we're liberating them from their own cruel and corrupt ruling classes; that we're introducing them to modern medicine and science, they'll welcome the Zionist state with open arms."

Father would respond to this with a despairing chuckle. "The rank superstitions of a Polish peasant," he'd say, "are nothing compared to the fatuous illusions of a progressive Labour Zionist. Don't you know *anything* about human nature? The Arabs want their own country, you fool, not your electricity. They want their own donkeys, not your motorcars. They want their own Bedouin desert, not your blooming Jewish orange groves. They want their own emirs, sheiks, and muftis, cruel and corrupt as they may be, not your irrigation.

"They dream of being masters in their own house, for heaven's sake. They don't dream of being ratepayers to Jewish utilities.

"How can Zionists not understand this? You're migrating to the most desolate region on earth to have your own country. You're building Israel in a mythical zone of scorching heat, stench, and squalor. If it was electricity or irrigation you were after, you'd never leave Europe. You're trading symphony orchestras for camel dung to have a flag of your own, and you think you'll bribe Arabs with low infant mortality?

"Time, patience, or education are not on your side. Education will spread more nationalism from Cairo to Damascus. As for time and patience, the Arabs will be patient all right. If they can't shoot you face to face right now, in time they'll shoot you in the back. Then they'll hack off your beards and spit on your graves. As a European liberal I can at least condemn them for it, but as a Zionist nationalist you can't even blame them. After all, they're fellow romantics. They want their own land. As for good Muslims, they would sooner starve in the House of Islam than feast in the House of Zion."

In spite of Hitler, my father retained more confidence in the West as a place of reason than in the Middle East. "If you were taking us to Palestine," he said to my uncle, "because of God's promise of 'next year in Jerusalem,' that would be one thing. But that isn't your quest. You're a secular Jew, with no mystical yearning for the promised land. You're in search of what you call 'a lifeboat' for your people. You're looking for peace and security—yet you're taking us to Palestine. To Palestine, for heaven's sake!

"Why are you doing this to your own people? Hitler is a nightmare that's almost over. Europe is about to wake up from it. But the Arabs have nothing to wake up from. Arab resistance to a Jewish national homeland is reality, not a bad dream. We will have to fight them for a piece of desert for the next ten generations."

Uncle remained unrepentant. He would often finish the discussion with an effective blow, delivered just under the belt.

"My, my, look at the time," he would say to my father. "You don't want to miss the curfew Goethe's descendants have imposed on the Diaspora. Why risk being caught in the street? Go home and soak up some European culture. I hear Furtwängler is conducting some first-rate Wagner tonight on the radio."

The curfew for Jews in Budapest was 5 p.m. People wearing a yellow star on their coats had to be inside the ghetto after that. Unstitching the yellow star had its own risks, though some Jews took a chance on it, including my father. Another ploy was to casually carry a newspaper or parcel in front of one's lapel. Many of our acquaintances got away with it, though we had also heard of some who did not.

The Germans brought in the rule in 1944, but left it to the Hungarians to enforce it, so the penalty for breaking the curfew was somewhat haphazard. It could range from a scolding, if caught by an ordinary policeman, to instant execution, if caught by a green-shirted Arrow Cross patrol. After October 1944, the Arrow Cross got into the habit of rounding up Jews in the streets. Often they just marched them to the Danube, lined them up along the lower ramparts facing the river, then dispatched them with rifle bullets. The practice was called "shooting Jews into the Danube" and it was a hit-and-miss operation. Many years later I met a woman in New York who had been shot into the Danube along with her husband. The green-shirts had missed her, but she had the presence of mind to jump into the water as the shots were fired. She let the turbid current carry her for a block or two, clambered to the rampart, and walked home. She said that looking back she saw the body of her husband, an architect, float by. My father, who had known them both, confirmed her story, adding that the architect had been a very nice man, which could not be said of his wife.[13]

Going back to my Zionist uncle, he turned out to be mistaken about meeting his end at the hand of an aberrant housepainter from Linz because he outlived Hitler by almost three years.

Uncle Árpád's survival was due to his short temper. The Arrow Cross men came to empty the ghetto in November 1944. In the apartments people meekly packed their rucksacks and stood around the courtyard waiting to be marched to the railway station, all except my Zionist uncle. He stubbornly stayed in bed and refused to let his anxious sister pack a rucksack. "I'm busy reading," he told her. "If I ever want to go hiking with Schicklgruber, I'll let you know."

A young greenshirt was sent upstairs to fetch the stragglers. "Get out of here, you horse's ass," my uncle said to him, "before I take my stick and break it over your head."

For some murky reason that would keep an army of psychologists puzzled, the greenshirt became uneasy at his tone. "Keep your shirt on, Gramps," he muttered, and backed out of the room. In the kitchen he discharged his rifle twice, then reported to his leader that he had shot two old Jews in the apartment upstairs. The same night Uncle Árpád and his sister dragged some bottled water and biscuits to the coal cellar and stayed there until the Red Army entered Budapest six weeks later. The greenshirt's bullet holes stayed in the kitchen ceiling. My Zionist uncle refused to have them fixed. "They're the finest monument to European humanity," he kept telling visitors after the war.

Uncle Árpád could still drain a glass of plum brandy to toast the partition vote in the United Nations in November 1947, and died only about a month before Israel was proclaimed a state. The ambulance came for him as the famous acacias of Üllői Street were beginning to sprout new leaves in the spring of 1948. He never saw them. During his last week in hospital he had been staring at the ceiling. "Well, I've outlived the housepainter Schicklgruber," he said to my father, who visited him every day. "I don't expect to outlive the mountain bandit Dzhugashvili."

"Don't worry, I'll outlive him for you," my father replied. He was sixty-five by then, but still an optimist. He believed that Stalin was a temporary aberration, just like Hitler.

Uncle Árpád shook his head. "You've no one left to put him in his place," he said. "Roosevelt is dead, and the English have thrown your friend Churchill out of office. Mind you, Dzhugashvili is a cut above Schicklgruber. At least he voted for partition. Maybe we can live with him."

"No, we can't," said my father. "You think the Soviets voted at the U.N.

for the Jews' sake? Stalin does things to suit himself. Only yesterday he had his Molotov make a pact with Hitler's Ribbentrop, remember? Tomorrow, if it suits him, he'll make a pact with the Arabs to push you into the sea."

"Why should you care?" asked Uncle Árpád. "You're a liberal. A European liberal, described perfectly by a British statesman more than a century ago. Remember George Canning? *'A steady patriot of the World alone, / The friend of every country but his own.'* That's you."

"I think you should get some rest," my father said. He could see that Uncle Árpád was becoming excited. As he stood up, the old man smiled at him.

"I suppose so," he said, "because I've a big journey ahead of me. Luckily I don't have to do much. I just close my eyes and start travelling, by the mercy of God. I think I'll leave my books to George."

My father kissed him, left, then a few days later made arrangements for his funeral. That's how I inherited my Zionist uncle's library. It was to have consequences, needless to say, like everything in life.

8

HISTORY HURTS

WHEN BUILDING (OR DEFENDING) a nation, people can cause harm in three different ways, as the example of Israel illustrates.

One, by ignorance—as when early Eurocentric Zionists assumed, honestly but obtusely, that in Palestine they would be setting their sights on "a land with no people for a people with no land."[14]

Two, by negligence—as when Israeli authorities let Lebanese Christian militias massacre women and children in the Palestinian refugee camps of Sabra and Shatila in West Beirut in 1982.

Three, by inevitable injury—as when Zionism by its very existence caused the harm that is a natural concomitant of nation-building or nation-defence. One might call it "attendant harm."

Innocent as such attendant harm may be—in the sense that it is independent of the intentions, designs, or ethics of the nation-builders or nation-defenders—it is probably the most fundamental harm. The mere declaration of a Jewish State was a catastrophe, or *nakba,* as seen by Palestinians.

Inevitable injury is more than collateral damage. It is what happens to any ecosystem, including political ecosystems, as a consequence of any human activity, no matter how necessary, legitimate, or protective of the "environment" it may be. Inevitable injury results even from the most justifiable examples of immigration or nation-building. The Earl of Selkirk's Scottish settlers meant no harm to anyone in the Hudson's Bay Company's lands in the early nineteenth century, but their very presence threatened the livelihood of Metis buffalo hunters in present-day Manitoba and resulted in what became known as the Pemmican War after an 1816 massacre of several colonists at Seven Oaks. The American Revolution uprooted about fifty thousand settlers from the Thirteen Colonies and caused them to emigrate to today's Nova Scotia, Quebec, and Ontario. The United Empire Loyalists suffered considerable hardship during their dislocation; they suffered losses of life and limb as well as of property. Their injury was the inevitable result of the Thirteen Colonies' justified desire for independence that eventually created the United States of America. There is no escaping the fact that history hurts.

9

GREAT-GRANDFATHER

MY GREAT-GRANDFATHER (on my mother's side), Adolf Klug, was born in 1845, three years before the great revolutions of 1848 that convulsed Europe. He did not turn out to be a child of his times, though. His perspective on life was not shaped by Mazzini, Garibaldi, Kossuth, or the other liberal-nationalist giants who were the contemporaries of his childhood.[15] Throughout his long life he continued to rely for his values on the Talmud. While the rest of my relatives and ancestors, especially on my father's side, embraced liberalism, nationalism, and assimilation—or liberalism and nationalism *without* assimilation if they were Zionists— great-grandfather remained sternly, austerely, and matter-of-factly Jewish.

Jewish, not Zionist. Theodore Herzl's ideas would have been as remote for great-grandfather Klug as Kossuth's or Garibaldi's. He simply remained an observant Jew who wanted to live in the realms of the Habsburgs. In peace and harmony, needless to say, but retaining all the distinctness of his tribe. He proposed to raise his twelve children and run his small business in the land of the Gentiles without becoming one of them. Unlike my grandfather on my father's side, Dr. Adolf Hübsch, proud recipient of the Order of Franz Joseph, who argued for the establishment of a kind of Unitarianism—non-denominational monotheism, as he called it in his book, "the religion of the future"—that would amalgamate the realm's Christians and Jews into one Judeo-Christian church as the ultimate act of Jewish assimilation, great-grandfather Klug was content with the ancestral faith. He had no quarrel with the Gentiles; he just saw no reason to join them. Nor did he see any reason to leave European civilization and pitch a tent in the desert. He wanted to worship Jehovah, but as a subject of Franz Joseph. He was content to see Jerusalem "next year," in the fullness of God's time. "I'll be going to Jerusalem with the Messiah, not with the Baron Rothschild," he remarked once.[16]

Great-grandfather Klug's children, though highly assimilated and barely observant any more, remained as matter-of-factly Jewish as their father until the third decade of the twentieth century. My grandfather and his siblings, along with their spouses, children, and grandchildren, converted to Christianity only after Hitler came to power in Germany during the 1930s.

For a person of great-grandfather's nature and character the conversion of his children would have been hurtful no matter what, but there was one element to make it worse. This was for his children to convert without a change of faith, as a matter of utility.

Changing one's faith as an expression of religious conviction was something Great-grandfather Klug could accept, at least in the abstract. The family consensus was that he could have accepted it even for his own children; with a broken heart, no doubt, but he could have accepted it. However, he would have viewed conversion as a way of making peace with Hitler beneath contempt.

Modern people would see it the other way around. They might not forgive genuine conversion, but would consider conversion to save one's life excusable, even natural. Great-grandfather Klug was clearly not a modern person.

The family solved the problem by keeping the news of their conversion from him. This was not hard, because by the time my grandparents became Lutherans, Great-grandfather Klug was a widower, well into his nineties, living with his unmarried daughter, Aunt Berta, who kept his house for him. Although he was alert and physically fit, he was no longer keeping a tight rein on his children. Not only were the children themselves grandparents by then, but since they came for the ritual Friday meal as before and lit the candles at the proper time, it never occurred to great-grandfather to inquire into their spiritual lives.

As a result I grew up in a family that was not even nominally Jewish. My grandparents and my mother were Lutherans, my father a Calvinist, my aunt and uncle Roman Catholics. Only Hitler and his followers continued to regard us as Jewish, proving that great-grandfather's pre-modern morality made a great deal of sense. One cannot bargain one's way out of hatred by an act of desertion.

In the room where I am writing these lines, there are two objects that belonged to great-grandfather Klug. One is a plain pocket chronometer, made by the Record Watch Company of Geneva about 130 years ago. It is still keeping the time. The other is an ebony walking cane with a silver handle in the shape of a tiger's head. It is of more recent design: textbook art nouveau. My great-grandfather carried it every day walking to his café. Now it stands against the wall. I do not have the courage to carry it, although I would like to.

Elsewhere in the house there is a framed photograph on the wall. It shows a severe Victorian gentleman with a Prussian-style haircut. Wearing a pince-nez, a high collar, and a bow tie, he is sitting stiffly in a wicker arm-chair with a stern expression on his face. Only the subject is Victorian; the photograph itself is from the late 1930s. Great-grandfather was ninety-five when it was taken.

He would go to the barber for a haircut every fortnight until the last week of his life. He disdained the family's suggestion to have the barber come to his house in the winter. One day in February, on his way back from the short walk to the barbershop, he got caught in a snowstorm. Somehow his overcoat became unbuttoned and he lost his hat. Passersby found him wandering disoriented in the city square and brought him home. He was ninety-six.

He lived for three more days. The family doctor came, but advised against removing him to a hospital. It was considered better to wait for the end in the greater familiarity and comfort of one's own room. In those days the act of dying may have been long on the aesthetic and spiritual benefits of stoicism and acceptance, but it was also long on suffering. There was a surfeit of dignity, and a short supply of palliative care. My great-grandfather's pneumonia was not treated with antibiotics; the water was not drained from his lungs; he received no oxygen. My father, who had lit-tle in common with him but admired his unbending spirit, stayed in his room to the end. Great-grandfather did not complain but was in evident discomfort.

"*Herr Klug, man muß Geduld haben,*" my father said to him at one point. Though they had spent the better part of their lives in Budapest, they always spoke German to each other. "One needs patience."

According to my father, my great-grandfather raised his eyes to him. "*Na ja,*" he replied in a weak but clear voice, "*es bleibt doch nichts mehr übrig.*"

Great-grandfather was right: there was nothing else left. He made no further remarks and died later that evening. It took many years before it dawned on me that, although he did not know it, he died the only person of the Jewish faith left in his entire family.

As a six-year-old I attended his funeral, holding my grandfather's hand as we followed on foot a black-draped cart carrying the coffin to the gravesite.

The walk took nearly ten minutes, and I could tell that my grandfather felt he ought to couple it with something that might further my education. After some thought he said: "See, this is a man's last journey." It was a somewhat pedantic remark, but it made sense. I still remember it, long after I've forgotten other observations, more original or more profound.

10

COUNTESS ILY'S DIARY

Somebody said that I am the last American living the tragedy of Europe.
—EZRA POUND

LEAFING THROUGH THE DIARY of Countess "Ily" Ilona,[17] widowed daughter-in-law of Admiral Miklós (Nicholas) Horthy de Nagybánya, Hungary's regent between 1920 and 1944, is like looking at an outtake from an old movie. The "visuals" in the diary are as if they came from a movie made by Britain's Pinewood Studios in the 1940s, but with dialogue written twenty years earlier.

The opening frame is the elegantly beautiful Countess Ilona Edelsheim-Gyulai, being married at twenty-two, in April 1940, in a fairy-tale wedding inside the old Calvinist Church of Budapest, attended by a glittering crowd of Hungary's aristocracy. The ceremony is followed by an airborne honeymoon to Italy, Turkey, and Egypt, with the groom himself piloting his magnificent steel-grey Arado 79 flying machine.

Dissolve to the widowed countess in August 1942, after her husband, Flight Lieutenant István (Steven) Horthy, the regent's son, dies in a plane crash at the Russian front. A span of only two years from a fabulous romance to stark and unredeemable tragedy. Rumour has it that the plane crash may have been brought about by Hungary's Teutonic allies, possibly because the Germans did not like either young Horthy's politics, or his father's. (Contemporary readers who may be puzzled by this should keep in mind that Hitler's crowd were Germans and Nazis, while their ally Horthy's were Magyars and Fascists. The two nationalities and movements did not always see eye to eye.)

In any event, Countess Ily spends the next two years serving the Axis war effort as a Red Cross nurse, quietly, demurely, and photogenically. She also raises, with the aid of considerable household help, little István Horthy, Jr., born in the first year of her marriage. She does all this while looking like Vivien Leigh, or at any rate someone who should be played by Vivien Leigh in the movies. Then in the late fall of 1944 she tries to assist her father-in-law, the regent, in his clumsy and belated attempt to desert his erstwhile ally, the Führer.

What the one-time Austro-Hungarian admiral has in mind is a separate peace with Britain and the United States if possible, and with the Soviet Union if necessary. Countess Ily/Vivien Leigh types documents for Horthy and sends messages on short-wave radio. The Nazis foil the plan, arrest the entire Horthy family, and transport most of them to Chateau Waldbichl in Bavaria.

There, in Baron Hirschberg's confiscated mansion southwest of München, overlooking the picturesque Bavarian Alps, the twenty-six-year-old countess begins her diary. It is now October 1944. The regent's younger son, Miklós, called "Nicky" by the family, is in German custody somewhere else.[18] The Nazis will not let him correspond with his parents, as German Foreign Minister Joachim von Ribbentrop, an old acquaintance, coldly informs Countess Ily in a personal letter. The remnants of the Horthy family are lodged on the first floor of the manor house, guarded by nine armed Gestapo soldiers, who are billeted on the main floor below and on the second floor above. In addition to Horthy and his wife (respectively nicknamed "Miklóspapa" and "Magdamama" by the countess), there are the countess herself, her three-year-old son, István Jr., a family governess named Ila, and a few of the last faithful retainers: an aide-de-camp, two butlers, one or two housemaids, and a cook. Later the regent's brother, Jenö Horthy, joins them. A barbed-wire fence encloses part of the large park surrounding the chateau, housing a hundred SS soldiers in barracks.

The conditions are comfortable as prisons go. Indeed, as Nazi prisons go, the conditions are spectacular. But Countess Ily has no basis for comparison; it is doubtful if she has ever heard of Dachau, which is some fifty miles north of Chateau Waldbichl. She matter-of-factly describes the family's breakfast at 8 a.m. in the private drawing room, and their lunch at 1 p.m. in the small dining room on the main floor, served by the butler (all except little Istvan Jr. and Ila the governess, who are served separately). The party dresses for dinner: tuxedos for the men, afternoon frocks for the ladies. Countess Ily never voices any complaint in her diary, but the way she notes their modest and monotonous schedule, she evidently believes that things speak for themselves. Later she describes how the regent and his wife share a cigarette because cigarettes have become in short supply, and she also notes that after December 11 their food rations are reduced to single-dish meals, or *"Eintopfgericht,"* usually rice- or potato-based, with just a tiny pat of butter and a thimbleful of jam. She and the governess save half of their own butter and jam rations for little István. She feels duty-bound to write down that she is constantly hungry, as are the others, though no one talks about it. She also notes the day—Friday, February 16, 1945—when Horthy leads his family out of the air-raid shelter without the SS Oberführer's permission. When the German later charges into the dining room to yell at the regent, Horthy replies: "How dare you talk to me like this?" which leaves the Nazi officer speechless.

"Maybe he knew nothing about us when they sent him here to guard the 'traitorous dogs,'" Countess Ily speculates, "and he only now begins to realize who we are."

The seventy-five-year-old regent does cut a fine, if somewhat operatic, figure. His Hungarian subjects call him "the mounted sailor" for his habit of wearing his admiral's uniform while astride a white charger. If he leaves an SS Oberführer speechless, it is probably because the Nazi cannot believe his eyes, or is dumbfounded at such obliviousness to reality—but Countess Ily would not be aware of this. She may be in her twenties, but already shares with her father-in-law the dignified obtuseness of the historic classes.

When Uncle Jenő arrives, he manages to smuggle a small radio into the chateau. This enables the family to listen to foreign broadcasts (until then they could only listen to German and Hungarian news on their "official" radio set) and so on April 29, 1945, they hear that Benito Mussolini was executed the day before at Lake Como by Italian partisans. The news prompts Countess Ily to make an extra diary entry. She notes that, in her father-in-law's opinion, Mussolini was Hungary's friend; he used to defend the country against Hitler.

"The [Horthy] parents," she writes, "had a totally different view of [Mussolini] than of Hitler. [Mussolini's] tragedy was that he let Hitler influence him, and so ruin the wise constructive work he began in the interest of his country."

Time out. The imaginary movie comes from another era, but even so it is difficult to suppress a giggle. Il Duce's Fascism as wise, constructive work, ruined only by Hitler's influence? Is it possible that that's how Countess Ily saw it? And is it possible that Hungary's hapless regent had been assessing himself in similar terms?

The answer is probably yes. Brainier people than the ex-admiral formed similar judgements about Mussolini, no less than about themselves. "A very human, imperfect character who lost his head," was how the American poet Ezra Pound described Il Duce in 1945. Such a remark serves as a reminder that Communists have no monopoly on being defensive about their youthful ideals or follies. Horthy no doubt saw himself as having saved Hungary from Béla Kun's Red Terror in 1919, which, as a matter of fact, he had. The admiral might have honestly regarded all the forces contending for his country's soul as worse than his own authoritarian and quasi-mediaeval ideals. The First War brought the collapse of the *ancien régime* and the dawn of extremely troubled times. Democracy appeared to be both weak and perpetually questioning. As a social system, it seemed to resemble what the French sociologist Émile Durkheim called the suicidal mind. "A mind that questions everything," Durkheim wrote, "unless strong enough to bear the weight of its ignorance, risks questioning itself and being engulfed in doubt."[19]

Democracy with its many clamouring voices certainly did not seem strong enough to bear the weight of its own ignorance. Self-doubt was becoming its middle name. Inflation was raging, markets were collapsing,

Bolshevism was spreading, public morals were decaying. Individual liberty was leading to anarchy and chaos. It all appeared to fit Durkheim's definition of the suicidal mind.

To some people, Mussolini's ideas were an attempt to humbly accept human nature for what it was, instead of trying to improve it. Ironically, when the French philosopher Michel Foucault wrote, "The strategic adversary is fascism... the fascism in us all, in our heads and in our everyday behavior, the fascism that causes us to love power, to desire the very thing that dominates and exploits us,"[20] it amounted to saying that humanity's strategic adversary is—human nature. On the other hand, when Mussolini wrote, "Fascism... believes neither in the possibility nor the utility of perpetual peace,"[21] it was hard to contend that his observation was less than honest with regard to Fascism, or less than factual with regard to peace. Of course, Il Duce made his observation with satisfaction rather than with regret, but that was a different matter.

There was an additional factor. If the French semiologist Jean Baudrillard was right in describing democracy as "the menopause of Western society" and Fascism as "its middle-age lust,"[22] it was not surprising that some people preferred passion, even lecherous passion, to climacteric's barrenness and frigidity.

Instead of denying human nature, the corporate state proposed to tame and contain human passions by benevolent and paternal control. This was Fascism's promise as well as its allure. It viewed patriotism as a great virtue: after all, was it not? The very irredentism of Fascist thought—*Italia irredenta,* or unredeemed Italy—echoed the Wilsonian principle of national self-determination.

Ignazio Silone wrote that "Fascism was a counter-revolution against a revolution that never took place."[23] This was true, but the revolution that Fascism forestalled in several countries would have been just as ugly. By 1937 Antonio Gramsci, the founder of Italy's Communist Party, lay dead in Mussolini's prison. Very brutal and shocking—except if we realize that the world would not have been a better place if it had been the other way around: i.e., if Gramsci had assumed power in Italy between 1922 and 1926, outlawed the Fascists, and sent Mussolini to die in jail.

Fascism as a cure for liberal democracy's ills turned out to be worse than the disease, but this was not as plain eighty years ago as it is today. Even people who had the gifts of Ezra Pound, Gabriele d'Annunzio, Louis-Ferdinand Céline, Knut Hamsun (who gave Joseph Goebbels his 1920 Nobel Prize medal as a present), Robert Brasillach, or Curzio Malaparte did not see it. Marguerite Duras, author of *Hiroshima Mon Amour,* failed to see it *twice,* first when she collaborated with the Nazis in Vichy France, and then when she turned to the Communists for a cure for democracy's ills after the war. Neither failure prevented her from becoming a cult figure. The mounted sailor Horthy could not reasonably be expected to have more prescience than such dazzling artists or intellectuals. Neither could Countess Ily, whether in person, or as she might have been played in a movie version by Vivien Leigh.

Today the words "Fascist" and "Nazi" are used interchangeably even by careful writers and speakers, who might reel off the names of Hitler and Mussolini as if they were identical items on the same list. But Hitler and Mussolini did not seem identical to contemporary observers—especially to those who knew them both. Whether this was because contemporary observers were shortsighted, or because we ourselves have lost sight of some essential differences, is a key question. (My answer is yes and yes.)

In any event, the old movie soon reaches the next dissolve. The Americans arrive. On Tuesday, May 1, 1945, General Alexander "Sandy" Patch of the U.S. 7th Army invites the regent of Hungary to surrender himself into his custody as a prisoner of war. He is allowed to bring his butler. Eventually Horthy goes into permanent exile in Portugal, along with his family, including his widowed daughter-in-law. Before the year is out, von Ribbentrop is hanged at Nuremberg.

Countess Ily's diary[24] remains like a bit of imaginary celluloid from the outtake bin at Pinewood Studios. There is Vivien Leigh gliding across the screen. The sets and costumes look spectacular.

11

HITLER AND PACELLI

We do not want, as the newspapers say, a Church that will move with
the world. We want a Church that will move the world.
—G. K. CHESTERTON

"RENDER UNTO CAESAR WHAT IS CAESAR'S, and render unto God what is God's." One interpretation of the well-known Biblical injunction is that the world passes, but the Church is eternal. It is not only proper but quite safe to render unto Caesar what belongs to him, as Caesar's rule is temporary, while God's rule is here to stay. The diarist Victor Klemperer notes a Saxon priest observing in 1935: "We have seen the Third Reich, and we shall see the fourth." In the same entry, Klemperer also quotes a Dresden chaplain, Dr. Baum, who remarks (pessimistically) that the Church "will avoid conflict [with the Nazis] as long as it can" because it believes that "everything else will pass and it will remain—so why risk trouble?"

This is a well-established view. It holds that the Church ought to concern itself with spiritual verities and keep aloof from matters of governance and state. Becoming entangled in shifting secular alliances and changing socio-political trends amounts to a trap into which the Church ought not to fall. Even when she is greatly tempted because of an apparent spiritual component in some worldly matters, it is a temptation the Church ought to resist because one cannot employ the rough measure of the world's political fashions to weigh heavenly truths. Keeping the Church unsullied by secular conflicts is among a prelate's main duties.

This view was probably at the bottom of Pope Pius XII's much-criticized failure to denounce the Nazi persecution of the Jews—denounce it, that is, with sufficient clarity and explicitness. The failure was almost certainly not due to the pontiff's alleged "anti-Semitism." As papal secretary of state, Cardinal Eugenio Pacelli did negotiate the concordat with Hitler in 1933, but he also drafted his predecessor Pope Pius XI's resounding encyclical condemning Nazism, entitled *Mit Brennende Sorge* (With Burning Concern) in 1937. When Pacelli was anointed Pope two years later, he no doubt recalled the fate of his predecessor, Barnaba Chiaramonti. It was Chiaramonti who, as Pius VII, consecrated the Emperor Napoleon in Paris, but when five years later he excommunicated the French invaders of the Holy See, Napoleon had the Pope arrested, took him to France, and forced him to sign a new concordat.

Napoleon did not erase the Papal States and allowed Chiaramonti to escape with his life: Hitler might not have been so fastidious. The Führer knew that Pacelli was principal author of Pope Pius XI's encyclical and was not kindly disposed either to him or to the Vatican. People who talk about Pacelli as "Hitler's Pope" (the title of one recent book) do not seem to understand that Pacelli had not negotiated the concordat with Hitler because he had a soft spot for Nazism, but because he had a soft spot for the Catholic Church.

It is a different matter that another pope might have considered denouncing Nazism fundamental for any Christian churchman. In such a pope's view, taking a clear position on Hitler would not be a failure to render unto Caesar what is Caesar's, but *not* taking a clear position would amount to a failure to render unto God what is God's. (One suspects that such might have been the view of the Polish priest Karol Wojtyla, had he been Pope John Paul II at the time.)

Still, Klemperer's Saxon priest had a point in 1935. Within ten years of his remark, the Church *had* seen the Third Reich, heralded to last a thousand years, pass the way of all Reichs. True, meanwhile six million Jews lost their lives, but (as the Church may have seen it) in the long run their lives would have been lost anyway, along with the lives of all other contemporary mortals.

This, alas, is the drawback of the "long view." This is why the long view, whether taken by the Church or any other institution, is colder than liquid air. "Vanity of vanities, saith the Preacher, vanity of vanities; all is vanity," but it is possible to take Ecclesiastes 1:2 too literally. Too keen a sense of *vanitatum vanitas* can lead holy men to abdicate to evil. This, in the end, may have been the tragedy of Eugenio Pacelli.

12

In Defence Of The Short View

An appraisal of Pacelli invites the observation that the long view is always cruel. Anyone who raises the prospect of long-term gain implies immediate pain. The German writer Erich Maria Remarque wrote (in his novel *Arc de Triomphe*) that it is easier to conduct business with a Jew than with a Frenchman, for a Jew will see the deal, but a Frenchmen will only see his cost.

Yet, if so, the Frenchman is more practical, for a "deal" can only be a future abstraction, while "cost" is a contemporary reality. Paying the price usually precedes enjoying the merchandise, and never guarantees it.

This does not mean, obviously, that people who take the long view are necessarily wrong. It only means that the cost of their transactions can be taken for granted, while their benefits can only be hoped for. In this sense, a buyer always takes the long view by definition, while a seller takes the short view. Either (or both) may turn out to be right; it is only that supporters of the long view release the bird in the hand for the two that are lurking in the bush. We can assume, therefore, that Cervantes (who first pointed out that "a bird in the hand is worth two in the bush") would not have been overly impressed by anyone insisting on the long view.

13

WHY GERMANY?

We should be careful to get out of an experience only the wisdom that
is in it—and stop there; lest we be like the cat that sits down on a hot stove-lid.
She will never sit down on a hot stove-lid again—and that is well; but
also she will never sit down on a cold one anymore.

—MARK TWAIN

IN THE SPRING OF 1996 Professor Daniel Jonah Goldhagen, an American scholar, published a book that created a splash in Germany, and a noticeable ripple around the world. *Hitler's Willing Executioners* is a lengthy tome, but its central points, at least as I understand them, can be summarized in two sentences.

1. The Holocaust was a singular event, unique in world history.
2. The Holocaust was not only the inevitable result of a singular and unique kind of group-hatred called anti-Semitism, but of a singular and unique kind of anti-Semitism, peculiar to Germans and Germany.

I spent the first ten years of my life in Nazi-occupied Europe. My immediate family and I survived the war by hiding. Since I kept no diary, had the Nazis found me as they had found Anne Frank, I would have disappeared without a trace.

This would undoubtedly have made the Holocaust a singular and unique event for me. I am less sure about the Holocaust having been a singular and unique event in world history. To me it seems that it was one of many horrifying holocausts, albeit of immense proportions. I also doubt that the Holocaust was the inevitable result of anti-Semitism, and especially that the Holocaust was inevitably caused by a singular and unique type of anti-Semitism peculiar to Germany.

Professor Goldhagen's thesis is that the Holocaust could never have happened without the participation of ordinary German men and women, and ordinary German men and women participated in the Holocaust because they were virulently anti-Semitic.

This is true enough as far as it goes, but it does not go very far. Saying that Hitler could not have killed six million Jews without the participation of many other people, and that people who participate in the wholesale slaughter of Jews are likely to be virulently anti-Semitic, is saying something singularly self-evident.

One would almost hope that the people who slaughtered Jews in Nazi Germany were anti-Semitic, because a person who kills and tortures men, women, and children without being convinced, no matter how erroneously, that they are somehow dangerous, evil, and a threat to him and to his nation, would be a worse kind of monster than a true-believing Nazi. It is more terrifying that there were probably some direct participants in the Holocaust who never thought much about Jews one way or another, who massacred and tortured human beings only for sadistic pleasure, or for some career advantage within the Nazi system (real or perceived), or simply because they found themselves in a situation where others in their group were killing and torturing Jews, and they were just going with the flow.

But many Germans were indeed anti-Semitic. Their direct participation in mass slaughter is hardly required for proof. Voters who elect a Nazi government are likely to be anti-Semitic, whether they personally participate in genocide or not. A Hitler-type regime cannot come to power without at least a substantial and vocal minority of the population being bona fide anti-Semites.

Accurate as Professor Goldhagen's statements are in this limited sense, they are hardly worth making. The interesting questions are different. And insofar as Professor Goldhagen raises them in his book, his answers, I believe, are wrong.

What exactly is "genocide"? How does it differ from non-genocidal mass slaughter?

In theory, genocide refers to one group's purpose to exterminate another group, or at least to physically expel or expunge it from a given geographic region. In the absence of such an overall design, killing members of other groups, even on a massive scale and with no reference to their combat status, age, or gender—for example, by the aerial bombardment of cities—is rarely called genocide. We do not normally speak of genocide when we consider the Allied bombing of Hiroshima, Dresden, Tokyo, or Nagasaki, or even the Axis bombing of London or Rotterdam. (The exceptions are people who use the term promiscuously and imprecisely or to score political points.)

One need not quarrel with this distinction in order to note it. There *is* a difference between acts of war—including even the terror-bombing of civilians—and Auschwitz. Yet it is also necessary to note that the results of such behaviour can be indistinguishable from genocide.[25]

The extinction of entire groups and cultures in a series of bloody conflicts is inseparable from genocide in its consequences, even in the absence of a genocidal intent. It may still be legitimate to distinguish between "incidental" genocide and genocide by design, for moral purposes as well as for purposes of academic classification, and a historian would certainly be entitled to do so. However, Professor Goldhagen does not take this approach. He simply asserts the uniqueness of the Holocaust. His book appears to view what the Germans did to the Jews, both during the Nazi period and before, in isolation from human history.

Needless to say, it's unnecessary to show the uniqueness of Nazi Germany in order to condemn it. The point is raised only because Professor Goldhagen sets out to show the *singularity* of the German people and their genocidal history. Unfortunately, it does not seem to have been singular. It was just one monstrous peak in the colossal mountain range of the world's genocidal history.

Does anti-Semitism lead to genocide? Does it lead to genocide inevitably if it is virulent enough? Are exclusionary measures—restrictions or quotas for certain groups—different from genocidal behaviour in kind or only in degree? Can exclusionary ideas and policies be viewed as precursors of genocidal behaviour?

Professor Goldhagen invites these questions by contending that German people and culture were anti-Semitic in a unique way that he calls "eliminationist." This singular German anti-Semitism would lie dormant, or only manifest itself in discriminatory policies and rhetoric within the civic sphere, until it erupted like a fulminating infection resulting in a holocaust. For proof, Professor Goldhagen documents the historic existence of German anti-Semitic ideas and policies exhaustively and convincingly.

The trouble is that German anti-Semitism hardly requires documentation. No one disputes it. What would assist Professor Goldhagen's thesis is proof of its singularity, coupled with proof that "eliminationist" anti-Semitism can be taken as a precursor to, or at least a portent of, genocide. However, *Hitler's Willing Executioners* offers no such proof.

Proof would be hard to come by, for history shows no *inevitable* link between anti-Semitism—or any other type of racial, ethnic, class, or religious prejudice or hatred—and genocide. There have been discriminatory measures aimed at various racial, ethnic, religious, social, and gender groups in many different cultures. Many have been as strict, or nearly as strict, as anti-Jewish policies in pre-Nazi Germany. Some have been much stricter. Examples range from denial of voting rights to outright slavery, from segregationist "Jim Crow"-type laws to occupational quotas or laws against miscegenation. All precede the German introduction of *numerus clausus*. Exclusionary measures such as "affirmative action" exist even in our current Western societies. Genocides, or at least atrocities, have undoubtedly coincided with some of these social policies, but not inevitably or even frequently. In short, while a potential link between group-hatred and genocide is self-evident, an inevitable link cannot be demonstrated.

Arguments showing that some affirmative action type of preferential policies may be justified are irrelevant. One need not argue that all exclusionary measures are equally *unjustified* to argue that all exclusionary measures are equally *exclusionary.* Justifiable or not, such measures have the effect of creating a group with diminished rights and opportunities—"second-class citizens"—because of some perceived social need or ideal. The extent to which the social standing of such groups is curtailed varies from culture to culture, along with the reasons offered in justification, but such variations do not alter the essence of *exclusion*, which always leads to decreased career and lifestyle opportunities, and often also to opprobrium and reduced social status for the affected group. On Professor Goldhagen's thesis, these measures should all presage a holocaust. In fact, they do not. Many societies exclude but only a few kill.

This, obviously, is no excuse for discrimination. Exclusion, civic hurdles, or even simple social snobbery directed against groups—to say nothing of persecution or enslavement—are evils in themselves. However, they do not necessarily lead to Auschwitz.

The degree or "virulence" of such a prejudice cannot, in itself, create a sufficient link between prejudice and genocide. Even if it could be shown that traditional German prejudice against Jews was more virulent than, say, traditional French, English, or Russian prejudice, it would still fall short of creating a causal connection.

In any event, such a showing cannot be made. Traditional German prejudice against Jews, though widespread and intense, was less acute than traditional Polish prejudice, and not significantly more acute than French prejudice. Before Hitler's times Jews often emigrated *to* Germany to escape worse discrimination elsewhere. In Czarist Russia exclusionary measures directed against Jews, viewed as socially acceptable, were far harsher than German exclusionary measures prior to the Nazi era.

Traditional German prejudice against Jews does not, in itself, explain the Nazi Holocaust. Illustrating the extent of this prejudice by a series of examples, or coining the term "eliminationist" to describe it, cannot serve to distinguish it in kind from the prejudice and hatred many other societies have directed against Jews (or other groups) throughout history.

Was anti-Semitism in general, or German anti-Semitism in particular, the only form of group-hatred that ever resulted in anything akin to the Holocaust?

The simple answer is no.

If "group-hatred" is defined as animosity directed against other human beings on the basis of their membership in a despised racial, ethnic, religious, or social group, and "holocaust" is defined as the deliberate and large-scale extermination or physical expulsion of such despised human beings regardless of their age, gender, or combat status, there have been many holocausts in human history, including the modern era. Listing them all would take an entire book.[26]

Some seek to narrow the definition of "holocaust" and exclude so-called humane expulsions of despised groups to regions of exile. Under this definition, the expulsion of the Japanese from Canada's West Coast during World War II would not qualify as a holocaust.

There is indeed much to distinguish the victims of the Japanese holocaust in British Columbia from the victims of the Jewish holocaust in Bergen-Belsen. In terms of misery and agony the two cannot be mentioned in the same breath. But while such a distinction might play a significant role at the trials of individuals charged with war crimes, it can scarcely justify *denying* a holocaust. The wholesale expropriation and expulsion of people from their homes in their ordinary regions of residence carries the potential of their destruction as a group. As such, it fully exhausts the dictionary definition of genocide.

It is immaterial in this regard whether a group is actually destroyed or not. Few groups are ever, in fact, totally destroyed. The Nazis themselves have not succeeded in eradicating the Jews of Europe. Most genocides are only attempted genocides.

If "holocaust" is defined, additionally, by sheer magnitude, it obviously becomes a much rarer event. Genocidal outbursts of group-hatred often claim only thousands rather than millions of victims. It is possible to regard the wholesale slaughter of human beings as an "atrocity" rather than a "holocaust" if the number of victims does not exceed some arbitrary figure—say, a million members of a targeted group. But even by this definition, Germany's Nazis come a distant second to the Soviet and Chinese Communists.

According to the "Black Book of Communism," an academic study published in Paris by a group of French historians in 1997, Marxist versions of socially and ideologically based group-hatred claimed 20 million victims in the former Soviet Union and between 45 and 72 million in China. The global tally adds to these figures between 4.3 and 5.3 million people in Cambodia, Vietnam, and North Korea, 1.7 million in Africa, 1.5 million in Afghanistan, one million in Eastern Europe, and 150,000 in Latin America.

These are not casualties of war or civil war. These human beings all perished in the "Gulag"-type labour and re-education camps of various Communist regimes, or in the cellars of their secret police. Many were deliberately starved to death. The total, taking the lower figures, is over 73 million people.

If the six million murdered by the Nazis pales in comparison, it does not prove that Communism is "worse" than Nazism. It only shows that defining holocausts by sheer magnitude is not a very productive exercise.

The problem with Professor Goldhagen's thesis is that even if the Holocaust had been the inevitable product of anti-Semitism—and of German anti-Semitism in particular—German anti-Semitism would only have produced another despicable and monstrous tragedy in world history. *One* of several such tragedies. It would not have produced a unique or singular event.

Is irrational hatred based on racial, ethnic, social, or religious differences the only type that inspires genocidal behaviour? Clearly not. Genocides, or attempted genocides, are just as often inspired by rational animosities, such as historically founded fear, territorial envy, or tribal revenge. In any event, hatred for another group, rational or otherwise, is not a requisite for genocidal behaviour. Genocide often follows militaristic or conquistadorial pursuits of booty or geopolitical influence.

When it is group-hatred that inspires genocidal behaviour, is anti-Semitism the only type? Again, clearly not. Far from being restricted to hatred against Jews, it need not even be hatred against a racial or ethnic group. The Communist holocausts were motivated by group-hatred based on *social* distinctions (or perhaps based on "religion," if one includes all creeds and ideologies under this heading). Religious or ideological hatred, along with class hatred, has been every bit as powerful a genocidal engine as racial or ethnic hatred, as demonstrated by recent historical figures from J.V. Stalin to Osama bin Laden.[27]

Was German anti-Semitism *before* the Hitler era materially different from anti-Semitism in other times and places? Not in my view. This assertion, though central to Professor Goldhagen's thesis, is not supported by any evidence in his book. Though he lists many examples of anti-Semitic legislation and opinion in Germany, I do not believe he offers any for which a parallel could not be found in the legislation and opinion of other cultures.

Professor Goldhagen makes out a convincing case for a strong thread of anti-Semitism running through Germany's social fabric long before Hitler came to power. This is not disputed. It is equally undisputed that "modern" forms of populist anti-Semitism emerging in the mid-nineteenth century were fundamentally different from the older, largely religious forms of anti-Semitic traditions throughout Christendom and Islam. It is undisputed that these modern forms were in many ways deadlier than the older forms as potential precursors of a holocaust.

The disputed question is whether modern anti-Semitism was or was not peculiar to Germany. I believe it was not.

Modern anti-Semitism developed side by side with nationalism, as older organizing principles of the social order weakened. Ironically, it came as a by-product of the Enlightenment. As the dynastic and religious systems by which groups used to define themselves were losing their grip, people were gradually beginning to think of themselves as "Russians" rather than subjects of the Romanov Tzars, or "Germans" rather than subjects of the Hohenzollern emperors. The one-time vassals of the Bourbons were turning into the Gallic sons and daughters of Marianne, the emblematic figure of the French Revolution. The pilgrims and warriors of Christendom or Islam were evolving into "Italians" or "Turks." Such definitions inevitably put a premium on ethnic identity. Suddenly Jews were no longer patches in the colourful tapestry of empires, but alien and potentially baneful cells in the bloodstream of nations. In earlier times a Jewish subject could escape the Inquisition by submitting to Isabella the Catholic and confessing the Christian faith, but in the new era he would have had to turn himself into a Spaniard, which was impossible. As dynasties and religions declined and national identities assumed greater importance, a new type of anti-Semitism was born.

But these modern, populist-nationalist-racist elements existed in the anti-Semitic laws and opinion of all contemporary cultures, not only in Germany's. They existed in France's and in England's. They existed, probably even more strongly, in Russia's and Poland's. They existed in the cultures whose descendants ended up going to war with Hitler's Germany in 1939.

The writers and thinkers who explored the themes of social Darwinism and imbued the *Zeitgeist*, directly or indirectly, with modern notions of ethnocentric nationalism certainly included many Germans, but were by no means restricted to them. The author of one of the most influential works, *Essai sur l'inégalité des races humaines,* published in 1853, was a Frenchman, Count Arthur de Gobineau. The man who originated the concept of ethnocentrism was the American Yale scholar, William Graham Sumner, whose seminal work "Folkways" was published in 1907 (the year the teenage Hitler first arrived in Vienna). And Houston Stewart Chamberlain was, of course, an Englishman, though he did become a German citizen later. His social Darwinist manifesto "Foundations of the 19th Century" appeared in 1899, when Hitler was still a schoolboy in Linz.

One cannot explain Caesar by listing the qualities Caesar had in common with all other men, as the novelist Petru Dumitriu pointed out half a century ago. Germans were anti-Semitic. So were Poles and Hungarians. So were the Russians, the French, and the English. Several nations had exclusionary practices far stricter than post-Bismarckian Germany's— Russia's infamous Pale of Settlement is one obvious example—and some had practices that were almost identical. Some had few or no such practices for a variety of reasons, but virtually all had similar sentiments.

The "Jewish question," so-called, was raised by almost every nation from the mid-nineteenth to the mid-twentieth century. Raising it was regarded as legitimate. Although a liberal strand in public opinion argued passionately against discrimination, in Germany no less than elsewhere, discussing measures of exclusion, or even acting on them, both in the private and the public sphere, was socially acceptable. Anti-Semitism was not "beyond the pale" in most countries. The trial of Captain Alfred Dreyfus happened in France, not in Germany. If anti-Semitism alone had been the cause of the Holocaust, it could have occurred in France or England as easily as in Germany, to say nothing of some other countries.

Why, then, did the Holocaust occur in Germany and not in some other country? This, finally, is the important question. Professor Goldhagen's answer is that anti-Semitism in general, and German anti-Semitism in particular, was uniquely virulent. As such, it could reach a critical mass, the mass required for an explosion.

We have already concluded that pre-Nazi German anti-Semitism was probably not unique, but let us assume for the sake of argument that it was. In this case Professor Goldhagen's explanation raises a prior question: *Why* did Germans hate Jews so much more than other people?

There is a danger of replying to this by attributing some peculiar evil to Germans as a group—i.e., as a "race." To his credit, Professor Goldhagen takes great pains to avoid it. He does not wish to demonize Germans. The problem is, unless we postulate evil, there is little in German history or culture to provide an alternative explanation.

Germany's traditions were no less rational, no less civilized, no less chivalrous, than other Western traditions during the same period. Her public laws and civic morality, the personal habits of her citizens, their ethical precepts, their customary religious beliefs, were not markedly different from those of the citizens of other European nations. German art, science, industry, and infrastructure were, if anything, more advanced. Although the governmental institutions in Germany's recent past were more autocratic than those of France and England, not to mention the United States, they were not nearly as autocratic as many other countries'. In any event, by the time Hitler came to power, the Weimar Republic was a full-fledged democracy.

The Jews in Germany were well integrated—not only far better than the Jews of Poland or Russia, but on the whole better than the Jews in many Western countries, including even the United States and Canada. Most German Jews were German patriots. They were far more likely to be indistinguishable from non-Jewish Germans in their language, demeanour, and cultural habits than American Jews were from non-Jewish Americans. Though after their emancipation in the mid-eighteenth century, their contribution to music, arts, sciences, commerce, literature, journalism, and even politics far exceeded their numbers (about one percent) in Germany's population, Germany's institutions were not overwhelmed by Jews (though this became a frequent explanation offered by anti-Semites for their anti-Semitism), not even to the extent that Austria's or Hungary's might have been. One looks in vain for a rational—or even irrational—explanation for a supposed "unique hatred" in the history of the actual relationship between Jews and Germans. Their *actual* relationship was better than the relationship between Jews and their host countries almost anywhere else. The search turns up nothing.

What, then, is the answer? Why did the Holocaust occur in Germany?

We can certainly view traditional German anti-Semitism as one contributing cause to the Holocaust. Hitler could probably never have persuaded Germans to exterminate, say, all people with red hair. In the absence of a tradition of prejudice against redheads, killing them would have appeared absurd to Germans, in a way that the notion of killing Jews did not.

Hitler himself must be considered a significant factor. If past fashions of historical analysis used to overestimate the influence of personalities on the course of events, modern fashions tend to underestimate them. But personalities do matter. A charismatic leader is like an ignition source, a spark: utterly insignificant in the absence of an explosive mixture, but the direct cause of a blow-up in a place filled with combustible fumes. In another country—or in Germany in another historic period—Hitler might have died unnoticed in a flophouse or in a mental institution. But he was where he was, therefore he did what he did. The Holocaust would not have happened without him.

There were many reasons for Germany being unlike other countries in the 1920s. Other countries lacked the shock that follows losing a war that the Germans believed they were winning almost until the last minute. The national trauma of that unexpected blow is still insufficiently understood outside Germany. It was inevitable for conspiracy theories to start flourishing after such a traumatic event. The soil for Nazism was prepared by

German indignation. It sparked an immediate search for scapegoats, for traitors who "stabbed Germany in the back." It seemed natural to include Jews in this conspiracy.

The super-inflation that started after the murder of Foreign Minister Walter Rathenau in 1922 and lasted until 1924 would have been devastating for any nation, but in a national psyche fixated on order, discipline, and stability, as Germany's undoubtedly was, it induced something close to derangement. "Nothing ever embittered the German people so much—it is important to remember this—nothing made them so furious with hate and so ripe for Hitler as the inflation," recalled Stefan Zweig in his autobiography, *The World of Yesterday.*[28]

The stock market crash of 1929 was undoubtedly a factor in the rise of Nazism, but the Depression was a worldwide phenomenon, and it did not necessarily lead to the rise of totalitarian systems elsewhere. More significant was the rare, maybe even unique, vulnerability of the Weimar Republic. Conventional analysis often blames the treaty of Versailles for the rise of Nazism, but the status of Germany as an adolescent democracy was at least as important. This developing, almost teenage-like stage in the nation's life probably had more to do with the irrational eruptions in Germany's soul than any other factor.

Mature democracies, such as the United States or Great Britain, with solid traditions of both individual liberty and checks and balances on the exercise of power, would have been far more resistant to the totalitarian nature of Nazism than Germany. Additionally, a class society such as Britain's, while somewhat more tolerant of authoritarianism than the United States, would have been far more resistant than the Weimar Republic to letting a party composed of tradesmen, subalterns, and petty officials grab the helm of the ship of the state. Social snobbery alone would have prevented a corporal like Hitler from becoming the supreme leader of England.

It is no accident that both Auschwitz and the Gulag had been created by a breed of leaders who rose from social milieux with no traditions of learning, leadership, or noblesse oblige. Germany may have been anti-Semitic from top to bottom, but the Nazis still emerged from the sewer of its underclass. It took an unemployed drifter, the son of an Austrian customs official, to come up with the idea of Auschwitz.

This was not merely a matter of morality, but of modernity. It required a new breed of Hitler's ilk to put slaughter on the assembly line. Members of the *ancien régime,* even if equally anti-Semitic, were not sufficiently up to date for the mass production of either Nuremberg-type rallies or Birkenau-type murder. Mass production became possible only in the age of the masses.

The last two elections in the Weimar Republic showed that only about one in ten Germans retained any faith in the old class society of traditional Germany, whose aristocratic-military or haute-bourgeois patriots were still clinging to power under the figurehead of their ancient general, Paul von Hindenburg. Four in ten Germans favoured a Western-style liberal democracy of one sort or another, while about five in ten were attracted to the millennial-totalitarian visions of the new mass age. Within this last group, however, only about two in ten preferred the Communists. Eight in ten wanted the Nazis, and in the end they got their wish.

The old ruling classes had been discredited by the 1920s, along with all their inhibitions. They had, as it seemed to many Germans, lost the honour of the Fatherland. It was the Führer who restored it. In a relatively short time his Nazi regime recaptured much of Germany's wealth, power, and influence among nations. If Hitler was right about so many things, why would he be wrong about the Jews? Why would he be wrong about the Final Solution?

But there is something even more important. The seemingly insurmountable hurdle of "Why in Germany?" vanishes if we stop insisting on the Holocaust as a unique and singular event. If it were unique, we could scarcely explain it, in spite of all the points listed above, except by attributing to Germans an inherent, subhuman barbarity that comes perilously close, no matter how we try to get around it, to the inherent, subhuman malice the Nazis attributed to Jews.

A race of barbarians with inherent streaks of virulent anti-Semitism does not metamorphose into a race of liberal humanists overnight, as Professor Goldhagen incongruously insists in his book. The influence of post-war education could not achieve such a miracle. If Germans are not genocidally anti-Semitic today—as indeed they are not—it is because Germans were never uniquely or inherently genocidal or anti-Semitic. They were just situational murderers between 1933 and 1945, as many groups have been at one period or another.

If we view the monstrous tragedy of the Holocaust as only one of many such monstrous tragedies in human history, then the accurate question becomes "Why *not* in Germany?" Why could Germans not do evil in the same way that so many other people have done?

"I would suggest that barbarism be considered as a permanent and universal human characteristic which becomes more or less pronounced according to the play of circumstances." It was the French Catholic philosopher Simone Weil, a converted Jew, who wrote these lines in an article entitled "Hitler and Roman Foreign Policy" in 1940. The half century that has elapsed since has given us no better insight.

A DIFFERENT QUESTION

If there is nothing unique about the Nazi Holocaust (aside perhaps from its dimension), why does it preoccupy us more than other holocausts?

Some may dispute the premise the question implies, but it is clear that the Holocaust perturbs us more than other holocausts, including holocausts of comparable proximity and magnitude. Match it, for instance, with our attitude to the Communist holocaust. While Nazi criminals who played a direct role in the murder of six million are still hunted down and tried, we rarely prosecute Communist criminals of similar degrees of responsibility. (Interestingly, almost all the exceptions occurred in Germany, which did prosecute some former East German officials after unification.) Elsewhere it has been more usual for ex-functionaries of KGB- or Gulag-type organizations to receive government positions or pensions.[29]

The Nazi Party was immediately outlawed in post-war Germany. The Communist Party, in contrast, is still the official opposition in the former Soviet Union. Ex-Nazi officials like Kurt Waldheim, once discovered, became international untouchables. Ex-Communist officials like Mikhail Gorbachev are still asked to join think-tanks or lecture at Western universities. It would be unthinkable for known ex-Nazis to be invited to the same diplomatic cocktail receptions in Western countries at which ex-Communists, or even current Communists, are honoured guests. And imagine a former Gestapo officer being accepted as the president of post-Nazi Germany, the way ex-KGB officer Vladimir Putin has been accepted as the president of post-Soviet Russia.

The representation of Nazis in literature, art, and the cinema as genocidal figures of pure evil exceeds by a wide margin any similar representation of Communists. Scholars teach the ideas of Karl Marx at Western universities in a manner no scholar could teach the ideas of Arthur de Gobineau without risking his tenure. One need not even object to this, but one cannot escape noting it. It is a fact.

Why do we react to the Nazi Holocaust and the Communist holocaust differently? I believe it is possible to postulate the following answers:

To begin with, as I noted earlier, the Holocaust provided people with the initial images of mass slaughter as the Nazi death camps were being liberated by the Allies. Cinemas around the world showed—for the first time in history—heaps of skeletal corpses being pushed into mass graves by bulldozers, along with mounds of footwear, gold teeth, artifacts alleged to have been made of human skin, and charred remains inside the incinerators of Auschwitz. The impact of that early documentary footage cannot be overestimated. No ordinary person had ever seen anything like it. In the manner of a childhood experience, those inaugural images literally shocked the world's conscience. "People will not believe this," remarked General Dwight Eisenhower, shaken by the sight, even though he already knew what he was going to see.

The Communist holocausts provided no comparable photo opportunities. The islands of the Gulag deep inside the Soviet Union or China remained inaccessible to the cameras of the Western media. Their millions of victims between the 1920s and the 1980s perished unseen. By the time a few snippets appeared on television screens, such as the aftermath of the holocaust in Cambodia, audiences had become inured to death and destruction through repeated exposure. Pictures of slaughter in people's living rooms became commonplace during the television coverage of the Vietnam War. By the end of the 1970s photographic images had lost their power to shock the same way as they had in the mid-1940s.

Another contributing reason, at least until recently, was the contrasting attitude many opinion makers had to Nazism as opposed to Communism. Identical as the two intoxicants may have been, intellectuals could get drunk on the wine of one far more easily than the other. Nazism never "travelled," to borrow an expression from viticulture. Communism did.

There were self-evident reasons for this. It would have been nonsensical for ideas of German superiority to become an export item for non-Germans, or ideas of Aryan superiority for non-Aryans. Marxist notions of the class struggle faced no similar obstacles. In addition, Nazism as a social theory could rely on nothing but the coldest and most selfish of human impulses to justify its call for conquest and slaughter, but Communism could also enlist warm and humane impulses of altruism to rationalize its own genocides. It may be a hopeful sign that more people— and better people—respond to calls for social justice than to calls for racial mastery, but it nevertheless enabled left-wing irrationality to disguise itself in a manner not available to right-wing irrationality.

Next, given that Nazism suffered an abject military defeat within a decade of its emergence, while Communism appeared to march from triumph to triumph until the mid-1980s, it is not surprising that generations of opinion makers in academia, journalism, and government have been reluctant to discuss acts of Communist genocide in the same breath with Nazi acts of genocide. To this day, Communist holocausts may be respectably denied in countries whose laws treat the denial of the Nazi Holocaust as a crime.

World opinion has also been affected by the fact that the largest single group of Hitler's victims were Jews. Murdering six million members of one group does not have exactly the same consequences as murdering six million members of another. Recent massacres of Mayans, Moluccans, or Kurds have not resulted in the same echo as earlier massacres of Armenians. The opprobrium that attaches to genocide will vary not only with the slaughter's magnitude, cruelty, irrationality, documentability, and scope, but also with the ability of its victims and survivors to attract attention and sympathy.

All victims are equal in their desire for, and entitlement to, the world's notice, but they are not always equal in their capacity to capture it. When Germans decided to exterminate the Jews, they picked the wrong group. As individuals, Jews tended to be gifted and articulate. As an aggregate, they were well placed to disseminate information, especially in the Western hemisphere. Traditional Jewish occupations, in addition to science, business, and the law, included such natural forums as the literary arts, the entertainment industry, and the media. What's more, the Diaspora spread Jews all over the globe. Many rose to prominence in various fields. Jews always amounted to a constituency in many key nations, at least in weight if not in numbers. "Jews are news," as an eminent Western scholar on Islam quipped in a speech in 2002, quoting an old witticism.[30]

Anti-Semites have often pounced on these characteristics, distorted them, or used them illegitimately, mixed with false ones of their own invention, to raise the spectre of a mythical "Jewish conspiracy." That is poisonous rubbish, but it does not mean that some of these characteristics do not exist. It is hardly surprising that Jews were traumatized by Nazism and resented being murdered. As they had the necessary attributes to attract public attention, they relied on them—especially after the Holocaust—in self-defence. They wanted the world to remember what happened.[31]

Still, the foremost reason for which we view the Holocaust not only as one of many such abysses in humanity's past, but as a unique occurrence and the epitome of evil, is probably different. I will attempt to illustrate it with a quote from the evidence of the camp survivor and writer Elie Wiesel at the 1987 trial of Klaus Barbie in Lyons.

"How do you describe the sorting out on arriving at Auschwitz, the separation of children who see a father or mother going away, never to be seen again?" Wiesel asked the French court. "How do you express the dumb grief of a little girl and the endless lines of women, children, and rabbis being driven across the Polish or Ukrainian landscapes to their deaths? No, I can't do it. And because I'm a writer and teacher, I don't understand how *Europe's most cultured nation* could have done that. For these men who killed with submachine guns in the Ukraine were university graduates. Afterwards they would go home and read a poem by Heine. So what happened?" (Emphasis added.)[32]

In a strict, literal sense, Wiesel was mistaken. Most men who killed with submachine guns in the Ukraine were neither university graduates nor readers of Heine. The hands-on murderers of the Holocaust tended to be former factory hands, agricultural workers, or petty civil servants. Such people entertained themselves at best with the waltzes of Johann Strauss the Younger, not with the cantatas of Johann Sebastian Bach. Readers of poetry were the exception, not the rule, among the executioners of the Third Reich (and even they would have been unlikely to read Heine, who as a Jew had been proscribed by the Nazis.)

But in a larger, more essential sense, Wiesel was touching on a key point.

Germany *was* Europe's most cultured nation. It was a nation of Kant, Beethoven, and Goethe. Even if only a minuscule minority of its Nazis read poetry or played Mozart on the piano, the gulf between the cultural history of Germany's inhabitants and their barbaric behaviour during the Nazi era was incomprehensibly wide. It stunned their victims as it stunned the world.

The scope and barbarity of the Holocaust would have been stunning even if carried out by headhunters from Borneo, but it was not. It was carried out by Germans. It may be difficult for post-war generations raised in the last half century—during which Germans became equated with the Nazi salute, not only in popular entertainment but also in political and academic discourse—to understand the sheer bewilderment people felt in the decade between the mid-1930s and the 1940s as they were gradually discovering the full extent of the base and vulgar brutality of Hitler's regime. It did not seem "typically" German, as we might think of it today, but fundamentally un-German. It did not fit. It made the world appear out of joint.

The German-Jewish diarist, Victor Klemperer, made the following diary entry for July 13, 1933:

[Kühn] said Mussolini's regime corresponded to the tyrannies of the Italian Renaissance, it is therefore evidently compatible with the Italian psyche and will last for example like the rule of the Medici, Este etc., it is a "southern" form of government. In Germany (and that is my opinion also after all) this form is nowhere to be found in its history. It is absolutely un-German and consequently will not have any kind of long-term duration.[33]

For Europe's Jews at the time, the singularity of the Holocaust did not arise (as Professor Goldhagen postulates) from their sense that Germans were more virulently anti-Semitic than any other group. On the contrary, it arose from their sense that Germans were more enlightened and civilized. It arose from their experience of reading German books, studying German philosophy, listening to German music, fighting alongside German comrades during the First War, and more than anything else, living among Germans. It arose from their experience that Germans were *less* intolerant than others, not more.

At the risk of trivializing a cataclysmic event by a facile metaphor, the Holocaust was like a society murder. Society murders become notorious because of the contrast between the criminal and the crime. Butchery in the slums hardly makes the back pages, but the same act committed in a mansion becomes headline news. The crimes of a serial killer would be noted in any event, but if Jack the Ripper turns out to be the Archbishop of Canterbury, it occupies a unique place in the annals of crime. It becomes singular. This, I suggest, is what happened in 1945 when the Allies entered Bergen-Belsen and revealed the Germans to the world as mass murderers.

Nations are different from one another, possibly in certain innate ways, and undoubtedly in their traditions and culture. But these differences define us much less than our fatal similarities. It is the human race that is genocidal, not the Germans. Saying this is not to excuse the Germans, but to note a fact. In one vital sense we are all Jews and we are all Germans, potentially, depending on the conditions in which we find ourselves. Remembering this may reduce the likelihood that we will ever be Jews or Germans again as Jews or Germans were during one nightmarish period between 1933 and 1945.

2
MAD COWS,
SACRED COWS

14

THE BEST

POLICY

A virtue to be serviceable must,
like gold, be alloyed with some commoner
but more durable metal.
—SAMUEL BUTLER

THE RULE OF THE SWASTIKA ended over the eastern half of Budapest on January 18, 1945. That was the good news. The bad news was that on the same day the rule of the hammer and sickle began. The Soviet emblem held sway over only one side of the city at first, the side where we lived, the side called Pest. In old Buda, on the western side of the Danube, the fighting continued for another three or four weeks. The Hungarian capital as a whole remained a war zone almost until the end of February.

After some days spent on a diet of dried peas cooked in melted snow, my father set out with my honest uncle in search of more interesting food. We called my uncle Moritz "honest uncle" not because the rest of the family's numerous uncles or cousins were less honest, but because they had other distinguishing features. Uncle Moritz had none—at least none that could be condensed into one telling word or phrase. Unlike my Zionist uncle, or my Communist uncle, or my anti-Communist uncle, or my great-uncle the Musical General, or my uncle Stiglitz the Nimrod, or my Viennese aunt, had we not called Uncle Moritz our "honest uncle," we could only have called him our "avionics designer uncle," which would have been cumbersome. According to my father, even "honest" was a misnomer because Uncle Moritz was guileless rather than simply honest, but he agreed that we could let it pass.

My honest uncle was an electrical engineer, specializing in avionics, i.e., navigation and communication equipment for aircraft. Other family members of his generation usually sojourned in Paris, Berlin, Vienna, or Rome during their formative years, but my honest uncle spent his in Schenectady. This mid-sized company town in eastern New York State (from which General Electric station WGY transmitted the world's first regular television program in 1928) was something of a Mecca for aficionados of electronics before World War II. His wife, Etelka Freund, a

"Aunt Etelka made an abysmal choice geographically." Etelka Freund with Béla Bartók in 1908.

noted concert pianist, had been a student of the German-Italian virtuoso Ferruccio Busoni as well as a close friend of the Hungarian composer Béla Bartók.

Clever as they had been about matters musical and electrical, Uncle Moritz and Aunt Etelka made an abysmal choice geographically. They decided to return from New York shortly before the war to join their oldest son, Endre, who had been studying in Vienna. The parents did somehow survive the years that followed; Endre did not. Luckily for their younger son, Miklós, Aunt Etelka and Uncle Moritz had left him in the United States to complete his studies, and he ended up in a happily uneventful career at the State Department.

Uncle Moritz and my father got on well together, despite—or perhaps because of—their personalities being so different. My honest uncle was serious to the point of being earnest; my father was sardonic to the point of being (or at least appearing to be) flippant. Father could not resist unstuffing stuffed shirts and might say things just *pour épater le bourgeois,* even if he did not mean them. My honest uncle would never say anything he did not mean. He was not stiff or pompous—just, well, *honest.*

Budapest was in ruins on that day in late January when the two of them set out to scrounge for food. It was bitterly cold. In the streets one could see little but rubble mixed with dead bodies, half-covered by snowdrifts. Some of the bodies had previously belonged to horses. They were an excellent source of protein, much in demand by the half-starved population. My father carried an empty pail and a large kitchen knife in anticipation of the bounty. My honest uncle, more realistically, had brought a handsaw, a pair of needle-nose pliers, and a hammer to tackle the frozen meat.

The occupation forces ruled the Pest side of the city, but things were still haphazard and disorganized. In the confusion, occupying troops could not count on maintenance or supplies any more than the occupied population. In addition to regular Red Army patrols, or units purposefully moving from one point to another, there were scores of stragglers, deserters, and marauders picking their way through the debris and detritus of the siege.

Turning a corner, my father and uncle encountered one such derelict. The Russian soldier was lost and in trouble. The front tire of his Zis 42 halftrack was not only flat but had almost come off the rim. It had split; it was beyond repair. The soldier had been so busy cursing, kicking, and pummelling it in his fury that at first he did not even notice my father and uncle.

This suited my father just fine. He would have been content to walk quietly by, but my uncle was intrigued by all mechanical problems. He stopped. The Russian turned and noticed him.

He was a young man, exhausted, suspicious, and angry. He had been trying to catch up with his unit, my father assumed, when his vehicle ran over some explosive or debris. Now he was stuck, alone in an enemy city, and in no mood to be trifled with.

"What are you staring at, you old fool?" he said to my uncle, speaking in Russian. "You never seen a shredded tire before?"

My uncle spoke no Russian, and he looked at my father for help. My father had no Russian either, but was fluent in both Czech and Slovak. He had little trouble understanding Russians or making himself understood by them.

"He wants to know if you've seen a shredded tire before," he translated for my uncle. Then, when my honest uncle nodded, he said to the soldier: "Yes—he says he has."

The soldier cursed. "Where's the tire depot? There's got to be one in this fucking city. I need a tire. Ask him."

"He wants you to tell him where to get a new tire," my father said, unperturbed.

My honest uncle was astounded. He could not believe his ears. He looked at the rubble, the snowdrifts, the utter devastation, then spread his arms wide.

"A *tire*?" he asked incredulously. "God, I don't know."

The Russian understood the gesture, and responded by levelling his submachine gun at my honest uncle. "You fucking saboteur," he said. "You don't know, eh? Now try to remember."

This time my father did not bother translating. "*He* doesn't know," he said to the soldier, "but I do."

The Russian looked at him. "Go down this street," said my father, pointing, "until you reach the third intersection. Then turn right, and walk half a kilometre. You'll see a square. Across the square, there's a narrow lane. At the end of the lane is the depot with tires."

The soldier lowered his gun, cursed again, hesitated for a second, then turned and started walking down the street at which my father was still pointing.

My honest uncle looked at my father in astonishment. "Is there a depot for tires at the end of that laneway?" he asked.

"I'm not sure," my father said, "but here's what I suggest. I'll be on my way now, looking for food. You stay here. You wait for that soldier. And when he comes back—ask him."

Postscript: I realize this sounds like a war story by the Baron Münchausen. Frankly, if I had heard it from my father, I would not have believed it. But I heard it from my honest uncle.

15

EUROSEX

Only child life is real life.
—GEORGE ORWELL

AT TWELVE I WAS A MAN WITH A PAST. I had a past like most twelve-year-olds, or perhaps more than most, because my past included the war. But even if the past of other twelve-year-olds does not include memories of the battlefield, it usually includes the most important events of their lives, or perhaps of life itself. Though everything is still to come at twelve, though the future seems like an empty book with blank pages, the things that really matter, the things that determine the rest, have usually all happened. The remainder is just commentary.

But this is hard to believe, even though saying it has become a commonplace. This is among the great contradictions that befuddle us all: the truth is a cliché. We all know the truth, therefore it has no effect on us, and we behave as if we were ignorant of that which we know. We feel the truth in our bones; we paint it, use it in speeches, put it into books, and then dismiss it. I certainly did for many years.

Like all men with a past, mine included women. It included a woman named Zsuzsi, one named Éva, and one whose name I can no longer recall. I will call her Juli-or-Mari, because servant girls were mostly called Juli or Mari, and she was a servant girl.

But Juli-or-Mari came much later. Zsuzsi came first, in point of time and perhaps also in importance. She and I were both six when we got into the habit of wandering off from our gossiping nannies to sit beside each other on a secluded bench in the Museum Garden. (Many years later my mother was to insist that Zsuzsi actually exclaimed once, "*Ach, wie praktisch!*" when she happened to observe me take out my penis to pee behind some bushes, but I wonder. Little girls exclaiming, "How practical!" on observing little boys using their penises to pee was just folklore. It was a story making the rounds at the time, and I think my mother simply appropriated it.) But Zsuzsi did have a keen interest in my body parts, of that there was no doubt.

The interest was mutual. I am not sure how it all began, but during the summer of 1941, when adults talked about the imminent fall of Britain or exchanged whispered rumours about the cellars of the Gestapo, Zsuzsi and I found ourselves in the dense botanical garden behind the playground, intently bending over each other's thighs and tummies. We mostly looked, but we also touched a little, with me doing most of the touching. What Zsuzsi liked was to take my hand and place it on her leg or lower body. Then she would lean back and close her eyes, while I drew straight lines or circles on her skin with my forefinger.

The lines or circles were not arbitrary. They had a specific meaning, according to the rules of our game. This was because, in spite of our complete innocence, we understood two things. The first was that we should always play our game in private, and the second that we should pretend, even to ourselves, that it was something other than what it was.

Zsuzsi would ask me to operate on her, to open her up and look inside, and in particular to cut off her leg. We enjoyed the procedure immensely, especially its aftermath, when Zsuzsi would lean on me and hop around the bench on one leg. We were convinced that we had invented the game. In some respects we may have, because requesting an amputation was probably an individual embellishment on Zsuzsi's part (her father happened to be an army surgeon), but what we did not know was that in playing doctor we were imitating six-year-olds all over the world. There were millions of children playing our private game, and we never knew it. Nor did we know that in our species there is a transitory sexual phase that flares up very early before it goes underground again to lie dormant until the awakening of puberty many years later.

It was grandmother who put an end to our game. She put an end to it as soon as she saw us together in the garden one day, but not because she suspected anything. She suspected only that Zsuzsi was a girl and I was a boy. For grandmother that was enough.

"My father found it hard to keep a straight face." Mother and Father being amused by my Victorian grandmother. This snapshot was taken on Kékes Mountain in 1943, a year before the German occupation of Hungary.

"I caught Gyuri with the army doctor's girl, that little Zsuzsi Schmidt," grandmother said to my father ominously at supper. "They were sitting on a bench in the bushes. Don't ask me where the nanny was."

My father found it hard to keep a straight face. He always referred to grandmother as "Vicky," only behind her back of course, because in his view she not only acted but looked like Queen Victoria. My grandmother and my father were the same age, born in the penultimate decade of the Victorian era, but my father considered himself a child of the twentieth century, which grandmother decidedly was not.

"Dear me," he said to her. "Gyuri and little Zsuzsi. What did you do when you discovered this Satanic plot?"

"Spanked them, what else?" Grandmother seemed puzzled. "Then I gave Zsuzsi to her nanny, and brought Gyuri home. I should have spanked Aliza, too"—that was my nanny, an Alsatian girl—"but I didn't want to create a scene."

"Very prudent," my father nodded. "Your wife is a prudent woman," he continued, turning to my grandfather. "She realizes that our Aliza must be handled with care."

My father warmed to the subject, as was his custom. "Consider," he said, "that Aliza's home region served as a *casus belli* in two world wars. True, Alsace gave us acetylsalicylic acid, Albert Schweitzer, Captain Alfred Dreyfus, a tasty dish called choucroute, and nannies in every capital of Europe, but choucroute causes indigestion, acetylsalicylic acid couldn't even be turned into Aspirin until the Germans figured out how, Schweitzer regressed from a splendid organist into a middling do-gooder, and Alsatian nannies carry on like the dickens when you spank them. This leaves only Dreyfus," my father added darkly.

"Pass the butter," my grandfather replied. He rarely made any reply without a practical component. "Prudent or not, my wife gave me dry toast tonight. How does she expect me to have my toast without butter? Tssk, eh, huh!"

Grandfather ended most of his remarks with the words "tssk, eh, huh!" The exclamation was meant to convey that the world was going to the dogs, and right-thinking people were powerless to do anything about it. When, many years later, I told

"The world was going to the dogs."
Grandfather, 87, and grandmother,
79, in the Museum Garden of
Budapest, 1962.

grandfather that I was off to America, goodbye, he again replied "Tssk, eh, huh!" except he immediately turned away because he started crying. I excused him because he was a very old man by then, well over eighty.

But I am cutting ahead of myself. This ends the tale of Zsuzsi Schmidt, Doctor-Major Schmidt's daughter, whatever became of her, and Éva is next. Oh, Éva.

If Zsuzsi was a creature of the flesh, Éva was one of the spirit. For me, at least, because I never laid a finger on Éva. All I wanted was for her to notice me. I still have no idea what I would have done if she ever had, for I was well past the age of playing doctor, but still too young for other games.

Éva was an older woman. She was twelve when I was nine, during the last summer of the war in Europe. In my mind Éva became intimately linked with the hostilities, but there was a special reason for that. The war had put into my hands the instrument with which I expected to seduce her.

By the summer of 1944 the Allied air raids on Budapest had turned from a sporadic into a daily event. Twice daily, in fact, because the Americans bombed during the daylight hours, and the British bombed during the night. The Russians also bombed the city, but at less predictable intervals. Everybody knew about an impending raid because the regular radio broadcast was interrupted by a male voice gravely intoning the German code, "*Achtung, Achtung, Lichtspiele, Krokodil gross,*" fifteen or twenty minutes before the bombs began to fall. "*Krokodil gross*" meant that a wave of bombers from an Allied base had crossed into southwestern Hungary. The planes were usually bound for Budapest if they came from that particular quadrant.

When bombs exploded, they burst into fragments. The resulting shrapnel was usually small, with the jagged pieces of metal ranging from less than an inch to three inches in length. They were often coloured by the explosion. Chemical residues combined to produce kaleidoscopic hues of blue and silver, strikingly beautiful sometimes, like gemstones. Fragments were like gemstones in another respect as well, because they soon became standard units of exchange in school. Big and flawless pieces were rare and valuable, like big sapphires or emeralds.

I had a shrapnel that was nearly half a foot long. Textured metallic blue and polished silver, it was a showstopper in class. Whenever I pulled it out of my pocket a crowd was certain to gather. Once I refused an offer of a three-horned toad for it, even though the toad came with a week's supply of flies and a ladder of twigs inside a jar, so that one could use it for a barometer. Toads were reputed to sense atmospheric pressure and climb up and down their ladders to forecast highs and lows, a feat for which a reliable toad was much in demand.

I knew about toads, but no one ever told me how to woo girls. Still, I had a clear understanding of the procedure. A boy attracted and impressed a girl by displaying his possessions. He might even offer her some of them as gifts. The girl, so attracted and impressed, would in turn bestow on the boy her company, and that was that.

Éva lived on the fifth floor of a block of flats designated as a Jewish ghetto by the authorities. We lived on the third floor. If I stood on the landing at certain times in the morning, Éva had to pass me on her way to school. My plan was to have the fragment in my hand, pretending to be engrossed in its aesthetic allure. Éva would find the shrapnel irresistible, like everyone else. She could not help stopping and admiring it as she was passing by, and the rest would naturally follow.

I still remember the first morning when I put the plan into operation. Éva was slim but fully developed, not given to girlish skipping or jumping. She ambled down the stairs at a comfortable pace, her blond plait neatly tied with a blue ribbon. Nibbling contentedly on the remnants of a yellow pear, she glanced at me with utter indifference before continuing on her way downstairs.

She simply walked by me. Evidently she never noticed the shrapnel.

The next morning I repeated the procedure, taking care to display the metal fragment in the plainest possible view, but the result was the same. Only the piece of fruit on which Éva nibbled was different: on this occasion it was a green apple.

I was more puzzled than dismayed. The idea that Éva might notice the shrapnel without it having any effect on her did not even enter my mind. I knew that the shrapnel was irresistible, and not only to my schoolmates. Even grandfather reached for it once and examined it from every angle before remarking "Tssk, eh, huh!" and handing it back to me.

Let me explain this carefully. The fact that Éva would look through *me* was not puzzling or dismaying. I took it for granted that a girl would pay no attention to me—not only a magnificent girl like Éva, with blond plaits, knee-length skirts, and visible breasts, but any girl. There was nothing about a boy to interest a girl, except for his possessions. That was why I was relying on the shrapnel. What amazed me was that Éva would reject the shrapnel in my hands.

In my view, shared by everyone in school, girls were wanted for themselves (as long as they were pretty: who would ever want an ugly girl?) but boys were wanted for what they had. Exclusively for what they had; what else could a girl possibly want a boy for?

But Éva was not responding. This was clear enough after my week-long vigil on the landing where she passed me every morning without a glance at my shrapnel. Still, the depths of her unresponsiveness became evident only a short while later. It was revealed by a game called Spaceship.

It happened during my first invitation to a gathering of older children who all lived in our block of flats. The coterie was very exclusive, including a majestic boy named Gordon who was almost sixteen. The group usually partied upstairs on the patio of flabby, cross-eyed, thick-lipped thirteen-year-old Miklós, a.k.a. Squinty, whose father rented the penthouse. Despite my possession of a unique shrapnel, I had never been asked to join this august company—at nine, I belonged to a lower order of beings—but for some reason they did ask me one day, along with my closest friend, a ten-year-old boy whose name I no longer recall. Éva was there, of course, and that's where I was introduced to the game.

I had no idea what Spaceship was all about when Miklós started handing out pencils and pieces of paper to everyone. "God, now we have to explain the whole thing to him all over again," he sighed. "Suppose the earth is about to be destroyed," he said to me in a condescending tone, "but you have this rocket. You can escape to the moon, but who will you take along? There's only room for one person. Okay? Okay, so write his or her name on top. Then, supposing you had room for two people, write down the name of your second choice, then the third, the fourth, and so on. There are twelve of us here. When you're finished, put your own name on the list. Whoever scores highest, wins."

"Just the people in this room?" I asked.

"Yeah, yeah, just in this room. Forget about your parents and everybody else."

In retrospect, what strikes me about this game now is its amazing cruelty. Letting people know exactly how we feel about them, ranking them in the order of our affection in relation to others, may be the most hurtful thing we can do. Did we know this? Were we just naïve at our age, or had we not yet learned to mask our desire to wound? Children are said to be more honest than grown-ups, but noting this only shows that honesty is a dubious commodity. In our hands it was rarely a virtue. A frank announcement of our hierarchy of friendship injured us all, and it may have scarred some of us for life.

My list was a particular disaster. I could not help putting Éva's name on top. It amounted to a humiliating confession of a crush on a girl who had never even glanced at me, but another thing made matters worse. Putting Éva on top bumped my closest friend to second place: my closest friend, the one who came with me to the party, and the only one in the group who had put my name first on his list.

Predictably, Éva's own list had majestic Gordon at the top. I was at the bottom. Even my friend's name came ahead of mine on her list. Éva would have taken everybody to the moon in preference to me. It was worse than devastating; it was shameful.

Next day I traded my shrapnel for the barometric toad. Naturally I stopped waiting for Éva on the landing, but the curious thing was this: until then I would keep bumping into her, by accident as often as by design, but as soon as I made up my mind to stop having a crush on her, I never saw her again, not even by chance, until well after the war.

By then I had long forgotten Éva, or just about, when one day I saw a puffy teenager chatting in a park with some friends. It was hard to credit, but it was Éva. There was no doubt about it. She had developed into an obese sixteen-year-old. I noticed in particular that her legs were thick and shapeless. It did not amount to a complete relief, but it made me feel much better.

Juli-or-Mari lived in our house. Her principal job was to keep it tidy, which usually occupied her from six o'clock in the morning, when she emerged from a narrow chamber near the service entrance, until about two o'clock in the afternoon. After that she was "underfoot" in the kitchen, as our cook, Old Panna, described her presence, until she could get rid of her by inventing some errand. Juli-or-Mari would announce her imminent departure by spreading an embroidered shawl over her blouse, then sticking her head, crowned with a wreath of thick, blond braids, into my mother's boudoir. "To the shop, now," she would elucidate. "Anything for Sir or Madam?"

Though Juli-or-Mari always referred to my parents in the customary third person, it would never have crossed her mind to be servile or even subservient. She was unassailable in her dignity as a peasant princess, with eyes the colour of amber, strong arms for carrying buckets of water, wide hips for bearing children, and a solemn mien for surveying the world. Her features were expressive enough—her eyebrows might wrinkle to convey stern urgency, or arch high to communicate astonishment or disapproval—but they would never break into anything as frivolous as a smile.

"Father says to be with Sir and Madam until I am eighteen next July," she announced to my mother when she took her on, "and then to be back in the village to marry."

"Whom are you marrying?" my mother asked.

"Father didn't say," replied Juli-or-Mari, unperturbed.

Mother consulted Old Panna about the new acquisition, as she always did, knowing that without the assent of the ranking servant the household could be in turmoil. Old Panna examined Juli-or-Mari in much the same way as she inspected live ducks or chickens at the market, even pinching her cheeks and lifting her braids to blow at the soft blond down at the back of her neck. Then she just said, "She'll do," and took Juli-or-Mari by the hand to the narrow chamber where she was to live for the next eleven months.

Old Panna was a childless widow. She regarded servant girls as foundlings, procured by my parents for her benefit in some misguided act of kindness. We lived in a downtown flat with no pasture, no garden, and no domestic animals. Old Panna had a tolerant view of the bookish classes, but she could never fathom why we thought that she could not handle the household chores all by herself, what with running water in the building and the milk and ice delivered to the door every day. Why spend good money on a servant girl and a laundress? "May God tear out my tongue before I say anything bad about this family," she explained to me once, "but my mother looked after nine of us, and we even had the seven acres, the two cows, and the pig."

"Oh yes," my father said sarcastically when I related Old Panna's remark to him. "I'm quite familiar with bucolic households like Old Panna's. You could eat off the floor, and the pig probably did, too."

Juli-or-Mari was rather smug about the fact that her father had sent her into service in town so that she might do "easy work" as a young girl before settling down to the serious business of a rural marriage. It was all a matter of perspective, because many people would not have viewed her duties in our household as easy work. In the winter it began with carrying cradles of wood from the cellar upstairs for the blue porcelain fireplaces—our flat, like most flats in Budapest at the time, lacked central heating. Once a week it was her task to drag the heavy carpets into the courtyard for a thorough beating because appliances like vacuum cleaners were just about unknown. On washdays she assisted the hunchback laundress who made her appearance at the monstrous metal tubs in the attic, along with the traditional caraway-seed soup, staple for laundry days, on the menu. There were no laundromats in the city and no one had electric machines for washing or drying.

Shopping, which Juli-or-Mari viewed as a pleasant diversion, entailed taking immense woven baskets on daily treks to the greengrocer, the butcher, the baker, the florist, the pharmacist, and the tobacconist. This was all in addition to her regular tasks of dusting, sweeping, scrubbing, making beds, polishing silver, ironing, and often also mending, because frayed cuffs and such were not worth the price of a seamstress or a tailor, nor would anyone have dreamed of throwing away a good pair of socks for a hole. Butter, milk, and other perishables were safe enough in the cool pantry until March, but between spring and autumn the iceman delivered big slabs of ice to the door that needed to be chopped into small pieces for the icebox. The refuse was ultimately disposed of by a janitor, but Juli-or-Mari had to carry it down to the courtyard every day in metal containers as incinerator chutes or plastic garbage bags had not yet come into existence.

But it was still easy work, because water did not have to be drawn from a well, septic tanks did not have to be drained, stables did not have to be mucked, gardens did not have to be weeded, fruits and vegetables did not have to be picked or dug up for the table, and livestock did not have to be fed, milked, or taken out to pasture. There were no sides of beef to hang in the shed or sausages to be cured or stuffed. Meat came from the butcher cut into steaks, strips, and chops, ready to be braised, fried, or boiled. Only chickens, ducks, and fish—usually horned pouts or splendid carps—needed to be gutted, plucked or scaled after they were brought home live from the market. This was Juli-or-Mari's job, but Old Panna never delegated the task of slaughtering to anyone. She did not fuss much with the fish before she banged them with a mallet, but she squeezed the poultry firmly between her thighs so that they would not wiggle as she bent back their necks and slit their throats with a serrated knife, carefully collecting the blood in a dish. Chicken blood was my due, fried with a little flour and onions for *Zehnuhrjause,* or elevenses, as it was believed to promote growth.

Juli-or-Mari called me "the young Sir" and regarded me with unabashed curiosity. At thirteen I was big for my age, possibly due to the liberal infusion of chicken blood in my diet, and something of a peripheral sex object for a healthy peasant girl of seventeen. She first expressed her interest by giving me a firm shove as I was passing near a divan in the blue salon. Except for Old Panna in the kitchen, we were alone in the flat.

Her sudden gesture was an invitation to roughhouse, such as a boy might extend to another in school. Naturally I turned and pushed her back. She grabbed my hand and held on. Though we were about the same size, she was marginally stronger. For a few seconds we tussled silently, until she managed to twist and pin me on the sofa. We lay there for a few more seconds, panting for breath. Her thick, blond braids came undone. So did the top buttons of her blouse, popping out one of her breasts almost to the nipple.

Juli-or-Mari's breasts were no novelty to me. They were objects of fascination from the moment she walked into our house. My glance skipped to them like a needle to a magnet when I first saw her, before I ever raised my eyes to her face. But on this occasion, before she shoved me, my mind had been on other things. Her ambush seemed utterly devoid of erotic content, and I started wrestling with her in earnest as if she had been a boy. Then suddenly I saw her naked breast protruding, only inches from my face.

My hands were free. I raised one to touch her, but then lost my nerve and stopped, not daring to complete the move. The heat of her skin shimmered at my fingertips. I became aware of a distressing tumescence pressing against the inside of my pants. She waited, and so did I. My hope was for some further gesture on her part, a shifting of her body perhaps, or maybe a sound of encouragement, but it never came. She only kept her steady gaze on me, with what seemed like a look of scorn in her amber eyes.

Finally she spoke. "If young Sir doesn't let me go," she said, "I'll scream."

I was not holding her at all. If anything, the weight of her body was pinning me down. I pulled my hand back from the vicinity of her breast, and she bounded up from the sofa, buttoning her blouse as she rose. Then she looked at me again with a sulky expression on her face. She seemed offended, which puzzled me because she started it. As I got up, I had to put a hand in my pocket to shift my painfully erect penis across the seam of my trousers.

"Why did you push me?" I asked.

She shrugged. "Young Sir was in my way," she said. "I've no time to fool around."

From that day we wrestled whenever we found ourselves alone in a room. Either of us might be the instigator, but whoever started it, Juli-or-Mari would grimly fight me off, though always careful not to make a noise. Once when she had scratched me, she immediately put a hand over my mouth to prevent me from crying out. We each employed different holds in our wrestling matches to suit our nature as men and women. I tried to trip, twist, or pin her down. Her holds included pinching my skin and pulling my hair. She also had a way of pressing her chin against my chest and squeezing my body in a bear hug that took my breath away, but she would never let me touch her breasts, no matter how hard I tried. Her cheeks would flush, her braids came tumbling down, and sometimes I could see tears in her eyes.

In retrospect, these fierce tussles were not only to disguise our mutual desire for sex. Our craving was obvious, even to us, but what we did not know was that, in addition, we were also practising strategies appropriate to our sex. Juli-or-Mari was testing my genetic fitness, having no interest in wasting her procreative chances on weaklings. I was curious to see if I could take a woman against her will and concluded that I could not. She tried to see if she could prevent a man from raping her and concluded that she could. We were probably both mistaken, but that was another matter.

I think we were lucky that our carnal awakening occurred half a century ago. Today our neo-Victorian contemporaries might call our wrestling matches assaults. I could be in trouble with the law as a male, or maybe as "a person in authority" over a servant girl. Juli-or-Mari might be in trouble with the law as an adult sexually addressing herself to a minor. But back then we only had to worry about my grandmother and a few other aging Victorians, and we did not have to worry about them much. Their fangs were already ground down, while their priggish successors had not yet grown fangs of their own. There was a lull. The worst period of insanity in political Europe coincided with a brief interlude of sanity in sexual matters.

That was why my non-relationship with Juli-or-Mari had such a sensible ending. She left our household after eleven months of service, just before her eighteenth birthday, and still very much a virgin. "Godspeed, young Sir," she said to me coldly in the doorway. Then, just as soon as my mother turned her back on us, she made a face at me and stuck out her comely, pink tongue.

16

FRANKENSTEINISM

It has been said that when human beings stop believing in God they believe in nothing. The truth is much worse: they believe in anything.
—MALCOLM MUGGERIDGE

PROFESSOR FRANKENSTEIN WAS NOT an evil man. He just thought that he could figure out everything. He was not alone. The Age of Enlightenment had turned most of us into mad professors.

In the last two hundred years we have been misled by science. Medicine became our hubris. Having learned to fix appendices, we thought that we could fix history. Western civilization shifted its worshipful glance from the black garb of the priest to the white lab coat of the technician.

Some noted this half a century ago. Among them was the ex-Communist Whittaker Chambers, the prosecution's witness in the Alger Hiss espionage case. In a foreword to his 1952 book *Witness*, Chambers remarked that the first commandment of Communism "is found, not in the *Communist Manifesto,* but in the first sentence of the physics primer: 'All of the progress of mankind to date results from the making of careful measurements.'"

The twentieth century became Professor Frankenstein's world. As World War I was winding down, the mad professor set up one laboratory in Russia, and another in Germany. Both were supposed to create a new man, scientifically, by careful measurements. Another idea, borrowed from the eighteenth-century French philosopher Claude Helvetius, held that in a modern scientific state citizens must be "put under the necessity of being virtuous." The legislators of virtue were to be specialists in disciplines ranging from torture to philosophy. (Professor Frankenstein's Georgian disciple, J.V. Stalin, actually took to describing the hack writers of the Communist state as "engineers of the human soul.") The credo that pupils were obliged to memorize in Soviet schools began, "We Communists are a different kind of people..." As it happened, no different kind of people emerged from Frankenstein's workshops in either Russia or Germany, but it took two more wars, World War II and the Cold War, to subdue the monsters they created.

In the twenty-first century there are some hopeful signs. We may be gradually relearning some of the things people knew in antiquity. For instance, we are beginning to comprehend again that fighting a war to end all wars makes about as much sense as eating a meal to end all meals. We do not conclude from this that we should despair of having meals or waging wars; we are just beginning to understand that a solution is not vain for being provisional. Modesty in expectations does not equal surrender. Taming fate is helpful, even if the ultimate secret is to endure it.

17

TIGER SHARK

How can we reconcile our desire for fairness and equity with the
brutal fact that people are not all alike?
—JUDITH RICH HARRIS

MATZKA-CZÁPA WAS OUR NICKNAME for a teacher in high school. I do not remember his real name, but I can still see him sauntering over to my bench. He looked at me quizzically while I stood at attention, the way pupils were supposed to, without meeting his eyes. Not rigidly, not military-style, just looking straight ahead, hands dangling at the seams of my trousers.

"You know nothing, Jonas," Matzka-Czápa remarked, seeming puzzled. "Your mind is a blank. Earlier in your career you were also very cheeky. One day you decided to stop being cheeky, but your mind is still a blank. Why is that, Jonas?"

The question Matzka-Czápa asked me was obviously rhetorical and there was no need to answer it. But it surprised me; surprised me enough to remember it nearly sixty years later. Not the part about knowing nothing—that was simply true—but the part about being cheeky.

I had never been cheeky with Matzka-Czápa. At least not knowingly, not by design. Was it possible, then, to be cheeky without knowing it? And not only that, but to suddenly stop being cheeky one day and not know that either? It must have been, because Matzka-Czápa was not given to making things up.

Matzka-Czápa was our favourite teacher because at the beginning of the year he offered us an understanding, and then kept it with meticulous fairness. Our part of the bargain was to sit still and try to pay attention to his subjects, biology and Latin, as well as we could for the first half of every period. If we did that, for the remaining thirty minutes he would read us passages from Gaston Leroux's *The Phantom of the Opera*. The French mystery writer's book was very popular just then, even though it had been published in 1911, more than a generation earlier, but after the war it was made into a Hollywood movie starring Claude Rains. The movie also starred Nelson Eddy and Jeanette MacDonald, but they did not matter. Claude Rains was the ticket. Whatever it was about Claude Rains that caught the fancy of Budapest high school students in 1946, ten specimens of Rains's purported autograph was worth one specimen of the purported autograph of Ferenc Puskás, the captain of Hungary's national soccer team. No other film star, not even Rita Hayworth, merited such an extravagant rate of exchange.

Matzka-Czápa's nickname originated in his lisp, which during his first appearance in our classroom caused him to describe an exotic form of marine life—a tiger shark, called *Macska-Cápa* in Hungarian—as tiger *Sark*, or Matzka-Czápa. The nickname became foreordained. The appellations we gave people were usually based on impediments of some sort, physical or psychological. This might appear cruel to modern sensibilities, but we took a different view. Our nicknames, like all caricatures, went to the heart, or at least to the jugular, of the matter. They also stayed with their recipients for a lifetime. Only ten years ago I got a letter from some ancient schoolmate, now living in Australia, that started, "Dear Hippo!"

Chief Cow, our music teacher, did not get his nickname from us. He gave it to himself, gravely and deliberately, with malice aforethought. He was a heavyweight in every sense of the word, bearing a massive frame and the forbidding features of a Beethoven death mask. His name was Zoltán Peskó. Professor Peskó happened to be a prominent organist in a city that prided itself on musical culture, and he resented being put in charge of a post-war U.N. program for distributing milk in schools.

He floated across our horizon like a towering cumulus the day the program started. "Did some of you think perhaps that this was a place of learning?" he asked. "Was it your illusion that I was here to acquaint you with a fugue by Handel? No, my dears, your minds and spirits are of no concern to me. I am here to suckle your disgusting bodies. This venerable institution has changed into a milk farm, courtesy of the United Nations, and I am the chief cow."

The milk was delivered in horse-drawn lorries before the morning classes, even to private or ecclesiastical schools like ours, because the victorious Allies deemed Europe's children to be undernourished. It happened to be a waste of milk in our school, where few children were poor and none went hungry, but Chief Cow had no choice. He was stuck with suckling us for the next year, except he was not obliged to put a good face on it, and he did not. He made no secret of hating us. He took positive delight in it. There was a persistent rumour that he was poisoning the milk, and one day a bold boy put it to him on a dare. He did not bother denying it at all, only chuckled darkly. "Drink up, my dear," he said to the boy. We did not like Chief Cow one bit, but we respected him.

Vizelet was another story.

To this day I cannot be sure why we picked on Vizelet. He was, as I remember him, an ordinary-looking young man. His skin had a sallow hue, his wooden voice lacked resonance, but he was not misshapen or freakish. He had narrow shoulders and a narrow head, topped with a mop of reddish hair. He bore some resemblance to a stream of congealed liquid waste, which was why we promptly dubbed him *Vizelet,* or Urine. But this was not our reason for refusing to put up with him. We would have been content to call him Urine and still cut him some slack, as we did most teachers, had it not been for something else.

I think Vizelet's misfortune was that he let a scent of fear escape from his exocrine glands when he walked into our classroom. It was, as we later discovered, his first teaching job, but it was still a grave error. We were like a pack of hyenas, possessed of sterling qualities like daring and loyalty, but we could smell fear and it made us merciless.

Vizelet, also a music teacher, had been hired to hold the fort for Chief Cow, whose burden of administrative duties often kept him away from the classroom. The substitution was doomed from the start. Submitting to a young man who smelled of fear was a deliberate insult to us, and we did not feel obliged to tolerate it. We submitted to teachers because, in spite of our nicknames for them, their authority was self-evident. It went beyond (though in many cases also included) superior physical strength. Submitting to superior forces involved no humiliation in our ethos, but submitting to weaklings was shameful. It was an indignity from which one could not recover. We were like Zulu braves who know that captives must die, but surrender only on condition that they be put to death by other warriors, not by youths or women. Ours was a traditional school and it understood this atavistic command. Keen as our masters were on discipline, they had no interest in breaking our spirit. They never tried to put schoolmistresses in charge of us, not even when there was a shortage of male teachers during the war. But Vizelet, whose fear we could smell, was more humiliating than a woman. Surrendering to him would have been a crushing indignity, and we were not prepared to do it.

None of this was spelled out, of course. We no more formulated our thoughts than sharks that gather around a thrashing swimmer at sea. We just sensed a vibration in the water and began circling by instinct. Vizelet survived his first class because we could not quite bring ourselves to believe that we might get away with murder, but at his second session we finished him off.

The attack began with whispered exchanges, rippling from bench to bench. Vizelet's repeated entreaties to please pay attention could not quell it. He then tried to be forceful, which made matters worse because his wooden voice broke when he attempted to raise it. Eventually he gave himself the *coup de grâce* by a reckless deadline. "Boys, settle down by the count of ten," he said, "or you're for it." As he began counting, we started counting with him in unison. We reached the count of ten together. There was a beat, then a cheer went up, and the class erupted around Vizelet in a crescendo of derision and laughter. Two boys started fighting in the aisle, another hurled an inkwell, and a fat boy named Skunk threw open the window to look at the scenery outside. No one paid the slightest attention to Vizelet any more. He might as well not have been in the room.

I can still see him standing helplessly in front of the blackboard, with tears welling up in his eyes. He must have tried to say something for we could see his lips move, but his voice was lost in the tumult. Then with a sudden jerk he turned and left the classroom, leaving the door ajar.

We did hope for a victory of some kind, but this was a rout. We could scarcely credit our triumph. No teacher had ever fled the classroom, not in our institution, certainly not in living memory. It was the start of a new era, and we could see no reason to contain ourselves. We climbed on the benches, yelled incoherent war cries, pummelled each other, and threw our books around. One boy kept repeating the word "Guatemala!" for no reason I could think of, then or since. Skunk hustled up to the blackboard and chalked the word VIZELET on it in block letters.

I cannot remember how long our celebration lasted, but it could not have been more than five minutes. Then the door flew open and Chief Cow marched in, with Vizelet in his shadow.

We froze.

The interesting thing was that Chief Cow, who could have said or done anything, chose to say or do nothing. He just stared coldly at us through his Beethoven death mask. He planted himself on the dais, treating us to the sight of his thick, grey hair and his massive shoulders. He seemed to be enjoying himself. He did not break the silence for two or three minutes as we stood at attention with eyes straight ahead and hands dangling by the seams of our pants. If an insect had walked across the floor, we would have heard it. Like a frame of film in a silenced projector we froze wherever we happened to be when the door opened. Unlucky Skunk was still cowering by the blackboard, holding a piece of chalk in his hand.

When Chief Cow finally spoke it was in a conversational tone. He directed his remarks to the nearest boy, without troubling to address the class. "There's some writing on the blackboard behind me," Chief Cow said. "Go and wipe it off, son."

Afterwards we could swear, and did, that Chief Cow never even glanced at the blackboard when he came into the room. How he could possibly notice Skunk's handiwork we could not say. Nor could we explain how he crushed our rebellion so promptly and completely. Chief Cow did not try to admonish, lecture, or shame us. He did not appeal to our better nature, and he uttered no words of reproach. Nor did he have any authority over us that would not have been equally available to Urine. Chief Cow had no special powers. Any teacher could select boys at random, keep them in school after class, write reprimands to be countersigned by their parents, or, in extreme cases, have them expelled by the bishop. Teachers also had the authority to slap a boy, or send him for a caning to the home room teacher, though that rarely happened. Corporal punishment was on the books as a disciplinary measure, but some unspoken consensus disdained its use in our school. Few of us had ever been caned, and none by Chief Cow.

But then how did Chief Cow do it? We argued about it afterwards, with one boy offering poisoned milk as a possible explanation. We laughed, but we were puzzled. It was a mystery.

Chief Cow's parting remarks to Vizelet were icy. "I can't imagine what happened," he said to his younger colleague, speaking loudly enough for us to hear. "As you can see, these boys aren't hard to manage. Finish the period, please. I'm sure you'll have no more trouble."

To say that Vizelet became pale would not do justice to the way the colour drained from his face. He turned albino. He did finish the period, then went home and never came back. Some said he resigned (which was probably all he did) but there were also rumours of suicide. In any case, after a month or two we forgot him. We were ignorant enough to think that he had taught us nothing.

18

A DANUBIAN INTERLUDE

Hypocrite lecteur, mon semblable, mon frère!
—CHARLES BAUDELAIRE

THE THREE OF US WERE HEADED for a small island in the Danube. We had a specific purpose. Tom steered his father's motorboat with a steely resolve inspired by lust, George the Elder affected a jaded posture of world-weariness, while George the Younger, as I was known, felt expectant if a trifle uncertain. We were on our way to a sexual encounter.

Most people would not view a half acre of scrubby, uninhabited mud flat in the middle of the Danube as a promising location for romance. It was the perfect place, though, for the three of us. Having despaired of ever "making" a girl, as the 1950s expression had it, we decided to make one for ourselves. Make one, literally, out of the local materials available. Like God.

Common as it is for adults to look back at their youth with nostalgia, it is rarely justified. Adolescence is almost as undesirable a condition as dotage, except it has a better prognosis. To be a teenage boy is to experience the strongest urges combined with the skimpiest opportunities to satisfy them. Virility comes at a price. Being brought to a state of arousal by the rhythmic bouncing of a car on a bumpy road, in the total absence of any sexual stimulus, is not a bliss but a bother. Yet it is at this superheated stage of his journey as a sexual being that a boy is least able to entice a girl. He is unlikely to have any of the standard qualifiers for attraction in males: status, power, money, sophistication, style, self-confidence, reliability—not even looks. All he is likely to have is pimples.

And, of course, an appetite—an insatiable appetite for food, for sex, for knowledge, and for approval. Also for being noticed—look, Ma, no hands—for better or worse. In short, a teenage boy is not a very attractive creature. He is probably unattractive to most people, but he is especially unattractive to a teenage girl. Unless an older woman takes pity on him by transmuting her motherly instincts into sexual succour, he is unlikely to get lucky when he needs it most.

Which is why we set out to an island in the Danube to fashion a receptacle for our passion. Tom had the motorboat, and George the Elder had the necessary sculpting skills. All I could contribute was my share of ardour. The reddish silt was plentiful, the fresh ooze marvellously pliant, and under George the Elder's inspired hands our Mud Maiden soon started taking shape. She rose out of the wet earth as a bas relief, with her head shyly turned to one side. Her well-developed torso was left enticingly exposed, but some tribal memory prompted us to cover her nakedness with a leaf—white maple, as fig was not available. Then, starting with Tom, we all had our way with her. George the Elder tried out his handiwork second. By the time my turn came the Mud Maiden's slushy locks were slightly disarrayed and she seemed to have sunk deeper into the bog, but she was a welcoming presence to the last.

Twenty years passed; George the Elder went on to became a maker of Hollywood movies; I took up scribbling, and we had both lost sight of Tom. In the late 1960s I recounted the episode to the Canadian writer Margaret Atwood, who promptly turned it into a parable (after duly noting that the story was told to her by "a traveller"). What seemed to attract Atwood to the Mud Maiden's tale was that it showed how men "objectify" women. As grist to the feminist mill, Atwood's moral was not illegitimate—though in fact, innocents as we were, we would have preferred a more animated sex object. In any event, the episode stuck in my mind for a different reason. It had to do with the order in which Tom, George, and I availed ourselves of the Mud Maiden's favours.

In the natural kingdom first go at available mates is governed by a pecking order, established by factors ranging from fighting prowess to relative age. In our little band that day the alpha male turned out to be Tom. It seemed self-evident to us that he should go first; we did not argue about it for a second, nor did we draw lots. Yet there was no obvious reason for it. Tom was not the eldest in our group, nor was he the natural leader. Both distinctions belonged to George. In addition, it was George who created the Mud Maiden. There *was* an obvious reason for me going last; I was the youngest, the low man on the totem pole. But why was Tom first?

The answer seemed as obvious to us then as it seems to me today: the motorboat was Tom's. At least, it belonged to Tom's father. Without this wonderful vessel, we could not have gained access to the Mud Maiden's domain in the first place. But it was more than that. The motorboat was property. It was his property or "territory" that gave Tom the prime prerogative. He possessed that which male songbirds proudly announce when they twitter, chirp, cluck, or warble at nesting time. In the hierarchy of sexual ranking, Tom preceded the rest of us. It was not only a question of how we felt about the matter ourselves. It was *she*. Even though we fashioned the girl out of mud, we were engaged in a ritual of courtship. We knew instinctively how the girl would feel. Tom had territory; we knew that the Mud Maiden would prefer Tom.

19

FATHER'S PERSPECTIVES

The psychoanalysis of individual human beings teaches us with quite special insis-
tence that the god of each of them is formed in the likeness of his father.
—SIGMUND FREUD

ON MAD COW DISEASE

FATHER CONSIDERED CLOSED SYSTEMS HOPELESS. He held that one should give a wide berth to a true believer for the same reason one gives a wide berth to a mad cow. "If you see a mad cow, you don't argue," he explained. "You don't say to her: 'Look, cow, it's like this or like that.' You just step out of her way."

As the Marxists started their stampede in Budapest after the war, Father viewed them as the same herd of crazed bovines as the Fascists and Nazis who preceded them. "They, too, have a short circuit between the ears," he said. "You can actually see the sparks."

If one asked Father to elaborate on mental short circuits, he illustrated with an old Jewish joke:

"Our rabbi talks to God every Saturday."

"What makes you think so?"

"The rabbi told us himself."

"What if the rabbi lies?"

"Don't be ridiculous. God wouldn't talk to a liar every Saturday."

When the Marxists assumed power in 1948, Father insisted that I should not be influenced by the official status of the current bovines. "Sometimes mad cows are elevated to sacred cows," he said, "but sacrament can take a cow only so far."

ON FEMININITY

Father would not have felt at home in our feminine (as well as feminist) times. Fond as he was of women, he had reservations about them. He might have agreed with extreme feminists, though, that men and women were intrinsically incompatible. He liked to use attraction as an example.

"There are many doors to a woman's heart," he would say. "Some may be erotic, but they also include utterly asexual doors marked 'position,' 'kindness,' 'intelligence,' 'income,' or 'security.' To a man's heart there are seldom more than two doors, and they're usually marked 'looks' and 'youth.' Sometimes there may be a third door marked 'vulnerability' but it has a rusty lock and you can't rely on it."

Once I told Father that I was dating a bright girl.

"How bright?" he asked.

"An IQ of 130, maybe more," I said proudly.

"Drop her instantly," said Father. "This minute. I beg of you."

He swivelled on the piano stool to face me. "Brains are a burden," he continued, "to both men and women. However, men are a little sturdier. They can cope with a slightly larger quantity of grey matter. Men usually start cracking around an IQ of 150. Women begin showing the strain around 125.

"Some people think that intelligent women aren't attractive. That's baseless prejudice. Intelligent women can be beautiful, and often are. They can also be affectionate lovers and excellent cooks. The problem's different.

"A woman of high IQ is likely to be unstable. Not always, obviously, but nine times out of ten. She'll be given to swings of mood and fits of temper—if not outright hallucinations. Steer clear."

Father felt that women had a tendency to trivialize life as well as mystify it with their peculiar concerns. As he put it more than once: "I've no time for misogynists, of course. One should keep a sense of proportion about women. Consider the ascetic, Francis of Paula. Francis was abducted from his cave by Louis XI, who hoped that his court might be blessed by the noted hermit's saintliness. Well, Francis ate only roots, and whenever he saw a woman, he screeched in horror. Now this is an exaggerated reaction, even if one can see the holy man's point."

At the time I thought that my father was joking, not only by pretending to understand the ascetic's reaction to women, but by making up the entire story. I grew up believing that Francis of Paula was just a product of my father's peculiar sense of humour. (I was not sure even about Louis XI, until the French king's existence was corroborated in history class.) It was only when I read, years later, a life of Erasmus of Rotterdam that I saw in print my father's story about Francis.[1] The hermit's stance was not only confirmed but embroidered by the attitudes of such forerunners of the Reformation as the adherents of a fifteenth-century religious movement known as *devotio moderna,* one of whose leaders, Egbert ter Beck, would avert his face and close his eyes when speaking to a woman. Consistent with this, ter Beck also held that harmony in music was unseemly ostentation, and true Christians should sing "as frogs croak" to appeal to God. Much as he understood ter Beck's reaction to women, for his musical views my father would have had no sympathy.

ON ARCHIMEDEAN POINTS

Once in a while my father would extol the virtues of what he called "a fixed point" for my benefit. Any fixed point, from patriotism to religion. He said that in one sense it did not matter much what it was, because the real purpose of a fixed point was to be fixed—as in Archimedes' quest to move the Earth, or as in a star to steer by.

"You need a compass, boy, or at least what you take to be a compass. Unless you have a needle in front of you that you believe points to true north, how can you navigate?

"You may be arrogant in your ignorance and say: 'Who needs a compass; I shall navigate by landmarks.' Except people can only navigate by landmarks on their *second* trip, not the first one, and as Omar Khayyám pointed out long ago, you pass this way only once. You may wander around in circles for a while, looking for landmarks, but sooner or later you'll turn to a compass like most people.

"And when you do, you'd better keep your fingers crossed that your compass isn't flawed, that it doesn't have a piece of iron stuck under it, because it will lead you hopelessly astray.

"Astray from what, you ask?" (I didn't.) "Ah, that's an excellent question. From your destination, obviously, whatever that may be. A compass, even a perfect compass, won't tell you if your destination is a good place or a bad place, or how many leagues away it is from you. It will only tell you which horizon it lies over."

ON FLATTERING THE JURY

It puzzled me that in popular films and novels poor people were always good, and usually got the better of rich people, who were invariably bad. It did not take me long to discover that life was different from books and movies. First, poor people rarely triumphed over rich people. Even more importantly, poor people were not necessarily good, nor were rich people necessarily bad.

I asked Father about this.

"Ah," he said. "Yes. There may be an innocent explanation for the first cliché. Writers let poor people triumph over rich people in stories, partly for wish-fulfillment, and partly because the unusual is more diverting. It's *news*, as in man bites dog. But there's no innocent explanation for cliché number two.

"Socialists say that the poor are made out to be good in fairy tales as a moral anaesthetic. They say portraying the poor as 'good' is a conspiracy by the rich to give poor people a sop, to calm them down, and reassure them of a reward in the Kingdom of Heaven.

"This is nonsense, of course, like most socialist beliefs. It presupposes intelligence on the part of the rich, as well as a master plan. There isn't a shred of evidence for either.

"I think writers portray the poor as good from economic self-interest. Writers know that most readers are poor, and they simply try to flatter the jury."

ON THE CLASH OF CIVILIZATIONS

Father passed away long before Samuel Huntington coined the phrase, but he had been aware of the concept. "In theory, all evil is the same," he would say. "In practice, choosing intelligently between evils can make the difference between life and death.

"Assume, for instance," he continued, "that you are a European Jew in the year 1944. As such, you must support everyone in the world against the Nazis, including the Communists. Once the Nazis are defeated, you can support everyone in the world against the Communists, including the Fascists. Once the Communists are vanquished, you may turn against the Fascists, and so on."

"Does it ever end?" I asked.

"Are you serious?" asked Father. "How could it possibly end? Evil is inexhaustible."

I asked Father about the future. "Simpler than you think," he replied. "Far simpler. You have to remember only one thing: People want to lord it over each other. Actually most living things do, even zooids.

"Human beings want supremacy. First for themselves as individuals, and then for their groups. They can't help it; that's the shape of the ladle into which the great Buttonmaker has poured them, to borrow an image from Ibsen.

"Hindus want to lord it over Muslims, Muslims over Hindus, and Christians over both. Ditto for Jews. All groups juggle for ascendancy over other groups. It's true even for children and parents, doctors and patients, or females and males.

"If there's one thing Europeans, Asians, and Africans have in common, it's an urge for primacy. The bottom dog may say that it's looking for equality and justice—it may even believe it—but it's not true. The bottom dog is looking to be the top dog.

"This is the rule. Confuse it with the exceptions at your peril.

"There are exceptions, yes. There are saints and freaks. There may be one in a hundred who genuinely seeks fairness rather than mastery. You may be one such person yourself, but for heaven's sake, don't count on your neighbour being one. The odds are hopelessly against it."

I was silent for a while. "But if this is so," I asked finally, "why were the Nazis wrong?"

"Trust me, the Nazis were wrong," Father replied, "but this isn't the point. The Nazis were your enemies: *that's* the point. Your enemy isn't always wrong, but he's always your enemy."

ON PLANNING VS. PRAYER

"if you're too timid, you'll never make your first cent." Father at age 19, on a visit home from Vienna, 1902.

For part of his life Father was a private banker. He liked to say, "If you're too bold, you'll lose your last cent, and if you're too timid, you'll never make your first cent." This was an inadvertent echo of a remark made by Bering Bank's nineteenth-century American president, Joshua Bates, who said, "By being too liberal we lose our money, and being insufficiently liberal we lose our business."

I am calling Father's echo inadvertent, because I doubt if he was familiar with Bates's dictum. In any case, this was a dilemma well known to entrepreneurs, not only in business, but in art, politics, science, and most other human quests.

Father thought highly of intelligence, but not of intellectuals. "An intellectual, is he?" he asked once disdainfully about someone. "I'm not impressed. An intellectual is a person who is clever enough to put down everything he is not clever enough to create. In particular, he likes to denigrate the wealth he is unable to accrue. At bottom all intellectuals are frauds."

His real point, seldom stated, was that much of everything in the world had to do with luck. Few successful people acknowledged publicly that their triumphs owed as much to chance as to their daring, skill, and wisdom, though many suspected it privately. Language itself suggested it, by using "fortune" as a synonym for "wealth." People knew that the same deal that brought profit for one person one year might bring ruin to another person a year later. This has always made prayer no less influential in human affairs than planning.

Father was keenly aware of the limits of planning and often quoted Robert Burns on "the best laid plans of mice and men." In Father's view it was no wonder that planning was the essence of socialism, the most inefficient system in modern history. Prayer, on the other hand, was *not* the essence of theocracies. The essence of theocracies was also "planning," as Father pointed out: that is, incessant scheming by theocrats. If the essence of theocracies had been prayer, they would simply have been monasteries and quite tolerable.

THE ATTACK-DEER OF NARA

Talking of monasteries, on one occasion I was able to translate Father's distaste for sacred cows and other revered ungulates into action. It happened in 1985, long after he had passed away. The place was the park surrounding the Todaiji temple in Nara, Japan. In addition to the Nio statues of fierce-looking creatures of many toes guarding a central statue of Buddha, the complex is home to a large population of singularly unpleasant and ill-tempered deer. The pony-sized reddish-brown pests are considered sacrosanct. They roam around at will under the watchful eye of priests or monks, whose function is not to protect worshippers and tourists from the pesky blights of Nara, but to make sure that the bold nuisances are not mistreated by visitors. The deer fully realize their privileged status and will attack any passerby who fails to provide them with a steady supply of cookies.

Selling deer cookies is key to the economy of the 1,200-year-old temple. The animals act as the enforcers. It is an efficient system, for what the brazen fawns lack in fighting equipment, they more than make up for in cunning and irascibility. Sometimes they sneak up behind one, and sometimes they bar one's path. With the priests watching carefully, one cannot kick or smack them. The only legitimate defence is to offer them a cracker, pronto. Unless one does, they nip. The wounds they inflict are not exactly mortal, but they can raise a decent welt through a thin shirt or on the naked skin. The climate at Nara is too warm for protective clothing.

My walking companion, Alissa Alexander, a cinematic costume designer in Japan for a location shoot, had not been forewarned and carried an insufficient supply of cookies. As a result she was soon black and blue. I

"A shameless doe nipped me in the midriff." Alissa Alexander and the author, surrounded by the attack-deer of Nara, Japan, in 1985.

was slightly better off, partly because I had heeded the admonition of my Japanese publisher and laid in a good supply of cookies, and partly because my bulk and menacing frown made even Nara's attack-deer somewhat wary. Still, eventually I became a target. A shameless doe nipped me in the midriff. At this point, inspired by the memory of my father, I improvised a foolproof defensive system: the surreptitious flick.

Deer have soft and sensitive noses. The flick of a middle finger, initially restrained by the thumb, then snapped firmly against the animal's nose, will cause even the peskiest deer to back off. A rubber band would work even better, but it might be observed by a priest. A flick of the finger is invisible. Soon I became so skillful that I could boldly smile at a stone-faced priestly guardian of the four-legged extortionists while inflicting painful pops on their sacred noses.

The deer were startled and indignant. Until now they had been untouchable. They could nip anyone with impunity and collect cookies in return. Now a stealthily snapping finger had turned their world upside down. I wondered if they viewed me as a mere aberration, a passing fluke, a transient nightmare, or if my middle finger had entered their cultural memory. At any rate, Ms. Alexander and I could complete our walk in serenity. My father's influence had touched the Orient.

20

BASIC GEOGRAPHY

MY FATHER'S WORLD ENDED IN 1948, the year the Communists took over the country. At sixty-five he found himself destitute. He gave my mother a small envelope for her birthday, containing a handwritten gift certificate. "I can't celebrate you the way I would like to this year," he wrote, "but I love you more than in all previous years combined. For now, my dear, be content with this belated confession of love and a simulated gift of three pairs of nylon stockings."

After writing my mother this note, my father lived for another twenty-four years. Unemployable in a Communist system, his property confiscated, he tried his hand once at building chicken coops. He lasted for a day. Thereafter he stayed at home, cooked meals, and played the piano (until he was forced to sell it). At no point did he lose his faith in what he fondly called "the long run." It was the same faith that sustained him under the Nazis. He seemed serene in his conviction that systems like Nazism or Communism could not last. It did not worry him that he was waiting for a miracle, because he considered the miracle inevitable. "I've nothing on my side," he would say, "except time."

Father was wrong in this, for time is rarely on any person's side. Empires may not last, but they usually outlast people—or their best years, anyway. Still, for a few days in 1956 it looked as if Father's faith in Communism's collapse would be vindicated not only in the long run, but instantly. On October 23 a spontaneous uprising broke out in Budapest that swept away the Communist government in about seventy-two hours. With the rebels (promptly dubbed "freedom fighters") ruling the streets in most cities, the Soviet forces that had been occupying the country under the Warsaw Pact began to withdraw. By the second day of November there appeared to be no Soviet troops on Hungarian soil.

On November 4 I woke up to the crackling of distant thunder around 5 a.m. The sound was unusual in that it did not start with a sharp clap diminishing into a rolling rumble. It was rather like a rugged ridge of bass notes without a break, and with hardly any peaks or valleys. It resembled the snarl of some predatory animal, crouching and ready to pounce.

"He considered the miracle inevitable." Father with mother on their balcony in Budapest, circa 1960.

I switched on the radio. Immediately I heard the familiar voice of Hungary's new prime minister, Imre Nagy. He was saying the words that were soon to be quoted in headlines around the world: "Soviet troops attacked our capital with the obvious aim of overthrowing the legitimate Hungarian democratic government. Our troops are fighting. The government is in its place." By then the rumbling noise had resolved itself to the unmistakable sound of a distant artillery barrage.

The Hungarian revolution was twelve days old at that point. In a military sense it was defeated within hours of the Soviet onslaught, though resistance continued for another two weeks, becoming increasingly sporadic. I left the country nineteen days later, on November 23.

Many years would pass before I saw the diary entry of the British politician and journalist Sir Harold Nicolson for that day. "November 4, 1956—... The Russians have sent seven divisions into Hungary and are closing in on Budapest with 1,000 tanks," wrote Sir Harold. "But we have no right to speak a word of criticism."

Few writers have illustrated the obtuseness of big powers as succinctly as this. In these two sentences, Sir Harold managed to equate the Soviet action in Hungary with the British-French action at the Suez Canal. The two occurred around the same time. Evidently for the British chattering classes, military action in one big power's sphere of interest appeared as legitimate (or illegitimate) as military action in another's. Sir Harold wrote as if Hungary had been under an obligation to the Soviet Union similar to Egypt's obligation to maritime law and the United Nations—or

"Played the piano until he was forced to sell it." Father at 65, after the Communist takeover of 1948.

as if the Soviet Union had created Hungary in much the same way as the West had created the Suez Canal. Moral equivalence ruled. Western politicians like Sir Harold could not distinguish between Abdul Nasser arbitrarily blockading or nationalizing international waterways—i.e., the Strait of Tiran and the Suez Canal—and Imre Nagy withdrawing a sovereign nation from a military alliance, the Warsaw Pact, that it never voluntarily joined.

The Soviets knew better. Following the uprising on October 23 they quickly pulled out of Hungary their regular Warsaw Pact troops—in other words, the troops of Soviet occupation who knew where they were. On November 4 they invaded with fresh divisions. The new troops had no idea where they were being deployed. The Kremlin was not keen on letting them know that they were invading a "fraternal" socialist country, at least not right away. Since most Soviet soldiers read only the Cyrillic alphabet and could not decipher the signage in Hungary, their commanders felt safe in telling them that they were fighting the British and French imperialists in Egypt, and that the Danube was—the Suez Canal.

The deception probably did not persist. In a day or two even the most unsophisticated Soviet troops would have realized that the ragtag freedom fighters facing them were not the regular armies of the West. The Russian soldiers must have been thankful for that. By the time I left the country, Hungary was firmly under Soviet control again.

If the Russians were under the illusion that they were in charge of Hungary's destiny, I was under the illusion that I was in charge of my own. Their mistake was no greater than mine. Sitting in the back of a stolen truck, on my way to the Austrian border, I caught a last glimpse of my father crossing the street. He was carrying two buckets of ice. The electricity was still unreliable, and my parents had a few days' worth of perishables left in the icebox.

21

PEOPLE IN TANKS

Unpredictability, too, can become monotonous.

—ERIC HOFFER

LET ME REWIND THE NARRATIVE BRIEFLY to tell a story of two tanks—or possibly one tank. Whether one or two were involved, the events occurred on November 5, 1956, eighteen days before I left Hungary. At twenty-one, I was a junior editor with Radio Budapest, but still living with my parents in Damjanich Street, near the square in which Stalin's statue had stood until two weeks earlier, on the west side of Városliget, Budapest's largest city park.

A boy who used to live in our apartment building died prematurely that day, partly because of historical developments, and partly because he happened to be slight and small. If Emil had not been slight and small, he would not have become a jockey, and if he had not become a jockey, he would not have lounged in the loft of the stables at the Budapest racetrack, near the Eastern Railway station.

As it was, Emil had been relaxing in the loft. It was a Monday afternoon, little more than twenty-four hours after Soviet forces began reoccupying Hungary following the uprising of October 23. Reclining on racks of hay, Emil and four or five other jockeys were watching a Russian tank make its leisurely way across the paddock area and the exercise track. There were still armed groups of people in Budapest resisting the occupation here and there, but Emil and his friends were resisting nothing, not even their curiosity. They were just sitting in the loft, squinting in the late autumn sunshine, looking at a tank drive across the service road.

They were still looking at the tank as it started swinging its turret in the direction of the stables. They made no move as the tank rumbled by about a hundred metres distant, with the muzzle of its cannon pointing straight at the loft. In a moment the tank clattered past the stables, driving away, the cannon aiming back at the loft. Which is when they saw a flash.

They saw a flash, a surviving jockey said later, but they never heard a sound. Emil's shoulder was torn off, and he lived just long enough to tell the rescuers what happened. "In the stables..." he explained. "Fucking Ivans...Mother, Mother..."

My friends and I knew nothing of this when, a few hours later, we watched a Russian tank proceeding along Budapest's Dózsa György Avenue at a leisurely pace, not far from the Eastern Railway station and the racetrack. It was keeping to the cobblestoned part of the wide roadway, closer to the houses on the west side, farther from the deserted Városliget on the east. Like a bull shaking its head, the tank was swinging its sloping turret from side to side.

No one could fathom what this lone Russian tank was doing all by itself, clattering along the wide avenue toward Dózsa György Square, where a robust statue of Stalin used to survey the city. Now, like Ozymandias in Shelley's poem, nothing remained of it except a pedestal with "two vast and trunkless legs," though not of stone, but of bronze. Stalin had been cut off at the knees with blowtorches in the early evening of October 23, then hauled through the streets by cables attached to a five-ton truck. The rebels dragged it to and fro all night, watching the immense torso strike showers of sparks on the cobblestones.

"*My name is Ozymandias, King of Kings, / Look on my Works ye Mighty, and despair!*" Very ironic, coming from a pair of boots; but all the same, we could now see one of Ozymandias's tanks making its way toward the defiled pedestal. A T-34/85, of late World War II vintage, still standard in Warsaw Pact countries eleven years after the war. Perhaps it was lost. Perhaps it was trying to withdraw, get out of town, scurry after its retreating mates. Even so, it had one 7.62 mm machine gun in its bow, another mounted coaxially, and an 85 mm cannon swinging in its steel turret. Maybe it was not lost. Maybe it had come to avenge its fallen master.

As if to underscore the point, there was a sudden flash from the gun's muzzle, then an explosion as a shell smashed into the wall of a house less than a hundred yards away. The damn thing was firing at something. Or at nothing. Perhaps it was just throwing its weight around, showing who was boss to whoever might be watching it. There was no one visible in the street, though, and even the buildings on the west side seemed deserted. On the east side there were only bushes and trees, in the crimson colours of the Budapest autumn. Swinging its muzzle the other way, the T-34 now fired into the park. The bushes responded with a billowing brown cloud of dust and smoke, underneath a parachute of red and yellow leaves, settling slowly.

Suddenly, just as the turret swung toward the row of stone mansions again, a nearby door opened and an old woman emerged. Holding a shopping net with a loaf of bread, she looked at the approaching tank and hesitated.

The next few seconds were a montage from a film:

City street. Ext. Day. Close on the muzzle of a 75 mm cannon swinging into the frame.

Cut to

City street. Ext. Day. Reverse angle: close-up of an old woman's mottled face underneath a black kerchief, lips parting.

Cut to

City street. Ext. Day. Wide shot.

The old woman's confusion was propelling her forward. She started shuffling across the avenue in front of the T-34, as if hoping to beat it. In almost the same instant she seemed to realize that she could not. She tried turning back, but even as she swung her body she knew that it was hopeless. Whether she moved forward or back, she could not clear the giant steel centipede bearing down on her. The cannon in the turret was pointing at the doorway behind her, but the machine gun in the bow was aiming straight at her head.

That was when the tank stopped. There was a moment's pause, then we saw the hatch swing open and the head of a soldier emerge, wearing a leather helmet. In a second the shoulders and torso followed as the tankman stood up. He bowed from the waist with a theatrical gesture, motioning *"aprez vous, madame!"* at the woman, like a cavalier of the old school. Then he waited until she shuffled across the cobblestones. He seemed unconcerned about Molotov cocktails smashing against the armour. He stood erect and exposed for an eternity as she crossed the avenue and disappeared into the park.

Then the hatch slammed shut again and the tank lurched forward. The next second there was a flash from its muzzle, followed by an explosion as the shell smashed into the wall of the adjoining mansion. The T-34 continued rumbling down Dózsa György Avenue, swinging its turret left and right, firing at random. As it might have fired into the loft of the stables at the racetrack. Assuming it was the same tank.

That evening I told my father about the tankman and the old woman, and asked him why he thought the Russians needed tanks to perform public relations gestures. My father could never resist a pun. "Well," he replied, "great powers are not keen on performing tankless tasks."

22

ACCIDENTAL LIFE

Death is not an event in life: we do not live to experience death.
—LUDWIG WITTGENSTEIN

ON SEVERAL OCCASIONS OVER THE YEARS, had I moved a few inches fore or aft, tilted my head this way or that, arrived at a junction a moment sooner or later, entered the next office instead of the first, I might not have lived to recount the experience. This is probably true for most people. If we bothered to make a list of the times we touched hands with mortal peril, we would appreciate the accidental nature of what we consider "our" lives. The burden of such knowledge might be rather crushing, though. Perhaps it is just as well that after successfully jumping away from a bus, most people forget about it.

I tend to forget about it myself, most of the time, but once in a while I remember.

TRIP TO THE COTTAGE: *1946*

I remember, for instance, a bullet whistling by my face, so close that I could feel a warm rush of air against my skin, like someone's breath. "Whistle" is not the right word, either. The slug really buzzed past my cheek, like a particularly large and angry horsefly.

I was not alarmed, only startled. "What was *that?*" I asked my grandfather.

"What was *what?*" he answered.

Grandfather had not noticed a thing. We had been walking next to the railway, along with dozens of people, lugging our suitcases, having just got off the train. It was 1946, the war had been over for almost a year, but trains still ran only sporadically, often stopping short of their destination because something was blocking the tracks. This was the case that day. The conductors made us get off and walk to the junction where they were going to transfer us to buses. Grandfather and I were on our way to his cottage in a resort village called Érdliget, some thirty kilometres west of Budapest.

We heard no shot. The bullet must have been fired from some distance by someone who may or may not have aimed his weapon at the passengers—or a particular passenger—getting off the Budapest train. The shot may have been accidental—a village urchin might have found a gun and pulled the trigger. There were many guns after the war for urchins to find, along with unexploded artillery shells and hand grenades.

In a second we heard a faint cry and a commotion as the bullet struck someone or something a considerable distance behind us. We did not go back to investigate. It was probably a spent bullet by then, and it may not have done much damage. Grandfather and I never found out who fired it and why. By common, if unspoken, consent, we never mentioned it when we got home.

TRIP ACROSS THE YARD: *1951*

The other thing I recall from those years is Tiny's truck. I graduated to Tiny's truck from being in charge of Sári and Bandi, the two stolid Mecklenburgians that drew a wagon on a weekly trip from Ujpest in the north all the way to the south end of Budapest. In the north end was the chemical plant where I had a summer job; in the south end there was a pungent glue factory. It was my task to help load the wagon with the bones of Sári's and Bandi's fallen colleagues, draft horses that died in harness, then drive the remains to the malodorous place that turned the bones into glue.

My initial problem was that I had never driven a team of horses before. "If I want them to turn right, what do I do?" I asked the stable master, who showed me how to harness the team.

The stable master considered the question. He seemed to dislike me a little less than most workers did at the factory. He called me "student boy."

"If you want them to turn right?" he asked slowly.

"Yeah."

He scratched his head. "Well, you can say, 'Hey, Sári, you cocksucker!' You could say that, student boy."

"All right; what if I want them to turn left?"

"Left, eh?"

"Yeah, left," I said patiently. At the chemical plant people moved swiftly but spoke deliberately, leaving one unsure if they got the point. "Left, you know—left? The other way?"

"Well, if you want them to turn left," the stable master said, "why'n't you say, 'Hey, Sári, you cocksucker!'"

"But that's the same command."

"Yeah, well, it's the same horse, student boy," said the stable master disdainfully, handing me a pair of feeding bags.

The stable master's advice turned out to be impeccable. Sári, the lead horse, responded to the same expletive by turning left *or* right, as the situation warranted. She knew the way to the glue factory and back far better than I did, just as she knew the location of every pub between the north and the south end of the city. She would stop in front of them in sequence and not move an inch until I tied the nosebag to her face. As for Bandi, no one ever talked to him. Sári was the boss; he just followed.

"Why Sári? Is it her personality?" I asked the stable master once.

"Personal-what-ity?" he replied. "Sári, she's a mare, and Bandi, he's a gelding. Stallions boss mares and mares boss geldings—horses or humans. It's just the way it is, student boy."

Driving bones to the glue factory was a peaceful job, but then I got transferred to Tiny's truck, which turned out not to be a peaceful job at all. First, there was Tiny himself, a giant of nearly seven feet, weighing about three hundred pounds. Men of such elephantine size are often pacific or even meek, but Tiny was not true to type. He was seething with fury. This was not because Tiny was a mean person—he was rather generous, in fact—but because he was trying to suppress some inner demon.

As a driver's helper on Tiny's truck, my job was to deal with the cargo and the paperwork, the latter being voluminous in socialist Hungary. In those days Budapest was surrounded with toll stations for internal customs, as many industrial and agricultural items could not be exchanged between the capital and the countryside, or at least not freely. Our cargo happened to be duty-free as it consisted chiefly of horse piss. The chemical plant—it was called Chinoin—manufactured estrogen, among other things, which was distilled in some fashion from the urine of pregnant mares. Chinoin had two sources for the raw material. One was its own herd of mares, serviced around the clock by two excitable stallions that seemed to be in a state of permanent arousal. The mares were squeezed into narrow stalls with their rear ends sticking out, while two men wearing rubber gloves guided the prancing stallions from one amatory experience to another in a rectangular enclosure behind the mares. (Summer students were never assigned this job, called "fuck-detail," unless they could convince the lab chief that they were no longer virgins. I drew the assignment one afternoon by mistake and concluded that sex is not what it is cracked up to be.)

Chinoin's other source for the raw material was Tiny and his truck. Pulling a trailer loaded with steel drums, and with an additional crew of two inside the cab, we would set out for the countryside. Sometimes we drove east toward the Great Plains, sometimes west toward Transdanubia. The villagers were instructed to collect horse piss in cisterns dug specially for the purpose—not just any horse piss, of course, only the product of gravid mares.

Peasants in Hungary tended to regard the government as being totally devoid of sense, and horse-piss collectors from Budapest, being in the category of government, were no exception. To the rural folks' amazement, city fools not only paid for the cisterns but offered to pay for their contents. If the government officials wanted to pay money for horse piss it was, of course, their lookout, but with the cisterns more than half empty, it would have been a crying shame to forgo half of the potential revenue. This led to a battle of wits between town and country. To prevent the supply from being adulterated, villagers were never notified ahead of time of a collection. Peasants being shrewd and flexible, though, a drill soon developed. A reception committee in a village would guide Tiny and his crew to the local tavern, where toasts would be offered to the socialist state and its scientific endeavours. Meanwhile, there would be urgent conversations in the vestibule.

"Hey, Panni! Stir your stumps, the government truck is here. Be off to the cistern like a shot, everybody. Get the old folk, the women, the children, and don't forget the blasted goats. It's cash for piss tonight."

Given the doubtful purity of the source, the quality of Hungarian estrogen may have left something to be desired, but the prime ingredient was certified one night by an eager customs man officiating at a toll booth outside Budapest. We were on our way home after a long day, and Tiny was not inclined to be helpful to the zealous minions of excise surrounding his truck.

"What's on your trailer?" asked the lead minion.

"Steel drums." Tiny spoke in the surliest tone he could muster.

"I can see that. What's inside them?"

"Horse piss."

"I'll teach you to talk to me like that," the minion replied. "Get out of that truck."

Such requests made Tiny's day. He stepped out of the cab. "I'm ready for the first lesson," he said in a drawl Clint Eastwood might have envied.

The excise man took a step back. "I don't care how big you are," he lied. "I want to see what's inside those drums."

"Go see, then," said Tiny, motioning to us to lower the side of the trailer. I took the iron bar we used to unscrew the stopper on the steel barrel.

"Which one do you want to see?"

"That one," said the unfortunate customs official, pointing to a particular drum. "Open it."

I unscrewed the stopper, taking my time. The excise man looked at us in turn, then reached deep inside the drum. He withdrew a glistening hand which was bathed in the freshly harvested liquid. Casting one last triumphant glance at us, he raised his finger to his mouth and licked it.

His face fell. "This is horse piss," he said.

"That's what I was trying to tell you," replied Tiny, suddenly in a much better mood.

This was Tiny, the man who very nearly killed me a few days later. The situation developed out of a combination of Tiny's temper and generosity. Unlike other truck drivers who rarely let their helpers sit behind the wheel, Tiny did not mind me driving the rig. And at sixteen I enjoyed driving perhaps more than anything else.

As the shift started one morning Tiny said, "Turn the rig around, kid, and meet me at the gate. I'm getting a cup of coffee."

I nodded happily. The truck and trailer stood facing away from the gate in a rather narrow yard, but I thought there was a way of turning around without uncoupling the trailer. As I proceeded to do so, Tiny came back with his coffee mug in his hand. Not realizing what I was doing, which was something different from what he would have done, he immediately lost his temper, and he started for me.

"You moron, I told you to turn around! What are you doing?"

"I'm turning around, Tiny."

"How are you gonna turn around like that, you idiot? Don't you ever listen to what I tell you? Get the fuck out of there before I pull your head off."

And he reached into the cab.

"Tiny, look, look," I said, desperately squeezing myself away from his grip. "I just go *there* and *there,* see? From there I'm already turned around. It's simple."

The interesting thing about Tiny was that if you could get in your point before he broke your neck, he would stop and listen to you. If what you said made sense to him, he would calm down. The same hair trigger that blew his lid would snap it back on again.

This is what happened this time. He looked in the direction I indicated and saw my point.

"Yeah. . . you can do that," he said slowly. "Sure. That makes sense. So go do it while I finish my coffee."

Heaving a sigh of relief, I turned the truck around, but my troubles were not over. Because Tiny was a good soul, whenever he lost his temper he became conscience-stricken. He started brooding, and thereafter he paid no attention to what he was doing.

I had parked the truck at the end of the yard with the engine running. The hood ornament was pointing at the gate. Tiny came out of the canteen in a pensive mood, got behind the wheel, and without a glance around engaged the gear and let out the clutch. I was still standing on the running board at the other side of the cab.

The fact that I was still outside the cab would not have mattered. My feet were on the running board and I was hanging on to the door of the cab. The problem was that the door had not been closed properly. As the truck lurched forward, it began to swing open, sweeping me with it. My feet came off the running board and for a second I was hanging in mid-air.

The thought flitted through my mind that a freak accident like this could only happen to me. In another instant I would be on the ground, with my head in front of the dual rear wheels of a ten-ton rig—a rig whose driver was brooding. Which is exactly what happened. In the next instant my head and shoulder were on the cobblestones in front of the wheels. Tiny had not noticed a thing.

A second later somehow he did notice. From the corner of his eye he glimpsed the open door and surmised what happened. The air brakes hissed as he stopped on a dime. Except by then it was too late. The dual wheels were exactly abeam my skull.

Abeam, not on top. The rim of the outer wheel missed my head by about an inch. Pure chance, because I fell like a rag doll, without being able to twist myself out of the way. And Tiny stopped a split second too late. Luckily the wheel passed by me. If a Cinquefoil Skipper had put a wingtip on the rubber, the other wingtip would have rested on my cheek.

Q: What is the difference between a writer and a road kill? A: The wingspan of a butterfly.

TRIP IN THE PARK: 1953

As soon as I was old enough for a licence, I joined a motorcycle racing club. My club, the seriously misnamed Hungarian Freedom Fighters Association,[2] was very unlike its Western counterparts. Stalin still ruled the Kremlin. In his Soviet empire, sporting clubs were not private but para-military, subsidized and controlled by the state. Youngsters could join such clubs for sports that had a military-related function, such as motorcycle racing, gliding, parachute jumping, or competitive target shooting.

The club boasted of about ten Hungarian-made Csepel motorcycles with two-stroke engines displacing 125 cc's; two or three 250 cc Csepels; one 350 cc German DKW (the type used by General Erwin Rommel's troops in the African desert during the war); and one four-stroke 350 cc BMW (strictly for show, because for racing it was even more useless than the others). The club did have one serious racing machine, a Czech-made 350 cc Jawa. This was the bike used by the head coach, a stern man of about thirty, whom we called "Uncle" Béla. Uncle Béla finished a thirty-lap race once on the twisty circuit leading through Buda's Castle Hill following a first-lap spill that left him with a broken wrist. Such things come with the sport, but it was still a stoic performance. In matters of pain threshold and tolerance for discomfort, Uncle Béla's was the standard to emulate.

In view of our attitude and equipment (which no technical scrutineer would have passed on a Western racetrack even then, let alone today), it was a miracle that we not only survived but escaped serious injuries. The closest I came to harm was not on the racetrack but in Budapest's city park, and not on a motorcycle but inside a four-passenger sedan.

It happened during a leisurely drive to the clubhouse in the club's only car, an ancient Renault. I was behind the wheel; my three passengers

"Tolerance for discomfort." Winter cross-country race in Soviet-era Hungary. Author is riding a 125 cc Csepel.

included two fellow racers in the back seat and the chief instructor of the club sitting beside me. There was virtually no traffic. The weather was fine, the road dry, and we were moving slowly.

The instructor, slightly older than the rest of us, but still a teenager, noticed some girls walking on the other side of the road. They were strolling in our direction. "Check 'em out, Jonas," the instructor instructed, and I obeyed. Slowing even further, I drifted to the wrong side of the road, closer to the girls. My view of the boulevard was unobstructed for some distance, and I could see no traffic ahead or behind. What I could see was the girls taking notice. Private cars were rare in Budapest in the 1950s and had a correspondingly high social cachet.

Suddenly and without warning, the instructor grabbed the steering wheel and twisted it in the direction of the girls, as if to run them down. A narrow and unstable car, the Renault protested the abrupt steering input by lifting two of its wheels off the pavement. They would probably have settled on the ground again if I hadn't overcorrected, but I was startled and inexperienced. I countered with a huge twist of the wheel in the opposite direction.

The Renault squealed and slammed down the two wheels it had raised—but it now raised two wheels on the other side. I overcorrected again and had the original two wheels come up once more, except this time higher. I did not know it, but I had hit a sweet spot, albeit the wrong one: I caught the perfect rhythm for tipping a car.

At my next overcorrection, the Renault gave up and flipped directly onto its roof.

The visual sensation when a car overturns is perceptible only as a revolution of the horizon. It is the earth that seems to turn upside down, not the car. I did not think that I was hurt after we slid to an inverted stop, but was convinced that the others must be. They would probably need help to get out. The engine was still running, and my main concern was to shut it down and reduce the chance of fire.

Our model of Renault had no ignition key. A push-pull knob on the instrument wall served as a kill-button. As I was groping for it, my passengers, all unhurt, as it turned out, became convinced that I was writhing in my final agony.

After a few seconds I found the knob and pulled it. The engine stopped. I tried the door: it opened. We all tumbled out of the car. The girls had wisely vanished; they must have thought that we were insane. (They were wrong: we were merely teenage boys, though the two conditions are clinically indistinguishable.) At any rate, we seemed to be alone in the vast city park. This was good, as the last thing we wanted was a discussion with the police. We heaved the car back onto its wheels, looking in amazement at the denticulated roof that ought to have squashed at least some of our heads. But the roof did nothing of the sort. We were literally unscratched. The old Renault decided to let down gently four elect fools who rolled a car with no five-point harnesses, no Kevlar body pads, no fire-retardant suits, and no racing helmets.

The engine started like a charm. It was a lucky escape, if only temporary. Some people suffer accidental death; most suffer accidental life. Then time passes, and all parallel lines meet in infinity.

TRIP TO THE IRON CURTAIN: 1956

The Iron Curtain was just a phrase by the time I first glimpsed it, a month after the uprising. The minefields had been deactivated two years earlier. Not that minefields can ever be swept flawlessly—the occasional stray cow or child will probably be blown up between Hungary and Austria even in the twenty-first century. But on that misty day in November when our little group reached the border zone in the Lake Fertő district in

Western Hungary, we were not worried about mines. We were worried about gypsies.

More precisely, we were worried about a particular gypsy, a friendly, well-built man in his thirties who looked a bit like Omar Sharif (not that we knew then what Omar Sharif looked like). He had approached us as we were getting off a truck in the village square. There were six of us, four men and two women.

The gypsy addressed Potyo, who at thirty-two was the oldest in our group.

"Are you after to cross, then?" he asked. His dialect sounded like everyone else's in those parts.

"Yes," said Potyo, after a moment's hesitation. It was obvious what six people in city clothes a kilometre or two from the Austrian border wanted. It seemed pointless to dissemble.

Our group was like countless other "dissidents," which is what escapees were called. Our leader, a cabaret writer nicknamed "Potyo," came with his wife, Rose, and a younger couple with the Biblical names of Joseph and Mary. The kid brother of a writer friend and I were tagging along. Thousands were fleeing the country, there were huge gaps in the Russian deployment, and the Hungarian border guards were half-hearted about stopping refugees. The border troops belonged to the green-tab security police, less hated than the blue-tab security forces of the state. The green-tabs were mainly conscripts; the blue-tabs were mostly volunteers. During the uprising many blue-tabs were unceremoniously shot by the rebels. Though the freedom fighters were beaten, the green-tabs were still hesitant to take sides.

Still, it would have been foolhardy to try crossing at an actual checkpoint, whether road or rail, without the necessary exit papers. Sneaking through fields, woods, marshes, and rivers presented its own problems, though, especially for escapees unfamiliar with the countryside. The unmarked border was a twisting line, often doubling back on itself. Even though the Austrians helpfully signed their side with flags every kilometre or so, the flags were easy to miss even during the day and quite impossible to see at night.

By the time we met the gypsy, the six of us had been trying for two days. The first night we were captured by Russians in a copse of woods—a lone Russian, actually, whose rifle jammed when he tried to fire a shot to alert his comrades, so he had to yell for help. We could have taken him perhaps, but the women started to cry so we just assisted the soldier in yelling, "*Idyi sooda, joptvoyematj!*"[3] and waited for his fellows. The Russians trucked us back to the city of Gyõr, about fifty kilometres from the border, where we were put inside the local prison and fed a surprisingly tasty goulash soup. We were bedded down in holding cells for the night. When no one came to feed us in the morning, after shouting and banging for a while, we tried opening the door. It was unlocked, and so was the main gate of the prison. Our guards had vanished. We thanked God for the unsettled times, took a train back to the border zone, then hitched a ride on a truck that dropped us in the gypsy's village.

We knew that we were only two or three kilometres from the border, but had no idea where to cross and how. We clearly needed a guide. The gypsy was eyeing us and we were eyeing the gypsy.

"Are you after some help, maybe?"

"Maybe," said Potyo cautiously. The revolution had been defeated, the Communist state was rapidly reasserting itself, and informers would be coming out of the woodwork. The gates of the prison might not be unlocked the next time. But if Omar Sharif was an informer, it was too late anyway.

"Walk up that path, see? You'll come to a bend. A hop, skip an' a jump, that's all. When it gets dark, go there and wait for me. I'll walk you across."

"You sure to show?" asked Potyo.

"I'll show," said Omar Sharif, flashing a smile. Then he turned and walked away.

We set out in search of a pub. It was damp and chilly, and we still had hours to kill before it would turn dark. We were feeling lucky, all except Potyo's wife, Rose, who said that she had a premonition. Considering that Rose had a premonition every day, this did not change our mood. What did change it gradually was that we were cold and hungry, and had walked to the end of the only street in the village without finding a tavern or even a store.

After we sauntered back to the square, we saw a woman waiting in front of a gate. She looked at Rose and said something to her.

Rose gave a little cry. The woman disappeared behind the gate.

"What did she say?" asked her husband.

"'Don't go with the gypsy.' That's what she said."

"What gypsy? What are you talking about?" Potyo was a calm man, but Rose had a way of getting under his skin sometimes.

"The gypsy you talked to. The gypsy who is meeting us on that path after dark. The gypsy who is going to rob and kill us all."

Until then we had no idea that Omar Sharif was a gypsy—at least, five of us did not. The fellow looked like everyone else. Only Rose claimed that she had recognized the man for a gypsy right away. Perhaps that was why she was having her premonition.

"Yes, and why did you have a premonition yesterday?" her husband asked. "We hadn't met any gypsies yesterday, had we?"

"Well, I won't say anything more. You just wait and see."

"It's a stupid prejudice that all gypsies are thieves," declared Potyo. "Only ignorant peasants believe such nonsense. Gypsies are like everybody else. Some steal, some tell fortunes, some play the violin, some..."

We looked at each other. "Yeah, okay—steal, tell fortunes, play the violin," said Tom. "What else?"

"This fellow," I said to Potyo, "didn't seem to be telling fortunes or playing the violin. Which, on your analysis, leaves only..."

"Stealing," said Rose helpfully. "And murdering," she added. "He'll also have to bury us, because if they find our bodies, everybody in the village will know that he had done it. He was seen talking with us by this woman."

"Unless he kills her, too," said Potyo sarcastically. "Burying six, seven people in the half-frozen ground is hard work, mind you—certainly for what he's going to get for robbing us. Navvying for a day at the railway station would pay him more."

"Yes—but we're still not going with him," said Joseph, a colourless fellow who rarely said much and had said nothing until then. "Potyo is probably right, but I'm not betting Mary's life on it." Mary and Joseph were practically newlyweds. "We can get across on our own."

This settled the matter, and we knocked on a window. "Which way is Austria?" Potyo said to the villager who stuck out his head. The question was not as impressive as Charles Lindbergh's "Which way is Ireland?" posed to a fisherman in the Atlantic twenty-nine years earlier, but it was still memorable. The man pointed, just as Lindbergh's fisherman had, and we struck across some soggy fields.

It was not yet dark but we were tired and did not care. Eventually we came to a meandering cow path that seemed to lead in the right direction. The clouds hung low and a greasy drizzle started to fall. We began hearing an eerie hum in the wind, and soon saw the telegraph wires. Close up, the wires shrieked like a chorus of banshees. Next came the railway trestle, a single line, extending in the direction of what had to be a bridge. A narrow river probably fed into Lake Fertõ, or Neusiedler See, as they called it on the Austrian side. Once we crossed the railway bridge, even if it had no walkway, even if we had to balance on the rails like tightrope walkers, we would be in Austria. The gypsy was probably harmless, but we did not need him anyway.

That was when we bumped into the green-tabs. They were two young men, high-cheek-boned Hungarian lads both, leaning against the wintry remnants of a haystack. We came upon them suddenly as we rounded a bend in the trail, with our eyes fixed on the distant railway bridge.

We were surprised. The green-tabs were not. They had either heard us coming or expected all escapees to end up on this cow path. It may have been the only trail for miles. The border guards made no move when we came around the bend, just continued smoking their cigarettes, as casually as young men do when they have the upper hand. They had their submachine guns leaning against the stack, within easy reach.

For a few seconds no one spoke. Then one of the soldiers said, without looking directly at any one of us, "Where do you think you're going?"

"Across the border," said Potyo in a measured voice. "Unless you shoot us."

"We don't shoot Hungarian people," said the other soldier.

There was silence again. The young green-tab seemed to speak earnestly. It would have been unkind to say that if he would not shoot Hungarian people he did not need a gun at all because no other kind of people wanted to cross this border.

"Hell, we should have gone with the gypsy," said Potyo dejectedly. He was speaking loudly enough but to no one in particular. His disappointment made his voice hoarse. Potyo wanted to get out of Hungary more than any of us, and the railway bridge was so close that he could almost touch it.

"Yeah, and you'd have a few extra holes in your ass if you had, maybe," said the first soldier. "You've a better chance with us. At least we're not gypsies."

It sounded like an invitation to talk turkey.

"I'm reaching into my jacket," Potyo said, "and it's only for my wallet."

"Go ahead." The green-tabs were clearly not alarmed. "That's all I can spare," said Potyo, extending four or five hundred forint bills. The green-tabs did not reach for them.

"I'll put them here under the stone," said Potyo, and he did. The soldiers continued smoking.

"I'll let you have my overcoat," I said, and started taking it off. It was a decent winter coat of English wool, pre-war.

"We don't take a man's coat," said one of the green-tabs.

I was glad to see that Hungary's military had standards. "That's all right," I replied, "I'm wearing two coats, look."

The green-tabs looked. My father had insisted that I put on two coats, no matter how cumbersome, and it turned out to be a wise precaution. I took off the top one, folded it, and put it on Potyo's stone. Joseph added something to the loot as well. Then we waited.

"Well, there's the bridge," said one of the soldiers after a while. "The other side is Austria."

"Good—thanks," Potyo said. We started walking. "Don't worry when you hear gunfire," called out one green-tab. "We'll be aiming over your heads."

We kept walking. I could feel my muscles tighten. "They'll shoot us," Rose whispered. "They'll cut us down like dogs. Why shouldn't they? It's their job to shoot us. We're illegals, dissidents. If they let us escape, they'll be punished. If they shoot us, they'll get a medal."

"Spare us your premonitions for the next few minutes, will you?" said her husband. He spoke angrily, but without conviction. This time Rose seemed right. Shooting us was enlightened self-interest for the border guards. Not shooting us was taking a wanton chance. Why risk a court martial for six strangers?

We heard the first burst. We were almost at the bridge. I involuntarily crouched as I started running. Rose broke into whimpering sobs and continually tried to look back as Potyo was dragging her along. Another short burst came, and then another. Tom stumbled and staggered, then regained his balance. Our footsteps reverberated with unexpected clangour as we crossed the iron trestle, drowning out the submachine guns. Or, possibly, the firing had stopped. Suddenly we were on the other side. We were out of breath. Now the only sound was the shrieking wind in the telegraph wires mixed with Rose's whimpering.

"Well, the lads did aim over our heads, it looks like," said Potyo after a while. "Or else they're very poor shots. Either way, Rose, cheer up."

I walked up to the Austrian flag planted in a ring of stones about fifty metres west of the riverbank. I felt neither tired nor cold, only bewildered.

There were about ten or twelve Austrian spectators, some with binoculars, standing within a hundred metres of the border. They were attracted by the bursts of gunfire, but kept their distance. Some wore the expectant smirk of ghouls gathered around a road accident. Later I learned that hundreds had gone to the border during November to watch the refugees as they first trickled, then streamed, then trickled again across the line. Some Austrians came to help, some came to watch the show. The exodus lasted for about eight weeks.

One spectator came up to me, trying to decide whether I spoke German. *"Wohin geht's?"* he asked finally.

I felt suddenly numb. *"Immer nach Westen,"* I replied.[4] We had made it; we were in the free world. We got what we wanted. Our troubles were about to begin.

3
TWELVE GOLDEN
MULLETS

23

A TOLERANCE FOR

QUEUES

We should often be ashamed of our finest actions if the world
understood all the motives behind them.
—FRANÇOIS, DUC DE LA ROCHEFOUCAULD

THE AUSTRIANS WERE AMAZINGLY HOSPITABLE to refugees from Hungary. It was common for passersby in the streets of Vienna to offer gifts of food, clothes, or money to bedraggled strangers. Their generosity was a notable departure from the petit-bourgeois small-mindedness that normally characterized Austria's inhabitants. One might have almost called it un-Austrian. The explanation probably included the fact that Austria itself had only recently been relieved of the Kremlin's military presence. The Soviets started withdrawing in 1954, and within a year the formal four-power Allied occupation had come to an end. The agreement to treat Austria as a liberated rather than a defeated nation resulted in Vienna becoming the only major city in Europe that, having been occupied by the Red Army, had been voluntarily vacated by it. A year later, observing in the streets their tattered and emaciated former compatriots in the Dual Monarchy, many Viennese were overcome by a feeling of but-for-the-grace-of-God. The contrast between the dismal refugees and the well-stocked, bustling, brightly lit, *gemütlich* ambiance of carefree Vienna was remarkable.

Another reason for the Austrians' hospitality was fashion. The mood of the 1950s was unlike the mood of the decades that preceded or followed them. It was an era in which public opinion was suspicious of Utopias and clenched-fisted salutes. The fellow-travellers of the thirties and forties were disenchanted, enfeebled, under deep cover, or dead. Most had exited (or were carried off) the world's stage. The next generation of fellow-travellers, the "New left" of the sixties and seventies, were still waiting in the wings. Sympathy for Communism was at a low ebb, temporarily. Being the first to take up arms against the overwhelming odds of a Yalta-mandated Kremlin, Hungary's freedom fighters cut a gallant figure—and, more importantly, a trendy one. Newspaper datelines like "Budapest, 1956" usually heralded uplifting stories of children fighting with Molotov cocktails against tanks. The revolution had a good press; the rebels made the front pages, and the solid citizens of Austria reacted accordingly.

Along with most of my friends, I suspected that it would not last. Like guests who overstay their welcome, Hungarian refugees would rapidly change from heroes to nuisances for their Austrian hosts. It was not just a matter of an inevitable shift in public mood. Even with the best of will, the small nation of Austria could not possibly absorb a sudden influx of more than two hundred thousand people, or about three percent of its population. No country in Europe was equipped for immigration on such a scale physically, economically, or psychologically.

In any case, like most of my fellow escapees, I did not want to stay in Europe. It was not only a question of putting some distance between myself and the lands of applied Marxism. No distance would have been too great for that, but I wanted to put a distance between myself and Europe altogether. This meant overseas—but over which seas? Africa was the closest, being a mere hop across the Mediterranean, but emigrating to Africa would no more have occurred to me than emigrating to Pluto. Asia was similarly out of the question: it would have brought me closer to the Soviet empire, not farther away from it. This left the countries of Anglophonie: the United States, the United Kingdom, Australia, New Zealand, and Canada. I immediately eliminated Australia and New Zealand as being too far—though if someone had asked me "Too far from *what?*" I would have had no answer.

I sat in my somewhat depressing hotel room near Taborstrasse, on the wrong side of the Danube canal, contemplating the question. My choices

"Too far from what?*" Crossing the English Channel, Ostend to Dover, in December 1956.*

seemed almost alarmingly infinite. Virtually no country would have refused asylum to a Hungarian in December 1956. The window of opportunity stood wide open, if only for a brief time: my friends and I suspected that soon it would be slammed shut by the same *Zeitgeist* that opened it. Meanwhile, however, the world was our oyster. We could choose, but we had better choose well.

I chose America.

The trouble was, so did most Hungarians. This became distressingly clear to me around nine o'clock the next morning. The line in front of the American embassy extended for about ten city blocks. Worse, it seemed not to be moving. My access to Llewellyn E. Thompson, Jr., U.S. Ambassador Extraordinary and Plenipotentiary—or to one of his visa-issuing minions— was blocked by about a thousand of my countrymen. It would have taken me all morning, possibly all day, to get near the front door.

I liked America, but my tolerance for queues did not extend to all-day vigils. With the spoiled impatience of youth, I promptly turned on my heels.

While turning, I caught a glimpse of a sign displayed on the door of the building at the tail end of the American queue. It said "Canadian Legation." Had there been a queue in front of it, I would have been the first person in line.

There was no line, though. The tail-enders waiting for their distant chance to emigrate to America did not even glance at me as I entered the doorway to Canada. As far as my fellow refugees were concerned, America's good neighbour to the north was having a bad hair day.

The old-fashioned office building did have an elevator in the lobby, but since the sign pointed to the second floor, I chose the wide, ornate staircase. On reaching the landing I saw a slim figure emerge from the door of the embassy suite. The young woman looked vaguely familiar, but I was too intent on my mission to pay her much attention.

"Jonas!" the woman exclaimed suddenly. "Is that you?"

It still took me a second to recognize Zsuzsa Szegõ, the second wife of the immensely popular Hungarian poet, George Faludy.[1] She was an ethereal beauty, the subject of one of the finest love poems in Hungarian literature. Faludy wrote it in a prison cell while waiting to be executed by the Communists in the morning. They did not garrotte him, as it turned out, but sent him to the infamous stone quarries of Recsk instead.

I knew the poem well, but had met Zsuzsa only once before.

"Do you want to go to Canada?" she asked me. She seemed quite enthusiastic about the idea, for some reason.

"Are you going yourselves?" I asked. "I didn't even know that you and Gyurka were in Vienna."

"Gyurka" was Faludy's nickname. He had been released from Recsk less than two years before the revolution. Zsuzsa had waited for him, in spite of being put under tremendous pressure to divorce her "American spy" husband. (Under interrogation Faludy confessed that while serving in the U.S. Air Force during the war, he had been recruited by two CIA officers: Lieutenant Walt Whitman and Captain Edgar Allan Poe. He expected his illiterate torturers to happily place this information in his file, which they did.)

"No, we're off to Costa Rica first, and then to South America," Zsuzsa said. "The Social Democratic International is sending Gyurka on a speaking tour."

This had to do with a furious internal dispute within the left. The Communists had been spreading the word that the uprising in Hungary was a kind of fascist counter-revolution. The Social Democrats wanted their comrades to know that it was a true-blue workers' uprising against the red fascism of the Communists. They were both wrong, though the Social Democrats were a shade closer to the truth.

I had little interest in the latest schisms in the serrated ranks of the progressive left. "So what are you doing here, then?" I asked Zsuzsa.

"I work here," Zsuzsa explained. "The Canadians gave me a temporary job as a translator. They've been expecting a flood of Hungarian refugees, but so far, you're it. They'll be so happy to see you."

"I'm not sure if I want to see them," I replied. Suddenly I wondered if other Hungarians knew something I did not know. It occurred to me that I had no clue about the country to which I was about to emigrate. I remembered it only as a white spot on a high school map, an uninhabited area atop the United States. Not quite uninhabited, actually, because two writers lived in the white void: Stephen Leacock and Mazo de la Roche. I knew them both by their works. When I was about twelve I devoured every Jalna book I could lay my hands on and thought they were marvellous. Later I read Stephen Leacock, who seemed to me nearly as amusing and shrewd an observer of people as Mark Twain.

What I did not know was how far removed these two authors were from contemporary Canada—but that was tomorrow's concern. Meanwhile I had a decision to make.

"It's a great country," said Zsuzsa firmly. "You'll be very happy there. I'll help you fill out the papers."

Such factors determine the future. If I had had a greater tolerance for queues, or a greater resistance to ethereal blondes—including ex-Communist blondes like Zsuzsa, trying to earn their keep as translators—today I would be writing these lines in America. It is also possible, of course, that I would be writing no lines, being just a name on the Vietnam memorial in Washington.

Had I gone to America, I would almost certainly have fought in the war. There was no way I would have dodged the draft. In fact, had I not been drafted, I would have volunteered. This was not because I supported the war in Vietnam. On the contrary, I opposed the war. I opposed it fundamentally, publicly, and with considerable vehemence, though for reasons entirely different from the reasons of most opponents of America's involvement in Vietnam.

I did not oppose the war because I thought that Communism was not so bad, or it was not really expanding, or it did not need to be stopped. Far from it: I thought Communism was hideous, it was spreading like cancer, and it needed to be stopped. I only thought that Southeast Asia was the wrong place in which to stop it.

It seemed incongruous to me, ridiculous even, that after virtually signing over Eastern Europe to Stalin and his successors, America would make a stand in Vietnam. Why Vietnam, of all places? In Europe most people neither wanted nor needed Communism. They knew that far from improving their lives, it would make them much worse. There was no place on the map between Berlin and Kiev that Communism would not reduce economically, psychologically, and technologically. It was a system that could only diminish and impoverish European countries, and most Europeans knew it.

Things were not nearly as clear-cut in Asia. Given the conditions of Asia's economies, technologies, and cultures, one could not say quite as categorically that Communism would bring no improvement, at least in some Asian countries, or to some segments of society, or in the short run. Most important of all, the inhabitants of these countries, the people of Vietnam, Laos, Cambodia, Korea, and China, were not sure themselves. They did not necessarily look at Communism the way most people looked at it in Dresden, Warsaw, Prague, Bucharest, or Minsk.

"Goodbye, Europe." Aboard the Empress of France, *on the way to* Canada, *in 1956.*

Preventing people who thought, however mistakenly, that Communism may do them some good from experimenting with it, while abandoning people who desperately wanted to be rescued from Communism, struck me as insane, morally as well as in a practical sense. Not that I would have advocated any attempt to liberate East-Central Europe by force—the West had long missed the boat on that—but having shied away from the good fight, America's insistence to engage in a bad, or at least far more dubious, battle, seemed nonsensical to me.

Yet, had I gone to America, I would have felt honour-bound to engage in such a dubious battle. I could not have sat it out. The idea of dodging the war of a country that took me in, that gave me shelter, would have struck me as unconscionable.

Here are the inevitable counterfactuals. Had I not been lazy, I would have stood in line. Having stood in line, I would have gone to America. Having gone to America, I would have gone to war. Having gone to war, I would have been killed. My laziness had saved my life.

None of this entered my head on that day in Vienna, of course. Though the French debacle at Diem Bien Phu had occurred two years earlier, Vietnam was not yet a factor in most people's thinking, in Europe or in America. It was certainly the last thing on my mind as I filled out the papers Zsuzsa put in front of me, along with a *Mocca,* a tiny cup of black coffee, Viennese style. As an early applicant, I was getting the Cadillac treatment.[2] A few days later I would be crossing the English Channel at Ostend. From there it was on to Dover, London, Liverpool, the Irish Sea, the Atlantic Ocean. *Goodbye,* Europe.

24

YESTERDAY'S FUTURE:

THE NEW EUROPE

I have ever deemed it fundamental for the United States never to take active part in the quarrels of Europe. Their political interests are entirely distinct from ours. Their mutual jealousies, their balance of power, their complicated alliances, their forms and principles of government, are all foreign to us. They are nations of eternal war.
—THOMAS JEFFERSON

THE SAME YEAR IN WHICH I BOARDED the *Empress of France* in Liverpool to put an ocean between myself and Europe's "nations of eternal war"—as Thomas Jefferson described them in an 1823 letter to President James

Monroe—the rival powers of Europe embarked on a road designed to lead them out of their perpetual conflicts.[3]

The Europe of the twenty-first century was conceived by nineteenth-century minds. The vision that seemed futuristic at the time, a vision of supranational cooperation, leading one day perhaps to a United States of Europe, was being shepherded through the intricate maze of continental and British politics by three statesmen. Though many shared the dream that went back to the pacifist intellectuals of the First War—writers like Stefan Zweig, Roger Martin du Garde, and Romain Rolland—its realization was chiefly due to the efforts of Jean Monnet and Robert Schuman of France, and Paul-Henri Spaak of Belgium.[4] All three were born in the nineteenth century. Spaak was in his late sixties and Monnet in his late seventies on April 8, 1965. This was the day of the Merger Treaty, when the three preliminary entities, the ECSC, the EEC, and Euratom, were subsumed into the European Community (EC). By then Schuman was already dead.

The EC adopted the European flag—azure field with a circle of twelve golden mullets—in 1986. The Maastricht Treaty was signed on February 7, 1992, replacing the EC with the European Union (EU). On that day, had they been still alive, Monnet and Schuman would have been 104 and 106 respectively, and even young Spaak would have been 93. The European Union was the future, all right, but it was the future as envisaged from the distant past: "yesterday's future," as former British prime minister Margaret Thatcher called it. She was speaking in The Hague as the European Union came into being in 1992.

Countries and commonwealths coalesce around organizing principles. Some are easy to list. In all periods and regions it is quite common to encounter: 1. dynastic, 2. tribal-historical, 3. cultural-linguistic, 4. ideological-religious, and 5. geographical organizing principles. A sixth organizing principle—economic—tends to serve as a core canon for common markets or trading blocs rather than countries. This list by no means excludes the possibility of others; it merely describes five or six that recur with considerable frequency. They may appear singly, but occur more often in combination.

When an organizing principle serves alongside another and complementary organizing principle, it strengthens the cohesion of a country or commonwealth. Any nation whose population shares a common tribal descent, language, and religion, in addition to being ruled by a native dynasty and inhabiting a well-defined geographic region (such as an island), has an unusually high degree of internal coherence. We might describe such a nation as "making sense."

Most countries are not like this. They do not "make sense," at least not perfect sense. Nor do they have to. Successful countries may comprise several different tribes and religions, or have geographically ill-defined borders. It is unnecessary for any country to be governed by a multiplicity of organizing principles acting in unison for a stable and coherent existence. Still, the rule seems to be that organizing principles strengthen one another, as long as they are equally active and do not act at cross-purposes.

The same organizing principle that helps to create stability and cohesion when it is complementary to another organizing principle within a nation has the potential of becoming a fault line under different circumstances. One obvious example is a multiethnic empire that has been organized primarily along dynastic and ideological principles. As soon as such an empire undergoes a weakening of its dynastic and ideological bonds—as happened to the Hapsburg empire in the early part of the twentieth century, among others—chances are that it will split up along its tribal, cultural, or geographic fault lines. Seventy years later the same thing happened to the Soviet empire when Communism, the "god" around which the state had organized itself, had failed.[5]

It appears that organizing principles are both the glue and the solvent of nationhood. An organizing principle that acts as a bonding agent in one historic period can be a fault line in another era. It is equally possible for one country's organizing principle to become another country's fault line. Ideology, for instance, in the shape of religion, became an organizing principle for Pakistan and a fault line for India after the end of the British Raj in 1947.

The sense in which I am using the term "nation-state" is one in which a nation coincides with a country within the confines of given geographic boundaries, acknowledged by most other countries.

Obviously not all countries are nation-states by this definition. Some nations encompass many states, while there are some states that comprise two or more nations.

After 931 B.C. the Hebrew nation consisted of two states, Israel and Judah. The German nation comprised several states during various periods of its history—most recently during the Cold War. Before that, the German nation had a multitude of states for two and a half centuries, between the Thirty Years War (1618) and Prince Bismarck's proclamation of Wilhelm I as German emperor (1871). Even today, after the unification of East and West Germany, the German *nation* may be said to consist of at least two *states*, namely Germany and Austria. The Arab nation has a great many states, of course, from Algeria to Yemen.

At the opposite end, Canada, Belgium, Iraq, and Switzerland are examples of states that comprise several nations. This is not merely because they have different "tribes"—that is, ethnic/cultural/linguistic entities—dwelling within their borders. Tribes do not necessarily stay separate. They may, and often do, coalesce into one nation, as the twelve tribes of Israel had done, at least until King Solomon's death in c. 922 B.C. Some tribes may coalesce even when they lack all kinship and descend from different ethnic, linguistic, and sometimes even racial stocks. The English nation that evolved after the battle of Hastings, with its intermingled Anglo-Saxon, Celtic, and Norman strains, is one historic example. China is another. "The Dutch, whether they speak Dutch, Limburger, or Frisian," Luigi Barzini observed, "know at all times they are Dutch." On the other hand, Canada, Belgium, Iraq, and Switzerland are examples of states whose tribes had not coalesced into one nation. "The Belgians can feel like Belgians only in life and death crises," Barzini noted. "At all other times they feel like Walloons or Flemings."[6]

This does not necessarily make such entities non-viable or unsuccessful as countries. It only makes them countries of several nations.

National distinctness does not stand in the way of a country's existence as long as the main principle around which the state has been organized remains intact. However, when this principle withers, crumbles, becomes discredited, or loses relevance for some other reason—and is not replaced by some other core principle—tribal kinship is likely to reassert itself.

People need a reason to consider themselves citizens of a country. Patriots require a *patria*. Countries must coalesce around some organizing principle. It need not be a tribal principle, and often it is not. It may be a dynasty, such as the Rome of the Flavian emperors, or an ideology, such as a republic based on Islam, or on the Communist Manifesto, or on the Declaration of Independence. Still, a fraternity of culture, language, "blood" (i.e., ethnicity), and shared history will usually come to the fore in the absence of some other, more compelling bond.

Ideological organizing principles can be quite strong. They can serve as core ideas by themselves; they can be sufficiently coherent for the creation and maintenance of countries. To function as a sole magnet, however, one that is powerful enough to hold together a nation, an ideological organizing principle needs to be exclusive. It must become a state religion, or close to it.

In societies held together by a multiplicity of organizing principles, the presence of different ideologies or religions causes less strain. Coherent nations need no established churches. Japan, for example, is bonded securely enough as a country by its dynastic, tribal/historic, cultural/linguistic, and geographic organizing principles to serenely accommodate its traditional Shinto faith with Buddhism, Confucianism, and Christianity. Some countries—the United States, for instance—make religious and ideological diversity part of their ideological organizing principle. Such societies are immunized against competing ideologies and religions, or at least they build up a tolerance for them. In such states different ideologies can coexist to a considerable extent.

But in states whose raison d'être, core idea for being, depends on a single ideological organizing principle, such diversity can be fatal. As soon as these societies admit the legitimacy of other ideological forces—even ones that seem utterly benign, apolitical, and non-competitive, such as the Falun Gong breathing exercise and meditation movement in China—the central magnet that holds the state together begins to lose its force.

The clearest example in the twentieth century was the Soviet Union. That country relied on the ideology of Communism as its sole organizing principle, as did the empire built up around it. There was no other organizing principle to define either the Soviet Union or the system of satellites in its orbit. Although the Russian nation was central to what became the "Great Socialist Fatherland"—and foreigners often used the word "Russia" as a synonym for the Soviet Union—the Soviet Union as a country consisted of too many different national and cultural/linguistic entities to ever view itself as Russia. On the contrary, ethnically and linguistically the Soviet Union was strained by concepts of Russification far more than organized by it. Other nationals from the Baltic to the Caucasus, from Estonia to Uzbekistan, even if proudly Soviet (as they sometimes were), did not consider themselves, and often resented being viewed, as "Russians."

As long as Communism was strong, vital, and unchallenged by competing ideologies or religions, the Marxist-Leninist organizing principle proved to be enough. After the rise of Soviet power, traditional religions were persecuted and suppressed at first, but by the end of World War II the regime's central organizing principle, Communist ideology, seemed entrenched and powerful enough to even permit some old religions (though not others) to emerge in a kind of shadowy, twilight existence.

For over seventy years, or nearly three generations, the organizing principle of Communism had enough cohesive power to hold a country together. Ideology, acting on its own, not only proved sufficient to create and maintain a distinct entity, but turned it into a superpower for a period of time.

Needless to say, the Soviet Union did not achieve this by the spiritual magic of its organizing principle alone. It did so through the coercive force of a brutal dictatorship, including mass murder, intimidation, and aggressive war. Still, all organizing principles include at least some degree of coercive force. The freest democracy might dissolve into anarchy and chaos without the state safeguarding and reinforcing the principles at which its people have consensually arrived. But while no state exists without some form of coercion, coercion is no substitute for organization. Coercion by itself can only create zones of occupation or colonial dependencies; it cannot create countries or commonwealths.

Once coercion becomes the state's sole raison d'être, it is likely to collapse. In the case of the Soviet Union, though the degree of coercion had been significant—indeed, totalitarian—once the key organizing principle had eroded, the collapse became rapid and spectacular.

What does this say about the future of the European Union? Prussian Chancellor Otto von Bismarck was unequivocal on the subject in the late nineteenth century: "Whoever speaks of Europe is wrong," he wrote. "It is a geographical expression."

Bismarck's celebrated view, scribbled on the margin of a letter from Russia's foreign minister, Prince Aleksandr Gorchakov, has often been quoted, though this alone would not validate it. The world has changed in many ways since 1876, when the Iron Chancellor made his observation. But no matter how much the world has changed, countries and commonwealths still need to be organized around some principles to be viable. Since the European Union is not designed to be organized around dynastic, tribal, historical, cultural, or linguistic principles, it leaves ideology and economics, plus the rather weak notion of geography, to serve as the core organizing principles of Europe.

Are they sufficient?

The probable answer is yes, with certain reservations. Economics as a core organizing principle is more suited for creating common markets or trading blocs than countries or commonwealths (and indeed, the European Union started out as the European Common Market). Geography alone is not a strong organizing principle, especially for large and diffuse entities, such as an arbitrary geographical "Europe" stretching between the French coast and the Ural Mountains, thus including the Kalmuk Steppe and the Caspian Desert, but excluding (arguably) the white cliffs of Dover.

"The United States had more or less a common philosophy, they were a society before they were a state," remarked Henry Kissinger. "Europe isn't a society. An election campaign that goes from Denmark to Sicily isn't operating in the same country. It would be easier to run it from Denmark to Maine."[7]

This leaves ideology as the chief bonding agent of the European Union.

As the example of the Soviet Union (among others) has shown, ideology is capable of serving as an organizing principle by itself. The objection that ideology may in time lose its force, though valid, is not particularly weighty, since historic changes can alter other bonds as well. Dynasties degenerate or die out, while migrations, epidemics, or wars, coupled with developments or mutations in technology, fashion, or even climate, dilute or break up tribal, historical, cultural, linguistic organizing principles as readily as ideological ones. Ideology as a core organizing principle is not necessarily less serviceable than other organizing principles. It is, however, likely to fully define the entity it creates. The lifespan of a country born of ideology will probably be limited to the lifespan of the ideology itself.

The contrasting examples of China and the Soviet Union illustrate the point. The Soviet Union could not go on existing as a country once it stopped being Communist; China obviously could. China would continue being China even if it completely renounced the ideology of Marxism-Maoism (which by now it has all but renounced economically, if not politically). The reason is self-evident: Marxism has not been a core organizing principle for China in the same way as it has been for the Soviet Union. Other than a shared Communist ideology, there was never a sufficient bond between Russia and, say, Uzbekistan to amount to a "Soviet nation" (and not enough even between Russia and Ukraine, as it turned out, in spite of a linguistic kinship). The internal bonds of China, on the other hand, based as they are on history, ethnicity, and culture, have been independent of ideology. China is a nation in a way the Soviet Union has never been.

If the European Union becomes a nation, it will be a nation in the way of the Soviet Union, and not in the way of China. This alone need not prevent it from being a prosperous and successful country—or, for that matter, a superpower—only from being a country with a redundancy of organizing principles. If the European Union were an aircraft, it would be a single-engine plane. Single-engine planes have no trouble flying; they fly splendidly, as long as the engine works. When it stops working for any reason, however, the plane must begin its inexorable glide back to earth.

25

SIC TRANSIT

A poet in history is divine, but a poet in the next room is a joke.

—MAX EASTMAN

I WILL PUT OFF DESCRIBING MY FIRST YEARS in the New World, and fast-forward to the mid-1960s, when I bought myself a white TR4. Tibor Polgár, a former Budapest conductor and composer who by then also made his home in Toronto, fancied the sporty two-seater. One day he asked me to give him a lift to New York. Polgár wanted to see an old friend and collaborator, the novelist Lajos Zilahy, who had an apartment somewhere in the East 70s near Second Avenue.

I jumped at the chance of meeting the famous author of the pre-war period. His novel *Ararát* (published under the title *The Dukays* by Prentice Hall in New York) was one of my childhood favourites. Zilahy had been likened to Tolstoy by his American publisher's blurb writer, which was something of a stretch, but he could probably have been accurately described as an amalgam of Ferenc Molnár and W. Somerset Maugham. In any case, he was the real thing, a skilled writer with several best-selling books and two Broadway plays to his credit.[8] He was also known as one of the best-dressed men of his time, a specimen of the European boulevardier. Other men-about-town were said to have become suffused with envy in his presence, while women-about-town experienced a weakness in the knees.

We set out before dawn and arrived in New York around lunchtime. Polgár, who was enchantingly vague about practical matters, had been fairly sure of the number of Zilahy's street in Manhattan but not the number of his house. Noticing an elderly caretaker fixing the sidewalk in front of a dilapidated building, Polgár asked him if he knew where Mr. Zilahy lived.

"I'm Zilahy," the caretaker replied, looking up. "Don't apologize. I've no idea who the devil you are, either."

The best-dressed man of his period wore baggy pants with a clown's mismatched buttons and a sweater over a shirt that at one point may have been white. Underneath his curled-up collar there was a neatly knotted tie, accompanied by a second tie knotted loosely and slightly askew above the first. As he rose from the sidewalk, I noticed that he had neglected to zip up his fly.

After sorting out who Polgár was, the writer offered us lunch. It took him some time to recollect setting up a date with the composer, but once he did, the two had much to reminisce about. Polgár, the one-time conductor of the Budapest Radio Orchestra, had written music for several films based on Zilahy's books, including the theme song for *Halálos Tavasz*, Fatal Spring, one of the great hits of the late 1930s, recorded originally by Budapest's favourite film star, Katalin Karády, and later by legendary chanteuses from Zarah Leander to Marlene Dietrich. Zilahy, a hands-on novelist, co-directed the movie himself. I tried to keep this firmly in mind, though it took some effort to associate *Fatal Spring*, an archetypal mixture of romantic elegance and Danubian gloom, with a fragile man in his eighties, fixing a sidewalk in Manhattan, wearing two ties.

Before going to lunch, Zilahy had us take a seat in his dressing room, leaving the door to his bathroom ajar, so he could talk to Polgár while he shaved. He took a straight razor from a black case, glancing at us in a way reminiscent of Sweeney Todd, the demon barber of Fleet Street, but to my relief he put it back and reached for a safety razor. As he lathered his face, he suddenly noticed the unorthodox arrangement of his ties. "Bizarre," he remarked thoughtfully, without doing anything to rectify the matter. He carefully shaved himself but did not bother removing the excess lather from his earlobes or the tip of his nose. "Best place on Second Avenue," he said when he finished. "Let's go."

His fly remained unzipped. I was on the verge of pointing it out to him—my lips were about to form the words—but then could not bring myself to utter them. How do you tell a literary and social icon, the best-dressed man of his period, that he forgot to button his fly? We walked to the restaurant.

It turned out to be a noisy canteen serving Hungarian-style dishes. Patrons lined up to buy their meal tickets at a cashier, then formed a queue again at a counter with their eating utensils in hand, waiting for a server to slop their food into their plates, military-style. Zilahy bought our tickets. When we had our bowls of stuffed cabbage in our hands, he led the way to a table in the back of the establishment. We sat on plastic chairs and drank water.

The stuffed cabbage was tasty as well as piping hot. It also provided the solution to Zilahy's sartorial defect. As he brought the first forkful of cabbage to his lips, a small piece of the sizzling meat fell straight into his open fly. This immediately brought the matter to Zilahy's attention. He winced, fished out the stuffed cabbage, then adjusted the offending garment with remarkable aplomb. Polgár was busy recounting an anecdote and paid no attention to anything else. (Polgár rarely paid attention to his environment. It did him no harm as a musician, though it rather diminished his effectiveness as a driver.)

I said little during lunch; frankly, I was too shocked to even listen. A fragment from Villon kept coming into in my mind. *Mais où sont les neiges d'antan*: where are the snows of yesteryear? Thirty years pass, and the wry chronicler of Europe's aristocratic twilight takes his lunch in a self-serve restaurant on Second Avenue. The master makes a guest appearance in "The Ballad of the Ladies of Bygone Times." The stylish author of *Fatal Spring* plays a cameo in Browning's recollection of a long-ago carnival in St. Mark's Square: *Oh Galuppi, Baldassaro, this is very sad to find! / I can hardly misconceive you; it would prove me deaf and blind.* Venice remembered on the Upper East Side, Maestro Zilahy with his fly unzipped, a tale in chords of plaintive thirds and commiserating sevenths. *Was a lady such a lady, cheeks so round and lips so red?* By what process does a noted European boulevardier turn into a baggy-panted caretaker fixing a sidewalk? Is it age, is it Alzheimer's, is it America? The three words start with the same letter, as Marshall McLuhan (or his ghost) would undoubtedly point out.

26

MY VIENNESE AUNT

We go to Europe to be Americanized.
—RALPH WALDO EMERSON

LET ME CONTINUE OUT OF SEQUENCE chronologically in order to stay in sequence thematically. In the spring of 1971 I had the use of a Mercedes convertible on the Côte d'Azure. Since my Viennese aunt and uncle were flying in to Nice for the weekend, I suggested that I pick them up at the airport. They were going to spend a day on the French Riviera before going to Monaco, where my uncle, formerly a maker of red and yellow bricks, but by now a manufacturer of decorative and ceremonial candles, had some business meetings.

Aunt Klari and her husband had emigrated to Austria shortly after the 1956 uprising. Unlike most people, they did not sneak across the border. By pulling some strings—my uncle was good at pulling strings—they had managed to exit Hungary legally. When years later I asked him how he did it, my uncle made a face and said, "Pfff!"

It took me many years to realize that my Viennese aunt embodied the attitudes of the European Union toward America. I did not know this at the time. I thought that Aunt Klari was merely quirky.

"What have you planned for us, dear?" my aunt inquired as she swept into the terminal, with my uncle trailing dutifully behind her. My mother's baby sister was then in her early sixties, slim, stylish, and looking at least ten years younger than her age. She inspected me, as she usually did, as if I were a puppy of dubious breeding one might fully expect to misbehave. "I do hope it's not going to be something terribly tedious, whatever it is," she said.

"Lunch and dinner," I replied, trying to project a confidence I did not feel. "Lunch at the Croisette, so uncle can audit the starlets at the Festival, then dinner at a very charming restaurant right back here in the old city of Nice."

I was staying in the town of Vallauris myself, not far from Cannes, at the rented villa of an old friend, the writer Stephen Vizinczey, whose novel *In Praise of Older Women*, published a few years earlier, had created a literary sensation. Vizinczey was still basking in the glory (and funds) his best-selling book had brought him, looking for excuses not to settle down to the brutally hard work of writing his next novel. For the duration of the Cannes Film Festival I became his excuse, as he played the attentive host, generously putting his villa and Mercedes at my disposal.

Aunt Klari narrowed her eyes, wrinkled her brow, and cocked her head when she heard me speak. It was to express her utter disbelief.

"Did you say a *charming* restaurant in the *old* city of Nice?" she asked. "Is this what you suggest we do in France? Tell me, how much time did you spend in America altogether?"

"I spent most of it in Canada, actually," I replied, "and it was about fifteen years."

My uncle used the opportunity to rest his leather travelling cases on the floor, but quickly picked them up when my aunt glanced at him. (He obeyed his wife, just as he had obeyed Fatime, the Turkish opera singer, when she wanted him to push his fist against her diaphragm thirty years earlier. Obeying women came naturally to my uncle, as did being nursed and mothered by them. Meek as he was, he was a man and a European. The idea of laying out his own socks in the morning would never have occurred to him.)

"Amazing," my aunt said as she started walking toward the exit. "Apparently in fifteen years a person becomes thoroughly *American*. Perhaps not American enough to have any money to speak of, but American enough to sail back to Europe as a *tourist*. He'll carry a Baedekker in his pocket, and start looking for charming old restaurants."

"He'll probably carry a Michelin guide," I murmured. "Americans are innocent of Baedekkers."

Aunt Klari let this pass. "Do you think we've come from Vienna all the way to Nice," she continued, "to dine in a charming old restaurant? *Mein*

Gott! There are about fifty charming old restaurants in Vienna within walk-ing distance of our flat. I see about seven of them if I look out the window, one older and more charming than the next."

"Sorry, Aunt," I said. "Very stupid of me. Where would you like to go?"

My aunt's expression became suffused with blissful expectation. As she looked at me, her eyes seemed radiant. "Plaza 2000," she said.

"Pardon?"

"Plaza 2000. You must have read about it. They opened it last year. Right on the seashore. The French are always a step ahead of everybody. It's the first genuine American-style shopping plaza in Europe."

Our exchange took on a theatrical tone. "Aunt Klari," I said, "you can't be serious. We're in Nice. There's the pure azure of the Mediterranean to our left and the pristine white of the French Maritime Alps to our right. Caesar's legions beheld these vistas, unless they were too drunk, and you want me to take you to some shopping plaza for polyester fabrics and hot dogs as if we were in an American suburb?"

Aunt Klari had stopped listening by then. She was looking around the parking lot. "Where is your car?" she asked. "Is that it, that tedious Mercedes? I was hoping it might be a Chevrolet. Never mind, dear, let's go."

My aunt's mysterious preference for a Chevrolet reminded me of earlier automotive experiences in her company. In the 1930s Aunt Klari had acquired the reputation of being a thoroughly modern woman, at least in Central European terms. One expression of her modernity was to insist that her husband set her up in business; the other to take instruction in dri-ving a motor car. The first endeavour turned out to be more costly (my uncle had to invest in a boutique for her, specializing in fancy hats) but the second was more menacing to the environment. For several years the only person who would get into a vehicle piloted by Aunt Klari was my grand-father—not because he was particularly gallant, but because he felt duty-bound to indulge his younger daughter.

"How was it?" my grandmother asked (according to family legend) after he returned from their first driving adventure.

"Fine," grandfather replied. "Klari mounted the sidewalk once, going

"I don't think I'm up to spending an entire evening with Americans." My Viennese aunt in Budapest, circa 1935.

around a corner, but then she got right back on the road."

"Then what are you doing with the *szilvorium*?" grandmother inquired as she saw her husband reaching for a bottle of plum brandy in the cupboard. "You don't usually take a drink at this time of the day."

"I refuse to be a slave to my habits."

As long as my uncle had a chauffeur he was safe from my aunt's driving, but after the war things changed rapidly. One fundamental difference between the New and the Old World was that until the end of the 1930s almost anybody could afford a chauffeur in Europe, but only a few people could afford a car. After World War II democracy and mass production made cars much easier to acquire, and chauffeurs much more difficult. Before long, gentlemen had to enlist their wives to drive them—that is, unless they were willing to learn to drive themselves, which my uncle refused to do. "I'm not mechanically inclined," he'd say. "My wife seems to enjoy this sort of thing. She's also rather handy with hats."

This made Aunt Klari the designated driver of the family Peugeot. (It was invariably a Peugeot, either because my uncle had a surfeit of brand loyalty or a lack of imagination.) For some reason Peugeot used to make cars with headlights set close together, which made them appear to have a permanent squint. "No wonder she's all over the place," my father remarked once. "That damn French car is cross-eyed."

My aunt was over seventy in 1979 when she picked me up in what turned out to be her last Peugeot. It was at the train station in the resort town of Baden, not far from Vienna, where she and my uncle had a summer condominium. By then I had almost forgotten about Aunt Klari's driving habits, but she soon reminded me.

"Oh dear," she said, as we turned the corner from the railway yards. "What's that silly bus doing in the ditch?"

"Trying to avoid you, Aunt," I murmured. "This is a one-way street, I believe."

My aunt cast me a withering glance.

"Don't be daft, dear boy," she said. "I *always* come this way."

Having said this, she continued driving the wrong way in what could only be described as a regal manner—to her doom, as I noted with some glee, because there was a policeman waiting at the end of the road. But my expectation proved that I had been away from Europe too long. The policeman only gave my aunt a charming Austrian salute, which she coolly acknowledged as her due.

Going back to the matter of Plaza 2000 and the Chevrolet, the fact that my aunt liked American *things* did not mean that she liked Americans. She did not—which was perhaps her most European feature. Actually, my aunt reminded me of the goat described by George Orwell in one of his Burma stories. The animal wanted a piece of bread Orwell was holding out, but it did not want the British essayist, and resolved the dilemma by alternately taking a bite of the bread then trying to butt Orwell in the stomach, evidently hoping that if it could drive the writer away, the bread would somehow remain hanging in mid-air. In the manner of many Europeans and Burmese goats, my aunt, too, tried to acquire American things—objects, systems, funds, and military protection—while keeping Americans, with their boorish voices and habits, at bay.

I was spending a few days in Vienna in the late 1970s with the Canadian criminal lawyer, Edward. L. Greenspan, and his wife, Suzy. Greenspan was attending a legal conference and I was doing research for a book. When I phoned Aunt Klari to say hello, she expressed a desire to see me. I suggested dinner.

"Perfect. Your uncle and I will take you to Sacher's."

"No, let me take you—I'm here with some Canadian friends."

"Obeying women came naturally to my uncle." Uncle "Nimrod" flanked by mother (l.) and her sister, shortly before my Viennese aunt's death, Baden, Austria, 1979.

There was a pause. "American friends?" asked my aunt, a touch frostily.

"Canadian."

"I suppose it's all right," she said, "though it means we'll have to speak English."

"It's a lawyer and his wife. You can speak French with her, if you prefer."

"Oh dear," said Aunt Klari. "I'm not sure if I'm up to speaking French with an American."

"Canadian—and she's from Morocco, actually. Schooled in Paris, I believe."

My aunt sighed again. "Oh dear."

We set a date, but she phoned me the day before. "You'll have to excuse me, dear," she said. "You know I've been having trouble with my vegetative nervous system. The doctor advises me to avoid strain. I don't think I'm up to spending an entire evening with Americans."

My aunt died rather unexpectedly at the age of seventy-two. We immediately suspected her vegetative nervous system. I commented, perhaps unkindly, that she must have broken her rule and spent an evening with some Americans. My uncle was devastated, having lost a chauffeur as well as a companion. He immediately offered to marry my mother, who was by then a widow of seventy-five herself. My mother did not think much of the idea. "Thanks, but I don't think you want to go to such lengths," she wrote back in reply. "You know I don't drive."

27

EUROPE:

THE ANTI-WAR UNION

War is an ugly thing, but not the ugliest
of things. The decayed and degraded state of moral and
patriotic feeling which thinks that nothing
is worth war is much worse.

—JOHN STUART MILL

THE AVOIDANCE OF WAR HAS BEEN ONE fundamental motive for the concept of a European Union from the beginning. The earliest architects of the union reasoned that since it was undisputed among people of intelligence and goodwill that war was a bad thing, and since war meant an armed conflict between nations, an obvious way to avoid war was to avoid nations. No nations, no war: it seemed as simple as that.

This was not merely a pacifist view. It was held by many intellectuals during and after World War I who did not necessarily dispute that some armed conflicts may be just, necessary, or at least unavoidable under the current organization of the world. What they wanted to change was the world's current organization. This meant doing away with both nations and war, partly because the former begot the latter, but mainly because they were both intrinsically undesirable. (Actually it was hard to tell which was viewed as the bigger evil: that nations begot war, or that war begot nations.)

During the Wilsonian period an idea gradually emerged, possibly for the first time in human history, that war had no cultural and spiritual value and no practical utility. Wars never "solved anything"; there was no merit in the so-called military virtues. This became an article of faith for the literati of the Western world, except for a few eccentric souls and, of course, for

171

followers of the fascist heresy. Coupled with the idea of the uselessness and unredeemed evil of war was a parallel notion: as Hannah Arendt put it, "the bankruptcy of the nation-state and its concept of sovereignty."[9] Nations were Out and world government was In, while sovereignty, whether national or individual, became another bad word. "Rugged individualism" had turned into a concept of ridicule, and sovereignty was seen as the rugged individualism of nations.

Pacific supranationalism was a key ingredient in the Petri dish that nurtured Brussels. The view from the dish was flat: few could see the intimate connection between shadow and light, evil and good, the wars of Europe and Europe's accomplishments. Among the exceptions was Milan Kundera, the brilliant Czech author of *The Unbearable Lightness of Being*, who wrote the following lines in 1991:

"War and culture, those are the two poles of Europe, her heaven and hell, her glory and shame, and they cannot be separated from one another. When one comes to an end, the other will end also and one cannot end without the other. The fact that no war has broken out in Europe for fifty years is connected in some mysterious way with the fact that for fifty years no new Picasso has appeared either."[10]

In his book Kundera puts these lines in the mouth of a character. Whether he does so with approval or not is less important than the fact that he observes the connection.

Great art usually emerges at a confluence of great personal gifts and great historical events. It comes at a point where a major talent is bolstered by major experiences, often involving bloody strife, conflict, and sacrifice. Significant art usually comes from significant artists living in significant places at significant times. The argument is not that it is "worth" having Napoleon invade Russia because it enables Tolstoy to write *War and Peace*; the argument is merely that looking for the second is futile in the absence of the first. If the EU ever succeeds in eliminating European conflict, it will also go a long way toward eliminating European art.

28

EUROPE: THE

ANTI-AMERICAN UNION

We often want one thing and pray for another,
not telling the truth even to the gods.

—SENECA

NATIONS BEHAVE RATHER LIKE PARTICLES: they jell into cohesive wholes by forces of attraction and repulsion. France would not exist without its inhabitants sharing a sense of "Frenchness" that is distinct from their neighbour's sense of "Englishness." This sense acts both as a magnet and a repellent: it attracts those who share it and repulses those who do not. Such a sense of nationhood is universal. The expression "un-American" could not exist without a shared feeling that there is something—a set of ideas, attributes, characteristics, tempers, and so on—that can be called "American." The organizing principles that generate such feelings of group cohesion or nationhood can vary, but whether they are tribal, dynastic, ideological/religious, linguistic/cultural, or geographic in their origins, or a mixture of them, they ultimately lead to a sense of inclusion and exclusion. Without such a sense of "we" and "they," discrete entities could not exist.

Needless to say, "repulsion" or "exclusion" do not necessarily translate into feelings of hostility, let alone belligerency. The words merely denote feelings of distinctness when used in this sense. They set out the psychological perimeters of groups. They are demarcations separating the home team from the visitors, the kin from the unrelated, the English from the French.

All the same, the maintenance of cohesion and distinctness *within* requires a certain amount of friction *without*: friction between those inside and outside the circle. Competition with "outsiders" is the lifeblood of cohesion among "insiders." There is usually an ostensible reason—a contentious issue, a border dispute, a quarrel over fishing rights, or some other *casus belli* that appears to have an objective reality—but the fact is that without a certain amount of jostling between groups, the internal equilibrium of groups could not be assured. Singularity needs some hostility as an ingredient. "I exclude, therefore I am" is the Cartesian motto of all groups, including nations.

It was clear from the outset that the creation of a supranational entity, such as a United Europe, required the substitution of a new system of attraction and repulsion. If France and Germany, subsumed in the new union, could no longer maintain their internal cohesion by mutually repelling each other, another sum of repulsion had to be found to balance the equation. The new European entity that was to replace France, Germany, and Britain needed an "other" to define itself just as France, Germany, and Britain needed each other to define themselves before. If they could no longer be each other's aliens, they required a substitute. One obvious candidate was the EU's own role model, the much-admired, much-envied, and much-resented superpower across the Atlantic, the United States.

People with a sense of history intuited this development before it occurred. If the chief gain of the European Union would be harmony in Europe, what would be the chief loss? When I asked Henry Kissinger this question, he replied: "Well, the chief loss could be the loss of the transatlantic relationship."

Kissinger recalled the head of a European commission saying at the conclusion of some agricultural agreement with South America that the Europeans made certain concessions that were not in their economic interest. "The reason we made the concessions which are not in our economic interest," the European negotiator explained, "is because they are in our political interest. It is a price we have to pay for breaking the hegemony of America."

Kissinger added that the European negotiator "wasn't a Frenchman, he was a Portuguese." The comment was very much to the point. As a Portuguese, the EU negotiator had no national axe to grind. He was not proposing to break the hegemony of America on behalf of a direct rival, however distant, such as France, but on behalf of the new European entity.

In the same conversation[11] Kissinger made a reference to one of his books, written many years earlier. It featured an apocryphal dialogue between Jean Monnet, one of the godfathers of the European Union, and General Charles de Gaulle. In this made-up conversation, as Kissinger recalled, "Monnet says to de Gaulle, you're crazy, you're trying to extract from the Americans what I will get them to give to me...and de Gaulle says, well, unless we *extract* it, it won't have any meaning to us."

This was a keen insight, not only into the nature of the general's nationalism, but also into the nature of nationalism in general. Free concessions, unlike extracted ones, have little value in national narratives. Kissinger's mythical dialogue foresaw the invention of a new "European civilization," not as a cultural concept of Western or Christian civilization (which would have some historic validity), but as a political concept designed to supplant the myths and narratives of the real nations that make up geographic Europe, and setting it up in opposition to "non-European" civilizations— primarily of the United States.

For many Russians the EU was a mere mask for a re-emergent Germany. Leonyd Slutskiy, deputy head of Russia's international affairs committee, writing in the influential *Nezavisimaya Gazeta* in 2000, described the "spectre" of a coming U.S.-German conflict for world domination being already "visible on the ruins of the Berlin Wall." Slutskiy posited that Americans had not yet recognized the "hidden but unavoidable" conflict between the United States and the emerging Europe.

Some observers discerned a German—or rather Franco-German— Europe reconstructing itself along the medieval lines of Charlemagne's Holy Roman Empire. The Russians were not alone in this view. Lee A. Casey and David B. Rivkin, Jr., pointed out in a 2001 issue of *Policy Review* that "many of the European Project's supporters today look to the Europe united under Charlemagne for precedent and inspiration." Indeed, every year a Karlspreis, or International Charlemagne Prize, is awarded to an individual to recognize the "most meritorious contribution serving European unification and the European community, serving humanity and world peace." (The 1999 winner was British Prime Minister Tony Blair.)

True enough, the EU resembles the ninth-century dominion of Charles the Great territorially, incorporating as it does France, Germany, and the Netherlands. Even more to the point, Brussels' budding pan-European empire recalls Charlemagne's universe in the ruling Eurocracy's imperious and supranational spirit. It is ironic, though not altogether surprising, that the chief ideologues of the emerging Eurocracy, such as Hong Kong's former governor, Chris Patten, have been compelled to counteract successive waves of older chauvinisms—surfacing in various movements led by personalities such as France's Jean-Marie Le Pen, Austria's Joerg Haider, or Holland's Pim Fortuyn[12]—by resorting to the construction and promotion of a new Euro-chauvinism. "A healthy European democracy will develop only when people begin to feel an emotional commitment to their European identity," wrote Patten in the British *Spectator* in the spring of 2002.

A new "European identity" would, of course, require people to feel less French, German, or British—or less "xenophobic," as Eurocrats would put it. Even more importantly, however, it would require them to feel more anti-American. It is "breaking the hegemony of America," to use the Portuguese negotiator's phrase in Kissinger's anecdote, that would give Patten's patriots their national purpose. Down with xenophobia à la Le Pen, long live anti-Americanism à la Patten. One might call it a chauvinism to end all chauvinisms.

The American commentator James C. Bennett put it in straightforward terms.[13] "The political purpose of the synthetic concept of 'European civilization' is obvious," he wrote. "It is a response to the failure of the Eurocratic elite to find any kind of socio-political glue to hold their creation together.

"United Europe does not have the 'mystic cords of memory' Lincoln evoked; rather, they belong to the nation-states whose strongest myths, narratives, and memories must be suppressed for the sake of Europeanism."

Bennett argued in his piece (and in others) that the raison d'être of the European project has been superseded by events. Europe today has far less to fear from internecine wars, to say nothing of being overrun by the Soviet Union, than it did when the EU's founding fathers, Jean Monnet, Robert Schumann, and Paul-Henri Spaak, first put their ideas into tentative practice during the 1950s. This leaves "nothing but economic rationalism as an argument for European unification," wrote Bennett. "Economic self-interest, in and of itself, is seldom a sufficiently strong glue to hold together a polity."

Bennett and others have used the word "Euro-Lepenism" to describe a glue that is much stronger: the Krazy Glue of anti-Americanism. "Perhaps the Eurocrats can eventually succeed in building a European superstate by eradicating enough authentic local and national identities and by scapegoating outsiders," wrote Bennett in another essay.[14] Scapegoating outsiders is key: "I'm not pro-Canadian, I'm anti-American" was how the Canadian nationalist Dave Godfrey put it in the early 1970s.[15] Thirty years later Brussels' creations are echoing the sentiment. A fundamental error of Europe's founding fathers was to think that by uniting Europe, and thereby doing away with the potential of conflict between, say, France and Germany, they could do away with conflict itself. They could not. They merely substituted the potential of conflict between the European Union and the United States.

29

EUROPEAN LOVERS: FIVE VIEWS

"WHEN AN AMERICAN HEIRESS wants to buy a man, she at once crosses the Atlantic. The only really materialistic people I have ever met have been Europeans," wrote the American essayist Mary McCarthy.[16] "No, dear," responded one of my cousins when he came upon her remark in an old issue of *Commentary* magazine, "she crosses the Atlantic because that's where she has to go to find a man worth buying."

Stendhal had a dimmer view of the available stock. "As a man, I can take refuge in having mistresses. The more of them I have, and the greater the scandal, the more I acquire reputation and brilliance in society." The French author wrote this to his twenty-nine-year-old sister Pauline in an 1804 letter as a stern warning for her to stay chaste.

One might call Stendhal an old-fashioned European. About 150 years later the aviator Antoine de Saint-Exupéry, a more modern and sensitive Frenchman, struck a different note. "Whoever loves above all the approach of love," he wrote, "will never know the joy of attaining it."[17]

Perhaps La Rochefoucauld had the same thing in mind when he remarked: "Too great a hurry to discharge an obligation is a kind of ingratitude."[18] At least, I always assumed the seventeenth-century aphorist was talking of a man's conjugal duty—but of course he may have been referring to some totally unrelated matter.

30

A EUROPEAN AUTOBIOGRAPHY

CONSIDER THE FOLLOWING LINES in a European autobiography written in the second decade of the twentieth century:

"Hunger was then my faithful bodyguard; he never left me for a moment and partook of all I had, share and share alike. Every book I acquired aroused his interest; a visit to the Opera prompted his attentions for days at a time; my life was a continuous struggle with this pitiless friend. And yet during this time I studied as never before. Aside from my architecture and my rare visits to the Opera, paid-for in hunger, I had but one pleasure: my books."

Just imagine: Hunger! Opera! Books! Just who was this destitute but contemplative and industrious European whose sole delights, purchased at the price of self-deprivation, were music and reading? And what became of him? Did his assiduous studies do him any good? Did he go on to become a noted writer, architect, or philosopher? Did he end up contributing to the welfare of mankind? Did his name go down in history?

The answer to the last question is affirmative. About seventy-five years later, at the dawn of the twenty-first century, most people still remember the name of Adolf Hitler.

While on the subject, near the Austrian city of Linz there is a picturesque little town called Leonding, which has a picturesque little cemetery. Among many picturesque little graves, there is one with an oval plaque on a grey memorial stone. A portrait on the plaque shows a dour-faced man of middle age with closely cropped hair and a walrus moustache. Below the plaque a smaller portrait affixed to the stone depicts a plain but younger-looking woman.

"Here rests in God," the inscription reads, "Alois Hitler, householder and senior official in the royal and imperial customs bureau, departed on the 3rd of January 1903, in the 65th year of his life. Alongside lies his spouse, Mrs. Klara Hitler, departed on the 21st of December 1907, in her 47th year. R.I.P."

Burnt stumps of votive candles still littered the grave of Hitler's parents in 2002. Cemetery officials cannot say who the visitors might be.

31

Non Morire: A Tribute

IN 1982 AN INDEPENDENT PRODUCER friend from Montreal, Tony Robinow, asked me to film an episode for a television series called *Masters of the Performing Arts*. My segment featured the Italian baritone Tito Gobbi, by then almost seventy. The legendary singer shuttled between master classes held in an austere rehearsal hall in the National Opera Studio in London and the splendid music room of his own villa near Rome. His pupils ranged from gifted voices in opera schools to established members of leading opera companies. Some were mature artists.

Robinow offered me a fee, though I would have gladly filmed Gobbi for nothing. False: I would have happily paid for the experience. As a teenager watching my first opera movie I recollected what seemed to me sheer magic: a production of Leoncavallo's *I Pagliacci,* in which the familiar stage set first expanded into a realistic countryside, then, unimaginably, combined the exquisite allure of Gina Lollobrigida's features in the role of Nedda with the equally exquisite allure of Onelia Fineschi's voice. To top off the celluloid miracle, there was Tito Gobbi himself, acting and singing all three baritone parts of the opera: the lover Silvio, the evil cripple Tonio, and the prophetic Prologue. Recalling Gobbi's rendition of the opera's opening line *"Si può...* *si può..."* still sends shivers down my spine.

Director Mario Costa's 1949 film was a tour de force, an early triumph of European cinema, opening the door to other memorable opera movies over the years. It was an experience that, at the age of fifteen, had a profound effect on me. It even impressed my father, who had sung Silvio himself at the Viennese Opera fifty years earlier. Gobbi's acting was bold yet believable. His versatility was remarkable not only for an opera singer but for any performer—in fact, even for the high-stakes, real-life role-playing of a con man or a spy. One of Gobbi's favourite stories involved a couple of downed American pilots during the war who had put on civilian clothes to avoid capture, but still looked hopelessly out of place in a little Tuscan village, until Gobbi figured out the problem and showed them how to *walk* Italian.

Gobbi's residence had a dusty patina—walls of faded Mediterranean pink, ironwork grills, wooden shutters, a large garden with a mossy stone fountain, verdant bushes mixed with the colour of ash, and two wily Roman cats that followed Gobbi around like dogs. On the first day of filming the maestro was in top form. He had just finished a tutorial with the radiant British-Australian soprano Rosamund Illing, who had performed Mimi's opening aria from Puccini's *La Bohème* in what Gobbi called her "charming Italian." We were sitting in the garden, waiting for the crew— French sound, British camera, Italian grip—to complete the set-up for the next master class. Gobbi was to take the robust Greek baritone, Louis Manikas, through his paces as the villain Scarpia in Puccini's *Tosca*.

Gobbi must have performed the role a thousand times. He was especially noted for his entrance in the first act. This is a scene in which Scarpia, the evil Baron, Rome's dreaded police chief, walks into the church of Sant'Andrea della Valle. In one of Gobbi's celebrated performances in Verona, the Baron actually rode into the church on horseback.

"Your entrance as Scarpia," I said, "is the stuff of legends."

Gobbi's eyes lit up. "Ah, but do you know why?" he asked.

"Well—why?"

"You know what I do when I come in?"

I shook my head.

"*No*-thing," said Gobbi, in an English at least as charming as Illing's Italian. "I do *no*-thing."

I must have looked a trifle blank because he grinned and tapped his finger on the side of his nose.

"And showed them how to walk Italian." Author looks on as Tito Gobbi rehearses with Canadian soprano Barbara Colliers in Rome, in 1982.

"Some singers, they compete with the music," he explained. "They fight with Puccini, the fools. They thump with the feet, roll with the eyes, scrunch up with the face. Look me, I'm such villain! But why do it? Puccini does it for you with the notes: bam-bam-bam. He tells everybody who is Scarpia. You try to act, you only take away from Puccini. If you want your audience to tremble like *tutti Roma*, you do *no*-thing."

By then Manikas had joined us in the garden. Gobbi looked at him. "The music is magnet. It is force, no? That's *dolce far niente*, my dear," he said. "It's sweet to do nothing—as long as the force is on your side."

"And if the force is not with you?" I asked.

"Then you act," Gobbi said. "You act till it hurts. You act to save your life. Whatever you do, *non morire*—don't die, that's what an old conductor, Santini, used to tell us at La Scala. During rehearsals, a little deaf, a little blind, he always stood in the back, waving his handkerchief. Keep acting. *Non morire*."

It sounded like excellent advice. My hope was that Gobbi would take it, but he did not. The greatest Scarpia—and Rigoletto, and Tonio, and Prologue—failed to listen to his own counsel. The baritone who once sang the entire soprano aria of Mimi before his class because he could not resist the "beautiful, touching music"; the actor who knew how to do *no*-thing when the theatre belonged to Puccini, even though he could also act until it hurt when the force was not with him; the film star who did alone what Gina Lollobrigida could only do in combination with Onelia Fineschi; the man who showed American pilots how to *walk* Italian; the master whose cats followed him like dogs: yes, even this lustrous and illustrious performer could not quite act to save his life. *Non morire*, he told us—but he did anyway, two years later, in Rome, at seventy-one.

Oh well. As Tonio put it to Nedda, *Affascinato io mi beavo:* watching you I was in heaven. Nor is it over because the maestro made it into the electronic age. *Si, si,* my dear, as he observed. It is all here in this little box: pink walls, Roman cats, opera in aspic. So what if we progressed from artists to nerds? We may never write music like Puccini or perform it like Gobbi again, but the nerds of today are spectacular at preserving what the artists of yesterday wrote and performed. And the nerds of tomorrow, they will be better still. *Viva* CD and DVD, *viva* life everlasting. *Non morire.*

32

EUROPE: BUT WILL IT FLY?

Europe has lived on its contradictions, flourished on its differences, and, constantly transcending itself thereby, has created a civilization on which the whole world depends even when rejecting it. This is why I do not believe in a Europe unified under the weight of an ideology or of a technocracy that overlooks these differences.
—ALBERT CAMUS, INTERVIEW IN *DEMAIN*, PARIS, OCTOBER 24, 1957

AS FLIGHT INSTRUCTORS NEVER TIRE of telling student pilots, the real danger of an airplane being loaded beyond its certified weight or out of its proper balance is not that it will not fly. The real danger is that it will. A plane that does not fly cannot hurt anyone. A poorly loaded plane hurts people precisely because it manages to stagger into the air. The European Union is such an aircraft. Its chief problem is not that it will not take off. Its chief problem is that it already has.

WHAT IS A EUROPEAN?

An Oklahoman is an American, and a Dane is a European. Accurate as this statement is, it would be a mistake to assume that a Dane is a European in the same way in which an Oklahoman is an American. Yet this is the unspoken—or perhaps unconsidered—assumption of many who contemplate a "United States" of Europe.

What confuses them is that America, too, is a country born of the union of different states across a continent, including states that are often remarkably unlike in size, economy, climate, culture, dialect, or ethnic composition. Sometimes such states seem to share little but the fact that they are located in North America. Yet their kinship is still infinitely greater than the kinship of states that share only the fact that they are located in geographic Europe.

The difference is history. All of America coalesced around the same ideological-geographic organizing principle, baked in the oven of a common conceptual heritage, made up from a shared set of civic habits, public morality, religion, laws, customs, and myths. In America, all states were born of a linguistic-cultural heritage that some recent writers, notably Neal Stephenson and James C. Bennett, have called "Anglosphere."

The states of Europe have no such shared roots. They have coalesced in several different cauldrons around several different organizing principles. The *least* that American states have in common is their shared tenancy of a continent, but this is the *most* that European states have in common.

The simplest illustration of the difference is that while an Oklahoman would naturally think of himself as an American even while riding a bus in Oklahoma City, it would rarely occur to a Dane riding a bus in Copenhagen to think of himself as a European. He would think of himself simply as a Dane. He would start thinking of himself as a European only if he found himself in Africa, Asia, or, God forbid, Oklahoma.

SMALL FISH IN A BIG POND

Some writers illustrate the success of the European ideal by pointing out that it cuts across a very wide spectrum. Small, exposed, insecure, and unsuccessful nations have been attracted to the concept of a European Union, and so have large, secure, confident, and successful nations. The observation is accurate, but what it does not take into account is that the two types of nations are attracted to the same ideal for entirely different reasons.

Underachieving nations hope that within the union they can rise to equality with their neighbours. Instead of having to approach successful nations with their tails between their legs, fawning for scraps, they hope to become entitled to a share in their fellow Europeans' fame and fortune. In contrast, overachieving nations hope that by joining the Union they will eventually come to possess it. They see the EU as a bloodless conquest, a new empire they can lead and dominate. (Dennis Healey, a British Labour politician, remarked in the 1960s, speaking of a small Europhile faction in the British Conservative Party, "Their Europeanism is nothing but imperialism with an inferiority complex."[19])

Romania, which would dearly wish to be admitted to the European club, exemplifies the spirit in which underachieving nations approach the union, while Germany exemplifies the spirit in which overachieving nations approach it. Germans expect that all of Europe will become German one day. "I believe that the European construction is accompanied by a de facto quest for German domination," remarked Henry Kissinger.[20]

Romanians do not expect, or desire, Europe to become Romanian. What they hope is that Romania might one day become French—or at least British.

A BOXER'S CLINCH

Two concepts drive the EU. One is hopeful, and the other defensive.

The first concept is the ever-glittering example of the United States. If uniting thirteen former colonies worked marvels in America, if unity resulted in history's biggest success story and ultimately the sole super-power on earth, why should the same thing not have the same result in Europe?

A sense of something like this emerged as far back as the eighteenth century. "People nowadays have such high hopes of America and the polit-ical conditions obtaining there that one might say the desires, at least the secret desires, of all enlightened Europeans are *deflected to the west*, like our magnetic needles," wrote the German philosopher G.C. Lichtenberg in his *Aphorisms*.[21]

The second concept driving the EU is quite different. Two persons holding one another in their arms might do so for two different reasons. First, they *might* be in a loving embrace. Conversely, they might be in a clinch, in the manner of boxers, each trying to prevent the other from knocking him down.

The EU is a boxer's clinch.

The Russian revolutionary Leon Trotsky gave an early expression to this view. He saw the European Union as a way of tying up nations that would otherwise continue pummelling each other. "The Federated Republic of Europe—the United States of Europe—that is what must be," he explained to an American communist sympathizer, John Reed. "National autonomy no longer suffices. Economic evolution demands the abolition of national frontiers. If Europe is to remain split into national groups, then Imperialism will recommence its work. Only a Federated Republic of Europe can give peace to the world."[22]

Trotsky's ambition was to run the Kremlin when he said this. He has been dead for a long time now, but the Kremlin is alive and well. Only it has relocated to Brussels.

THE CANADIAN SICKNESS

Statist assaults on liberalism came in three major waves during the twenti-eth century. The first two, Fascism and Communism, were defeated, largely or completely. The third wave has now been rolling over the world for some time.

This Third Wave (a.k.a. the "Third Way" or, as Canada's former prime minister Jean Chrétien called it, somewhat petulantly but not inaccurately, "The Canadian Way") has shed the crude trappings of the first two waves. It is the glossiest, the most sophisticated, and the most up-to-date version of the illiberal state. It is not, on the face of it, unreasonable. In some ways the Canadian sickness is not even unattractive.

The entity it creates is unmistakable, though, for those who know the prototype. A Canadian columnist described it succinctly. "The European Union is run by an unelected Commission and a secretive Council," wrote Mark Steyn, "and given a fig leaf of respectability by a parliament of EUnuchs with no real power."[23]

The new commissars do not look or sound like the old ones. Both sartorially and in personal style they resemble Tony Blair far more than Hermann Göring. Far from goose-stepping, they speak in the dulcet tones of upscale maitre d's. They *are* in fact different—except what is different about them is reduced to insignificance by the thing they have in common, which is statism. Under the guise of civilization, the mandarins of Brussels seek to insulate themselves from vulgar realities, such as their own electorates. "The direct accountability of parliaments," observed the British columnist Michael Gove, "is being supplanted by the closed power-broking of European bodies insulated from effective scrutiny."[24] If the assault of Eurocrats is successful, statism will defeat liberalism as conclusively as if it had been defeated by the darkest forces in Hitler's Berchtesgaden or in the Kremlin.

Third Wave statism may not be as bloody as the first two. It may not come complete with gas chambers and Gulags. Its commissars may not be as quick to resort to dungeons and truncheons as the commissars of the Gestapo or the GPU (though they, too, will resort to them when they run out of other choices). Third Wave statism may not be as harmful to the bodies of individuals as the first two waves, but it is equally harmful to the liberty, dignity, and sovereignty of their souls.

It is revealing how rapidly "progressive" people have come to terms with the new world order. "It is odd but true," the British-American journalist John O'Sullivan observed in 2002, "that the Left in general adapted much more quickly and surefootedly to post-communism than did the Right."[25]

As the new century begins, judas goats of "security" and "human rights" are ambling toward Brussels, leading the sheep to slaughter. Europe's dumb creatures that successfully evaded the lasso in the twentieth century might not be able to evade the lure.

WELCOME TO DIRIGISTE HEAVEN

The great Western philosopher, Mae West, remarked once, "When choosing between two evils, I'd like to try the one I've never tried before." If Eurocrats had the ability to achieve such a penetrating insight, they might distance themselves from central planning, social engineering, and the command economy. As it is, *dirigisme* is a main feature of Brussels.

Historians sympathetic to socialism, such as Mark Mazower, write when discussing World War II that "the war itself, with the new roles assumed by government in managing the economy and society, demonstrated the truth of the reformers' argument: democracy was indeed compatible with the interventionist state."[26] Such a statement is true enough, only it is largely meaningless. The interventionist state may well be compatible with democracy, but this does not take us very far. Even outright tyranny is compatible with democracy in the sense that voters may elect tyrants for fixed terms, as they did in some city-states in ancient Greece. The "turranos" of Syracuse was an elected official.

What the interventionist state is not compatible with is liberty.

If one uses the word "democracy" only in its primary sense, to mean a method of governmental succession, then the statement "democracy is compatible with the interventionist state" is accurate, albeit irrelevant. But if one uses the word "democracy" to mean a free society (as most writers and speakers use it), then the notion is no longer accurate. Democracy, meaning a free society, is not compatible with the interventionist state.

This isn't a matter of opinion, but of logic. If words mean anything, "intervention" means an outside force prescribing or proscribing conduct, which makes it contrary to volition. One may argue whether such restriction is good or bad in individual instances, but one cannot deny that it exists. To the extent that A can intervene in B's conduct—even in B's own interest, let alone in A's interest or some third party's interest—B is not free. This may be fine with B, and so "democratic," but a tyrant with a mandate is still a tyrant. A majority of voters may elect to live in an interventionist state, but this will not make the state any the less interventionist.

Libertarians do not flinch from carrying this logic to its extreme and regard anarchy as the only social system that is truly free. In contrast, anarchy is the point at which classical liberals draw the line. They believe, however, that liberty must verge on anarchy before it becomes undesirable and needs to be curtailed—and that very few societies come close to this limit.

VICTORS' COURTS, LOSERS' JUSTICE

About thirty years ago I did a radio interview for the Canadian Broadcasting Corporation with a leading figure of Canadian nationalism. Dave Godfrey, co-founder (with Dennis Lee) of the avant-garde publisher The House of Anansi, was the author of such books as *The New Ancestors* and *Death Goes Better with Coca-Cola*. Godfrey was an honest man. His first statement on the air was, "I'm a nationalist, but not because I'm pro-Canadian. I'm anti-American."

"Describe your ideal country," I asked him.

"Easy," he said. "It's a peaceful place where power and privilege are most equally distributed among all the people."

"And what country, past or present, approximates this ideal most closely?"

"That's also easy," Godfrey replied. "China."

"To avoid misunderstanding," I said, "let's repeat this. You say your ideal is a country where power and privilege are shared among all people *most equally*?"

"Yes."

"And the country that comes closest to this ideal is, in your view, *Communist China*?"

"Yes."

"Okay," I said, "maybe we should change the subject. How do you feel about goldfish?"[27]

Though Godfrey and I were on opposite sides of the political fence, it was his publishing house, Anansi, that had published my first three books of poems. Our conversation (which I'm quoting from memory) was not hostile. I was simply curious about how an obviously bright person's mind worked when he equated the ostensible objects of his desire—peace, prosperity, and the devolution of political power among the widest possible number of people—with Mao's China. I found it absurd for someone to see China as a symbol of equality and liberty, while seeing America as the symbol of Coca-Cola and death.

Absurd, that is, unless there was another explanation. It seemed to me that many partisans of national or political ideals or entities around the world were acting not so much in support of their ideas as in opposition to what Henry Luce had called "the American century." They appeared to resent the success of a mighty republic with a popular economic and political system, and felt a psychological compulsion to set up something in opposition to it.

Many supporters of Canadian nationalism in the 1960s, whether they admitted it as honestly as Godfrey or not, were anti-American rather than pro-Canadian. It drove some to quite senseless positions: they would have embraced the bubonic plague if they thought that America opposed it. What fuelled them was resentment. The fear that they would forever have to walk in America's shadow made them embrace causes that were the very opposite of their ideals—certainly their professed ideals, but often their real ideals as well. It frequently made them look at tyrants like Mao as distributors rather than stockpilers of power and privilege. (Godfrey actually said to me with reference to Mao, "Well, naturally, you have to collect all the power before you can distribute it."[28])

Today some supporters of the European Union view the Eurocracy's concentration of power in Brussels in a similar vein. They include people who are ardent Fleming, Scottish, or Basque nationalists vis à vis such entities as Belgium, Britain, or Spain, but see nothing incongruous about considering themselves pan-European patriots.

The Canadian legal scholar Hudson Janisch described to me a conversation he had with a Basque law student while lecturing in Spain during the

1990s. Apparently the student considered himself a Basque separatist, but also a good European. He was a confirmed devolutionist with regard to Madrid, but a committed centralist when it came to Brussels. He rejected the organizing principle of *Reino de Espagña* for two million Basques in northern Spain, even with provisions of regional autonomy, but felt that the sturdy Guernica oak, symbolizing the lost sovereignty of his people, would flourish again in the soil of the European Union. His idea seemed to be that the power gathered up by Eurocrats and centralized in Brussels would somehow devolve to the inhabitants of the present-day Basque Euskadi, the Basque heirs of the Kingdom of Navarre, as they were before their rude annexation by the Castile and Aragón kingdom of Ferdinand and Isabella. This annexation happened in 1512, which may seem like a long time ago, but Old World clocks ring a different chime. "To have a face, in the European sense of the word, it would seem that one must not only enjoy and suffer but also desire to preserve the memory of even the most humiliating and unpleasant experiences of the past," observed W.H. Auden.[29] Looking at ethnic minority supporters of the Maastricht Treaty, it is hard to escape the feeling that the EU has become the revenge of the losing parties of Europe's internecine conflicts over the centuries.

FORKED TONGUES

It is interesting to note that the European Union, which has always been a Franco-German project economically and politically, is fast becoming English linguistically. About sixty percent of its working documents have been circulated in English in 2002. Of the remainder, about forty percent have been in French and a mere one percent in German.

One can speculate about the reasons for this, and the Germans as well as the French have speculated a great deal. "French diplomats were heard muttering darkly about Anglo-Saxon plots to undermine the EU," reported Alexander Rose, writing in Canada's *National Post* in the winter of 2002. Apparently there is a view that if English is becoming the lingua franca of Europe in the twenty-first century, the way mediaeval Latin used to be, it is not a natural phenomenon but the result of some sinister conspiracy.

Tempting as it is to postulate the shadowy existence of a "Protocols of the Elders of Anglosphere," the explanation is simpler. The irony of Britain, the most Eurosceptic nation, providing Europe's new Union with a common language has to do mainly with America. English happens to be the language of the United States, the world's only superpower. English is also an official language in India, Pakistan, and much of Africa, in addition to Canada, Australia, and New Zealand. When combined, that is nearly half of the world's population and more than half of its wealth. The exquisite language of Molière cannot compete with such numbers and riches; the exquisite language of Goethe is not even in the running. Poets may hate this, but language and culture are shameless camp followers. They tag after the troops and the money.

WILL EUROPE BECOME A NATION?

The European Union mimics a nation like a homosexual union mimics a marriage. "An invented identity," wrote John O'Sullivan in 1996, "will model itself on an existing one. Homosexual families mimic traditional families by copying the parental role and demanding such perquisites as pension rights for domestic partners. But they are unable to perform important aspects of the role, such as child-bearing, and they are often unwilling to accept its disciplines, such as sexual fidelity. Invented national identities similarly copy the outward shell of real nations. For instance the European Union is gradually acquiring a flag, an anthem, citizenship, and even an army without the prior substance of a single European people with a sense of community and allegiance."[30]

True as this is, it does not dispose of the question. No union, no matter how traditional, is assured of success or permanence. At the same time some unions, no matter how peculiar, can be viable and lasting. Whether the future of the European Union is mirrored in the history of the Soviet Union rather than in the history of the United States is impossible to say. Europhiles and Eurosceptics alike refrain from predictions. "I don't think it will just dissolve," said Henry Kissinger when I asked him in the winter of 2001. "I think something will remain. Maybe like the Holy Roman Empire."

33

VIVE LA DIFFÉRENCE

The Bible tells us to love our neighbors and also to love our enemies; probably
because they are generally the same people.
—MARK TWAIN

HUMAN BEINGS HAVE MUCH IN COMMON, but cultures and national tempers still vary. Shakespeare's question in *The Merchant of Venice*—Shylock asking, "If you prick us, do we not bleed?"—is not as telling as it seems. For instance, it could be posed with equal force by an animal rights activist: "If you prick a chicken, does it not bleed?" Adroit as the question may be, it underlines the commonality of living beings only on a biological level. It is meaningless if offered as proof of their general commonality. Jews and chickens both bleed if you prick them, but this does not make a Jew a chicken or a chicken a Jew. Nor does mere bleeding in common make an Italian a Dane. Of course, an Italian is significantly closer to being a Dane than a chicken is to being a Jew, but Italians are still Italians and Danes are still Danes, and the European Union can do nothing about it.

Needless to say, the EU does not have to change Italians into Danes or vice versa in order to function, just as supranational dynasties could function well (or at least adequately) through long historical periods without trying to homogenize their constituent nationalities. The EU's problem, though, is that it may not be able to resist trying. The bureaucracy of Brussels is enamoured of "harmonization." It will not limit itself to harmonizing things that can be harmonized with relative impunity— say, the fat content of sausage—but will start trying to harmonize things that cannot be harmonized, at least not without grievous upheavals, such as national tempers. It may take many rejections, such as the French and the Dutch voters handed to their Eurocratic elites in the summer of

2005, before the gnomes of Brussels begin to recognize what Bismarck saw more than a hundred years ago, namely that Europe is a location, not a nation.

THE RUSSIAN SOUL

During the siege of Budapest the woman who became my first wife was a twelve-year-old girl. The armies of Marshals Malinovsky and Tolbukhin, after surrounding the city on Christmas Eve in 1944, fought a pitched battle for its possession with the defending German and Hungarian forces. Combat conditions lasted for about eight weeks, from late December to the middle of February. The population was starving, most buildings were in ruins, the streets were blocked by rubble, burned-out trucks, hulks of tanks, broken artillery pieces, and dismembered horses, all buried in snow-drifts. Fortunately the winter was unusually cold, so there were no epidemics. All bridges were down between Buda and Pest, but pedestrians and even trucks could cross the solidly frozen Danube.

The victorious troops of Marshal Tolbukhin's 3rd Ukrainian Front included many Soviet nationalities, among them, naturally, a number of Russians. It was a Russian soldier who first entered the cellar of the apartment building in which my future wife, Sylvia, was hiding with her mother. The fighting was over in that sector, and the soldier was looking for loot. The front-line troops of the Red Army, in addition to liberating victims of the Nazi occupation, were also intent on liberating every object of value that they could lay their hands on. The soldier in Sylvia's cellar was collecting watches and jewellery. Like many front-line soldiers in the Red Army, he was inebriated.

Central heating being rare at the time, apartment buildings had large coal- and firewood cellars that served as air-raid shelters during the siege. Families huddled on makeshift bunks in every corner. The soldier was going from bunk to bunk, saying *"Davay chasy!"* (hand over the watches!) to the cowering civilians, occasionally firing his pistol into the concrete ceiling for emphasis. People kept their heads down as the cement chips flew, along with ricocheting bullets and copper casings.

When the drunken marauder reached Sylvia's bunk, he hesitated. He saw a little girl, petite and pretty. She also happened to be sick at the time, running a high fever. The soldier, though proud bearer of the ancient plundering privileges of front-line troops, was a Russian. He needed to obey his national temper, whose hereditary components included many attributes. Whatever marauding warriors of other cultures may do, Russians rarely rob sick children. If anything, they feed them, pet them, and bring them things. Hurting children is simply an un-Russian thing to do.

The psychological conflict of an intoxicated Russian soldier to continue looting while also obeying the commands of his national temper resolved itself in a remarkable way. He mumbled *"Nu charasho"* (all right, then) and left the cellar. Half an hour later he returned, carrying an enormous velvet box filled with silver, which he deposited on Sylvia's bunk. Her mother immediately recognized the box, all the more so because the knives, forks, and spoons bore her monograms. Evidently the soldier went upstairs, broke into the first apartment he saw, and stole the silver as a present for the sick child. The fact that it happened to be her own silver was just a coincidence; it took nothing away from the magnanimity of the Russian's gesture.

An equally magnanimous Russian subaltern nearly choked me to death around the same time. My father, who was fluent in two Slavic languages, conducted elaborate negotiations with Soviet soldiers in the days following the siege. The object was to secure food for the family—slabs of reddish marmalade, sacks of dried peas or beans, and loaves of army-issue *khleba*, a kind of sticky black bread. In exchange for these commodities, my father would offer items from his dwindling supply of pearl cufflinks, silver cigarette cases, and Schaffhausen wristwatches. He usually took me along on his shopping trips, knowing that the presence of a child—I was ten at the time—would reduce his chances of being robbed. Children, along with old people, acted as cultural inhibitors on the aggression and piracy of Russian soldiers. It was a matter of national temper, amounting to a tribal taboo. Such taboos would not have inhibited occupying German troops, at least not as reliably.

Seeing me put the Russian subaltern in a reflective mood. First he produced a faded photograph from a burlap satchel to show my father that he, too, had a young son at home, just like me. Then he unscrewed the top of his metal flask, picked me up with one hand, and forced some kind of burning liquid down my throat with the other. I nearly choked and tried to resist, but my father was unsympathetic.

"Drink, you little abomination," he said to me in Hungarian, while smiling at the Russian soldier.

Having no choice, I drank. My reward was an extra slice of *khleba* with a generous dollop of marmalade when we got home. I considered it a fair deal, because in the early months of 1945 my dreams at night were mainly of food.

THROUGH A PLATE GLASS, DARKLY

Italians are volatile; Hungarians are phlegmatic. Though this is moderated by individual as well as regional differences—few people would find the Milanese particularly volatile or the inhabitants of Budapest particularly phlegmatic—as a general observation it is accurate enough. It is a statistical truth, as opposed to a scientific one: a rule proven by exceptions rather than a rule to be falsified by experiment. Hungarian visitors to Venice used to be amazed by the spirited disputes of gondoliers on il Canale Grande over matters as minor as a few drops of water being shipped by the oar of one into the gondola of the other. What amazed Hungarians most was that disputes of such sound and fury rarely, if ever, produced any blood. In their native land it would have been the other way around.

A typical village anecdote in the Great Plains of Hungary has two antagonists sitting side by side on a bench, smoking their pipes, from sunrise to sunset, without exchanging a word. At dusk, one of the men asks the other, "That's the way it is, then?" to which the second man replies, "Uh-hm." Having thus exhausted the verbal part of their dispute, the grudge-holders pull their knives from their boot-tops and stab each other.

This story is apocryphal, but the journalist Barbara Amiel (of whom more later) and I witnessed a demonstration of the national temper that might produce it. One summer evening in the 1970s we were having dinner in the courtyard of a then fashionable Toronto café, called the

Coffee Mill. The continental-style restaurant still exists, but in those years it was situated in the Lothian Mews, a passageway of expensive shops with large display windows. We had just started looking at the menu when we became aware of a commotion. An Italian customer had begun a heated dispute over some matter with a Hungarian waitress. Amiel and I missed the beginning of the argument, so we had no idea what it was about; we only noticed a young Italian shouting and gesturing, then walking theatrically away from the waitress, who stood in the doorway with her arms akimbo. The Italian would walk to the shop windows, then turn around, hurtle himself back through a narrow semi-circle between the tables, calling on the heavens to protest the treatment he thought he had received at the waitress's hands. He kept repeating the performance of walking away and returning over the next number of minutes, with ever-increasing volume, his gold chains jangling on his hirsute chest over his half-open shirt.

Amiel could not help laughing. The Italian's display was such a comic cliché that she found it more amusing than irritating, but that was evidently not the way it struck a Hungarian guest who was sitting alone at a small wrought-iron table in the volatile Italian's path. The Hungarian, a stocky man, continued eating his dinner without raising his head from his plate, but every time the Italian walked by his table, he tensed up quite visibly. Still, he did nothing until the Italian had the misfortune of brushing against his elbow on one of his return trips to confront the waitress. At this the Hungarian put down his knife and fork, and as the Italian walked by him again, without saying anything—indeed, barely bothering to get up—he knocked him through the plate glass window of one of the stores. Then he sat down again and continued eating his dinner.

Miraculously, the Italian was not hurt. He extracted himself from between the jagged blades of glass, muttered something, but this time *sotto voce*, then quickly walked away. Someone had rung for the police, but it was obvious that by the time they responded the victim would be gone, and no one in the restaurant would finger the perpetrator. The latter calmly finished his meal, still saying nothing, not even when the waitress came to refill his glass. Only when his plates were being cleared away did the

Hungarian look up and remark, speaking to no one in particular, *"Baszd meg az olasz anyád."* This is how I knew for sure that he was a Hungarian.

"What did he say?" asked Amiel.

"You don't want to know," I replied.[31]

THEFT YES, MURDER NO

A different manifestation of national temper occurred in Florence, in front of a *pensione* named California, on Via Ricasoli, a street leading into the celebrated Piazza del Duomo. It was the mid-1960s, and the novelist Stephen Vizinczey had just published the first of his international best-sellers, *In Praise of Older Women.* On the proceeds he purchased a magnificent Mercedes convertible—the one he lent me when my Viennese aunt visited the French Riviera—then put the remaining $35,000 into a suitcase and set out with his wife, Gloria, on a tour of Italy.

Thirty-five thousand dollars was a handsome sum in those days, and most people would not have carried it around in a suitcase, but Vizinczey wanted to be close to his money. After all, he had never had any before. A person does not shut his money up in a bank when he is just making his first acquaintance with it. Even Vizinczey drew the line at carrying his fortune in cash, but what he did amounted to almost the same thing: imitating his literary hero, Felix Krull, he carried it as a letter of credit.

At one point Stephen and Gloria needed to interrupt their trip and return to London, where the author had his headquarters. They deposited Gloria's two daughters from a previous marriage (to the Canadian actor-writer Don Harron) with their grandfather in Florence, left the magnificent Mercedes (locals referred to it simply as "La Macchina") at the Fiumicino airport outside Rome, and carried the $35,000 suitcase back with them to London. Gloria was in charge of the luggage, as always.

Vizinczey's business in England took longer than expected, and a month passed before Stephen and Gloria could pick up La Macchina in Rome again. From Fiumicino they drove directly to Florence, where Gloria's daughters, Martha and Mary, were waiting for them at the Pensione California. Gloria's father needed to go to Velletri, leaving the

"Had just published the first of his international bestsellers." Stephen and Gloria Vizinczey in the south of France, circa 1971.

owner of the lodgings, Signora Vitti, in charge of the girls. Martha and Mary required little chaperoning, but they were young and Gloria was anxious to see them. It was a mutual anxiety, because by the time Stephen pulled up at the front entrance, the girls were shouting and waving from a fourth-floor balcony. There was some confusion as Gloria tried unloading the luggage while waving and shouting back at her daughters. Vizinczey was engaged in his own quest, quite daunting in Florence, of trying to find a place to park the car. When it was finally accomplished, he joined his family on the fourth floor.

By then the emotions of the first greeting between mother and daughters had subsided, and Gloria was looking around the room. The sight seemed to make her a trifle uneasy. "Oh-oh," she said to her husband. "I think we're missing a suitcase."

"Which one?" asked Vizinczey, suspecting the worst.

"The one with the money," Gloria said. "I think I left it in front of the entrance. On the street."

Vizinczey tore down from the fourth floor. The entrance and the street were still where Gloria left them, but the suitcase was gone.

Hungarians may be phlegmatic and Canadians may be reserved, but Stephen has never been particularly representative of the national temper of either his native or his adopted country. His behaviour, though some might call it extreme, was not inappropriate to a man who had just lost everything. There was nothing left in his wallet, nothing in his bank account, nothing in his safe—in fact, he *had* no bank account or safe. All he ever had was a suitcase with $35,000 in it, and now it was gone. He had no means of replacing it, either, short of writing another bestseller—about the same statistical chance as being struck by lightning twice. From the street, he started yelling bloodcurdling threats at his wife, who was looking down from the balcony. In a manner that could only be described as convincing, he promised to wring her neck. His performance came complete with bulging veins at the temple and flecks of foam at the mouth—probably not because Vizinczey was such an accomplished method actor, but because he meant it.

The Italians in Via Ricasoli were impressed. Foreigners rarely rise to sufficient heights of theatricality to make a dispute memorable to a Florentine audience, but the balcony scene between Stephen and Gloria came close. More importantly, it started making the spectators uneasy. Since the participants were not Italians, it was hard to say where all this might lead. They did not understand Stephen's words, but his gestures spelled murder. Perhaps when a foreigner tells his wife that he will wring her neck, he might actually do it. In any event, the Italian who took the suitcase decided to take no chances.

He was the owner of a little *latteria* next door to Signora Vitti's lodgings. After listening to Vizinczey's performance with growing concern, he went to fetch the suitcase, which he had put in the back of his shop—for safekeeping, as he explained it.

The owner of the *latteria* might not have been averse to relieving careless tourists of their extra suitcases, but he evidently drew the line at being a party to homicide. Had Vizinczey reacted like a phlegmatic Hungarian (or a reserved Canadian) that day in Via Ricasoli, he would have been $35,000 poorer. Under the circumstances, behaving like an Italian was a wise choice.

TRAINS WITH WHIPPED CREAM

The Scots have a reputation for parsimony, but they are not a patch on the Austrians. A Scot may want to save himself some money, but a petit bourgeois Viennese wants to save every penny for everybody in the world, and damn the cost.

I was late for the Orient Express leaving Vienna one day in the 1960s. In my rush to check out from the hotel I missed my morning coffee, so when I reached the railway station with about ten minutes to spare, I went to the coffee shop straightaway. The drill at the Westbahnhof was to line up at a cashier's booth, purchase a ticket for the item of one's choice, then line up again at a counter and exchange the ticket for the item itself. Making customers line up twice is common throughout the continent: it is part of the genius of European organization.

I bought my ticket at the cashier and took it to the counter without looking at it. I carried it between my teeth, actually, because my hands were occupied with my suitcases. It was only when the counter maiden said, *"Sofortbitt'schöneinkaffeemitsahne"* that I discovered my mistake.

"I don't want the whipped cream, thanks," I said to her.

The girl seemed puzzled. *"Ja, doch, ein Kaffee mit Sahne,"* she repeated, looking at my ticket. "You bought a ticket for a coffee with whipped cream."

"My mistake. Just hold the whipped cream."

"You don't understand," said the girl, realizing that she was dealing with a foreigner, someone slow-witted, possibly even American. "You bought a ticket for a coffee with whipped cream, you see? It costs two schillings more. If you changed your mind and don't want whipped cream, that's fine. Just take the ticket back to the cashier. She'll give you back two schillings and a ticket for plain coffee."

"No, Fräulein, you don't understand. I'm late for my train. I don't care about two schillings, just give me a plain coffee before I miss my . . . "

"Sir, I'm trying to explain. I can't let you pay two schillings for nothing, when all you have to do is go the cashier and . . . "

Two Austrian schillings in the 1960s were worth about nine cents. The loudspeaker was announcing the Orient Express. I wanted my coffee desperately. There was no way this daughter of Austrian officialdom and lower-middle-class prudence was going to give it to me for nine cents more than it was worth. I harmonized my habits with local requirements and had my morning coffee with whipped cream.

Let us put this into context. The European Union was still in the future, but the Merger Treaty of April 8, 1965, had come into being. Soon it was to combine the European Coal and Steel Community (ECSC), the European Economic Community (EEC), and the European Atomic Energy

Community (Euratom) into a single entity to be called the European Community (EC). The Rhine maidens had begun to weave their immense bureaucratic net. The engine of missed trains and whipped cream had left the station.

34

NO FREE LUNCH IN REALPOLITIK

I can see . . . only one safe rule for the historian: that he should recognize in the development of human destinies the play of the contingent and the unforeseen.
—H.A.L. FISHER

THROUGHOUT THE COLD WAR, Europeans and Americans, the staunch Atlantic allies, stood poised, if not to commit treachery at a moment's notice, at least to convince each other that they might. They wanted their allies to know that they each carried a hidden weapon of potential treachery in their diplomatic bags, and would unhesitatingly produce it if their interests were threatened. This became especially true during the final phases of the Vietnam War. As Henry Kissinger explained it to China's Zhou Enlai in 1973, during the years of détente, America wanted to create the appearance of keeping "slightly to the left of the West Europeans" in its relations with the Kremlin "because then they will be afraid we will make a separate arrangement with the Soviet Union and that will worry them sufficiently so that they start thinking about their own defense."[32]

The Europeans were indeed worried. The problem was that the way in which they started thinking about their own defence was to consider making separate arrangement with the Soviet Union themselves. This became especially true of France, but to a lesser extent also of other members of the North Atlantic Treaty Organization. During the years of détente NATO allies were continually looking over their shoulders. The fear that America might sell out Europe, or vice versa, engendered a doctrine of preemptive sellout in both parties.

Though it was Kissinger who considered such complex policies necessary, he was also aware of their danger. In his memoirs he notes that these policies "might start a race to Moscow among our allies."[33]

As it happened, Europe's fear of American realpolitik did not start a race to Moscow. What it did, though, was to hasten the birth of the European Union.

4

ON BEING A
MARTIAN

35

A Tale Of Two

Functionaries

Truth is stranger than fiction,
but it is because Fiction is obliged to
stick to possibilities; Truth isn't.
—Mark Twain

THE YOUNG WRITER WAS LOOKING forward to the greatest event in a young writer's life. His first play had been accepted for production in a provincial theatre. The cast was being assembled, rehearsals had begun, and a date was set for the premiere. All the young writer had to do was to have his blue suit cleaned and mended for the curtain calls, and clear a space in his desk drawer for the rave reviews.

It was at this point that he was summoned to an office in the Ministry of Culture. Although Stalin had been dead for almost three years, the Communist state still held full sway in Hungary, as in all other parts of the Soviet empire. The state owned all theatres, whether live stage or motion picture, and made the final (and also often the initial) decisions about what the public would see. But since the young writer had been encouraged by the ministry's bureaucrats before—he saw clusters of the little red-tape worms as his manuscript was being shepherded through various desks before its acceptance for production—he had no reason to feel concerned about another meeting. There was a spring in his step as he proceeded to the grey building on Kossuth Lajos Square. When he arrived, he was ushered into an office and offered a cup of coffee. He had just raised the cup to his lips when a mournful functionary began explaining to him that, regrettably, because of the current political situation, it had become necessary to call off the premiere of his stage play for the time being.

The young writer was devastated. If he had had reservations about the nature of Communism before, the functionary's perfidy confirmed them. When the Hungarian revolution broke out a few months later, he joined it lustily. (Advice to regimes: Do not call off the first productions of aspiring playwrights if you expect them not to shoot you the minute they get their hands on a pistol.) Alas, pistols proved to be insufficient against Soviet tanks in the fall of 1956. The freedom fighters were defeated, and the young writer joined the exodus that followed. Eventually he found himself in Montreal, where after a few years of honing his language skills he submitted his first documentary screenplay to Canada's National Film Board. To his delight, the script was accepted, with a date set for the filming to begin.

Leaving one's native land is never easy, and it is especially burdensome for writers, for whom language is a working tool. Still, it seemed to the young writer that when he traded a system of statism for the free world he had made the right choice. Here, at last, his work would be judged on its merits—with luck, artistic, but even at worst, commercial—instead of the whims of a Kafkaesque bureaucracy.

In this happy frame of mind he responded to a summons from a functionary of the National Film Board. It was a pleasant summer afternoon, just a few days before his screenplay's first day of principal photography. There was a spring in the young writer's step as he proceeded to NFB's headquarters on the Côte-de-Liesse Road in Montreal. There he was ushered into an office and offered a cup of coffee. He had just raised the cup to his lips when a mournful functionary began explaining to him that, regrettably, on account of the current political situation, it had become necessary to call off the filming of his script for the time being.

It was not only the same situation. That would have been merely ironic. What made it farcical was that it was *the same functionary.*

The 1956 uprising that dislodged the young writer from his native country also dislodged about two hundred thousand other

Hungarians. They included certain officials in the bureaucracy of the Communist state. These functionaries chose to leave either because they first supported the revolution (which started out as a kind of reform-Communist putsch before it grew from a good-natured palace revolution into a fierce revolt of anti-Communism) or because they became frightened of it.[1] Once these ex-officials found themselves abroad, as bureaucrats they naturally gravitated to the bureaucracies of their adopted countries. Canada's state-run National Film Board was a logical choice of employment for a refugee functionary from Hungary's Communist Ministry of Culture.

Postscript: The young writer was Stephen Vizinczey. He told me the story many years ago. I waited for him to use it in a book, but for some reason he never did.

I knew the functionary myself. He later made the switch not only from one statist bureaucracy to another, but from state enterprise to private enterprise. He ended up a Hollywood producer. He was successful enough, though somehow never quite comfortable in his new role. When he co-produced a movie based on one of my books, I nicknamed him "Eeyore," after the pessimistic donkey in Winnie-the-Pooh. There was something about his metamorphosis from a policy entrepreneur to a real entrepreneur that made him sad. He had seemed happier as a caterpillar than as a butterfly. Perhaps it was because in his new incarnation he had to risk some of his own money rather than the state's.

36

A Square Peg

No doubt the artist is the child
of his time; but woe to him if he is also
its disciple, or even its favourite.
—Friedrich von Schiller

I WAS ALMOST COMPLETELY INNOCENT of English when I boarded the *Empress of France* at Liverpool in December 1956. My only previous exposure had been a German text called *Englisch lernen ein Vergnügen*, from which I quickly concluded that learning English, in spite of the title's promise, would be anything but a joy. I also had a few lessons from Mr. Csaba, who taught English and geography in our Budapest high school before he switched to teaching us geography and Russian. He announced the change with a resigned Latin phrase as he came into class one morning in 1948. "*Tempora mutantur,*" he said. It was an understatement. The times, they were a-changing, even while they stubbornly remained the same.

I learned little Russian from Mr. Csaba, but what I did learn from him was just as useful: I learned how little one needs to know of a subject to teach it. Our teacher was exactly one chapter ahead of us in the Russian text that he used for our instruction. The first time he entered class in his capacity as our Russian coach, we all rose, as customary in those days, but instead of waving us back to our seats, he whipped out his text and flipped through it until he found the word he wanted. "*Sadyees!*" he said in his spanking new Russian as he motioned for us to sit down, proud as a peacock. Keeping one step ahead of his students remained a point of honour with him.

Mr. Csaba's English lessons had been more sophisticated than his bold forays into Russian, but in Liverpool the only thing I could remember from them was the word "Massachusetts." Why he taught us the word, and why I remembered it, was a complete mystery—but it would not have mattered if I had remembered more English words, for the language spoken in Liverpool was Scouse. If Scouse had a relationship to English, as some claimed that it did, it was not transparent to a Hungarian who spoke neither.

Next day I embarked on the transatlantic voyage in the company of about four hundred of my compatriots, most of whom had the same communication skills as I. This worried the authorities who were responsible for us on board, for we appeared to be savages beyond the reach of verbal contact. Interpreters were considered essential for at least three officials—the ship's captain, the ship's purser, and the ship's doctor—but no one seemed eager to come forward. Eventually a Hungarian put up his hand, and he was assigned to the skipper. Then another Hungarian volunteered, and he became the purser's translator. This was it, though; there were no other applicants.

After a minute or so, I raised my hand. To this day I do not know why. I certainly spoke no English, nor was I under the illusion that I did. Any linguistic illusions I had would have been about Latin—the doctor's as much as mine. I thought that, with luck, between the two of us we could manage whatever medical exchange needed to pass between ship's doctor and refugees.

Now I think that if my theory had to be put to a test the results would have been grim. I spoke next to no Latin, and the doctor spoke less. There is little relationship between reading texts in a dead language and asking a live patient to list his allergies. It was fortunate that about fourteen years earlier a Nazi submarine had torpedoed the doctor's ship in the North Atlantic. The Germans fished him out, shipped him to some lager near Schweinfurt, and kept him in a prison camp for the duration. As a result, the doctor spoke fluent German, drunk or sober, but especially drunk. We lost no patient during the eight-day voyage, and just before docking the purser called me to his office and paid me a pound. It was the first money I earned in the West, and it was for acting as an interpreter in a language I did not speak. It made me feel rather at home. Eastern Europe was evidently not the only place for smoke and mirrors.

The immigration authorities in Saint John, New Brunswick, had pre-pared themselves for the onslaught of freedom fighters from Hungary by acquiring one interpreter. He was a splendid specimen with a walrus moustache, quite fluent in English—and Polish. To his credit, he tried everything. While bravely attempting to talk to Hungarians in Polish, a lan-guage they understood as little as English, he also tried explaining to Canada's officials that the distances between the languages of Europe were not as negligible as they believed. His advice was shrugged off by the bureaucrats, who continued to think of such distinctions as petty.

Apparently my fame as an intrepid interpreter preceded me, because as soon as I landed the immigration authorities offered me a job. It was a tempting situation, entailing room and board, an official blazer, and the then princely sum of $400 a month. I promptly turned it down, although not for the right reasons. I should have turned it down, obvi-ously, because I spoke no English, but in fact I turned it down thinking that if such a generous job offer was to be had in Saint John, New Brunswick, the job offers in the economic heartland—say, in Toronto, Ontario—would be even better. This was a grave error. That position in Saint John was just about the last spontaneous offer of a job I ever had in Canada.

The lack of offers in Toronto did not dismay me, at least not initially. In my experience so far, one was likely to be offered a job only if one was totally unqualified for it. By this logic I continued to be an ideal candidate in the employment market, for I was unqualified for most jobs—certainly unqualified for all jobs that required the use of any language other than German or Hungarian—which meant that I should be the first to be offered them. Nevertheless, unselfishly, and at the risk of reducing my chances of finding gainful employment, I decided to learn English.

The question was how to go about it. I was quite at sea, having never formally studied a language before. My first language, German, was *von Haus aus:* it simply happened to be the language spoken by the adults in my home, at least the adults who mattered, such as my parents and my governess. *Tante* Amanda (all governesses were called *Tante,* or "auntie") was a prim lady of indeterminate age. She adored the English detective story writer Edgar Wallace, though she knew him only in German translation. My first literary experience was listening to long passages from a book by Wallace called, in German, *Die Gelbe Schlange* (The Yellow Serpent) which *Tante* Amanda enjoyed reading to, or rather at, me. In my mind a German text would forever conjure up a yellow serpent, undulating on the breakfast table, smelling faintly of mint, like *Tante* Amanda.

Hungarian as a language evoked a different image. It was a pair of breasts, substantial and shapely, floating above snowy paths in the declivitous hills of Buda. The breasts came into my life because, as I turned five, it suddenly dawned on my parents that, in a year's time, I was due to go to school in Budapest without knowing the language of instruction. *Tante* Amanda was replaced—temporarily—by Karolina, a young Hungarian girl of cheerful disposition and athletic habits. In spite of my tender age I must have paid attention primarily to her mammary glands, for I remember little else about the winter I spent in her company. She would take me for endless walks in the picturesque laneways and mews of old Buda, talking to me in Hungarian, a language I associate with mammillae to this day. As learning tools, Karolina's breasts certainly worked, for they took me from zero to fluency in less than a year.

My next language was Russian—not Mr. Csaba's brave attempts to teach it in school, but the idiomatic Russian of the Red Army as heard in the streets of Budapest in 1945. It was a language of masculine words spoken with a remarkably soft, almost feminine, lilt: *idy suda, davay chasy, hore ruky, nu kharasho.*[2] What distilled the linguistic experience for me was the reaction of a theatre audience in Budapest around 1950, when a visiting Moscow company offered an excellent production of Hamlet in Russian. During Act One, as the Ghost's voice called out plaintively from the battlements of Helsingore, *"Gamlet, idy suda!"* (Hamlet, come here!), the audience broke up. They continued in unison, *"Davay chas!"* (Give me your watch!) while rolling in the aisles.

Picking up a language is a breeze at five and easy enough at ten, but it is no longer available at twenty-one. A person can still *learn* it, of course, and I resigned myself to learning English instead of picking it up. The question of who was going to teach it to me resolved itself when I heard about the University of Toronto's generous offer of free language lessons to new immigrants. I certainly had no money for private lessons—in fact, unless I learned enough English to land a job soon, I was not going to have money for my staple diet of tinned New Brunswick sardines and Christie's whole-wheat bread. The next evening I betook myself to a campus classroom at Queen's Park.

Three hours later I was walking home again, dejected and dismayed. The classroom had been comfortable, the reception obliging, the young volunteer teacher kindly and bright, but there were about twenty newcomers in class, and naturally the tempo of instruction had to be geared to the slowest pupil. He happened to be a gentleman from Salonika, and he was very slow indeed. For that matter, the fastest student in class was slow. If I was going to learn English at that speed, I would be forty before I uttered my first declarative sentence. The free language lessons suddenly became very costly. If time was money, I could not afford them.

It seemed that I would have to pick up my own English, after all. I simply did not have the time to have someone teach it to me. I proceeded to get myself a grammar book, a tape recorder, and a job, in that order. The job was in the gatehouse of the Granite Club. This bastion of old Toronto, the model for Stephen Leacock's *The Mausoleum Club,* was situated on St. Clair Avenue in those days. My duty was to wait for members at the main entrance, then take their cars and park them in the club's garage.

Many members were millionaires, and all members—this was 1957—were white Anglo-Saxon Protestants (not counting two or three white Anglo-Saxon Catholics). The gatehouse staff, meaning the drivers, were Irish or Scottish, and the kitchen–dining room staff were Italian with a sprinkling of French. The rest of the world was represented by a pert blond Finnish waitress and me.

It turned out to be an excellent job for picking up English. The Irish drivers were talkative and enjoyed being tape-recorded, while the gatehouse boss, Dave, was a Scottish devolutionist. The main reason he took me on was because he liked the idea of having a "freedom fighter" on his staff—which would have made the upstairs folk at the club shudder, had they known about it. But the upstairs people knew little about the down-

"Martian, are you?" In London, 1971.

stairs people at the Granite Club. They certainly knew nothing about the short-wave receiver in the gatehouse, around which some Scottish drivers gathered at night to listen to Radio Free Glasgow. (For a Hungarian this was vaguely amusing, but it showed that oppression, like beauty, is often in the eyes of the beholder.) At any rate, the broadcasts became my main language tool, along with the abundant blarney of the Irish contingent. They shaped my early English into a functional pattern of varied vocabulary, marginal grammar, and idiosyncratic regional syntax, delivered with a faint overlay of a Celtic lilt. After a while people could no longer trace my accent, which pleased me. (One club member made up his mind that I was a Martian. "Let the Martian park my car," he said whenever he came to the gatehouse. This popped into my mind many years later, when a suspicious reporter asked me to empty my briefcase in the offices of the London *Observer,* where I went to see the editor. It was a period when the IRA was on a bombing spree in England. "I don't think the IRA uses Martians," I said to him. "Oh," he said, "Martian, are you? Oh. Sorry about that.")

It was my German, though, that landed me my next job. The owner of a downtown driving school needed an instructor for an influx of German-speaking immigrants, most of whom knew how to drive, but needed a Canadian licence. My task was not so much to give them tips on driving, but to explain that during their road test when the examiner told them "right" he meant *rechts* and when he said, "Straight ahead," he meant *gerade aus.* In short, I was to be a language teacher rather than a driving instructor, which was fine by me. First I had to acquire a driving instructor's licence, though, which in those days meant standing for an examination at the Strachan Avenue police garage, then handing "Milos," as I will call the owner of the driving school, twenty dollars, which he would slip to the examiner, "Lieutenant Palmer," to make sure that I passed. There was no way for me to know, of course, who was going to palm the twenty dollars, "Milos" or "Lieutenant Palmer."[3] Either way, the arrangement comforted me. It cushioned the cultural shock of emigration. As an East European, it made me feel right at home in Canada.

I followed these preliminary skirmishes in the job market with a lengthy and slightly more lucrative stint as a cab driver. The extra remuneration did not come from my primary occupation, but from a sideline. Day drivers had to rely on their fares and tips, but there were three additional activities available for drivers willing to cope with the annoyances and hazards of a night shift. They could run working girls. They could bootleg booze—in those days buying alcoholic beverages in Ontario required a liquor licence, and government-run liquor stores closed at six o'clock—or they could service a floating crap game. Most drivers preferred booze, which required laying in a supply of bottles, or "mickeys," during the day, then selling them to thirsty customers at night at whatever premium the market would bear. A few drivers chose working girls, collecting a tip from the johns and also a cut from the suppliers. I preferred a floating crap game. Apart from matters of taste, it required the least effort and gave rise to the fewest possible complications. Around noon I'd receive a message with an address, then at night when a fare asked, "Where's the action?" I'd drive him to it. If a customer looked like an undercover policeman, I'd say, "Haven't a clue, buddy," and that was that. My sideline gave me a few extra bucks, and enough time for some tentative attempts at writing poetry in English. Also for marrying my first wife, Sylvia, which I did in New York during a Category 5 hurricane named Donna.

A vivacious redhead, Sylvia was a divorcee. Picture Zsa-Zsa Gabor with a penchant for archaeology and a taste for penniless scribblers. Previously she had been married to a Manhattan doctor. When we separated, she gave an accurate summary of our years together in a newspaper interview. "Marry a gynecologist," she explained to the reporter, "and you'll appreciate poetry. If you want to appreciate money, marry a poet."

After selling a short story, the first I had written in English, to a radio program of the Canadian Broadcasting Corporation,[4] I took a deep breath and applied for a job with the public broadcaster. At the time it seemed a logical thing to do, considering my background. Until the uprising I had been a program editor for Hungary's state-run broadcaster, Radio Budapest, and before that I had worked as a "dramaturge"—a kind of script editor—for one of the provincial theatres in Hungary.[5] Modelled after the BBC, more or less, the CBC appeared to be a natural home for someone interested in writing and producing "serious" dramas and documentaries.

Born of a marriage between show business and the Post Office, the CBC did not inherit the best features of either parent. My first exchange with the corporation's personnel manager, a crisply tailored lady named Marjorie Hand, gave me a premonition of things to come. After noting my qualifications—essentially, a junior's background in broadcasting and theatre—Mrs. Hand contemplated me dubiously.

"I must tell you," she said, "you'll be facing stiff competition. Only this morning I had an application from a young woman with a degree in psychology."

I suppressed the remarks rising to my lips. I refrained from saying that I thought I was applying to an organization in show business, not to an institution in mental hygiene. I stifled the suggestion that in a corporation producing information and entertainment my competition should come from people whose backgrounds in journalism and the performing arts were more extensive or distinguished than mine (God knows, easy enough), not from young women with psychology degrees. But, apart from getting me off on the wrong foot with Mrs. Hand, saying such things would only have shown how little I understood the CBC.

Even years later, when I understood it better, the CBC could still surprise me. As a junior staffer I took a program idea to an erudite and witty executive named Eric Koch, who also came from a European milieu. Koch glanced at the one-page outline, chuckled, then handed it back to me.

"Well, do you like it?" I asked.

"Oh yes," he replied. "It's good."

"Great, so you'll put it on the air."

"Of course not," Koch said. "Are you mad? Do you forget who you're talking to? I'm Koch, K-o-c-h, from Frankfurt am Main. If *I* like something, nobody in Canada will."

The notion that if something appealed to *them*, it would be beyond the grasp of the great unwashed television masses was an article of faith among the CBC brass—even though most of them did not hail from Frankfurt but from places as Canadian as Moose Jaw, Yellowknife, or Napanee. CBC mandarins reversed a classic show business maxim: they went broke underestimating the audience.

"To appreciate money, marry a poet." Sylvia in Toronto, circa 1960.

After a stint as a freelance play reader, I was offered a staff position by Hugh Kemp, a former CBS executive, who came back from the United States to set up a national script department for the CBC. He seemed amused by my reassurance that, though a Hungarian, I was not a professional revolutionary. Mrs. Hand, who did the paperwork for my hiring, was gracious if puzzled. I worked my way up (after, presumably, beating some woman with a psychology degree in a competition for a handhold on the greasy pole), from a reader of the "slush pile"—unsolicited manuscripts—at $1.50 a pop in 1960 to television producer in 1971, passing such exalted ranks as script editor and chief story editor on the way. It was not a brilliant career. The corporation and I were ill-matched in three major ways (in addition to many minor ones.) First, the CBC was left-wing, in political stance as well as in social attitudes and style, and I was not. Second, the CBC, if only by virtue of being in the mass media, was down-market, and I was not. Third, as a public broadcaster, the CBC tried to counterbalance being down-market by burping up big dollops of high-minded cant. Sadly for my advancement on the corporate ladder, high-minded cant nauseated me. I would have preferred to be unapologetically down-market. It was not a marriage made in heaven.[6]

The CBC's dramatic programs throughout the 1970s and 80s were for the most part indigestible blobs of stodgy sententiousness offered as "social relevance" and covered with thick sauces of leftist sentimentality. During my tenure, Canada's public broadcaster specialized in shows that managed to be earnest without being serious and trendy without being innovative or original. If America's low-end television was mindless, coarse, or "violent" during the same period, it was generally fast-paced and fun to watch (or at least mildly diverting). The CBC, taking what it thought was the high road, combined vulgarity with stuffiness. Being mindless and pompous at the same time was a challenge, but CBC programmers responded admirably to it.

Mother CBC practised political correctness long before the expression surfaced in North America. In 1974, for instance, when I produced a black comedy written by Mordecai Richler, the brass tried to pull it—for anti-Semitism, no less. Pulling it for mediocrity would have made much more sense (the show was not very good), but what annoyed the brass was not the production's innumerable flaws but its solitary virtue: irreverence. In the end the CBC was forced to reinstate the program, but only because I took the precaution of privately screening it for Robert Fulford, a prominent critic, who wrote about the show before the air date. The ensuing scandal was front-page news for a week: a genuine tempest in a teapot. Needless to say, it did not raise my stock in head office.

Stuffy pomposity was not the entire story. In a huge organization—the CBC employed over ten thousand staffers at its most bloated—some gifted people inevitably slipped through.[7] They squeezed by the CBC's preferred candidates, the women with psychology degrees, and insinuated themselves into programming. Despite the best efforts of the CBC's corporate culture, such people produced some decent shows. Once in a while they put on the air productions that were poignant, memorable, incisive, or amusing. At times one might walk down a CBC hallway and observe the best and the worst in Canadian show business at work in adjoining offices.

The best included the legendary Andrew Allan, founding head of CBC drama. In addition to his other gifts, the unflappable Scotsman was quick on his feet. During live broadcasts—in his days "live" meant live-to-air, not live-to-tape—a radio producer's duties included following the script, stopwatch in hand, to make sure the show was coming out on time. One evening Allan saw that he was losing the battle of the clock as he was shepherding the actors through their paces. Speeding up the reading might have ruined the performance, which left adjusting the script the better alternative. Cutting a script on the fly, though, was no easy task.

According to legend, Allan remained undaunted. He pressed the button of the intercom connecting the studio floor with the control room.

"Cut pages 26 to 39," he said *sotto voce*, "and substitute the word 'but.'"

Allan's tenure as drama head was before my time, but he was still working as an occasional performer when his successor in the boss's chair, the almost equally legendary Esse W. Ljungh, gave me—reluctantly—my first chance to direct a radio play. The brooding Swede insisted on casting the show himself ("Let's not overload you, kid," he told me). Coming into Studio G, I was startled to see Allan sitting at the rehearsal table, script in hand. It was Ljungh's revenge for being forced (as he saw it) to give me a crack at the controls.

I was resolved not to let the mercurial drama boss spook me—yet by making me direct his larger-than-life predecessor in my first show he was off to a good start. Before calling for the read-through, I walked over to the former drama chief. I was ready to flop on my back in submission and pee like a puppy.

In television studios the tone tended to be breezy, but in the "senior service"—radio—it was *de rigueur* to speak formally. "Mr. Allan," I said, "I'm new at this. If I need to ask you questions, will you answer me?"

"If I do, Mr. Jonas," said Allan, "will you listen to my answer?"

I longed to say no, but what I said was, "Of course."

"Sorry to hear that," Allan replied. "Then perhaps you aren't cut out to be a director."

Allan scored a bull's eye, for born directors are born with the bit between their teeth. They stick to their ideas, whether they are right or wrong—which is why born directors are not necessarily good directors. Good directors are born directors who also happen to be right, at least more often than not. Allan himself was such a director, and so was Ljungh, whose Scandinavian soul combined excellence with a touch of grim pugnacity. He believed in live performances, and resented all editing. Once he took umbrage at my suggestion that we tape certain scenes and select the best takes for the show. He stopped the rehearsal, gradually working himself into a rage as he explained to me how taping segments ruins the flow of a performance. Eventually he concluded that my mechanistic approach threatened the very existence of the performing arts, and the only way to rescue broadcast drama from my baneful influence was to kill me. At this point he dismissed the actors, grabbed a fire-axe from the wall, and started chasing me around the rehearsal table. He would have whacked me, too, but in 1964 I was only twenty-nine and, at over sixty, Ljungh did not stand a chance of catching me. After a while he ran out of breath, put down the axe, and invited me to join him for a drink at the Celebrity Club across Jarvis Street.

Not surprisingly, Ljungh soon gave up the helm in the junior service. During the 1960s the split between radio and television became complete, with television attracting most of the younger, more casual, and less literate members of CBC's establishment. Still, TV had its share of gifted mavericks, too, though they barely belonged to the same species. I worked with one such eccentric for a few years as his associate producer. Paddy Sampson had escaped from the shipyards of Belfast and worked his way through London's music halls as a lighting technician and stagehand before fetching up in Canada. A man of genuine sparkle, untainted by any education, he managed to talk himself into a variety producer's job at CBC-TV. Soon major figures in the music industry, from Duke Ellington to Harry Belafonte, expressed a preference for working with Sampson, sometimes to the point of refusing to work with anyone else. More than once the corporation needed to give Sampson a leave of absence so he could produce Belafonte's TV shows in Europe and Japan.

As Sampson's associate, I had my own encounter with Ellington. It was when the fabled musician arrived for a live-to-tape TV concert set up in the lobby of a Toronto airport hotel. The Duke appeared cool, calm, collected—and nearly three hours late.

Having left me in charge, Sampson expected me to roll tape ages ago. I was livid, but the delay appeared to affect no one else. The waiting band members seemed especially unconcerned. Before I could open my mouth, Duke came over to me and kissed me on the forehead.

"Don't fret, kid," he said to me kindly. "I'm on coloured time."

In the early 1970s TV's new drama head, Fletcher Markle, wanted me in his department mainly as an interpreter. Markle was an erudite, elaborate, even pedantic man. He knew, or rather sensed, that Sampson had good ideas, but he could not understand them. It was not so much Sampson's dockyard diction as his cryptic style, in which things were hinted at or alluded to rather than expressed, that defeated Markle. After departmental meetings he would beckon me to stay behind.

"All right, now what did our little Irish friend say?" he would ask.

I did not exactly know myself, but my Budapest brain cells must have linked up with Sampson's Belfast brain cells on some faraway wavelength, because I usually had an inkling. This way I continued to earn my living as a translator in Canada, as I first did aboard *The Empress of France*, between languages I did not really speak—in this case, Sampsonite and Marklese.

Allan, Ljungh, Sampson, and a handful of their peers were excellent programmers. The CBC bureaucracy hit upon a clever move, though, to neutralize excellence, or even competence. As soon as it hired a person to do a job, it hired another person whose only job was to prevent the first person from doing *his* job. The method worked.

One should perhaps underline that this was in entertainment programming. Information programming was worse. A person of my political outlook, for instance, would not have been allowed near any part of information programming in the CBC. The political left had public affairs television sewn up. (During the 1960s the executive offices next to the main transmission tower on Jarvis Street were actually nicknamed, with inadvertent accuracy, "the Kremlin.") To say that most people in TV public affairs were NDP supporters—as the newspapers put it from time to time—was the least of it. Current affairs types were not mere social democrats, but committed opponents of free-enterprise liberal democracy. There were probably producers in public affairs who might have drawn the line at working for the Soviet Union as agents of influence, but they would have been regarded by their colleagues as right-of-centre.

It happened only once that I offered to do an information program. In 1981 the upcoming twenty-fifth anniversary of the Hungarian revolution called for a commemorative show. I went to Knowlton Nash, then head of TV Information Programming, and suggested that I might be a rather natural choice to produce it. Nash was noncommittal, and I heard nothing for some months.

One day I received a phone call in Children's TV, where I was licking my wounds following an earlier corporate battle. (Children's TV was CBC's Siberia. Except for a few people who genuinely wanted to do children's programming, the brass used it for warehousing troublemakers, alcoholics, right-wingers, and other derelicts.) A very English voice on the phone explained that he was a BBC producer in town on loan to the CBC to mount an anniversary show on the 1956 revolution. The show was to cover Hungarians in Canada as well.

"It's a super gig," the voice explained cheerfully, "but to be frank with you, I don't know very much about the Hungarian revolution, and absolutely nothing about Hungarians in Canada. Some chaps here said you might give me some pointers."

He sounded like a decent fellow and I did give him some pointers. Later I heard that the program turned out passably well. I could not bring myself to watch it.

That I did not thrive in this ambiance was no wonder. The wonder was that I tried for thirty-five years. An even bigger wonder was that the CBC put up with me trying before finally getting rid of me—first from staff in 1985, then altogether about ten years later. After firing me from staff, ostensibly as a cost-saving measure, the corporation retained me as a contract producer for the next ten years at more than double my previous salary. The brass had no choice: the day they fired me I was in mid-season of producing the CBC's most popular docudrama series for radio, which eventually became a highly rated show on television. A legal action followed. One peculiarity of the public broadcaster was that one could sue it and work for it at the same time. Some years later, the CBC and I reached a negotiated settlement, the terms of which we agreed not to disclose.[8]

Was it thirty-five wasted years? Perhaps not completely. First, my tenure at "the Corpse" enabled me to produce a handful of programs I rather liked (as did other people, for they had top ratings and won all kinds of awards). Second, my job left me with enough time to write a number of books, some of which I liked even more (as did others, for they became bestsellers and won all kinds of awards). Third, the CBC paid me enough money—most of it willingly, and some under compulsion—to let me pursue my avocations, motorcycle racing and flying, along with some moto- and aviation- journalism (which also won awards). Finally, my years were not wasted for therapeutic reasons: they helped me gain some insight into myself.

The flaw was not only in what Fletcher Markle called the Corporation's little red-tape worms. The defect was in me. I refused to pay my dues, and reacted to CBC types like a White Russian nobleman in exile working as a concierge might react to some nouveau riche hotel guests. Instead of either serving with a smile or quitting, I pouted and hung on. When John Hirsch (a fellow Hungarian Jew) took over the TV Drama Department, I would neither become his doxy, figuratively or literally, nor tell him to take his job and stuff it.[9] Lacking both the courage to give up the security of a public service position and the willingness to make the compromises necessary to fit in, I merited Seneca's contemptuous description of a wretch. The Roman Stoic minced no words about my type: "Most men ebb and flow in wretchedness between the fear of death and the hardship of life; they are unwilling to live, and yet they do not know how to die."

My thirty-five years as an outsider inside show business demonstrated that, although I was not a loner, no community was to my taste. I liked many individuals, but found no group congenial. I might cherish a given writer or actor, but writers or actors in bulk did nothing for me. All the groups to which I nominally belonged left me cold—lyric poets, motorcycle racers, film people, news people, broadcasters, scribblers, Hungarians, Canadians, Jews, conservatives, libertarians, cultural functionaries, bohemians, men-about-town, blood relations, dog fanciers, pilots: the lot. Minimally, they bored me, and sometimes they filled me with distaste—not necessarily as human beings, but as aggregates, with their inevitable causes, conversations, buzzwords, pressures, and interests. All groups seemed like labour unions to me, looking for dues that I could not and would not pay.

Being an outsider had no romantic allure for me, either. It was simply a condition, like having webbed toes. "You're a square peg in a round hole," one of my exasperated CBC bosses told me once, but it was worse than that. It was not just a question of being a square peg in one particular round hole, but being a square peg in a world of round holes. Nor was it the fault of the round holes. They were what they were, just as I was what I was. Not exactly anti-social, not exactly friendless, perhaps not even unpopular, only profoundly alien—a Martian, as that prescient member of the Granite Club so accurately observed many years ago.

Historically, this put me in illustrious company. "I am a citizen of the world, known to all and to all a stranger," said Erasmus of Rotterdam, on being offered citizenship in Basle (which he declined). He did not say it with pride, though. He said it with regret.

37

A JEWISH WEDDING

We make out of the quarrel with others, rhetoric,
but of the quarrel with ourselves, poetry.
—W. B. YEATS

IN THE EARLY FALL OF 1974 the Toronto rabbi Dr. Gunther Plaut called Barbara Amiel and myself to his office for a brief examination in Jewish lore. The kindly scholar had no intention of giving us a hard time. His test in the Hebraic rites and liturgy was an exceedingly easy one, encompassing the barest minimum required for a Jewish wedding.

Amiel passed the test—scraping by, as it seemed to me, by the skin of her teeth. I failed miserably. After much prompting and lowering of hurdles for me, the rabbi finally gave up.

"I can't marry you," he said. "How do I know that you are Jewish?"

I could see Plaut's dilemma, though I had none myself. "Rabbi," I replied cockily, "if I was good enough for Hitler, I'm good enough for you."

I doubt if Rabbi Plaut consented to performing the ceremony because he was swayed by my argument. In any event the marriage did not last (though a close friendship with Amiel, now Lady Black, did). But why we sought to have a synagogue wedding in the first place is part of a conundrum. Before exploring it, let me digress.

My first impression of Amiel was thoroughly unpleasant. The setting was a shabby outer office in the Radio Building, so called to distinguish it from the newer Television Building at the back of the Canadian Broadcasting Corporation's parking lot. The one-time girl's school, incongruously nestled at the foot of a bulky broadcast tower, along with TV Studios 6 and 7, and the small executive building referred to as "the Kremlin," made up the Jarvis Street complex of the CBC in Toronto in the winter of 1964.

Guarding the outer office, Amiel was denying me access to her boss, Eric Koch, then second-in-command of CBC-TV's department of public affairs. She did so in a slightly twisted posture, displaying her upper body in profile, while speaking in a disdainful voice, suffused (as it seemed to me) with sexual challenge.

"I'm going to rise to the bait," I said to my friend Potyo, after Amiel, moving sideways like a seductive crab, withdrew to the inner office. This was the same Potyo in whose company I sneaked into Austria. Now we were trying to gain admittance to Koch's august presence to pitch him a story idea.

"What bait?" Potyo asked. "This girl is obviously beautiful. English, by the sound of her, possibly from a good family. She won't give you the time of day."

I remembered thinking about Potyo's remark some eight years later, as Amiel and I were standing in the vestibule of Toronto's Holy Blossom

"Moving sideways like a seductive crab." Barbara Amiel in Toronto, circa 1973.

Synagogue, about to be married. What was running through my mind was not that Potyo had been wrong, but that he was probably right.

For the sake of brevity and decorum, I will reduce here my great passion for Amiel to a couple of poems. Like lyric poems in general, they are reliable only in describing their author, not their subject. My earliest feelings were summed up in two stanzas, which I wrote shortly after Amiel and I had driven to what was then called Malton Airport for our first date, several months after meeting in Koch's office. I called the poem *Eight Lines for a Script Girl.*

I almost know you now. You are your name,
The substance of your skin, the movement of your eyes,
The line of your lips, the texture of your hair,
Your phone number, the colour of your voice.

You are your breasts' shape, the full length of your limbs,
You are your smile, your nailpolish, your dress.
Later I'll know you more. Still later
I'll know you even less.

Our first date came about by chance. Driving down Spadina Road one day, I noticed Amiel crossing the street. She was weighed down with more baggage than a ten-hand army mule, her load including a lamp shade. I slowed my car and honked at her. She narrowed her eyes in a peculiar way in which she could turn even short-sightedness into an asset.

"Don't tell me," I said. "You just robbed a dwelling and can't remember where you parked the getaway car."

"Close," she replied. "I just split up with my husband."

"Great. Let's go have coffee."

"Can't," she said. "Have to unload all this stuff before seven. Call me tomorrow if you like."

By then I had met Amiel several times, but only at large gatherings or in various office settings. We both worked at the CBC. I was a script editor, and Amiel had advanced from being a typist on a popular Canadian TV variety program, the *Juliette Show*, to becoming Eric Koch's secretary. A short time later, after Koch demoted himself from broadcast executive to TV producer to escape the *This Hour Has Seven Days* scandal—one of many periodic tempests in CBC's teapot, the details of which escape me—Amiel became his script assistant.

Koch mentored Amiel in the earliest stages of her career, as he mentored several other women who ended up becoming household names in Canada. Koch had an eye for female talent. If it included a lecherous eye, as it would have been unnatural for it not to, it never expressed itself as such because Koch was a gentleman of the old school. A sardonic and erudite German Jew, he could not resist collecting gifted and ambitious women. He took pleasure in scouting and grooming them as another person might scout and groom thoroughbreds. His prize fillies soon outpaced him because Koch himself—though a prolific writer, in addition to being a ranking broadcast administrator (he eventually retired from the CBC as Head of English Services in Montreal)—was not a particularly high achiever, at least not by the standards of his sparkling discoveries, who went on to become heads of state like Adrienne Clarkson or national icons like Barbara Frum.[10]

But in 1965 this was all in the future. After his judicious self-demotion, Koch became a producer for an afternoon TV show called *Take 30*, with Amiel as his script assistant and Clarkson, a glossy Chinese-Canadian broadcaster, as one of his on-camera hostesses. The Koch-Amiel team was distinguished by the fact that before attempting to mount their first show neither of them had seen the inside of a TV studio in any capacity other than that of a visitor. For them to actually record a live-to-tape television program was not unlike two pilots trying to land an aircraft without having been in the cockpit before. Even a relatively simple talk and variety show such as *Take 30* requires choreographing a number of performers and technicians in real time. It was a credit, perhaps not so much to the team's dexterity but to its determination, that it succeeded without a major mishap, though Koch did become legendary in technical circles for being the only producer ever to make two pedestal cameras collide head-on in Studio 6.

Clarkson had intellectual ambitions, which included having an opinion on books. It pleased Koch's sense of mischief to bring a sofa on the set and have Clarkson recline on it while talking about some book she was holding in her hand. Koch nicknamed his hostess "Madame Recamier"—a sobriquet probably no one ever used in her presence.

People who end up making their mark in the world need not resemble each other in other ways. Amiel and Clarkson certainly did not. The Chinese-Canadian, still in her twenties, moved with the studied grace of a society matron; the Anglo-Jew undulated like a sexy seal. Clarkson took herself seriously; Amiel's humour was keen and self-deprecating. Clarkson was poised—almost unbecomingly so, considering her youth; Amiel achieved her paradox by cultivated spontaneity.

If the image of Clarkson in the 1960s conjures up Madame Recamier reclining in Jacques-Louis David's famous painting, Amiel's image pops up as a black-and-white kinescope from CBC's archives recording a summer day in Toronto's old Riverdale Zoo. Amiel had advanced from script assistant to on-camera interviewer by then. Her assignment on that particular day was to talk with a then fashionable anthropologist, the improbably named Lionel Tiger, about men and women.

Amiel was facing the camera in front of the elephant's enclosure. The curious pachyderm seemed fascinated by a CBC interview in progress, and it started moving closer and closer. Amiel, concentrating on her subject, failed to notice an elephant breathing down her neck. She was coming to the key question of the interview.

"But *why* do you think," she asked, furrowing her brow, "that men and women are fundamentally different?"

Amiel was wearing a dress with a rather daring décolletage. Before the anthropologist could answer, the elephant did. It cheerfully extended its trunk over Amiel's shoulder, and placed it unerringly into her cleavage.

The elephant never got an award for creating what might have been the finest moment in Canadian television. The kinescope itself, showing Amiel trying to bravely continue the interview with a massive trunk fumbling in her bra, became an underground classic.

The times were a heady mixture of the frivolous and the profound (which would probably describe most times). The ideas of many journalists, especially in television, were defined by whatever was blowing in the wind. This in itself was routine; but what happened to be blowing in the wind just then was radical chic. It influenced minor TV journalists like Clarkson in much the same way as it did major ones like Frum. In this field Amiel stood out just by having a measure of intellectual curiosity. Her mind was only informed by prevailing trends, not determined by them. Adventurous to a fault, in everyday matters as well as in exploring issues, Amiel ran the risk of mindless iconoclasm at times, but never of mindless conformity.

People who rule the world today had their ideas shaped, and sometimes their souls forged, during the 1960s. Despite the trendy times, the real problem of the sixties generation was not that they were like leaves blowing in the winds of fashion—after all, most generations are like that. The problem was that the winds of fashion in those years were not blowing from favourable quadrants.

During the period that coincided with the Vietnam War most members of the chattering classes wandered about in what Tom Wolfe would later describe as "a quasi-Marxist fog." Amiel was an exception. In later years there were suggestions that she had switched from left to right under my influence (one newspaper account used the word "Svengali"), but this was not remotely true. By the time I met Amiel, her Pauline conversion was behind her. She encountered her Damascus on the road to Helsinki as a Canadian delegate to the Communist World Youth Festival sponsored by the Soviet Union in 1962. I am not going to describe her journey here; interested readers can look at Amiel's own account in her 1980 book *Confessions*.

By the time Amiel and I met she was twenty-four, I was thirty, and we saw the world in much the same light. Politically we were classical liberals (a creed that soon came to be called, inaccurately enough, "neoconservative"). Our hobbies did not overlap—clothes bored me, and motorcycles bored her—but our fundamental interests were almost identical. Amiel may have been more affected by the visual arts than I was—including films—but letters, ideas, and music enraptured us equally. In addition to a mutual passion, we never lacked attunement, or what people in the sixties called "chemistry." If Potyo's remark nevertheless flashed through my mind as Amiel and I stood before Rabbi Plaut about to be married ("She won't give you the time of the day"), it was not because I doubted our compatibility. The problem was more serious. By the fall of 1974 Amiel and I had known each other for ten years, and had lived together for two. We were only too compatible. Plainly put, we had all-too-similar natures.[11]

Returning to the conundrum of why two non-religious people wanted a synagogue wedding, my response to Rabbi Plaut in 1974 was not merely a quip. It was an updated (and flippant) version of the view expounded by the seventeenth-century Dutch-Jewish philosopher Baruch Spinoza. The author of *Ethics* believed that Jews, with regard to their survival as a group, have been protected by anti-Semitism as much as they have been imperiled by it. Jewish existence through four millennia, Spinoza wrote in the 1670s, has been preserved "in great measure by Gentile hatred."

I had no need to decide whether Spinoza's thesis was generally accurate or not. For me, personally, it always had the ring of truth. My own Jewishness was not defined by dietary laws, Friday candles, or Hebrew phrases in a prayer book. It was defined by a yellow star sewn to my lapel by my mother, in my native Budapest, as required by Nazi law, in April 1944. Until then, except for some anxious remarks overheard as a child, I had little awareness of being a Jew.

Certainly no *religious* awareness. As I mentioned earlier, I was brought up without any instruction in Judaism. My maternal grandparents' nominal religion was Lutheran, as was my mother's. Her sister and her husband were Catholics; my father a Calvinist. They had all "converted" to Christianity in 1938 when I was three.

I have been intrigued by Spinoza's argument ever since I first heard about it from my father after the war. My father was given to reading Spinoza and even copying out passages from his *Ethics* partly because they impressed him and partly because family legend viewed the Jewish sage of Amsterdam as having been related to the Jaffes, which was our family's name before it was changed to Hübsch. (How I came to be Jonas is another story.[12])

The Jaffe family was compelled to Germanize its name in the late eighteenth century during the reign of the Habsburg Emperor Joseph II. Joseph emancipated the Jews to spite his mother, the anti-Semitic Empress Maria-Theresa, in my father's view, and his series of liberal edicts were in many ways a mixed blessing. For instance, they permitted free choice of residence and schooling for Jews, but also compelled name changes, taxation, and military service. Nevertheless, they enabled those Jews lucky enough to live within the vast lands of the Habsburgs to metamorphose from outcasts to citizens.

The Hübsches emerged from Joseph II's empire as a thoroughly Jewish but also thoroughly secular, assimilated, non-observant, and rather colourful assortment of lawyers, musicians, bohemians, bluestockings, cocaine addicts, and business people. Great-uncle Edouard began his career as a trumpet player, but ended up as General Edouard von Hübsch for composing a number of musical pieces that pleased the King of Romania, including the royal anthem. My paternal grandfather, Adolph, a lawyer, was also the author of a book-length early Unitarian pamphlet, entitled *Monotheismus ohne Confession: die Religion der Zukunft* (Non-Denominational Monotheism: The Religion of the Future), the only surviving copy of which is now on my bookshelf.

It is important to note that my paternal grandparents' generation never thought of converting to Christianity. There was nothing for them to convert *from*, because they were no longer religious. They were simply Jewish. Their "rabbis" were the French and Scottish philosophers of liberalism. These Jews placed their faith in the Age of Enlightenment that had brought about their political and civic emancipation. If my forebears believed in anything other than classical liberalism, it was just a vague monotheism, a belief in one God. In their view it was precisely the sectarianism of religion, the splitting of the Judeo-Christian faith into a bewildering and hostile array of competing creeds, that had been responsible for the exclusion and oppression of Jews throughout the ages. Viewed from this perspective, rabbis were almost as bad for Jews as priests, and synagogues as hazardous as churches.

Had anyone suggested to my paternal grandfather that, as a natural consequence of his views, he must consider the survival of the Jews as a group to be of no importance, he would have been astounded. My grandparents took the intrinsic value of their own group's continued existence for granted. Their surviving papers, books, and correspondence all attest to this. They were proud to be Jews.

Had the further suggestion been made to them that, if Jewish survival was of value, then the emancipator Joseph II was a more dangerous enemy to the Jews than Sennacherib, the Assyrian king of Biblical fame who tried his utmost to destroy Jerusalem in 701 B.C., I suspect my grandparents would have been amused. They were not, of course, unfamiliar with Spinoza's thesis; they simply considered it irrelevant. After all, Spinoza lived long before the Age of Enlightenment. He could not have envisaged the triumph of humanism or of the holy trinity of Equality, Liberty, and Fraternity.

How could the gifts of liberalism be incompatible with Jewish survival? The whole point of the modern era was progress. Progress led to certain inalienable rights: to life, to liberty, and to the pursuit of happiness, laid down as self-evident truths in that great American Declaration of Independence with which my grandfather was fully and approvingly familiar. Henceforth people, alone or in groups, would be free to speak, to write, to worship (or not worship), to assemble, to travel, to compete, and to define themselves.

And if this was to be so, why would Jews not continue to define themselves as Jews?

Naturally, this led to the question of who *is* a Jew? A person of a certain faith? The member of a nation? A tribe? Or is he or she a person of a certain cultural tradition? Since freedom of religion also included freedom *from* religion, it meant not only that a person could be an atheist or an agnostic but also that no person would be obliged to confess adherence to a given dogma in order to retain an ethnic, cultural, or national identity. In short, a person would not have to be Jewish to be a Jew. He or she could even become a Christian or a Buddhist. If an Italian agnostic could abandon Catholicism without the risk of ceasing to be an Italian, why should not a Jewish agnostic be able to abandon Judaism without the risk of ceasing to be a Jew?

Did this mean, then, that Jewishness was a nationality? Not according to my family. They were not in the least attracted to the budding Zionism of their period. The Hübsches had already chosen their nationalities. They were not only German or French or Austro-Hungarian citizens, but were usually German or French or Austro-Hungarian *patriots.*

This left only tribal affiliation, coupled with cultural choice, as a determinant of Jewishness. You were a Jew primarily if you were of Jewish descent, and continued to define yourself as Jewish. You could also become a Jew by marriage or conversion, though this kind of secondary Jewishness would not take root—whatever taking root might mean—until the second or third generation.

The tribal element was an important factor. My grandparents would have regarded it as nonsensical to deny an ethnic affiliation that was plainly etched in people's features. Although genetic chance produced countless exceptions—and there was more than a single Jewish "type" in any event—many individual Jews in Europe, whether Ashkenazi or Sephardi, had distinct physical characteristics, as recognizable as any other group's. It would have defied logic to deny kinship among individuals whose ethnic identity could often be determined from a painting or a photograph.

But if so, could a person ever opt out of being Jewish? Yes, no doubt, in a secular society, my grandfather would have said—but why should he? Why would a person start identifying himself as a Gentile if (a) he was not, or (b) he did not have to?

In my grandfather's times, and even in my father's, the numbers would have supported this assessment. Though Jews could have converted or

married non-Jews in Western and Central Europe without any legal imped-
iment and even without much social stigma for well over a century,
relatively few had elected to do so. In my own family I could trace only
three of forty-four men between 1800 and 1922 who had married non-
Jewish spouses. As for my female relatives, forty-one of forty-eight married
Jews. The rest stayed unmarried.

Who is to say whether this would have changed if Hitler had not
appeared on the stage of history? Perhaps without the Nazis the rate of
Jewish intermarriage would have begun to soar in Europe during the
1920s as it did in North America and in Britain forty years later. But the
fact is, Hitler did appear. His cataclysmic regime very nearly wiped out the
Jews of Europe (my paternal grandmother, two aunts, an uncle, and almost
a score of cousins, among 5.9 million others) but it greatly strengthened
the Jewish identity of the survivors, and it played an indirect but possibly
decisive role in the founding of Israel. In this sense, at least, Spinoza's theories carried the day.

Hitler, of course, never established his dominion over Britain and
North America. Still, the very existence of Nazism probably had a conserv-
ing and cohesive influence among Jews even in this hemisphere. Although
Britain encouraged assimilation at least as much as the Habsburg and
Hohenzollern empires, and America's melting pot encouraged it even
more, in 1944 intermarriage among Jews had still only risen to 2.6 percent
from a low of about one percent in the 1920s.

The trauma of Gentile hatred, if that's what it was, must have persisted
long after the defeat of Hitler. Intermarriage figures in America rose only
moderately, to an estimated six percent by the early 1960s. The quantum
leap occurred during that decade. Though Amiel and I could not have been
aware of this in 1974, by the end of the 1980s more Jews were marrying
outside their community than within.

In a few years the alarm was sounded. "The great chain of Jewish continuity, stretching back some four thousand years," wrote England's Chief
Rabbi, Jonathan Sacks, in 1994, "is in danger of breaking in a single generation." The holocaust of love was proving deadlier to Jews as a tribe than
the Holocaust of hate.

According to figures quoted by Rabbi Sacks—whose book *Will We Have Jewish Grandchildren?* played a major part in rekindling the debate—the overall rate of intermarriage between American Jews and non-Jews was reported to have risen almost tenfold in thirty years, from six percent in 1960 to an astounding fifty-seven percent at the end of the 1980s.

Intermarriage as a syndrome appears to surface in the fourth generation of settlement in an inclusive society. Over three generations—original immigrants, their children, and their grandchildren—the ancestral identity is capable of being preserved. In the fourth generation, according to Rabbi Sacks, "ties of kinship and ethnicity weaken and mixed marriage soars." In mixed marriages only about five percent of the non-Jewish partners convert to Judaism. Almost half (forty-one percent) of the children born in such marriages are raised in the religion of the non-Jewish partner, while thirty-one percent are raised without any religion at all.[13]

The cure, according to Rabbi Sacks, as well as some other writers such as the American journalist Irving Kristol, is religion. Not orthodoxy, but some peculiarly Jewish mystery of "continuity," centred on the children and compatible with an open, liberal society, yet still fuelled by a metaphysical fire. "The new challenge," wrote Kristol in a piece entitled *Why Religion Is Good for the Jews,* "is how to live as equals in American society without committing demographic suicide. The opportunity is one for the American Jewish community to reestablish a Jewish core, a religious core, as a key to its identity."

When Amiel and I turned up in Rabbi Plaut's study in 1974 it was not because we had considered these matters. The synagogue wedding was Amiel's idea—as a Jew, but also as a person wishing to give the event a sense of occasion instead of having to surrender a private union to the dreary bureaucracy of the state. For myself, I was curious to see what the inside of a synagogue looked like. Jewish continuity was the furthest thing from my mind. When we first met, neither of us even knew that the other was Jewish. (Amiel, apparently, thought about it briefly and concluded that I was not, while I had no idea what she was and could not have cared less.)

Yet, looking back, I wonder. Perhaps there was a mysterious pull toward an ancestral tradition, fleeting and transitory as it may have been for both of us. It was not only that I considered a Jewish wedding "a lark" (though I suspect this was an element in it) but also that it corresponded with something felt, deeply if dimly, in my otherwise secular being. The ceremony moved us. The irony, as we both remarked at the time, was that if it had been much more traditional, much more orthodox, it might have moved us even more—except that then it would never have been performed. No Orthodox rabbi would have consented to marrying two such apostates.

The all-too-similar nature Amiel and I shared contained a strong streak of defiance. It was our defiance that insisted on a Jewish wedding, while deliberately rejecting religion or any traditional sense of community. Defiance was also the leitmotif of three stanzas I wrote around this time, entitled *A Love Poem:*

May I tell you the truth?

When I dropped the sailboat's anchor
on the skull of the fish, its mouth opened wide
but only in agony, not supplication
as knowing no mercy pikes ask for none;
but fighting well for a body of fourteen
pounds of muscle and slippery green skin,
pulling a deep-keeled boat a quarter of a mile
surviving a keen slap of the paddle between the eyes
a pair of pliers drawing a three-pronged hook
out of its gullet, taking whatever came with it,
and still biting the fisherman's finger with three rows
of immaculate teeth set in its dead jaws

may I tell you the truth—
cover girl without eyelashes lipstick
I saw your face.

If the analogy was even half-accurate, the surprising thing was not that our marriage did not last, but that it did last for five years. Amiel and I separated in the fall of 1979. Far from resolving the dilemma of Jewish continuity, we did not even address it at the time. We had what seemed to us far more urgent things on our minds. We stayed Jewish (naturally), but when we married again, we both married Gentiles and had Catholic weddings to please our spouses-to-be.[14]

I still have no metaphysical bone in my body. I am no more religious than I have ever been, yet I am more and more convinced that religion, if it is to matter, has to be more than a vague cultural fringe on the clothes of Jewish (or any other) tradition. Since religion is not available to me even as a fringe, I retreat into my room to read my grandfather's treatise, noting that in his fashion he was a very religious man. He quotes the early nineteenth-century British Conservative prime minister George Canning with approval: "Respect for religion once eradicated—the name of God once erased from the human heart—it is easy to pour into a heart so void, a spirit of hatred towards its fellow creatures." Old Tory rubbish? It took less than twenty years after Canning wrote these lines for Hitler's unwitting philosophical idol, Nietzsche, to be born.

I ponder these contradictions: the world's, my grandfather's, and my own. This too is Jewish continuity, I suppose.

38

MY LIFE IN LAW

ONE DAY, WHEN I WAS AROUND SEVENTEEN, my father said to me, rather out of the blue: "Go get a law degree."

Seeing the puzzled expression on my face, he continued:

"You don't have to practise if you find that the law bores you. Your grandfather had a law degree and he never practised; I have a law degree and I barely practised. Having a law degree commits you to nothing."

It was true that my paternal grandfather, who had died long before I was born, never practised law. He practised amateur philosophy and local politics instead. It was also true that my father never really practised, except for a brief stint as in-house counsel to a railroad. But these biographical facts still provided me with no impetus for going to law school.

"Dad," I asked my father, "if my goal in life is not to practise law, can't I also achieve it by not getting a law degree?"

Father thought about this for a second. "I suppose you could, yes," he allowed, whereupon I solemnly undertook to follow the family tradition and stay away from the practice of law but, unlike my immediate ancestors, accomplish this feat *without* a law degree.

It did not quite turn out this way. If my progenitors acquired a legal education but avoided legal practice, I avoided a legal education but acquired a legal practice of sorts. During the 1970s I drifted into legal journalism, first in print, then in radio and television, and stayed with it (intermittently) for the next twenty years.

The instigator was Barbara Amiel. She became fascinated by a high-profile murder case in 1973, and persuaded me to write a book about it with her.[15] It took some effort to persuade me, for at the time my interest in police matters and criminal law was just about nil, but Amiel could be uncommonly persuasive. While researching the book, I met Edward L. (Eddie) Greenspan, who was to become arguably the best, and unarguably the best-known, criminal lawyer in Canada. When the book became a best-seller, matters gathered their own momentum. The pressure of agents and publishers and the allure of money certainly played a part, but there was another incentive: curiosity. Night-long conversations with Greenspan, as well as with his many friends, colleagues, law students, rivals, and opponents, kindled my interest in the relationship between ideas, politics, and the legal system. I accepted an invitation to write a column for a new monthly called *The Canadian Lawyer,* started a law-related radio and later television series with Greenspan as host,[16] and eventually co-authored a book with him about *his* life in law.[17]

The physical Eddie was nearly as impressive as the intellectual one back in the 1970s. The Eddie of the mind was a giant, but at three hundred pounds the Eddie of the flesh was a near match. Eddie the Brain's gargantuan capacity for work, wisdom, and wit was almost equalled by

Eddie the Body's colossal capacity for calories. Eddie at table, dispatching dishes serenely, resembled a Cyclops digging into his nightly flock of sheep. An eye in the middle of his forehead would have made the illusion perfect, but even without it the resemblance was marked. Alas, the fabled figure eventually succumbed to the pressure of medical fashion. It may have been therapeutically wise, but it was aesthetically disappointing when, in the 1980s, after nearly a year of a stringent sashimi diet, Eddie emerged at about 220 pounds, reduced forever from a character of Greek mythology to a slightly corpulent Canadian lawyer.

"Reduced forever from a character of Greek mythology to a slightly corpulent Canadian lawyer." From l. to r., Eddie Greenspan and the author with Count Alfred de Marigny during a film shoot in the Bahamas. (Fifty years earlier de Marigny was acquitted of the "murder of the century" in the death of Sir Harry Oakes.)

If anyone, Greenspan might have kept me exploring legal topics, but after a while I found myself growing restless. There is a pressure for specialization in most occupations, including writing, but there has always been a significant pressure against specialization in my own mind. It is congenial to move from topic to topic, medium to medium, genre to genre. I enjoy writing prose one day and poetry the next. In my newspaper columns I have covered subjects from aviation to international intrigue. I like fiction and non-fiction; stage plays and television scripts; essays and opera librettos; song lyrics and investigative pieces, and over the years I have dabbled in most. But there is a penalty. Being a social butterfly is one thing; being a professional butterfly is quite another. The flattering way to describe people with my tendency is to call them "Renaissance men" but it is also possible to describe them as "jack of all trades, master of none."

"Master of none" is how agents, editors, producers, and critics tend to think of Renaissance men, and not without justification. Specialization enhances facility as well as expertise—after all, practice makes perfect—and the best people in any field are usually specialists. But I wanted to be an unhyphenated writer: a *writer,* not a crime-, screen-, political-, legal-, or thriller-writer. Much as I enjoyed telling and analyzing stories of crime and punishment, I came to resent being the chronicler of thieves, rapists, or terrorists, and of the people who hunted, prosecuted, or defended them. Going to my grave as a biographer of crooks and their lawyers, though potentially lucrative, seemed insufficiently rewarding. In the end I wanted to tell no legal stories except those that were larger than themselves.

Which led me directly to the show trials of our times.

39

SHOW TRIALS SHIFT FROM MOSCOW
TO OTTAWA

The sound of a kiss is not so loud as that of
a cannon, but its echo lasts a great deal longer.
—OLIVER WENDELL HOLMES, SR.

JUSTICE IN HIGH HEELS

ON FEBRUARY 14, 2002, the Supreme Court of Canada ruled in a 5–4 split decision that the Crown could proceed against former Nova Scotia premier Gerald Regan on seven counts of alleged sexual offences against women. The case against the former provincial leader had a troubling history. No woman ever came forward to accuse him. In July 1993, a political opponent, relying on some information obtained from a TV show—produced but never aired by the Canadian Broadcasting Corporation—filed a complaint with the Royal Canadian Mounted Police. In October the same year, before any charges were laid, the RCMP publicly revealed that Regan was being investigated for sexual assault.

Revealing such information before laying a charge is against RCMP policy and practice. Making the information public became the first of many irregularities in the investigation and prosecution of the ex-premier. Further flaws included a Crown attorney named Susan Potts contemplating "judge shopping," a practice the Supreme Court later called "offensive" and "unacceptable." They also included the prosecution team "homogenizing" its functions with the police and conducting a series of pre-charge interviews with complainants. A Nova Scotia Supreme Court trial judge, Mr. Justice Michael Macdonald, eventually found that at least some of these interviews were designed "to have reluctant complainants change their minds and come forward to lay charges."

Even though Susan Potts was no longer on the Crown's team by the time the Crown preferred an indictment against Regan, the trial judge felt the prosecution had become tainted. In April 1998, he employed a constitutional remedy for abuse of process to stay nine of eighteen charges against the ex-premier. Regan went on trial on the remaining nine counts. Defended by Eddie Greenspan, he was acquitted of all charges by a jury on December 18.

The Crown appealed Mr. Justice Macdonald's decision to stay nine charges against Regan. The judge called the charges minor, which they no doubt were. They consisted of allegations that Regan—a 1960s-style Liberal politician, whose social manners may have coincided with the "make love, not war" spirit of the times—stole a kiss or "copped a feel" some twenty-four to thirty-four years earlier. At the time these transgressions occurred (assuming they did) people would have viewed them, at worst, as churlish rather than criminal.

The quality of the Crown's evidence was illustrated by one complainant, who first recollected only a stolen kiss in 1969. Later she became "99.9 percent" sure that Regan also touched her breast over her clothes. It was such 99.9 percent certainties that the prosecution was proposing to turn into 100 percent criminal convictions. In spite of this, in a split (2 to 1) decision, the Nova Scotia Court of Appeal had reinstated the nine charges. Two of them were subsequently dismissed by the prosecution itself. What the Supreme Court's majority dismissed on February 14 was Regan's appeal from the Nova Scotia Court of Appeal's judgement.

There was no disagreement between the majority and the minority of the Court that the police and the prosecution had abused the process to a "troubling" extent. The dispute was over how much abuse should the process take in what the Supreme Court viewed as a good cause.

"Society has a strong interest in having the matter adjudicated," wrote Mr. Justice LeBel for the majority. "I conclude that... the cumulative effect of these actions, while troubling in some respects, does not rise to the level of abuse of process which... would offend the community's sense of decency and fair play."

But the abuse clearly offended the sense of decency and fair play of six Canadian judges. It caused the original trial judge to throw out nine charges, and five justices (in two appeal courts) sided with him. For the dissenters in the Supreme Court, Mr. Justice Binnie wrote: "It was [the trial judge's] view, after an 18-day hearing, that Crown prosecutors had manifested such a lack of objectivity in seeking the conviction of a prominent politician 'at all costs' as to taint the integrity of the administration of justice in Nova Scotia."

Ultimately there were two differences between the Court's majority and minority. One was that the majority[18] preferred policy to fairness, while the dissenters[19] favoured fairness over policy. The second difference lay in the two factions' understanding of "societal interest." The dissenters felt society itself had an interest in fairness; the majority saw fairness as being of interest only to the accused. Between the lines of the majority's reasons was the unmistakable whiff of a new state religion: feminism. Its message was that the matriarchy means business; that a politicized justice system cares mainly about "empowering" women, and that in Canada's gender wars an allegation of a sexual nature by any woman, no matter how minor, unsupported, or distant in time, reduces any man to a terrorist suspect, an unlawful combatant, to whom the Geneva conventions no longer apply.

In the end it was the Nova Scotia prosecutors who decided to drop the dubious charges the Supreme Court would have permitted to stand. The Crown's decision came as a relief, indicating that, at the dawn of the twenty-first century, the chances of a man charged with a sexual offence receiving a fair trial in Canada's matriarchal justice system was still better than the chances of a Jew receiving a fair trial in Nazi Germany—if only just.

The political nature of the judgement was celebrated by those who supported the politics. "The Supreme Court has shown a willingness," crowed one newspaper editorial, "to make the legal system more responsive to the victims of sexual assault."[20]

In fact, the willingness the majority of the Court showed was to achieve a policy objective at the expense of procedural fairness. As the old judicial maxim warns, though, "policy is an unruly horse." It is this skittish animal that has become the favourite mount of judicial cowboys.

JUDICIAL COWBOYS

When we believe ourselves in possession
of the only truth, we are likely to be indifferent
to common everyday truths.
—ERIC HOFFER

Beware of anyone talking about "evolving law." Expressions like "the living Constitution" usually signal a person intending to use the law for an instrument of social engineering. This is the main distinction between "purposive" judges, so-called, and strict constructionists. Strict constructionists try to read and apply the law as set down by legislature or precedent in their original context. When purposive jurists talk about "contextual" judgements, it usually means taking words and ideas out of the context in which they were used by the legislators or courts that pronounced them, and putting them into some other context of the purposive jurists' fancy.

Purposive jurists not only feel free to use the law as a platform for their political philosophy but come to believe that there is a moral imperative for them to do so. They feel not only licensed but commanded by history: they think that by "updating" the law, or "reading-in"—that is, smuggling into—a statute or the Constitution whatever strikes them as equitable or socially desirable, they are performing a benevolent or "progressive" function.

The opposite is more likely. Elevating human desires to human rights can destroy the rule of law even when such desires are equitable and well merited. Obviously this applies even more strongly to human desires that are neither.

What complicates matters is this. Although judicial activism gives rise to grave dangers, *all* judges are bound to interpret and apply the law. They cannot help it; it is their duty. Courts are obliged to measure a given piece of legislation against the principles of the country's constitution, written or unwritten. Very often judges need to divine the intent of the legislators, as far as their intent can be discerned, by using settled rules of statutory interpretation. Courts may also be required to gauge statutes against the principles of common law, as established by judicial precedent.

This is not the same as judicial activism. Legislators and citizens fully expect courts to interpret statutory or common law, measure it against the supreme law of the constitution, then apply it to the cases they hear. Testing statutes and legal procedures against constitutional and common-law principles is what judges *do*—all judges, whether they are strict constructionists or judicial cowboys. What separates the two tribes is that judges belonging to the first are willing and able to uncouple their own personal social and political philosophies from their obligations as jurists, while those in the second tribe are unable or unwilling to do so.

None of this is new, though it is salutary to restate it from time to time. However, what is almost never noted is that in democracies, whether based on parliamentary or congressional models, legislators often *want* judges to usurp their functions. The reason is simple. Legislators who pass unpopular laws, or laws that turn out to have unintended side effects, must put their jobs on the line. Rather than expressing their own social philosophy by passing laws and risking the censure of the voters, lawmakers and governments often find it more convenient to appoint like-minded judges. Like-minded is not enough, of course; they must also be judicial activists who can be counted on to "read-in" or strike down legislation that elected representatives do not dare to create or strike down themselves. Far from usurping the function of legislatures, such judges act as their dummies.

Stacking the courts with ideologically sympathetic appointees, then using them to implement policies, started out as a liberal device under the New Deal. Though not invented by Franklin Delano Roosevelt, it was perfected by him. The practice continued with a vengeance during the 1960s. By now conservatives have learned to utilize it as well. All it requires on both sides of the political spectrum is to seek out judicial candidates whose zeal exceeds their principles, or who know which side their bread is buttered on and are willing to be turned into political hacks.

40

INTERNATIONAL TRIBUNALS: A CAUTION

In doing good, we are generally cold, and languid, and sluggish;
and of all things afraid of being too much in the right. But the works of malice
and injustice are quite in another style. They are finished with a bold, masterly
hand; touched as they are with the spirit of those vehement passions that
call forth all our energies, whenever we oppress and persecute.

—EDMUND BURKE

THE HAGUE

ON JANUARY 16, 2001, Yugoslav president Vojislav Kostunica refused to meet with the prosecutor of the U.N. International Criminal Tribunal, Carla Del Ponte. Kostunica used the occasion to reiterate that he had no intention of allowing the former president of Yugoslavia, Slobodan Milosevic, to be extradited for war crimes.

Kostunica had been Milosevic's opponent, and a bitter opponent at that. He probably had no doubt in his own mind that Milosevic was a criminal. Kostunica, though a Serb nationalist himself, always disagreed with Milosevic's methods, and to some extent even with his aims. He also recognized Serbia's need to mend fences with the West. Still, Kostunica felt that letting international tribunals declare some policies to be crimes when pursued by one side in a conflict, then bring political figures to trial for their policies, or even for the means they employed in pursuit of their policies, would cause the fate of all nations to be decided in some foreign courtroom. Inasmuch as the rulings of international tribunals would be enforced by the military of the European Union or the United States (or both), the future of all countries from Serbia to Indonesia would ultimately be settled in Brussels or Washington.

One might argue that, myths of sovereignty notwithstanding, big powers have always shaped the affairs of little powers. True as this is, new systems of international tribunals go a step further. They propose to stamp certain historical realities—the big tend to rule the small; the *Zeitgeist* supersedes all other considerations, and so on—with the hallowed seal of virtue. Power politics and the rule of fashion are distasteful enough; covering power politics and fashion with a false veneer of equity is worse. It injures and diminishes not only the affected parties, but justice itself.

Kostunica appeared to understand this in January 2001. Unfortunately, six months later Yugoslavia's government could not resist a bribe of US$1 billion and delivered its former head of state to The Hague.[21] The Americans made an immense mistake when they promoted and facilitated the deal. Insisting on the extradition of Milosevic to a politicized international tribunal was an error that has already come back to haunt America, and will haunt other liberal democracies.

THE ICC

The next step in the evolution of international tribunals was the International Criminal Court (ICC), established by the Rome statutes of 1998 and ratified by the requisite number of countries over the next two years. The court became operational in the summer of 2002.[22]

The ICC likes to trace its origins to the war crimes tribunals of Nuremberg and Tokyo. There are two problems with claiming such descent. First, the antecedents themselves are badly flawed. No group deserved to be tried for its crimes more than the Nazis, but Nuremberg was still a victor's court. With the Soviets on the bench, it also became something of a farce. Stalin's henchmen could no doubt recognize a crime against humanity when they saw one, but having the masters of the Gulag prosecute the masters of Auschwitz still turned justice into a mockery. With Andrei I. Vishinsky—Stalin's former prosecutor during the "purge trials" of 1936–1938—supervising a Soviet team of judges and prosecutors, Nuremberg could safely be described as Al Capone sitting in judgement over Jack the Ripper.

But the ICC claim of descent of even such flawed ancestry has been less than legitimate. Unlike Nuremberg, the court cannot even lay claim to being "victor's justice," in the sense of being an institution set up by victorious powers exercising traditional territorial jurisdiction after assuming sovereignty over a conquered region. Nor is the ICC—unlike the ad hoc courts of the United Nations, such as the tribunal trying Milosevic in The Hague—subject to the U.N. Security Council. The court derives its power from no source of discernible legitimacy. It is designed to be a law unto itself. The judges and prosecutors are unelected officials arrogating jurisdiction to themselves across all lines of national sovereignty.

They are not just any unelected outsiders, however. The ICC's bandwagon is pushed by an informal coalition of interest groups, supported by what South African Justice and former U.N. chief prosecutor Richard Goldstone has approvingly described as "like-minded states." While not in a class with U.S. president George W. Bush's "axis of evil,"[23] the ICC coalition is an anti-American feminist environmentalist axis of left-leaning liberals.

Supporters of the court have a variety of agendas. The EU, for instance, hopes that supranational bodies like the ICC will enable it to do endruns around the United States. Losing parties in a conflict envision using the court to punish the winners (as an Argentinean group in 2000 attempted to demand the extradition of Margaret Thatcher for her role in the sinking of the Argentinean warship *General Belgrano* during the 1982 Falklands war). Since "severe damage to the environment" is regarded as a war crime by the ICC, and so is intentional attack on non-military facilities such as power stations or factories, Serb groups could attempt (but for a technicality) to use the court to prosecute NATO leaders for having ordered the bombing of Yugoslavia during the Kosovo conflict. The technicality that prevents this is an exclusion of offences before the ICC became functional in 2002, but such prosecutions would be available in future conflicts. In short, the ICC holds the potential of adding the insult of "loser's justice" to the injury of "winner's justice."

Needless to say, neither winner's justice nor loser's justice has anything to do with justice. The safeguards ostensibly set up to eliminate frivolous prosecutions achieve something entirely different: they ensure the selective prosecution of identical conduct. In this context the very word "safeguards" means a bow to political realities and fashions.

Aspiring supranational bureaucrats—U.N. functionaries, "progressive" academics, feminist law professors—see in the court a vehicle with the potential to transport them to their future power base, from which they may exercise a kind of Platonic guardianship of the world. These budding commissars are unlike the guardians in Plato's *Republic* in one significant respect: Plato assumed that good people would not wish to take on such a role and would have to be compelled to do so. In contrast, the ICC's guardians are all volunteers. A prescient Stephen Leacock must have foreseen the ICC crowd when he wrote about immoral little toads swelling themselves to the bursting point in their desire to be moral oxen.

Non-governmental organizations are strong supporters of the ICC as it holds the promise of criminalizing conduct of which they disapprove. There are trouble spots in the world, from the Middle East to the Indian subcontinent, where the criminalization of a conflict would be equally welcome, especially by the side that cannot prevail on the battlefield. The ink was hardly dry on the Rome agreement when Syria started urging that Israel be charged with war crimes for building settlements in the disputed territories. "The Israeli Settlement Act," Syria proclaimed, "is a form of ethnic cleansing." The ICC may end up holding that settlers who move into an "occupied territory" perpetrate a war crime, and prosecute them accordingly.

America's leaders ought to have foreseen these consequences but they did not. Had they foreseen them, they might not have bribed the Serbs to extradite Milosevic to The Hague. The results of the ICC's operations are likely to range from the farcical to the tragic—or, at best, will include examples of both. This can no longer be helped. Some strings have to be played out before the false notes become evident to all, including those with tin ears.

Ultimately the worst thing about the ICC is that it amounts to moral deception. This is why it is more harmful than a display of naked power. The imposition of *force majeure* at least creates no ethical confusion. Institutions like the ICC do. They are political fashion hiding behind a mask of justice.

41

ON FLIGHT INSTRUCTORS AND

CHINESE PROVERBS

It is not worth the while to go round the world to count the cats in Zanzibar.
—HENRY DAVID THOREAU

IN 1987 I MADE UP MY MIND to indulge myself. Having published three books in the previous four years gave me a little breathing space.[24] Though at fifty-two I was too old for a proper midlife crisis, I decided to set up a motorcycle racing team and return to the track for a final fling. I thought I could justify the self-indulgence by writing a book about it.

The problem was, racing teams cost money. I had none myself beyond what I needed to live on, and no experience in raising funds. All I knew about the business side of racing was that it was probably a very bad business. Even investing in the movies might be a sound venture in comparison.

Having decided on a simple pitch, I called some well-to-do friends. "Whenever you make an investment," I told them, "you spend sleepless nights wondering how it'll turn out. Invest with me and sleep like a baby. The outcome is guaranteed. You sign the cheque, and the money is gone."

"And return to the track for a final fling." Aboard a vintage Norton at Shannonville, 1988.

My friends chuckled, and a few of them signed cheques.[25] One day a man I barely knew telephoned. His name was Monty Beber, a developer.

"I hear you're going around town telling people you've got a surefire thing."

"Yeah."

"It's an investment they don't have to lose any sleep over, you say."

"Yeah."

"I hear you tell them they sign you a cheque and their money is gone."

"You've got it."

"Well," said Beber, "what's wrong with my cheque?"

There was nothing wrong with Monty Beber's cheque. Motorsport's bottomless pit swallowed it up along with the cheques of all others. They had nothing to show for it, except the thrill of sponsorship along with my gratitude. What I had to show for it two years later was some memories, some photographs, and a couple of broken ribs. Also a book, published in 1989.[26]

It was time to look for a more sedate hobby. I bought a used Cessna Cardinal RG and asked an airline pilot friend, David Frid, to teach me to fly it.

A superb pilot and an excellent instructor, Frid was patient and gentle while he introduced me to the art of aviation. He continued to be forgiving and serene during my clumsy attempts to practise my skills, at least for as long as he considered it reasonable for a below-average student's learning curve. He accepted that it was hard to teach an old dog new tricks. He made me all the allowances a naturally gifted person makes for someone for whom acquiring a craft is a struggle.

There was a point, though, at which he snapped. If I continued to be all thumbs beyond that critical juncture, as I often was, my friendly flight instructor metamorphosed into a Marine drill sergeant—and that was on good days. On bad days, he turned into a werewolf. His canines seemed to grow an inch as he snarled at me: "*Right* rudder! Where *are* you going? *Fire* that nose down the centreline!"

On in-between days Frid resembled an animal trainer. He never actually bopped me over the head with a rolled-up chart, though I would have preferred it to what he did do, which was to suddenly grab the dual flight controls and give an exaggerated demonstration of what I had done wrong, and of the required correction. Often he did not even precede his abrupt inputs with the customary "My plane" or "I have control." As a result, I might unexpectedly find myself in a steep bank or sickening skid, sometimes not far above the surface of a runway.

But Frid's tough-love method worked—at least it worked for me. He would get my attention, snap me out of my lassitude, and fix the proper drill firmly in my mind. After startling me out of my daydreams, he would, very much like an animal trainer, reward me with the treat of an encouraging word. Soon, pleasing Frid became a main object of my flying. Like one of Professor Skinner's rats, I lived for avoiding the electric shocks of his unexpected control inputs, and be rewarded by the savoury treats of his praise.

On November 23, 1993, we were practising cross-wind landings at Burlington Airpark's 2,900-foot Runway 14, about twenty-five miles west of Toronto. The weather was 1,800 feet overcast with a visibility of fifteen miles, and a south wind of about ten knots. Frid wanted me to practise side-slipping from circuit altitude all the way to the southeast-oriented runway. Giving me some room for practice required extending the northwest downwind leg after entering the circuit from the southwest.

Extended downwind legs, though normal in training, are viewed as something of a hazard. Landing and departing aircraft follow each other around non-towered, uncontrolled fields, such as Burlington, in a standard rectangular pattern. Planes enter the downwind leg and fly opposite and beyond the point of intended landing for a reasonable distance, then turn 90 degrees onto the base leg, perpendicular to the direction of the landing runway, before turning another 90 degrees for final approach. The risk of an extended downwind is that the plane following in the circuit may "cut off" the stretched-out flier by turning on the base leg before him. This sets up a situation for the first and second plane to arrive simultaneously in the same spot and at about the same altitude. Both will be roughly three-quarters of a mile from the runway's threshold, in the corner where the base leg and final approach meet.

Two planes cannot occupy the same piece of sky at the same time, at least not without dire consequences. To avoid mid-air collisions, pilots must look, speak, and listen. They announce their position and intentions in the circuit on the common radio frequency, and listen to other pilots announcing *their* positions and intentions. In addition, they keep their heads on a swivel. The official rule in visual meteorological conditions requires pilots "to see and avoid" each other.

All pilots try. Most succeed. Some do not.

Hankering after my reward of praise, I flew the circuit meticulously. Entering downwind, I announced my intention to extend it. I looked and listened but could see and hear nothing. Being the only plane in the circuit was not unusual at Burlington, so I concentrated on my direction, air speed, and altitude. I did my downwind checklist, extended the flaps, lowered the gear, turned onto the base leg about a mile and a half from the airport, and started setting up for my final approach.

I had done everything by the book, as far as I could tell. As I started turning final, having first checked right to make sure we were not cutting off another plane, I expected, if anything, some words of praise. Instead, the next thing I felt was a violent pitch down, followed by a brief moment of weightlessness, as my instructor pushed his control wheel forward.

For a split second I was puzzled. Frid had done exactly what he would do in a demonstration of angry censure after I had done something wrong, after I made some mistake he considered unacceptable at my level of training. But I could not think of anything. I flew that circuit *right,* so why did he ...

At that instant my peripheral vision registered a shape in my left side window, half-obscured by the doorpost. Although it was gone almost immediately, as if jerked upwards by an invisible wire, I recognized the stubby wing of the local flight school's Piper Seneca, a twin-engine aircraft I had flown myself once from Goderich, Ontario, to Burlington. The twin's wing seemed to jerk up only because we dove underneath it. In reality it continued banking serenely, completing its own base turn to final. The pilot who had cut us off never saw us.

My first reaction when I glimpsed the Seneca's wing was one of immense relief. So *that* was all that it was, a near miss, nothing more. I had only been facing death, not my instructor's censure.[27]

"On bad days, he turned into a werewolf." With David Frid at Burlington Airpark, Ontario, in 2001.

The experience illustrated the limits of enlightened self-interest. I had always known that it was easier for an infantryman at Ypres to go over the top than to face his comrades' contempt, but after I saw the Seneca's wing close up I understood it viscerally. Without meaning to teach me anything but side-slipping, Frid had taught me about my own hierarchy of values. Peer approval—his approval, anyway—mattered more to me than life.

A Chinese proverb holds that people should avoid being prominent for the same reason pigs should avoid being fat. Fame kills. This particular truism may be one-third true.

Once, many years ago, I fell off a horse. (I know one is supposed to say "I was thrown by a horse" but in my case I just fell off). I fell on my head, was feeling a bit queasy afterwards, and had myself driven to a Toronto hospital. This was in the 1960s. No one knew me, and consequently no one paid the slightest attention to me. I waited in the emergency ward for about three hours. During the fourth hour I went to the nurses' station.

"Do you think someone could look at me?"

"Wait your turn, sir. We have very sick people here. Do you want me to show you some?"

The nurse was just handing out freshly brewed coffee to a group of other nurses and interns. The atmosphere was supremely relaxed.

"No, I don't want a guided tour just now, thanks," I said. "It's only that if you're too busy I'll try the hospital across the street."

"Nothing much wrong with you if you can walk, sir, is there?"

"Nurse, as a snap diagnostician you're tops. Goodbye."

"Wait," the nurse said, putting down her coffee cup. "You can't leave here until you sign this release form."

"See if you can round up enough interns to stop me," I said and walked out. In the 1960s it would have taken quite a few interns. On the other hand, the nurse had been right: there was nothing much wrong with me. The minute I reached the street I felt fine. Mentally, though, I was seething. The nurse's disdain brought home to me the inevitable fate of the poor, the insignificant, the anonymous. Had I not come from the land of scientific socialism, the experience might have suggested to me that I should change the world. As it was, it suggested that I should change myself. There being no place where the poor, the insignificant, and the anonymous would not be treated with callous disdain, the answer was to stop being poor, insignificant, and anonymous.

In the years that followed I tried, and to some small extent succeeded. The next time I found myself in the emergency ward of a Toronto hospital (the one across the street from the first one, actually) was about twenty years later. My old Norton motorcycle had gone down in a spot of oil on the racetrack at Shannonville, and I was sure I had broken a few ribs (as it turned out, I had). This time I was not quite as anonymous and the head nurse on duty recognized me.

"You're the journalist, aren't you? I read you in the paper sometimes."

"That's good ... ah ... is the doctor? ..."

"He's coming.... Now *I* could tell you some things to write about."

"Yes, I'm sure ..."

"See this place, this waiting room? Look! See what we have to put up with?"

"Well ... ah ... turning's a bit tricky for me...."

"They treat nurses here like galley slaves. You patients come and go, but we have to be here every day...."

There was no stopping her. I thought I actually preferred the nurse across the street from twenty years ago. The ancient Chinese were definitely on to something in that proverb about prominence and pigs.

About ten years later the emergency physician recognized me, too. This happened in Phoenix, Arizona. The year was 1998. A few hours earlier I had landed at Scottsdale airport after an FAA examiner had put me through my paces for the biannual test I needed to renew my U.S. pilot's licence. As I was following him back to his office across the tarmac, I felt an unusual ache in my throat. The pain became a pressure in my chest a short time later, suggesting a heart attack.

"Ah, you're the columnist, Jonas," the doctor said to me at the hospital. "I'm from Canada, too, from Calgary. A refugee from socialized medicine. Well, you're having a heart attack."

"Any other good news?"

"Thank your lucky stars that you're a conservative columnist. If you were the other kind, I'd let you die like a dog. As it is, don't worry about a thing. I'll get you the best damn cardiologist in town."

And he did. So much for the Chinese and their proverbs. Far from killing you, fame extends your life. Dr. James J. Hines had the reputation of being the best heart man in the golden-age city of Phoenix—a bit like being the best bone-setter in the ski resort of Zermatt. It was the only time in my life when being mistaken for a conservative was to my benefit.

It would have served no purpose to explain to my compatriot from Calgary that I did not see myself as a conservative but as a classical liberal. What did it matter, anyway? I was finally in America, the country for which I had been too lazy to line up forty-two years earlier. I resolved to have my heart attack in peace.

5

THE INDISPOSED
EMPIRE

42

KISSINGER'S

GAMBIT

The public, with its mob yearning to
be instructed, edified and pulled by the nose,
demands certainties; it must be told definitely and a
bit raucously that this is true and that is false.
But there are no certainties.

—H.L. MENCKEN

"THAT MAN IS AN IDIOT," said Henry Kissinger to Mordecai Richler, referring
to Ronald Reagan. The year was 1980; Richler was a Book-of-the-Month
Club judge in New York, and Dr. Kissinger was a luncheon guest at the
club's editorial offices. By then Richard Nixon's and Gerald Ford's former
secretary of state was supporting John Connally, Jr., for the Republican
party's presidential nomination.

Richler recounted the anecdote in *Saturday Night* magazine,[1] to illustrate how easy it is to be mistaken in assessing someone's future political
significance. I am relating Richler's story here for a different reason.

Kissinger's remark, though intemperate, was not inaccurate. From his
vantage point, describing the future president of the United States as an
idiot was not unreasonable. Compared to Kissinger himself—probably
one of the most erudite men ever to have held a U.S. cabinet post—the former Hollywood actor of average IQ and uncertain grasp of geography and
history may well have appeared to be a simple-minded soul.

But the race is not always to the swift. Perhaps Reagan, the simple,
maybe even simplistic American, did not have a fraction of Kissinger's

256

extensive, sophisticated, and ultimately *European* understanding of history and human affairs. Yet in the end the brilliant pragmatist Kissinger's principal legacy has been America's ignominious withdrawal from Vietnam. His 1973 ceasefire, his Chamberlainian "peace with honour," was in many ways a disgraceful rout, the sacrifice of a principle (as well as a vulnerable ally) to realpolitik. Kissinger and Le Duc Tho shared a Nobel Peace Prize,[2] while thousands of South Vietnamese shared imprisonment, torture, death—and ultimately a Communist system that persists to this day. In contrast, the naively idealistic Reagan's legacy has been the collapse of the Evil Empire: the demise of this century's deadliest tyranny that was the scourge of one-fifth of the world and a grave threat to the rest.

Some might object that this is an unfair assessment of Kissinger's legacy. For one thing, by the time Kissinger stepped onto the world's stage, the best the United States could hope to achieve in Vietnam was to cut its losses. For another, the Nixon-Kissinger policy of making separate peace (as it were) with Communist China in 1972, thereby isolating it from the Soviet Union, paved the way for the collapse of the latter.

Is this objection valid? Vietnam *was* probably lost by the time Kissinger came along. But America's China policy is another matter. The Nixon administration's geopolitical strategy was nothing short of grandiose. As Kissinger describes it in the concluding volume of his memoirs, "Our strategic objective was...to transform the two-power world of the Cold War into a triangle and then to manage the triangle in such a way that we would be closer to each of the contenders than they were to each other, thereby maximizing our options."[3]

The conventional view is that this policy fatally weakened Communism by dividing the monolith. Another view is that it may have had the opposite effect.

In this view, whatever harm Kissinger's rapprochement with the Forbidden City had done to the Kremlin, it has allowed Communism to survive in China, instead of perishing along with Soviet-style Communism twenty years later. As the Evil Empire drowned in Europe, it would have dragged the Evil Empire in the Far East down with it, had

Kissinger not helped to cut Beijing loose from Moscow. If so, saving a Mao-jacketed Marx to fight another day may turn out to be the most insidious legacy of Kissinger's realpolitik. There is such a thing as being too clever by half. In the twenty-first century the very success of Kissinger's strategy may come back to haunt us, as a gigantic and reinvigorated China emerges to threaten the Pacific region as well as the rest of the world.

Tempting as the assessment may be, what complicates matters is that the world's stage is rarely static. Nations, outlooks, perceptions, and technologies change, sometimes from year to year. The winning policy in a given moment of historic time can be a grievous error in another. During the last great expansionary cycle of Communism—roughly between the 1957 launching of Sputnik and the end of the Vietnam War in 1975—a deft walk on the tightrope between containment and détente may have been the wisest policy option for the West. Reagan's uncompromising stance (or at least rhetoric) on the Evil Empire, so effective in the 1980s, might have been disastrous a decade earlier. It is possible that circumstances called for Kissinger's European-style pragmatism in the 1960s and 70s, in the same way, and for the same reason, as Reagan's American idealism became the answer in the 1980s. It was simply Nixon's and Kissinger's misfortune that their tenure coincided with a less glorious cycle.

A FOOTNOTE

Here is a curious fact. Western liberals, especially those with some illusions about the Soviet and Maoist empires, have always disliked Richard Nixon and Henry Kissinger more than they disliked other American leaders, including such staunch anti-Communists as Harry Truman or even Ronald Reagan. At first blush the liberals' dislike seems surprising, considering that Nixon and Kissinger were the very statesmen who extracted America from Vietnam, engineered détente with the Soviet Union, paved the way to the Helsinki Accords of 1975, and opened the door to the West's rapprochement with Communist China.

Though Nixon and Kissinger were on the political right, their actual policies were "softer" on Communism than the policies of most of their predecessors and successors. Between 1969 and 1976 Nixon and Kissinger instituted and nurtured modalities of coexistence with the major Communist powers to a far greater extent than other U.S. statesmen. America's liberals might have been expected to applaud them, but they despised them instead.

One speculates that what idealists and self-styled sophisticates resented most was that it was these pragmatic opponents of Communism, rather than liberal idealists, who first managed to make major deals with the Communists. America's liberals could not forgive Nixon for getting along with Leonid Brezhnev and Mao Tse-Tung, while their own idol, Jack Kennedy, had been savaged by Fidel Castro within eighty-seven days of his inauguration at the Bay of Pigs, then mauled by Nikita Khrushchev at their 1961 Vienna meeting a year later. Perhaps Kennedy was not foppish and weak, or certainly not merely so, but that is how he impressed the Communists. To persuade Khrushchev otherwise, the shining court of Camelot had to risk destroying the world during the Cuban missile crisis a year later. The confrontation engendered in liberals the uneasy feeling that if their aim was to reduce the risk of a nuclear holocaust, they had backed the wrong horse in 1960. Khrushchev might have been far less tempted to test Nixon's resolve by putting Russian missiles on Cuban soil.

Even worse, by coming to terms with the rulers of the Kremlin and the Forbidden City in the early 1970s, Nixon and Kissinger revealed the heirs of Marx and Lenin for what they really were: not harbingers of a Utopian future, but traditional, if rather thuggish, players of power politics. This was not how Ho Chi Minh's and "Che" Guevara's allies were envisaged by Jane Fonda, or even by George McGovern. The quixotic crusaders of the 1960s, hoping to see Tancred (or at least Torquemada) in Moscow's and Beijing's corridors of power, were suddenly confronted with the fleshy face of Al Capone. Western liberals could never forgive Nixon and Kissinger for destroying their illusions.

43

WHY LOSING SUCKS

FOR THIRTY YEARS, BETWEEN 1950 AND 1980, America seemed to be gradually losing the Cold War.

It is not human losses alone that create a sense of tragedy. Americans lost more soldiers in World War I (114,000 killed) than in Vietnam and Korea combined (58,000 and 33,000 killed, respectively.) In World War II, America's losses exceeded Vietnam, Korea, *and* the First War combined (292,000 killed.) Yet American memories and myths of the two world wars are on the whole uplifting, even glorious, while Korea, and especially Vietnam, appear as national nightmares.

Some historians attempt to explain the difference by the superior moral underpinnings of the two world wars. To me this seems fatuous. The moral underpinnings of World War I were by no means self-evident, and while fighting the Axis powers in World War II was undoubtedly an eminently moral cause, resisting Communism—a sordid system that, as we now know, claimed at least seventy million victims worldwide in the twentieth century—was no less righteous than resisting Nazism.

I think the difference is simpler, and it has nothing to do with morality. Although the United States paid a bloody price, America and its allies were victorious in both world wars. But in Korea, Americans managed to fight their enemies only to a draw, and in Vietnam they lost. To make matters worse, in both arenas they were defeated or fought to a standstill by an enemy that was militarily, technologically, and economically inferior. In other words, Americans lost ignominiously.

The defeated side rarely has fond historic memories of a war. This is especially true of defeat in a war that has not been entirely unavoidable. Sometimes a nation can retain pride in an unavoidable and purely defensive conflict bravely fought and lost against overwhelming odds,[4] but lofty national myths and memories are usually born of triumph. In historical recollections and legends, no less than in life itself, there is no substitute for victory.

44

TALES OF DÉTENTE

As long as justice and injustice have not terminated
their ever-renewing fight for ascendancy in the affairs
of mankind, human beings must be willing, when need is,
to do battle for the one against the other.
—JOHN STUART MILL

1. LAUGHING IN THE DARK

EVEN BEFORE THE REPUGNANT Helsinki Accords of 1975, which ratified Soviet dominance over Eastern Europe, I regarded détente with the Kremlin as a matter of taste. My memories of the 1970s centre on my visits to the Soviet empire with Canadian girls. Bright and inquisitive, these young women wanted to learn as much as they could about the mysterious Communist system that their own world had confusingly embraced, along with détente, in a *danse macabre* of MAD, mutual assured destruction. While appreciating their curiosity, I had my own agenda for these trips that had little to do with their education. It all worked out in the end, since most of our designs could be pursued in conjunction.

One girl seemed fascinated by the notion of political cabaret. She sensed it was different from comedy routines in Toronto or Chicago, including political comedy routines, but was not sure why. My explanation—"What makes cabaret funny in dictatorships is people on stage coming close to saying what everyone in the audience is thinking"—was too abstract for her.

"Can we go to a performance?" she asked.

"Yes, of course, but you won't understand it. We're in Budapest. You don't speak the language."

"I speak the body language. I'm smart. I know theatre."

"Fine, we're going tonight," I replied and rang the concierge for tickets.

The small theatre was crowded. The master of ceremonies—a well-known figure of political cabaret, Dezsõ Kellér by name, still active in 1972—parted the curtain. He came to the edge of the podium, using a characteristic gesture to let the curtain fall behind him. You could hear a pin drop as he eyed the audience. Then he spoke a line in a soft voice.

It brought the house down. People were clapping, hooting, hollering, literally rolling in the aisles. As a response to one line, no performer could have asked for more.

"What did he say, what did he say?" my companion demanded.

"You'll be disappointed."

"Never mind that; what did he say?"

"He said: 'Perhaps we should open the window and let in some fresh air.'"

The girl from Canada was crestfallen. When she finally accepted that I was not making it up, she concluded that people in Budapest must have a very peculiar sense of humour. In that she was not entirely wrong, though the reason the audience was rolling in the aisles was not because they shared a peculiar sense of humour, but shared a peculiar sense of being enslaved. "Fresh air" served as the trigger. The explosive reaction was a puncture in tyranny's balloon, the momentary release of a yearning for freedom.

There are genres that thrive only under adverse conditions. The soil of repression kills most art forms, but it nurtures poetry and political cabaret. In free countries where newspapers routinely call governments and officials idiotic or corrupt it is not necessary to turn to metaphors, allusions, or humour to disguise a civic discourse. When talking politics, neither writers nor audiences have to pretend that they are engaged in comedy or art. But in a king's court only a fool can tell the truth.

Cabaret and poetry flourish in tyrannies as substitutes for newspaper editorials and political rallies. In post-tyrannical societies they lose such borrowed relevance and retain only the values intrinsic to their art forms. Cabarets struggle in Budapest today, and poetry readings attract audiences of a dozen people or so, just as in London or New York. The chattering classes of the West, who thought that the readings of Yevgeny Yevtushenko during the 1960s attracted crowds of thirty thousand because of the Russians' love for poetry, were missing the point as usual.

2. WALKING IN THE DARK

An experience of a different kind involved a late-night walk with a girl through the deserted streets of an East European capital. Very different cities, such as Budapest, Bucharest, Warsaw, East Berlin, and Prague, had certain things in common during the Communist era, including the years of détente. One was that their Koestlerian "darkness at noon" was complemented by a literal, pitch-black darkness at night. There were no neon signs over shop windows, no strings of coloured lights over parking lots, no flashing advertisements in the sky. There being few cars, there were few headlights. Other than the occasional pale circle around the solitary sentinel of a lamppost—in desolate Bucharest, every third or fourth lamppost—urban areas resembled the countryside on a moonless night. Darker, in fact, because a permanent Soviet-style smog obscured even the stars. Office and apartment buildings showed no lights. With their entrance doors sternly locked, they loomed merely as black shadows. For visitors used to the sparkle of Western cities, night walks in a Communist capital seemed puzzling and unnerving.

I could feel my Canadian companion tensing up as we walked back to our hotel along the Grand Boulevard of Budapest. She reached for my hand and huddled closer to me. It was not a romantic gesture, but one of apprehension. I wondered how to reassure her. Though her fear in a strange, dark, and deserted avenue was entirely natural, we were in fact in less danger than we would have been in the brightly illuminated centre of any American city. Public safety was relatively high in Communist regimes. The only unlawful activities that flourished were smuggling and petty thievery. Holdups were rare; muggers almost non-existent. This was not surprising; after all, criminals are private entrepreneurs, and the authorities had expropriated most private ventures. In the Communist state, crime was nationalized, along with other human endeavours. The state reserved the privilege to rob, mug, and murder to itself.

To reassure my companion, I tried to convey this in a sentence.

"Relax," I said. "You're in Hungary. Here you've nothing to worry about, until you see a policeman."

Thirty years have passed. As I am writing this, the streets are brightly lit in East Europe's capitals once again. Along with the bright lights comes individual enterprise; along with individual enterprise comes crime. My companion would be less safe walking in Budapest's crowded and well-illuminated shopping districts today than she was in the dark and deserted Grand Boulevard thirty years ago. She would be even less safe in Moscow, where the overall squalor of a Marxist tyranny has been replaced by the moral squalor of a criminal oligarchy. For better? For worse? This may be a matter of taste, just as détente with the Evil Empire was a matter of taste, but I think being less safe in Moscow is a definite improvement. It is better to be frightened of muggers than to be frightened of policemen.

3. THINKING IN THE DARK

My earliest tale of détente actually predates détente, usually viewed as the period between 1972 and 1975, after which it matured into the era of the baneful Helsinki Accords. But the spirit of accommodation was already evident in the mid-1960s, and it became especially acute during the Prague Spring of 1968, when the illusion of "Communism with a human face" was at its zenith. This fantasy persisted in the West even after the "velvet revolution" of Czechoslovakia's reformers had been unceremoniously crushed by the tanks of the Warsaw Pact, and Alexander Dubcek was sent to Moscow in handcuffs. As the Beatles were releasing their white album, including "Revolution," which became a kind of battle hymn among the young intellectuals of Prague, the cant among Western pundits centred on the fundamental difference between the hard-line "Stalinist" Communism of the old Kremlin and the soft, enlightened, contemporary Communism of Stalin's successors.

It was not surprising to me that Western pundits held this view. After all, they persistently got everything wrong. There was no reason why they should not get wrong the nature of Leonid Brezhnev's Kremlin as well, even while Czech patriots were immolating themselves in protest.[5] What did surprise me was to encounter a similar view inside the Soviet empire.

I first returned to Budapest for a visit in the summer of 1969. Thirteen years had passed since the uprising. I felt safe enough; I was a Canadian citizen, and earlier the Communist state had declared an amnesty for ex-Hungarians who left illegally in 1956 and had become foreign nationals. The Communists' reason for the amnesty was their need for hard currency; my reason for the visit was a desire to see my parents, coupled with general curiosity and a modicum of homesickness. My father was eighty-six by then, and even my mother was turning sixty-four. I was also eager to see what had happened to some old friends.

One friend I met on the fourth or fifth day of my trip was a theatre director by the name of Robert Földeák. In 1955 he and I had spent a year together at a provincial theatre in western Hungary, sharing not only a room for a while, but literally a bed. Lodgings were almost impossible to find, and we were grateful for the unheated room with a single bed, a single chair, a washstand, and a basin of water, usually crusted with ice by morning. I was twenty at the time, and Robert was around twenty-seven.

Földeák stayed in Hungary after the uprising, despite the fact that his mother was living in New York. He was no fan of the regime, but he had a child, an actress wife, and probably no confidence in his ability to start from scratch in the competitive world of show business in a foreign language. There were many people who submitted to living with the Communists, and with the Nazis before them, for the same reason.

He suggested a late lunch at the Hotel Royal on Nagykörút, the Grand Boulevard of Budapest. There were few guests left by the time we were seated in the cavernous dining room, and when we finished our meal we were virtually alone. I sensed that Földeák wanted to say something to me, to explain why he elected to stay in Budapest, to justify his choice—not that it needed any justification. My choice to leave needed no justification either; people did what they did. But Földeák wanted to make sure I understood why he had made the right decision.

He looked around the empty room and lowered his voice. "I want you to understand something," he said to me. "This country is not like the country you left thirteen years ago."

Földeák moved closer, looked around again, and lowered his voice even further. "Stalin is gone," he said. "Things are different today," he whispered, casting an anxious glance over his shoulder. "Today, this is a free country," he continued after a pause, checking out a distant waiter. Then, almost inaudibly: "You can say whatever you like."

I thanked him and called for the bill. Two days later I was back on the train, bound for Vienna.

45

ON SEEING THE LIGHT TOO SOON

*Ages are no more infallible than individuals; every age
having held many opinions which subsequent ages have deemed
not only false but absurd; and it is certain that many opinions, now
general, will be rejected by future ages, as it is that many,
once general, are rejected by the present.*
—JOHN STUART MILL

"IT IS A GREAT ADVANTAGE FOR A system of philosophy to be substantially true," said George Santayana. It is an advantage that Marxism has never had. Nevertheless, it became the calling card of the literati in the twentieth century. "The survival of the Communist idea," remarked the French historian François Furet, "indicates the depths of its roots and its seemingly limitless capacity to survive experience."[6]

This did not mean that one had to be a card-carrying Communist throughout the twentieth century to keep one's intellectual credentials or to safeguard one's reputation as a caring human being. One did not even have to be a sympathizer with, or an apologist for, Communism. But being an *anti*-anti-Communist, as it was often called, became all but a *sine qua non* in the polite society of scholarly and media circles.

Insistence on this requirement waxed and waned at various times in America and Europe between 1917 and 1991, i.e., the rise and the fall of the Soviet Union. In America, for instance, it waned for a few years after the Molotov-Ribbentrop pact, waxed after Hitler invaded Russia, waned during the McCarthy era, then waxed again after the 1957 launch of *Sputnik I*. After that it simply persisted until the end of the Vietnam War, or almost until the end of the Carter presidency. The difference between the various periods was a matter of degree rather than a matter of kind, because some "understanding" for Communists and fellow-travellers was always *de rigueur* among opinion makers. It was part of the climate. "As early as 1934 or 1935 it was considered eccentric in literary circles not to be more or less 'left,'" wrote George Orwell in his 1940 collection of essays, *Inside the Whale*.

The habit of mind to view Communism in this light became ingrained even among those unaffected by it. The eminent American journalist Henry Grunwald, editor-in-chief of *Time* magazine during the 1980s, looking back at his formative years decades later felt compelled to explain, almost apologetically, why he had *not* been a Communist sympathizer. "So why was I not drawn to Communism and never had been?" he asks in his splendid autobiography, *One Man's America*. "I had often wondered about that. Wasn't it a character flaw not to go through a radical phase?"

Grunwald has no trouble answering the question in his book, but what illustrates the syndrome is that he finds it necessary to raise it. After all, asking such a question comes close to doubting one's character for never having been attracted to mass murder. It is absurd. Substitute "Nazism" for "Communism" and Grunwald's query becomes nonsensical. No American journalist would suspect himself of a character flaw for not having gone through a radical *Nazi* phase.

To view a lack of sympathy for Communism as a possible character flaw, in America as well as in Europe, affected mainly individuals of above-average learning, intellect, and moral preoccupation (or conceit). Ordinary people had less trouble seeing the similarity between various totalitarian systems of repression. The clerisy were more easily confused. Certain errors require high IQs.

There was another factor, which I came to think of as "the syndrome of the Communist uncle." While few intellectuals had Fascist or Nazi relatives, almost every intellectual—certainly almost every Jewish intellectual—had a Communist uncle or cousin. As often as not, they were kindly and accomplished people. They were certainly not ogres, which made it difficult to think of their creed as monstrous. It is a common misconception that monstrous creeds attract monstrous followers. One wishes that it were so, for it would make monstrous creeds easier to identify. But it is not so; not by a long chalk.

My own Communist cousin, for instance, was a highly accomplished person, respected in the literary community. A 1987 article described him, posthumously, as "one of the most cultivated book publishers in America."[7] The son of a great-uncle on my father's side, Ben Huebsch emigrated to the United States long before I was born. As one of the founders of Viking Press in New York, Cousin Ben became the publisher of such renowned authors (among others) as Stefan Zweig, Leon Feuchtwanger, Patrick White, and Saul Bellow. (It was a matter of pride for my father that Zweig spoke highly of Ben in his autobiography, *The World of Yesterday*.[8])

Like many Jewish men of letters in those years—and even many non-Jewish men of letters—my cousin was on the political left. He flirted with Communism, whether or not he had gone all the way. I should really describe him as an *alleged* Communist, because there was a continuing dispute about the matter that in 2000 spilled over into a correspondence in *The Journal of American History*. According to Sam Tanenhaus, the biographer of Whittaker Chambers, it always puzzled the novelist Lionel Trilling why his publisher, Viking, did not reissue Trilling's 1947 novel, *The Middle of the Journey*, during the Whittaker Chambers–Alger Hiss spy scandal of 1948–49, when it would have made some business sense to do so. "Since the book bore many intriguing parallels to the Hiss Case, it was likely to excite fresh interest," wrote Tanenhaus in a footnote, then continued, "Unbeknownst to Trilling, Viking's publisher, Ben Huebsch, was a

Communist and had quietly offered his services to the Hiss defense."

This footnote was cited by the noted essayist and critic Hilton Kramer in his 1999 book, *The Twilight of the Intellectuals,* for which he was taken to task by Michael Wreszin, a respected academic who reviewed Kramer's book for *The Journal.* Wreszin thought that describing Cousin Ben as a Communist amounted to "careless and uninformed name calling...symptomatic of the wild charges so easily made by cold warriors."

I cannot settle the dispute and, frankly, it is a matter of indifference to me whether Cousin Ben's surreptitious necking with the Red Harlot proceeded to full intercourse or not. But the mere possibility that it might have done so turned fellow-travelling into a family matter. My cousin's story illustrated why it became debatable in intellectual, especially Jewish intellectual, circles which was the greater character flaw: to be a Communist or "not to go through a radical phase."

Like other Jewish families, we also had relatives on the opposite side of the political divide. Not Nazis, obviously—as totalitarians, they would have been on the same side, anyway—but firm anti-Communists. Their problem turned out to be that they saw the light too soon.

One such cousin, a Toronto businessman named Paul ("Pali") Rigor, was about twenty-five years my senior. It was he who manufactured the family's false papers in Budapest, the documents that allowed us to go into hiding and survive the Nazis. He was well-read and quick-witted, but a man of affairs, not an intellectual. Born in what was then the Slovak region of the Austro-Hungarian monarchy, he emigrated to Canada soon after World War II. One day in the early 1970s I saw him muttering indignantly behind the counter of his pastry shop, holding a copy of *Time* magazine in his hand.

"What's the matter?" I asked him.

"Look at this idiot," he said, thrusting the magazine at me. The issue carried an interview with an ex-minister in Czechoslovakian premier Oldrich Cernik's cabinet: a disenchanted former Communist who escaped from Prague after Warsaw Pact forces crushed Alexander Dubcek's "reform-Communists" in August 1968.

"See? He's trying to convince this American journalist that

"Who is being interviewed by Time, *him or me?" My prescient cousin Paul Rigor walks with my son Alex in Toronto in 1976.*

Communism doesn't work," my cousin said. "When he was at school with me in Bratislava in 1931, I was trying to convince *him*. He wouldn't believe me."

"Why are you upset?" I asked. "You turned out to be right."

"That's the point," my cousin said resentfully. "*I* saw it forty years ago. *I* saw it in 1931. Yet who is being interviewed by *Time,* him or me?"

I could see why this would upset my cousin, but I could not resist needling him. "Cousin," I said, "only a very stupid person could have seen this as far back as 1931."

My cruel wisecrack was at best a half-truth. Some brilliant people saw the nature of Communism quite clearly by 1931; some had probably seen it as soon as they read The Communist Manifesto in 1847. But the fact remained that after the Bolsheviks came to power in Russia, it was more usual for Communism to be assessed realistically—and, in consequence, resisted and opposed—by ordinary people of conventional minds than by clever people of erudition and distinction. Whether or not religion was the opiate of the masses, as Marx had it, in the twentieth century Marxism took over as the opiate of the intellectuals. Edmund Wilson pointed this out during the Carter era[9] but an earlier variation by Clare Boothe Luce expressed the same idea with even more vigour. "Communism is the opiate of the intellectuals," she was quoted in *Newsweek* magazine. "[It has] no cure except as a guillotine might be called a cure for dandruff."[10]

46

IN DEFENCE OF ILLITERACY

*No amount of learning can cure stupidity, and formal
education positively fortifies it.*
—STEPHEN VIZINCZEY

IN THE NOT TOO DISTANT PAST, people who were illiterate could neither read
nor write. These days they can, with disastrous results for the culture.

Illiterates are consumers, like everyone else. If they are able to read,
they create a demand for printed matter. Having enough leisure time and
disposable income for disc drives and wall space, they create a demand for
art and music. The market serves them, naturally, as it serves all consumers,
which causes Gresham's law to kick in. The coinage of illiterate taste does
to art what low-grade coinage does to currency. Bad art drives out good
art, as surely as bad money drives out good money in Sir Thomas
Gresham's famous formulation. As Arthur Koestler observed in *The Lotus
and the Robot,* "We live in a state of cultural osmosis where influences per-
colate across the porous frontiers, native traditions wane, and the
movement toward a uniform, mechanized, stereotyped culture-pattern
becomes irresistible.... What makes the emerging patterns so vulgar is the
emergence of the underprivileged class with their underdeveloped tastes as
consumers of mass-culture."[11]

Examples abound. Book chains stock the latest bestsellers; they cannot
spare shelf space for literary works with slow turnovers. A novel that does
not get on the bestseller list is likely to go out of print within a year.
Populists often dumb down works of art by various devices, such as changing the original characters into contemporary ones or by reducing poetic
language into prose. Sometimes they rearrange music and superimpose a
contemporary beat on it. They create "fusions" of classical music and jazz;
they recruit opera singers to perform popular tunes. What this does is to

diminish the enjoyment of poetry or opera for those who like poetry or opera, in order to enhance the enjoyment of those who have no taste for poetry or opera in the first place. It is a puzzle why some think that striking false notes will somehow benefit people with tin ears, but populists swear by it. Reducing soaring spirits into plodding spirits is the populists' stock-in-trade, as exemplified by various contemporary translations of the King James Bible.

My father referred to this as putting whipped cream on a hamburger: making sure that the meal was ruined for those who liked beef as well as for those who preferred sweets.

The meal was certainly ruined for the renowned conductor, Otto Klemperer, when friends took him to a supper club after one of his Budapest concerts, shortly before the Communists came to power. The caviar was first-rate, but the entertainer happened to be a *diseuse* named Anny Kapitany, the rage of the town at the time, rendering American-style ballads in a particularly deep and throaty voice.

Klemperer's musical tastes were not catholic. He had just been conducting Schubert's Symphony no. 8 in B Minor, the "Unfinished," at the Conservatory of Music. When the first sounds emerged from Anny's larynx, he promptly rose from the table.

"I cannot cope with a double bass during a meal," he remarked on his way out, not bothering to speak *sotto voce*.

Anny was a star herself and used to having the last word. "But you still have to pay your bill," she shouted after the departing representative of high culture, to the amusement of the irreverent Budapest audience.

The *diseuse*'s parting shot went to the heart of the matter. The question of who pays the bill has always been central to any discussion of elite versus popular art. Anny's unrefined vocal chords may have sounded like a death rattle (according to my father), but her music was paying its own way in the supper club, while Schubert's sublime symphony could not have been performed in a concert hall without a subsidy of some sort.

There is a perennial dispute between elitists and populists, and it takes many forms. Elitists often say that populists lack "integrity," that they are "market-driven," but things are not that simple. Taking the low road does not invariably pay, and taking the high road does not invariably lead to bankruptcy. It is not enough to be down-market; one also needs to be good. Quality, fashion, packaging, and promotion influence success and failure in both elite and popular culture. It is just that people with a taste for low culture outnumber people with a taste for high culture by definition. Numbers are inexorable, and when elitists compete with populists in the same market for the same consumer dollar, elitists must lose. "I readily concede that here and there I am probably hard to read," wrote Saul Bellow, "and I am likely to become harder as the illiteracy of the public increases."[12]

In the days when socio-economic walls separated high culture from low culture, this friction was not so acute. The upper or upper-middle classes went to their art galleries and theatres, and common people went bowling or gawked at freak shows at the fair. Music halls did not feel compelled to accommodate Maestro Klemperer's taste, and admirers of vulgar soubrettes felt no obligation to attend Schubert concerts. Whatever was wrong with cultural apartheid, it promoted purity.

But with the dawn of American-style democracy, the definition of a "book" or a "ballet" needed to be filtered through the consciousness of people who were not inclined to read books or go to ballets in the first place. This was when the fundamental changes occurred. To continue functioning in this environment, art galleries and operas had to please people who did not much *like* art galleries and operas. At this point elitists retreated into angry obscurity, while populists embraced corruption with missionary zeal. The mercury of verbal, visual, and aural literacy stopped rising. There were no successors to Beethoven and Tolstoy. Western art, music, and literature peaked at various points during the nineteenth century, then went into gradual decline.

The worst effect of compulsory universal education was that it educated people beyond their intellectual means. It taught illiterates to read and write, without making them remotely literate.[13] It created cultural consumers without culture. Adding purchasing power to their tastes became the hallmark of the American century.

In periods where illiterates were incapable of reading and writing—that is, in most periods—literature remained free of their baneful influence. In civilizations where illiterates had negligible leisure time and disposable income, art and music flourished as well. Whatever benefits short work-weeks, high wages, and universal education conferred on humanity (and they did bring benefits galore), trading the classes for the masses did nothing for arts and letters. Mass cultures replaced gems with hogwash—not surprisingly perhaps, as casting pearls before swine serves neither an aesthetic nor a nutritional purpose.

6

THE SHRIMP LEARNS
TO WHISTLE

47

THE FALL OF THE

EVIL EMPIRE

A state without the means of some change is
without the means of its conservation.
—EDMUND BURKE

"THOSE WHO WAIT FOR [the Soviet Union to reject Communism] must wait until a shrimp learns to whistle," said Soviet Premier Nikita Khrushchev on September 17, 1955.

A little more than thirty-six years later, on December 31, 1991, the shrimp began to whistle. It whistled loud and clear while the red flag with the hammer and sickle was lowered from the flagpole of the Kremlin for the last time. To many people's surprise, the shrimp proved to be quite musical. It whistled with great feeling and very melodiously.

Actually the shrimp started making whistling noises earlier—for instance, on August 23, 1991, when the Communist hardliners' coup against President Mikhail Gorbachev collapsed; or on the next day, when Gorbachev suspended the Communist Party; or on September 5, 1991, when Gorbachev persuaded the All-Soviet Congress to surrender power; or on the next day, when Gorbachev recognized the independence of the Baltic republics; and then again on December 8, 1991, when Gorbachev and Boris Yeltsin signed the Commonwealth of Independent States into being, ending all attempts to preserve the USSR.

Arguably the shrimp had begun to whistle earlier still. Possibly it first whistled within about a year of Khrushchev's original remark, when the Hungarians marched on the offices of Radio Budapest on October 23, 1956.

(I happened to be standing in the street outside Radio Budapest that evening, and I thought I heard the sound of a whistling shrimp quite distinctly.) Or on the night of August 20, 1968, when the Soviets felt the need to invade Czechoslovakia because they discerned in the feeble protests voiced by the "reform-Communist" Alexander Dubcek the sound of a whistling shrimp.

The matter is far from settled. As the twenty-first century begins, the shrimp is still whistling. Whether it will hang on to its new-found skill, only time will tell.

48

THE CODE CLERK AND THE SENATOR:

A COLD WAR TALE

SVETLANA'S GARDEN

THE GARDEN PARTY IN THE EARLY FALL OF 1995 could have been a church social or a meeting of an extended clan. There was plenty of cold beer, along with plastic glasses of fruit punch for the children. The focus of the gathering was a woman in her early seventies, with unusually blue and mischievous eyes, offering plates of food, kissing new arrivals and departing guests on the cheek, with a one-year-old girl, her clone in miniature, clutching at her skirt.

The guests were family and friends, men and women of all ages, casually dressed, nibbling crackers, taking snapshots of each other and playing with the toddlers. Nothing in the bucolic scene hinted at historic distinction or international intrigue. Just salt-of-the-earth folk getting together to honour some occasion in a local grandmother's life.

This, in fact, was what many at the party assumed. They had just dropped by to say hello to their neighbour, a Russian lady, who along with her late husband had been living next door to them for the past forty-odd years. The occasion, as they understood it, was her fiftieth anniversary in Canada. They would have been astounded by some of the telegrams in a white envelope lying on a table next to the rest of the anniversary gifts.

But the telegrams were shown only to family members and a few selected guests. One was from Conrad Black, another from William F. Buckley, Jr., and a third—handwritten, in Russian—from Nathan (Anatoli) Shcharansky.[1]

A fourth telegram read, in part, "When you and your husband crossed over to freedom, you began the long process that led to the eventual collapse of the Soviet Union. His revelation helped the West to face up to the reality of communist subversion and tyranny. Those of us who later fought the battle for freedom to its climax in 1989 and 1991 were greatly in his debt—and in yours." It was signed Margaret Thatcher.

Britain's former prime minister must have sealed the envelope herself because there was a small packet of artificial sugar in it. Lady Thatcher happened to be on a diet at the time.

THE COLD WAR

The Cold War began on a Wednesday, September 5, 1945, a few minutes after 8 p.m. The event was probably observed by several Canadian passersby, although no one would have paid much attention to a young, slight, nondescript man closing the door of an embassy building on Charlotte Street and walking out into the humid Ottawa evening.

When a twenty-six-year-old code clerk named Igor Gouzenko emerged from the Soviet Embassy he was delivering what he thought was a simple message. It was that Canada and her allies, having just concluded a victorious war, were at war once again. They were at war with their former Soviet partners, whether they realized it or not.

Gouzenko understood that for many this might sound like a far-fetched suggestion. He did not expect people to take his word for it. He carried with him a number of documents as proof.

During August 1945, while the atomic bombs were exploding over Hiroshima and Nagasaki, Gouzenko had been discussing his defection with his wife, Svetlana, in their small apartment on Somerset Street. Their final decision was prompted by two factors. A minor one was Igor's attraction to Canada, the country where his son was born and where Svetlana was now expecting another child. The major one was his belief that they might not survive their recall to Moscow.

"More than half a century ago."
Svetlana Gouzenko in Ontario, circa 1948.

As a cipher clerk, Gouzenko knew a great deal about a Soviet spy ring operating through the office of GRU (military intelligence) Colonel Nikolai Zabotin. The aim of Zabotin's spy ring was to secure atomic secrets. While being privy to such information might lead to a brilliant career in the Soviet apparat, it might also, Gouzenko suspected, lead to the Gulag.

Having made his decision, Gouzenko took 109 documents from the Soviet Embassy and hid them under his shirt. The same night he went to the editorial offices of the *Ottawa Journal,* thinking that it would be safer to report his defection to the newspapers than to the police. He was wrong. The puzzled night city editor of the *Journal,* Chester Frowde, turned him away.

For two harrowing days, with his pregnant wife and their two-year-old son in tow, Gouzenko tried to convince incredulous Canadian journalists and Ministry of Justice officials that he was worthy of a hearing. Having failed, the family sought refuge with a neighbour, R.C.A.F. Sergeant Harold Main. By then Soviet agents were breaking down their apartment door. In the end it was this act of the Soviets that prompted Sergeant Main to call the police.

After five months of debriefing and the hearings of the Kellock-Taschereau Royal Commission of 1946, Gouzenko's documents led to the conviction of eleven Canadians and Britons. They included a sitting member of Parliament, Fred Rose, the atomic-energy scientist Allan Nunn May, and the organizing secretary of Canada's Communist Party, Sam Carr. In America his evidence led the FBI to the trail of such figures of atomic espionage as Klaus Fuchs, Harry Gold, and Julius and Ethel Rosenberg. Gouzenko's revelations heralded the start of the Cold War, a process that ended in the collapse of the Soviet empire forty-five years later.

The Gouzenkos made a choice and paid a price. Family members left behind in the Soviet Union perished under interrogation or in labour camps. In Canada—after a brief period of being lionized in the early 1950s—Gouzenko suffered the usual fate of Cassandras, aggravated by the changing climate during the Vietnam era. Soon his name was mentioned only in terms of resentment and denigration. Choosing the West also entailed a lifetime of clandestine existence. Svetlana and her family lived under assumed names for the rest of their lives. As part of the security precautions, the children were told nothing about their backgrounds and were not allowed to learn any Russian.

The balance sheet did have another side. By the time of Svetlana's garden party in 1995, the Gouzenkos had produced eight children, sixteen grandchildren, and six great-grandchildren—perhaps to replace the family lost in the camps of Stalin and his successors. Their heritage could not be replaced, though. None of Gouzenko's children could read Shcharansky's Russian-language telegram.

Gouzenko himself did not expect to survive for more than five years. Media people of leftist sympathies talked him into using his trademark security measure—a Klansman-type hood, worn at rare TV interviews—then used it to ridicule and discredit him. Though he died of natural causes in 1982, it was not because the Kremlin forgave his defection. The last known "sleeper" sent to assassinate him was activated after nearly twenty years. The agent had second thoughts and gave himself up to the Royal Canadian Mounted Police instead.

TWO SCOOPS

As it turned out, Gouzenko's life in Canada was book-ended by two scoops. It began with the *Ottawa Journal* refusing the scoop of his defection. The last scoop came when the Canadian journalist Peter

Worthington, who had kept in touch with Gouzenko to the end, encountered Barbara Amiel, then associate editor of the *Toronto Sun*, in downtown Toronto. It was just hours after Gouzenko's death. His heart failure, though sudden, was not entirely unexpected; Gouzenko had suffered from diabetes and had lost his sight during the last years of his life.

"Igor Gouzenko just died," Worthington said to Amiel as they stood next to each other on a street corner, waiting for the light to change. Amiel asked no further questions. She was in a rush, being late for an interview with the radio talk show host, Andy Barrie. Assuming that *Sun* editor Worthington's scoop had already made the wire services, Amiel mentioned it during her interview on the air. This made a rather obscure radio show the first news outlet in the world to report Gouzenko's death. As associate editor of the *Sun*, Amiel managed to scoop her own paper. The echo was predictable. Barbara's nickname "Scoop Amiel" persisted in press circles long after the episode that gave rise to it was forgotten.

THE 110TH DOCUMENT

History records that Gouzenko took 109 documents from the Soviet Embassy. According to Svetlana,[2] there was an additional piece of paper that never saw the light of day for the following reason:

Spymaster Colonel Zabotin was a handsome man. Whether or not his masculine appeal was overrated (Svetlana believed that it was), he looked good enough in his Red Army colonel's uniform to catch the eye of an Ottawa society lady at an embassy reception. Ostensibly Zabotin was a military attaché, a legitimate diplomat, and the society lady saw nothing wrong with inviting him to lunch.

Zabotin accepted, partly because as spymaster it was his business to cultivate well-connected Canadians, and partly because he needed some social advice. He was an educated man, but not sufficiently familiar with Western customs. He suspected that some of his staff might appear boorish to Canadians. A certain Major Romanov in particular was prone to social blunders. Zabotin wanted to find out about proper Ottawa etiquette before his key people committed any more faux pas.

So he said yes to the lady, but then became a bit concerned. "What should I do at lunch?" he asked Major Sokolov, another agent attached to the Soviet Commercial Counsellor.

"Act like a man," was Sokolov's advice.

Unfortunately for Zabotin the conversation was conducted within earshot of Mrs. Zabotin, who was noted for her jealous temperament. She employed unmistakable terms to acquaint her husband with her views on the matter, and did so in a voice loud enough to shake the walls of the embassy. "I hope," Gouzenko said to his wife later, "that if I ever have to do something like Zabotin in the line of duty, you won't put me through this."

In spite of Mrs. Zabotin's views, the lunch proceeded as scheduled. Apparently Zabotin acted like a man, because on the fateful evening of September 5, 1945, while gathering up documents in the cipher room, Gouzenko came upon a handwritten note on the society lady's letterhead. It was an appreciative and rather indiscreet note, and Gouzenko put it under his shirt along with the rest of the papers.

Three days later, at Gouzenko's initial debriefing, the documents were sorted into two separate piles by RCMP Assistant Commissioner Charles Rivett-Cornac. Those in Russian were taken by a Czech-speaking RCMP agent named Leopold into another room, while Rivett-Cornac, who spoke no Slavic languages, looked over the ones written in English. Most were photographic copies of top secret papers stolen by Zabotin's Canadian recruits, such as Durnford Smith and Edward Mazerall, from the National Research Council.

When Rivett-Cornac came to the society lady's note he went red in the face. The veins stood out on his neck as he looked at Gouzenko in silence.

"Was she an agent, too?" he asked finally.

"No, no," Gouzenko replied. "No, she was just . . . well, you know."

"I see," said the assistant commissioner. He paused, then put the hand-written note in the ashtray and shook some embers on it from his pipe. By the time Leopold came back into the room there was only a small pile of ashes. "Count those documents again," Rivett-Cornac said to Leopold. "I make it a total of 109."

Svetlana said that the society lady was a personal friend of Prime Minister Mackenzie King. Out of respect for what she called a gentleman's agreement between Gouzenko and Rivett-Cornac, she would not reveal her name.

There is another footnote to Colonel Zabotin's story, equally unrecorded, but much more doleful. It is known that after Gouzenko's defection Zabotin was recalled to Moscow and, despite his considerable achievements in gathering vital intelligence for the Kremlin, either ended up in the Gulag or (according to some sources) was executed in transit.

What is not known, however, is that on September 7, 1945, Zabotin put out feelers to his Canadian contacts in order to explore the possibility of asylum in this country. He knew only too well that Moscow would blame him for Gouzenko's defection. He obeyed Moscow's recall only after Canada turned him down—whether because of mistrust, a misunderstanding, or because our authorities felt overwhelmed by a sudden influx of Soviet defectors. This, at least, is what Svetlana believed. After all, Mackenzie King's government could not even decide what to do about the Gouzenkos and for a brief period actually considered returning them.

SIC TRANSIT

In the early fall of 2001, fifty-six years after the Cold War began and ten years after it ended, Svetlana Gouzenko lay on her deathbed in a Mississauga hospital. She had sent word shortly after her admission that she wanted to see me so that she might impart the sum of her observations, the final words of her legacy. Her eldest daughter, Evy, would be at hand to video-record the conversation. It was to be a monologue rather than an interview because Svetlana's hearing was too far gone to respond to questions. The shrewd, strong-willed, fatalistic woman retained only a modicum of coherence by then. She seemed obsessed by Jews, talking about them with a mixture of admiration and suspicion, though without making any discernible point. She appeared to believe that Stalin himself was a Jew, which had been carefully hidden from everyone, but was at the root of the Soviet leader's fabled anti-Semitism. As I gradually tuned out of what seemed to me a flight of paranoid fancy, a curiously Russian kind of conspiracy theory, I marvelled at the irony of people at the centre of genuine, tangible, even epic conspiracies having the emotional need to construct a dreamlike layer of conspiracy fiction, a substitute history, to cover a reality that was either too mundane or, perhaps, too haphazard. After all, if Stalin had been a Jew, it would tie up all sorts of loose ends into a neat package, especially for visceral, albeit subconscious, anti-Semites.

Svetlana's monologue was interrupted by a black Labrador named Daisy. My wife, Maya, who is blind, came along to the Mississauga hospital accompanied by her guide dog. While Svetlana continued talking about Stalin's secret Jewishness with growing agitation, Daisy kept edging closer to her bed. Trained for pet therapy and accustomed to hospital visits, Daisy considered it her function to calm patients by inviting them to pet her. Suddenly, she leapt on Svetlana's bed, wagging her tail, thrusting her muzzle into her hand, disrupting the historic monologue.

Svetlana lay back on her pillow, exhausted. She turned to the window to look at the grey, roiling, foam-speckled waters of Lake Ontario. This was what she would have seen day after day from her window at Camp X, the Royal Canadian Mounted Police's wartime training camp for agents and infiltrators, to which she and her husband were taken in great secrecy after their defection more than half a century ago.

The association entered my mind; I had no way of knowing if it had entered hers. A few days later she was dead. She passed away in the evening of September 4, 2001, one day short of fifty-six years after helping her husband to trigger, or at least herald, the Cold War.

THE LAST LAUGH

It was a year after Svetlana's death that Peter Worthington and I drove to the Springcreek Cemetery in Mississauga. Canada's government decided to proclaim the Gouzenko defection an official "historic event" and commemorate it by unveiling a plaque at Igor's and Svetlana's gravesite. Worthington, one-time Moscow correspondent of the *Toronto Telegram*, remained perhaps the only Canadian journalist to retain Gouzenko's trust. He was to say a few words at the ceremony, while I was to read a brief note from Conrad Black, who could not attend. The speaker on behalf of the Canadian government was going to be Senator Laurier LaPierre.

LaPierre, who had been a broadcaster, author, and academic before his appointment to the Senate by the Liberal government of Jean Chrétien, was a left-leaning intellectual. His sinistral stance, a position cultivated by many of Canada's literati, only enhanced his reputation as a gifted and gutsy personality. But while lionized in scholarly and journalistic circles, left-leaning intellectuals stood for everything Gouzenko held in contempt. The cipher clerk would have viewed them as epitomes of Lenin's "useful idiots": dupes of moral equivalence, if not fellow travellers. He would have despised Helsinki-acolytes as moral Rip Van Winkles, comatose in the insensate slumber of Western intellectuals, the very media-types Gouzenko had tried, in vain, to arouse from their quasi-Marxist dreams. It was the senator's ideological nest-mates (though not LaPierre personally) who flocked to mock Gouzenko, belittle his message, ascribe mental instability or base financial motives to his sacrifice, spread slanderous stories about his aloholism or avarice, and trick him into adopting the image of the comic-opera defector with a bag over his head. Now, as if to add insult to injury, Canada's government dispatched a bird of this feather to perch at Gouzenko's gravestone.

When LaPierre began speaking, I caught myself waiting for some sign to signify the turbulence of the late cipher clerk's soul—perhaps the ground to heave as he was turning in his grave. But there was nothing, only the occasional chirp of a nearby cicada and the French lilt of LaPierre's well-modulated voice.

Then another thought entered my mind. I wondered who was having the last laugh. Was it Canada's left-liberal utopians, managing to mock Cassandra even in death? Or was it Gouzenko, forcing his very detractors to pay homage to his memory?

There was another ceremony in 2003 when the City of Ottawa unveiled its own plaque "to commemorate Igor and Svetlana Gouzenko in recognition of their historic flight to freedom in 1945." I could not bring myself to attend. The plaque is in Dundonald Park, though, on the corner of Somerset Street. That was where Igor and Svetlana debated, in the stifling August heat of their small apartment, whether or not to launch the Cold War.

49

THE YELLOW BRICK ROAD TO HELL

LIBERAL APOLOGISTS FOR COMMUNISM ought to have been mindful of the French mathematician and philosopher Blaise Pascal's dictum "Men never do evil so fully and cheerfully as when we do it out of conscience." He also said, "Man is neither angel nor brute, and the pity of it is that he who wants to play the angel acts the brute."[3]

Pascal made these observations in the seventeenth century, but no one demonstrated them as clearly as V.I. Lenin and his disciples did about 250 years later. The complacent delusions of altruistic evil-doers preceded the Soviet empire, and survived it as well. "I am a Communist because I believe that the Communist idea is a state form of Christianity," said a Byelorussian deputy named Alexander Zhuravlyov in 1991, as quoted by the *Observer*.[4] Was it pathologically smug for Zhuravlyov to equate his socio-political notions with the Sermon on the Mount? If it was, he was not alone. "Communism, my friend, is more than Marxism, just as Catholicism...is more than the Roman Curia. There is a *mystique* as well as a *politique*....Catholics and Communists have committed great crimes, but at least they have not stood aside, like an established society, and been indifferent. I would rather have blood on my hands than water like Pilate," proclaims Dr. Magiot in Graham Greene's *The Comedians*. Greene himself probably endorsed his character's sentiment, considering that in his introduction to the British traitor Kim Philby's autobiography he wrote: "He was serving a cause and not himself, so my old liking for him comes back."[5]

How much worse was the cause Philby served (Communism) than the system it replaced in Russia (Czarism), keeping in mind that the semi-feudal monarchy of the Romanov Czars was itself a cruel, corrupt, repressive, and inefficient system? I feel comfortable putting a numerical value on it: Communism was 71.4 times worse. The population of forced labour camps serves as a cogent general measurement. In 1916, just before the Revolution, the number of forced labourers in Czarist Russia, called *katorga* convicts, was 28,600 souls. The annual average of *katorga* inmates in the Soviet Gulag became two million. When it came to inhumanity, Lenin and Stalin outperformed Czar Nicholas II by a factor of 70+.[6]

"A faith is something you die for, a doctrine is something you kill for. There is all the difference in the world." The British Labour politician Tony Benn made this remark on a television broadcast in 1989.[7] By this definition, is Communism a doctrine or a faith? The accurate answer is not very helpful, as Communism has been a faith for some and a doctrine for others, but for many it has been both a faith and a doctrine. They have killed as well as died for it.

I heard more than one true-believing Western Marxist remark that if the Saviour were alive today, he would be a Communist. One specifically ventured that Jesus would support Stalin—but that was before Soviet leader Nikita Khrushchev first spoke of Stalin's crimes in his "secret" speech to the 20th Congress of the Communist Party in 1956.

50

THE SEXINESS OF THE VANQUISHED

"WHY ARE RUSSIAN WOMEN SO BEAUTIFUL?" asked Barbara Amiel. She was phoning from St. Petersburg in the late summer of 2000, on her first visit to Russia since the fall of Communism. Given that Russia was still an economic basket case, Amiel expected Russian women to look as drab and dismal as she found them on her previous visits. Instead, she was surprised to discover that they often looked unexpectedly radiant.

The women of defeated nations flower. This could be seen as readily in Germany after World War II as in Russia after the collapse of the Soviet empire. It was as if women sensed that their men were benumbed, wounded, impotent, or dead, and their best chance for survival was exerting an effort to entice the conqueror, and the world at large. "The GIs received a lot of attention from the girls," recalled a Polish Holocaust survivor in Germany at the end of the war. "The natives were so friendly that the men wondered why it had taken so long to win the war."[8]

The reaction seems almost physiological. Women of defeated nations appear to develop feminine charms the way animals grow fur in the winter. France noted the syndrome, too, after the Germans marched into Paris. The Austrian writer Stefan Zweig remarked on the "pathetic eroticism" of German women following World War I. "To be sixteen and still under suspicion of virginity would have been considered a disgrace in any school in Berlin at that time," Zweig wrote in his autobiography.[9] Women also blossomed in Japan and Korea following their respective wars, resulting in an infusion of Oriental brides in the United States. By the 1990s the latest communication technology came into play, and the World Wide Web was reverberating with pictures from unexpectedly comely Russian girls offering themselves to the world as spouses or playmates.

51

POST-SOVIET RUSSIA: FROM LENINISM TO GORCHAKOVISM

VLADIMIR PUTIN, THE EX-KGB OFFICER who succeeded Boris Yeltsin to become the second leader of post-Soviet Russia, appears highly enigmatic to Westerners. This is because Russia's president, despite his KGB past, seems no longer moved by the spirit of Marxism-Leninism, and few in the West are familiar with the spirit of Gorchakovism.

Alexander Gorchakov was a pivotal figure in Russian diplomacy in the days of Czars Alexander I, Nicholas I, and Alexander II. As Russia's foreign minister for twenty-five years, he's credited with rehabilitating his country's standing in the world in the wake of the disastrous Crimean War of 1853–1856. After Sevastopol fell to British and French expeditionary forces in 1855, Russia's stock as a world power sank almost as low as it did following the collapse of the Berlin Wall 135 years later. It took Prince Gorchakov fifteen years of cool, unhurried diplomacy to rebuild it. Working under his master, Alexander II—the "reformist" czar who emancipated Russia's serfs—Gorchakov took his country from the Peace of Paris, which closed the Black Sea to Russia's warships, to the 1871 Convention of London, which compensated Russia for its losses in the Crimean War.

This remarkable achievement was brought about by a realistic alignment of power relationships, culminating in clever Russian treaties with Germany and Persia. For his patient pursuit of realpolitik, Gorchakov has been compared with Bismarck (or with Henry Kissinger). Be that as it may, he became Putin's hero, as well as ex-prime minister Yevgeny Primakov's. A laudatory piece by Primakov on Gorchakov appeared in a 1998 issue of the Russian *Journal of International Affairs*.

When Yevgeny Primakov was still foreign minister of Russia, *Itogi* magazine's Alexander Golts asked him how the Kremlin's struggles of the moment affected Russia's foreign policy (Boris Yeltsin was fighting one of his periodic battles for political survival in 1996). As Golts reported it, Primakov replied: "Russia pursues its foreign policy not according to some considerations of the current moment, but on the basis of its historic role."

If this sounds familiar, there is a reason. Taking a long view and casting a deliberately cold eye on the alliances of the day was one of the hallmarks of nineteenth-century statecraft. It was Lord Palmerston, foreign secretary of Britain, who remarked about 150 years earlier: "England has no eternal friends, no eternal enemies, only eternal interests."

History appears to alternate between epochs of cold pragmatism and "hot," highly charged, ideological periods. The twentieth century was deeply ideological, but Russia's current leaders seem to believe that the twenty-first century will resemble the nineteenth century rather than the twentieth. Ideological divisions will count for less than realpolitik, spheres of influence, and balance of power.

A revival of communism, or any messianic ideology, is not on the Kremlin's current agenda. Domestic reform is quite in tune with the Gorchakovian tradition, as long as it is combined with building a Russia-China-India axis in Eurasia, and persuading the West—even the United

States, if possible—that its true interest lies in encouraging the development of a multi-polar world in which Russia takes her rightful place. This lies at the centre of Putin's diplomacy. Though he makes few historical allusions himself, in April 2001 his foreign minister, Igor Ivanov, conferred the A.M. Gorchakov Commemorative Medal on former prime minister Primakov.[10]

52

DEMOCRACY IS A

MICKEY MOUSE T-SHIRT

So foul a sky clears not without a storm.
—SHAKESPEARE: *King John.*

MY CBC COLLEAGUE ERICH KOCH remarked once that Germany's great misfortune after World War I was that it "never had a revolution." Although the Kaiser abdicated at the end of the war, Germany's bureaucracy, its judges, administrators, and officer corps remained in place. The nation's ruling classes were still of the *ancien régime*. German officials were steeped in the old imperial tradition and were not replaced with progressive, democratic, liberal blood under the Weimar Republic.

This is certainly what happened to Russia and the rest of the nations in the former Soviet empire following the collapse of the Soviet Union. Except for a handful of abdicating "Kaisers" at the top, such as Mikhail Gorbachev himself, post-Communist societies retained their former ruling classes largely intact.

The Hungarian poet George Faludy tells an amusing anecdote about this. Faludy had lived in exile until the fall of Communism, but visited Hungary a few times during the last years of the regime. As a British subject, he needed to have visas stamped into his passport whenever he returned to Budapest. A lady colonel with generous bosoms performed this task on the second floor of the Interior Ministry, where she sat behind an imposing desk, resplendent in her Interior Ministry (AVO) police uniform with blue and gold shoulder tabs.

After the Communist regime collapsed, Faludy continued to visit Budapest. He still required a visa in his passport, and the stamping was done in the same Interior Ministry building, on the same floor, at the same desk, by the same ample-busted lady colonel. Only one thing was different. Instead of her gold and blue shoulder tabs, she was now sporting a Mickey Mouse T-shirt.

The changing of the guard within the Soviet empire tended to result in such cosmetic or sartorial changes, and little else. There was never a question of "de-Nazifying" the lands of applied Marxism the way German society was de-Nazified after the war. Doing so would have been impractical. Nazism was in a position to appoint officials for no longer than twelve years. In contrast, Soviet power had lasted for over seventy years in the Soviet Union, and for over forty years in East Europe's "people's democracies"—in other words, for two or three generations. After Hitler's fall, Germany still had skilled and educated Germans untainted by Nazism. In 1991, Communist countries had no skilled and educated people untainted by Communism. No qualified people existed in these nations to fill leadership positions, other than graduates of the Soviet system.

Given these conditions, the consequences naturally followed. Ex-Nazis were usually repudiated after the fall of Nazism, but after the fall of Communism ex-Communists were usually not repudiated. Former United Nations secretary general Kurt Waldheim became *persona non grata* as soon as it came to light that as a young officer he may have played some role in the Nazi regime, while the world simply noted that Russia's leader, Vladimir Putin, had once been a KGB officer. Even when there were scandals, they passed virtually without comment outside the countries affected. In the summer of 2002, for instance, when it emerged that Hungary's newly elected prime minister, Peter Medgyessy, had been "agent D-209" with the rank of first lieutenant in Hungary's Communist Interior Ministry, the world's press—the same press that two years earlier went ballistic over the election of Austria's Joerg Haider—hardly took notice.[11] The irony was that, unlike Medgyessy, Haider was accused merely of being soft on Nazism; he was too young to have played any role during the Nazi era. But the media were more sensitive about a politician's possible sympathy with the wicked regimes of the far right than about his actual participation in the wicked regimes of the far left.

As a result, state autocracy atrophied in former Fascist and Nazi countries, while in former Communist countries it simply changed shirts. "It is difficult," as Faludy wrote, "to build democracies without democrats."

53

DEMOCRACY AND FREEDOM

THE RULE OF MAJORITY IS A SYMBOL for the rule of force. It is one side claiming victory, as it would in battle, because it outnumbers the other. If, say, Germany in a dispute with Denmark put the matter to a vote by the combined population of the two countries and let the majority carry the day, it would be rule by force no less than if Germany invaded Denmark.

This, incidentally, is hardly a new discovery. The American journalist Walter Lippman pointed out more than seventy-five years ago that "except in the sacred tests of democracy and in the incantations of the orators, we hardly take the trouble to pretend that the rule of the majority is not at bottom a rule of force."[12]

Majority rule is tantamount to saying, "Why suffer casualties when the outcome is inevitable? There are more of us, and if we fought, we'd defeat you. So why not accept defeat after a show of hands; it's painless and it amounts to the same thing."

There is much logic in this, making majority rule sensible and practical. But it does not make majority rule morally superior to minority rule, at least not intrinsically. We have come to think it is the method by which decisions are arrived at that determine their morality, but it is not. Decisions are moral or immoral on their merits, whether they are achieved through ballots or bullets.

Right and wrong are not synonyms for peace and violence. There are bloody rights and bloodless wrongs.

A democratic state can oppress and restrict a citizen as much as an aristocratic state. Majority rule does not guarantee freedom; in fact, it can be its mortal enemy. What few people understand about the American constitution is that, to a significant extent, it was devised to protect individual liberty from democracy.

54

LEFT AND RIGHT

AFTER THE LEFT WAS PROVEN PLAINLY and abysmally wrong by events in the twentieth century; after the dismal failure of all social, educational, and economic systems that have been based on Marxist, quasi-Marxist, Fabianist, Marcusian, Maoist, Castroite, or other collectivist and statist ideals, left-leaning academics and intellectuals were suddenly struck by an illuminating insight. They discovered that divisions of left and right had never made any sense in politics or in life—and even if they had made sense at one time, by now they have become thoroughly outmoded. Crude concepts such as right and left, left-liberal intellectuals started saying, belong to the antediluvian era of the Cold War, and can now only serve to distort or limit the way we think about human affairs in our enlightened, microchipped, and globalized times. Some recent works, such as the Canadian writer Hugh Graham's *The Vestibule of Hell*, have been largely devoted to this proposition.

It is a brave and amusing try, somewhat like attempting to blur all distinction between the gauche and the adroit to spare the feelings of southpaws. But it takes more than juggling words to make the sinistral dexterous.

55

MICROCHIPISM

The world belongs to me because I understand it.
—HONORÉ DE BALZAC

WHY DID THE SOVIET EMPIRE IMPLODE? Did it have to do with the computer age? Was it due to a quantum leap in information technology?

Americans who might say yes to such questions would probably out-number Europeans. This is because Americans give more weight to delivery systems, while Europeans give more weight to what systems deliver.

Here is an analogy. A person requires six glasses of water a day for drinking, a potful for cooking, and a basinful for washing. Naturally, it will make a difference to him whether he has to fetch his water from a distant stream or can draw it from a well in his own courtyard—or, better still, if he can have running water inside his house. It is important to recognize, though, how the difference will manifest itself.

If a person's supply of water has been adequate from a lake or a well, having a tap inside his house is unlikely to make him drink more. Even if he drinks more, it will not benefit him much. He may use more water for cooking and washing, which may benefit him somewhat, but the advantage will be at the margins. The substantial difference will be in the time and effort he saves by having a well in his yard as opposed to fetching water from a stream, or by acquiring running water inside the house as opposed to trudging to the well with a bucket. He will have more time for doing something productive, entertaining, or restful.

The same is true for information. The substantial difference lies in the speed, ease, and efficiency with which an information system delivers the data, and in the volume of data that is being delivered. The difference does not lie in the data's nature or content. Speed, ease, efficiency, and volume are important, of course, but they do not *by themselves* alter equations of knowledge, let alone judgement.

Speed, ease, efficiency, and volume constitute the major difference between different ages of information—before and after the invention of papyrus, say, or before and after Gutenberg's printing press. Or before and after the microprocessor.

The electronic information age offers benefits in addition to speed, ease, efficiency, and volume, but they are subtle and marginal, and come with a price tag. The most dramatic increase in flow does not improve or elevate the content. The Ten Commandments would not have been more profound if, instead of carving them into stone, God had e-mailed them to Moses.

There is a school of thought, of which the *New York Times*'s foreign affairs columnist Thomas L. Friedman is an example, that sees the Soviet Union and Pan American Airlines collapsing for essentially the same reason: their inability to adapt to the microchip age. It is not quite that simple, though; the trap here lies in the fallacy of observed similarities. Looking at two animals, it is possible to get so caught up in the accurate observation that both are vertebrates, as to lose sight of the fact that one is an elephant and the other a mouse.

Two anecdotes from the Middle East, more than half a century apart, illustrate the limits of ascribing technological explanations to cultural conduct. One is told by Friedman in his influential book *The Lexus and the Olive Tree*. A Syrian guide named Walid, watching superior Israeli yogurt containers on television in 1998, remarks resentfully, "It's not fair that we're a hundred years behind the Israelis and they just got here."

The other story is recounted by the poet George Faludy. Walking on a Moroccan beach during World War II, he notices some spectacular cliffs. He wants to climb them, and asks an elderly Arab for the way up. The old man spits in the sand, then says bitterly, "You can't reach those cliffs, because the accursed French never built a road."

Friedman postulates that feelings of jealousy and resentment, whether they lead to a desire to emulate or to destroy, are peculiar to the information age. Walid has noticed the yogurt containers on *television*; the signal may have reached him via a *satellite dish*. His attitudes, Friedman believes, are being shaped by technology. But Faludy's anecdote from 1942 demonstrates that Arab attitudes were similar fifty-six years earlier, long before microchips and satellite dishes. Their expression may have been triggered by different experiences, but that is all. The medium is not necessarily the message.

Another example of microchipism has Friedman explaining in *The Lexus and the Olive Tree* that an effective contemporary journalist is a kind of information arbitrageur who knows how to cull information from different perspectives and then "weave it all together to produce a picture of the world that you would never have if you looked at it from only one perspective."

"In a world where we are all so much more interconnected," Friedman tells his readers, "the ability to read the connections, and to connect the dots, is the real value added by the journalist. If you don't see the connections, you don't see the world."

A European might find this amusing, not because he disagrees with Friedman, but because Friedman seems to believe that he came up with the idea. As a true microchipist, he also seems to think that such a discovery could come to light only in modern times, "in a world where we are all so much more interconnected."

Alas, "connecting the dots" was a cliché much favoured by my father, born in 1883, except he called it "the grand connections." "Substantial people see the grand connections," he used to say, wagging his finger. He was quite right, just as Friedman is right, except my father never thought that he was contributing an original idea made possible by microchips, globalization, and the Internet. He only tried to reiterate an eternal verity.

For Europeans, one irritating aspect of the globalized, i.e., Americanized, culture of modern times is the solemn air with which New World gurus are urging commonplaces on everybody. There is nothing new about this; the very practice is shopworn. "As a rule we develop a borrowed European idea forward, and Europe develops a borrowed American idea backwards," wrote Mark Twain over a hundred years ago.[13]

A borrowed American idea developed backwards describes the European Union perfectly.

The American century believes that it has discovered hemorrhoids. It believes that it has discovered all body parts and functions. An early sign of people becoming Americanized is televised discussions about bad breath. Dwelling on such topics makes them feel open and democratic. They think that they are discarding the vices of the old world, when all they are discarding are its virtues. But even while it mimics America, Europe retains its sense of aesthetic and moral superiority. This gives European-American relations a split personality. Gone are the days when William James could remark, as he did in 1902, somewhat resentfully, that "it seems the natural thing for us to listen whilst the Europeans talk."[14] These days Americans do the talking and Europeans do both the listening and the resenting. One reason for their resentment is a Yankee propensity to Friedmanisms: Americans, when they become adept at using something—and they often do—tend to conclude that they invented it. Nothing shakes the average American's belief in the idea that the world moved from prehistoric times directly to *his* times; a kind of jump-cut from the Flintstones to CNN, to put it in American terms. If it is news to Americans, it must be news to everyone. This irks Europeans no end, though some try to put a good face on it.

7
THE JEWISH
QUESTION

56

CHAIRMAN

ARAFAT

That war is an evil is something that we all know, and it would
be pointless to go on cataloguing all the disadvantages involved in it. No
one is forced into war by ignorance, nor, if he thinks he will gain from it, is he
kept out of it by fear. The fact is that one side thinks that the profits to be won
outweigh the risks to be incurred, and the other side is ready to face
danger rather than accept an immediate loss.

—THUCYDIDES

AFTER SOME FALSE STARTS, Yasser Arafat's Palestinian Liberation Organization discovered that the way to the world's sympathy and support was to pretend that it simply wanted to reverse the outcome of the 1967 war. In truth, the PLO's real aim has always been to reverse the outcome of the 1948 war, if not the outcome of the 1917 Balfour Declaration.

As many will recall, the 1967 war was the conflict that resulted in Israel occupying various territories on the West Bank, Gaza, the Golan Heights, and Jerusalem. The 1948 war, of course, resulted in the establishment of the State of Israel. As for the 1917 Balfour Declaration, it called for a Jewish homeland in Palestine. Reversing 1948 and perhaps even 1917, under the guise of reversing 1967, has been Yasser Arafat's *ruse de guerre*. It turned out to be a tactical masterstroke.

Arafat's actual goal was spelled out in a conversation with the Italian journalist Oriana Fallaci in 1972.[1]

"We don't want peace," Arafat explained to Fallaci. "We want war, victory. Peace for us means the destruction of Israel and nothing else. What you call peace is for Israel and the imperialists. For us it is injustice and shame. We will fight until victory. Decades if necessary, generations."

This made perfect sense. Considering that Israel's war aim has been to exist, while the Arab war aim has been for Israel not to exist, peace would mean that Israel has achieved her war aims. It could not mean anything else. For Arafat peace meant defeat, by definition.

As Arafat matured in politics, he saw it as his task to obscure the truth that he blurted out to Fallaci in 1972. Then he had said to the Italian journalist: "The end of Israel is the goal of our struggle, and it allows for neither compromise nor mediation." Now he had to obscure his goal not only from Americans and Europeans, but from as many Israelis as possible. The slogan "land for peace" became Arafat's version of the Nazi inscription on the gate to Auschwitz: *Arbeit macht Frei.*[2] At the same time he had to make sure that his real goal was *not* obscured from Palestinians and others in the Arab/Muslim world. This was vital, otherwise many Arabs would have accepted peace as inevitable and sunk into complacency, while a fanatical minority, had they been taken in by Arafat's deception, might not have rested until he had been assassinated. It was a tightrope walk, an acrobatic performance, but Arafat accomplished it. He balanced on the high wire, without a net, and for a long time. No one can take that away from him.

Of course, a long time as measured in the lifespan of human beings is only a blink of an eye in history. Arafat succeeded masterfully in the short run; he did as well as Hitler in deceiving the West. One could draw a straight line from Neville Chamberlain's Munich through Bill Clinton's Oslo to George W. Bush's Road Map. But eventually all deceptions come to light. Even before the chairman passed away in the fall of 2004, the coin had begun to drop. Luckily for the late chairman's agenda, it is dropping in slow motion.

"Land" is to "peace" what *"Arbeit"* is to *"Frei."* By the time all Jews realized in Auschwitz that work was not going to set them free, it was too late. Whether Israelis and their allies will discover that land will not buy them peace—discover it, that is, before the gas chambers become operational— is anybody's guess.

57

THE COURTYARD INTERLUDE

Without stirring abroad,
One can know the whole world;
Without looking out of the window
One can see the way of heaven.
The further one goes
The less one knows.

—LAO-TZU

IN THE LATE 1970s, while the Arab world plotted to push the Jews into the sea, and the Soviets were hard at work to deliver the *coup de grâce* to the West, Canada's fellow-travelling prime minister, Pierre Elliott Trudeau, made a remark that was extreme even for him. Embarrassed by some leaked revelations indicating that détente-struck Canada was letting the KGB run loose in the country, the leftist philosopher-prince declared that while rogue elements in the KGB might wish Canada ill, the Soviet Union as a whole was a friend. Trudeau went on to compare the KGB to the CIA, saying that just as the White House might be unaware of certain things the CIA does, the Kremlin would be unaware of some things that its state security and espionage forces might be doing.[3]

This put the lid on it for Peter Worthington, then editor-in-chief of the *Toronto Sun*. He was one of a handful of Canadian journalists not blinded by the Red Sun either in Ottawa or in Moscow.[4] Worthington promptly published sixteen abbreviated case histories of Soviet espionage and subversion in Canada, based on a supposedly top secret but previously leaked and shopworn government document called *Canadian-related Activities of the Russian* (sic) *Intelligence Service*. The document was filled with embarrassing details about Canadians known to have been recruited for espionage or other subversive activities by the Soviets through blackmail, bribes, or persuasion—with none of the coerced, bribed, trapped, or seduced people being charged and prosecuted. It was the very information Canada's prime minister wanted to sweep under the carpet.

Incensed and resolved to extract vengeance, Trudeau had Worthington and his publisher, Douglas Creighton, charged under Canada's Official Secrets Act.[5] The baseless charges (eventually dismissed) were pure examples of administrative malice, and prompted the apolitical but ever-mischievous Dusty Cohl, non-practising lawyer and co-founder of the Toronto Film Festival, to have a batch of "Free Peter Worthington" T-shirts printed up and distributed among his sizeable group of friends. Cohl, though significantly more benevolent than the average Mafioso, was just as persuasive. If he gave you a T-shirt, you *wore* it.

Cohl wore his own "Free Peter Worthington" T-shirt at the Courtyard Café in Toronto's Windsor Arms Hotel, where he had invited me for breakfast to hand me mine. Jean Chrétien, later to be Canada's prime minister, but in 1978 minister of finance in the Trudeau cabinet, was sitting at the next table, having breakfast alone. After casting a series of disapproving glances at Cohl's offending garment, Chrétien leaned over and said, wagging a censorious finger at Cohl, "We 'ave laws in this country, you know."

The mischief-maker and the finance minister were not social acquaintances, but for the Courtyard Café the episode was not unusual. "The Yard," as the regulars referred to it, functioned somewhat like a club. Located midtown, part of a small but fashionable hotel that also had a popular bar and other restaurants, the café was designed to resemble a glitzy and gilded version of a *fin-de-siècle* railway station in Paris. It opened early in the morning and closed late at night, and would accommodate patrons at any time with anything from a snack to a full-course meal. Though the food was middling and the service spotty, there was something about the ambiance that attracted politicians, journalists, entrepreneurs, high-profile lawyers, literary and show business types, society ladies, men-about-town—in short, the crowd newspapers liked to call the "glitterati," along with their retinue. In the small pond of Toronto, the Courtyard Café was where some of the big fish lurked, at least for a while. The Yard's glory days lasted about ten years, roughly between 1975 and 1985.

In those years there was always an exotic car or two parked outside the Windsor Arms Hotel. The Courtyard's peak came at the tail end of a period where cars and women still had a coactive relationship, not always easy to interpret. My wife, Maya, claimed that she made up her mind to keep seeing me when, after our first date, she saw me open the door of a Lamborghini Urraco. Women often gauged men by their cars, not necessarily (or solely) for wealth or earning potential, but for nature, panache, perhaps even character. Some women would have been turned off by an exotic sportscar; my future wife would have been turned off by a Chevrolet. The most spectacular cars did not invariably belong to the richest people. A young engineer of my acquaintance—everybody called him "Uncle Sigi" for some reason—owned a classic Bentley, a rare German DKW, and a third peculiar car—a Lancia Fulvia Coupe, I think. I had no idea how he could afford them until one day he invited me to tea: he lived in his garage, where he had a hot plate and a camp bed. The showiest car parked outside the Courtyard Café, a Lamborghini Espada, was not owned by a playboy millionaire but by Roy Krost, a working producer of films and TV commercials.

The last date I ever took to The Yard was Maya, on our first date. It was the spring of 1986. Having just met the pretty Oriental girl, I asked her to lunch. I was hoping to go to bed with her, but had to leave for Europe the next day. It was a research trip that was going to keep me overseas for about two months.

"I'd like to have dinner with you," I said at the end of our lunch, "but I'm afraid it'll have to be sometime later this summer. Unless—do you want to have dinner with me next week in Paris?"

It was a spur-of-the-moment question. I expected her to laugh, then say that she would love to but could not. Instead of which she said, "Yes."

So I wrote her a cheque for the airfare and a week later we had dinner in Paris. In due course we got married. The Courtyard years were over.

In 1981 they were still at their zenith, though, so I was not surprised to bump into Nick Harris in the foyer leading to the Windsor Arms Hotel one day. Harris was a publisher, head of the Canadian branch of William Collins and Sons, himself originally from Britain.

I was more surprised when he said that I was the fellow he wanted to see. "Do you know Malcolm Lester?" he asked. "He and I have a project that may interest you."

I knew Lester better than I knew Harris, actually. He was then the head of a small but elite publishing house called Lester & Orpen Dennys (now defunct). His partner, Eve Orpen, had been a little girl in Vienna at the time of the *Anschluss,* the 1938 annexation of Austria. She was Jewish, but also very cute, so when Hitler made his triumphant entry some local organizers sent her to hand a bunch of flowers to the unsuspecting Führer. (As a four-year-old, Eve was unsuspecting herself.) Lester's other partner was Louise Dennys, niece of the British author Graham Greene. A joint project between Collins and Lester & Orpen Dennys seemed rather unusual.

"You're making me curious," I said.

"I was hoping I might," Harris replied. "Can you meet us in Malcolm's office tomorrow?"

Lester's office was off Spadina Avenue in downtown Toronto, in an area devoted to the needle trade, not unlike parts of the Lower East Side in Manhattan. When I arrived at the appointed time, Harris and Lester were waiting for me in the company of a nondescript man. He was introduced by a first name I no longer remember, and we had a general conversation for about fifteen minutes. Other than the fact that he was an Israeli, evident from his accent, I learned nothing about him. Had he asked me questions I would probably have answered them, but as he did not, he could not have learned much about me either. At the end of what seemed to be a brief and rather pointless meeting, Harris asked me to wait in the reception area. By the time he and Lester invited me to join them again, the Israeli was gone. He had obviously left through some other exit. I was puzzled.

"I expect you'll tell me what this is all about," I said.

Lester handed me a script of about ten pages. It appeared to be a synopsis of sorts. He asked me to read it, and then tell him if I had an interest in pursuing the matter. If my answer was yes, the publishers involved— they included Collins of Great Britain in addition to Collins of Canada and Lester & Orpen Dennys—would fund a period of research. It would entail me travelling to various parts of the world, then writing a brief report about what I had found out. If at that point the publishers and I felt that my research justified a book, they would ask me to write it.

The synopsis described the story of a hit team assembled by Israel after the Munich massacre of 1972. The terrorist incident was well known: a Palestinian organization called Black September tried to take Israeli athletes hostage at the Munich Olympic Games. The unsuccessful attempt resulted in the death of eleven Israelis. Some of the terrorists also died, but they were only foot soldiers. Israeli Prime Minister Golda Meir's government wanted to "cut off the head of the snake," to punish the planners, the organizers, the architects of the terrorist action at Munich. The Mossad—Israel's equivalent of the CIA—supposedly set up a counterterrorist team, which in two years' time hunted down six of eleven people named on their hit list, and played a part in the killing of another three. According to the synopsis Lester handed to me, the team also ended up killing or wounding six people not on the original list, losing three of its own five members in the process.

"Was this fellow in your office supposed to have been involved in this?" I asked Lester.

"Yes."

"Did he want to meet me? He asked me no questions."

"He wanted to meet you."

I was very intrigued, but far from certain that this amounted to a book. In addition, I was not sure why the consortium approached me. Although in 1981 I was fairly "hot" (or at least lukewarm) as an author—one award-winning bestseller and a recent novel that was a *succès d'estime*[6]—I had no background in international intrigue. I lacked Middle East expertise and had never worked as a foreign or war correspondent. I was not even an investigative reporter, strictly speaking.

I tried to analyze the question. The publishers had made their own inquires about the bona fides of their Israeli source before contacting me, but they would not share the details. This was fair enough, for such information might influence or taint my own inquiries. The publishers wanted me to start with a clean slate. The question was, what could I possibly draw on it?

It was evident that the publishers' own research had cleared the preliminary hurdles for them. Both Collins and Lester & Orpen Dennys were well positioned for research in this area. They had contacts, better contacts than I. Harris, like many Brits in the book business, had a personal background in hush-hush affairs, while Louise Dennys, in addition to being Graham Greene's niece (Greene had been in British intelligence during the war), was the daughter of a retired counterintelligence officer. I understood that her father had been the head of the Middle East desk in MI5 (the designation for British counterintelligence). I had no comparable contacts in the world of official secrets.

It was evident to me that, if I said yes to the research phase, I could not rely on the standard journalistic method of checking with "sources," either on or off the record. Facts for a story of this type could not be verified by asking people whether they were true. Those who might know would not speak—and even worse, if they did, could not be relied on to tell the truth—while those who did speak could not be relied on to know.

I could count on no official help. In the 1980s, unlike these days, counterterrorist teams did not operate on television. Israel had not yet admitted a policy of targeted assassinations. There were no pictures showing U.S. Predator missiles streaking toward their targets. The notion that a country would engage in extraterritorial and extrajudicial acts, even in self-defence, even in the best of causes, was still highly controversial. While unofficially Israel did not discourage rumours of counterterrorist teams, officially it refused to confirm them.

In any event, for a book one needed texture and details. Texture could not be supplied by people in head office, even if they decided to tell all. Details could only come from people in the field—but there had to be a way to verify their stories.

I needed a research method over which I had some control. After some thought, I concluded that the only one available to me was the method used by ordinary police investigators. The story obviously came from an Israeli agent who decided to go public, to tell tales out of school—the first one to do so, at that time, as far as anyone knew. Since the value of the information hinged on the veracity of the principal informer, I could, like any homicide detective, ask him questions about physical details—details to which he ought to know the answer, and which I could then verify with my own eyes or from an unimpeachable source. I could ask my informer for a detailed description of a street corner or public park that was the supposed location of an event in his story. I could ask him for the weather on a certain day. He could neither anticipate my question nor invent the accurate answer. If he could tell me the location and approximate number of light switches in an apartment lobby in Rome, it would be safe for me to conclude that he had been there.

Despite the need for secrecy, I discussed the matter with Eddie Greenspan, partly because he was my closest friend and I valued his judgement, but also because we were collaborating on a CBC series. No matter how confidential the Lester/Harris project was, I needed to synchronize my schedule with Greenspan's in order to do out-of-town research. It would have been impossible to invent stories about why I had to disappear for weeks at a time. Telling him the truth was more sensible than trying to withstand a cross-examination by the keenest cross-examiner in the country. Lester agreed, so Greenspan became privy to the project virtually from the start.

I was free enough to do the research once I squared away my production schedule. I did have family obligations, but no geographical ties. My father had passed away ten years earlier, and my mother had stayed in Budapest. My first wife, Sylvia, lived in New York. My second wife, Barbara, was moving back to London. My son, Alexander (from my first marriage), was about to embark on his studies as an undergraduate at Cornell University in Ithaca, New York. My then girlfriend, a willowy blonde who taught French at Havergal College, was sophisticated, independent, and discreet. As a Romanian—she had been Romania's Twiggy on the silver screen before she fetched up in Canada—she was used to asking no "political" questions. Hailing from the mad tyrant Ceausescu's realm had few advantages, but it made one an ideal companion for a writer engaged in clandestine projects. I could ask her to meet me in Rouen or Bucharest (and did, as it turned out) and she would not only be agreeable but incurious. Her attitude was that what she did not know could not hurt her.

The funding publishers were to be mainly Collins of Great Britain, with Lester & Orpen Dennys and Collins of Canada assuming the creative roles.[7] The funds for the research, while not lavish, seemed adequate. The advance, in case the project reached that stage, was to be more than I had received for my previous books. The final royalties, of course, would depend on sales. The topic was likely to generate some international interest.

"My then girlfriend, a willowy blonde." Romania's Twiggy in Toronto in 1982.

In the end, though, all these became minor considerations. I said yes to the project to satisfy a nagging personal question. I wanted to face the dilemma of the Jewish state in my own mind. I wanted to see whether, by taking a closer look at Israel, I could settle for myself that old argument between my Zionist uncle and non-Zionist father—the argument to which I listened night after night throughout a distant summer in 1944.

POSTSCRIPT: THE MOVIE VERSION

The book, published in 1984 under the title of *Vengeance: The True Story of an Israeli Counter-Terrorist Team*, reached twenty-one editions in thirteen languages. It was controversial in more ways than one. Some critics believed the story, some did not. In Britain, *Vengeance* became the only book to make both the fiction and non-fiction bestseller list.

Eventually *Vengeance* spawned two movies. The first, called *Sword of Gideon*, was made in 1985, the year after the book had been published. It was produced by Robert Lantos and directed by Michael Anderson.[8] The second, made twenty years later, was acquired initially by Barry Mendel for Universal Studios, but ended up being co-produced and

"Eventually Vengeance *spawned two movies." On the set of* Sword of Gideon *with (r. to l.) Michael York, Steven Bauer, and producer Robert Lantos.*

directed—in essence, auteured—by Steven Spielberg.[9]

I researched and wrote my book in 1982–1983. By the time Spielberg's film was released, the world had become a different place. In 1972, when the Munich massacre occurred, government-sanctioned acts of counterterrorism were still top secret. Even in 1984, when *Vengeance* was first published, no state admitted sending hit teams abroad to perform extrajudicial killings. It was not until the 1990s that some governments actually acknowledged their past participation in actions of this type. By the time the twentieth century ended, the targeted assassination of prominent terrorists had become regular television fare.

There was also a shift in popular perception. People had adjusted considerably their sense of right and wrong. The morality of counterterrorist violence might have been questioned thirty years ago—which was why governments covered up such acts—but the immorality of terrorist violence would have been beyond dispute. In 1972 the hooded terrorists of Black September were the bad guys. Even terrorist chieftains like Yasser Arafat tried to distance themselves from Munich-type massacres. By 2005, however, matters were more equivocal. Terrorists and counterterrorists alike were coming out of the closet. Far from being abashed, both were flaunting their stuff on TV. Security forces put targeted assassinations on CNN News, while video spots on al-Jazeera portrayed the beheadings of hostages and the apotheosis of suicide bombers. Disputing the moral high ground of counterterrorists, terrorists started claiming justification and legitimacy for their acts themselves. Soon the media were describing hijackers and shoe-bombers as "militants" and "insurgents," elevating the blowing up of shoppers and travellers to legitimate methods of political self-assertion. Terrorism was no longer just a bestial means *pour décourager les autres.* Political murder started to be respectable. News clips of airliners slamming into the World Trade Center sent people into the street dancing throughout the Arab world. The new millennium was turning into the Terrorist Century.

Different as the Lantos and Spielberg movies were, they did have one thing in common. Neither had much to do with my book. Of course, film scripts are not loyalty tests. The quality of motion pictures is not determined by how faithful they are to the books (or events) that inform or inspire them. All the same, writers whose stories are turned into movies can benefit from Graham Greene's advice. The author of *Our Man in Havana* suggested that if a writer wanted to avoid apoplexy, he should never look at his work translated into any language he could understand. Nor, I would add, should he go to see the Hollywood version.

58

ISRAEL'S PRESS

There is no precedent, either in our history
or in any other, to teach us that political measures can
conjure away hereditary antipathies which
are fed by constant agitation.
—ROBERT CECIL, LORD SALISBURY

WORLD SUPPORT FOR ISRAEL REACHED its high-water mark during the 1960s. It peaked following the 1967 Six Day War. Israel probably had its best press during a three-year period, roughly between June 7, 1967, after its troops took the Arab part of Jerusalem and incorporated it with the rest of the city, and September 6, 1970, when Palestinian militants successfully hijacked a TWA 707 and a Swissair DC-8 and blew them up on an airstrip outside Amman, Jordan.

From its high plateau between the summers of 1967 and 1970, Israel's press in the world entered a gradual decline. The descent was slow at first and more rapid later. It became precipitous after the collapse of the Soviet Union in 1991.

THE HOLOCAUST

There were several reasons behind Israel's abandonment by world opinion. During the first two Arab-Israeli wars, fought in 1948–1949 and in 1956, the spectre of the Holocaust still loomed over the conflict in the Middle East. World War II had barely ended when Egypt, Syria, Transjordan, Lebanon, and Iraq attempted to crush the five-hour-old Jewish state on May 15, 1948. The world's memory was still fresh. Even in 1956, when Egyptian president Gamal Abdel Nasser triggered an Israeli-British-French attack on his country by nationalizing the Suez Canal, Hitler had been dead for only eleven years. It was not just his ghost that had not yet been laid to rest: neither had six million other ghosts. The cause of Israel was still buoyed by the world's feeling of guilt. Even more to the point, most people also took the necessity for Israel's existence for granted. The record had shown Jews to be in mortal peril without the safe haven of a state of their own.

It was in the nature of things for the Holocaust to diminish as a factor in the Arab-Israeli conflict. By 1967 a generation had grown up for whom the Nazis were only history. This included soldiers fighting on both sides in the Six Day War. As the years continued to pass, people with personal memories of Hitler's times became an ever-shrinking minority, not only in the world, but in Israel itself. By the time the Soviet Union collapsed in 1991, the concept of Israel as a lifeboat for Jews seemed outdated. Jewish people were no longer in danger without Israel. They could safely live, worship, and prosper in all Western countries, as well as in several others. The world did not need to help preserve Israel as a refuge. On the contrary. It was the Jewish state that was turning into the most dangerous place for Jews in the world.

THE COLD WAR ALLY

The really precipitous decline began in the world's support for Israel after 1991. This puzzled some analysts. After the collapse of the Soviet empire and all it stood for, the loser ought to have been its erstwhile ally, the Arab side, in the Mideast conflict. This seemed especially true in relation to Yasser Arafat. The PLO derived a significant part of its support, moral as well as material, directly from the Kremlin. Much of the rest came from the Saudis and the Gulf States. When Arafat sided with Iraq's Saddam Hussein in 1990, the PLO had lost another important source of its funding. It seemed that Arafat had allied himself with the losing side in the Gulf War, just as much of the Arab world allied itself with what turned out to be the losing side in the Cold War. Why, then, was it not the Arab side that was losing the battle of public opinion in the Arab-Israeli conflict?

Posing this question was predicated on the assumption that the West's support for Israel—and, specifically, America's support—was more than situational. The West upheld Israel's right to exist not just because the Jewish state happened to be a strategic ally in the Cold War, but also because support for Israel meant supporting the rule of law in international affairs. Israel had been created by a vote in the United Nations. Assisting Israel meant championing the only democracy in the authoritarian or theocratic Mideast. Even people who viewed America and Europe as colonial powers rather than champions of liberal democracy took it for granted that Israel would always enjoy the West's support as a spearhead (or last bastion) of European colonialism.

Had this been true, public and media support for Israel would not have diminished after the demise of the Soviet Union. But the premise turned out to be false.

Western public opinion did vaguely favour democratic Israel over Arab autocracies or Muslim theocracies in the Middle East, but few people in Europe or in the United States would have crossed the street to give this preference any effect. Supporting the rule of law in international affairs depended almost entirely on a perception of rights and wrongs in the region, which after the November 10, 1975, resolution in the United Nations that equated Zionism with racism became highly equivocal. Though U.S. ambassador Patrick Moynihan described the resolution as "infamous" and the General Assembly grudgingly rescinded it in 1991, by then the resolution's baneful influence on the public's—and the media's— perception had become strong.

This meant the West's support for Israel hinged mainly on Israel being a trusty ally in the Cold War. Unfortunately for the Jewish state, it turned out to be a trusted ally in a conflict that was over and no longer mattered. The Soviet empire had vanished; the Cold War was history. Israel, like Shakespeare's Moor, had done its duty: the Moor could go. After 1991 the West's interests as well as the sentiments of many Westerners—many Europeans, in particular—favoured the Arab world more than Israel. The Arabs represented markets and resources (oil, to mention only the most obvious) while Israel represented only a sinkhole for money, attention, diplomatic efforts, and occasionally blood. Having Israel as an ally in the Middle East became a nuisance.

While Israel needed the West as much as ever, the West no longer needed Israel. The barometer of public opinion soon sensed this, and then it became gradually reflected in the media. The same realization seeped into Israeli public opinion as well. One of its effects was post-Zionism.

POST-ZIONISM

Post-Zionism arose for several reasons, but two were directly tied to the collapse of Communism. Different groups of Israelis read the meaning of the collapse differently, but their response to it was often the same.

One group understood that with the end of the Cold War Israel had lost its strategic importance to the West, as outlined above. The Arabs, being no fools, would soon discover that Israel, having outlived its useful- ness, was now on its own in a sea of Arab and Muslim hostility. This group of post-Zionists felt that only revising the basic idea of the Jewish state would ensure the physical survival of its population, the alternative being a prolonged and bloody conflict for generations. They thought that safety for Israeli Jews was to be found in changing Israel from a specifically Jewish state into a multicultural and multiethnic society.

Another group of Israelis reached the same conclusion for the opposite reason. They concluded that the Arab world, and specifically Arafat and the

PLO, suffered a grave setback in 1991. This being so, Jews no longer needed the special protection of their own state as envisaged by Zionism. It was safe to dismantle Israel and replace it with a "post-Zionist" state of pluralistic secularism, somewhat like Canada or the United States. Palestinian Arabs and Israeli Jews could live side by side in such a non-tribal, non-religious, multicultural democracy as full-fledged and equal citizens.

The two groups rarely enunciated their underlying reasons for their post-Zionist stance. Some post-Zionists may not even have understood them. They did not always realize that post-Zionism was either a counsel of hope ("We do not need a lifeboat any more") or a counsel of despair ("Our lifeboat has sprung a leak, so we had better abandon it"). Many post-Zionists, as well as their critics, traced post-Zionism to much older strains of Jewish intellectual anti-nationalism.

This lineage was not without validity. "Post-Zionism" existed in Israel for many years, long before the expression was ever used. Many intellectuals, and not only Jewish ones, viewed nationalism as the root cause of human strife in general, and of anti-Semitism in particular. George Orwell described nationalism as a disease (in his 1945 essay "*Antisemitism in Britain*") and viewed anti-Semitism as a manifestation or symptom of it.

Many early Zionists believed that Jewish nationalism was fundamentally different from other nationalisms. It was an article of faith among most pioneers of the Zionist movement that their longing for a Jewish homeland was entirely benign. Their form of nationalism, they assumed, could build a nation-state without harming anyone. In 1928 Ben-Gurion made his famous remark, no doubt sincerely, that "according to my moral outlook we do not have the right to harm a single Arab child, even if by dint of such harm we should achieve all that we desire." Only a minority of the early Zionists, such as Zeev (Vladimir) Jabotinsky, understood that nation-building inevitably entails strife and bloodshed, and might, whether the nation-builders intend it or not, uproot and displace other cultures. But Jabotinsky's insights were buried under two optimistic myths of early Zionism. One was that Palestine, a Turkish possession first, and then a British mandate, was some kind of a tabula rasa, a blank sheet, which could be viewed as "a land with no people for a people with no land." We now see that this early Zionist slogan was obtuse as well as Eurocentric, but at the time it appeared almost self-evident. The slogan was especially convincing when coupled with a parallel myth: the irresistible power of progress, i.e., modernity. The example everyone used for progress was irrigation. The "irrigation myth" held that downtrodden and poverty-stricken Palestinian villagers or nomads would be so elated by the Jews bringing modern technology, hygiene, medicine, agriculture, and European enlightenment to their barren land that they would welcome the Jewish state as a means of their liberation, their deliverance from mediaeval conditions and their cruel Arab or Turkish overlords.

These illusions were arrogant and naïve, albeit without malice. The British shared none of them. They had far more experience in nation-building as well as in the administration of diverse people and far-flung territories than the early Zionists could possibly have had. The Russian, Romanian, Austro-Hungarian, or Polish Jews who became inspired by Theodor Herzl's vision had mainly been people of trade, of books, of commerce. They started out with almost no understanding of what the settlement of territory or the creation and administration of a state might entail. It especially failed to register with early Zionists that the same rising spirit of nationalism that fuelled their quest during the late nineteenth century would soon fuel Arab nationalism and the Palestinians' quest for a state as well.

In time, it was the realization that the People of the Book aren't exempt from the laws of history, and that tribal nationalism, whether Jewish, Arab, or any other, is a very powerful and potentially malignant force, that contributed to the emergence of post-Zionism. In one sense, post-Zionism was born on the day Israel came into being. It was a parallel development with Zionism, though during the successful decades of Israeli nation-building it remained almost invisible. After Israel's first military reverses, however, around the time of the Yom Kippur War of 1973, post-Zionism, which had long been an undercurrent in Israel's culture and politics, gradually started emerging from the shadows. It first seeped into the country's academic and intellectual life, as trends usually do. By the time of Oslo, post-Zionism had come close to being a dominant force, not in Israel's body politic perhaps, but in the culture of Israel's elite. Just when the Palestinian elite was reaching the conclusion that the time was ripe to replace the Jewish state with a Palestinian state, the Israeli elite was coming to believe that the Jewish state was an anachronism and should be replaced, if not with a Palestinian state, at least with a pluralistic and multicultural one. In this atmosphere, it was hardly surprising that by the time of Yasser Arafat's death many Palestinians viewed settlement with the Jewish state as a poor substitute for victory.

INTERNATIONAL TERROR

For Israelis, as well as for much of the world, the military and economic miracle of Israel masked all other realities for about twenty-two years, from 1948 to 1970. Those were the years when in the eyes of Western public opinion Israel could practically do no wrong. During that period Israelis were hardly ever viewed by the world as "occupiers" or "colonists," but as people who planted orange groves and made the desert bloom.

This era came to an end on September 6, 1970, when the PFLP, the Popular Front for the Liberation of Palestine, hijacked a Swissair DC-8 and a TWA Boeing 707, then, six days later, a BOAC VC10. After holding the passengers for several weeks, the Palestinians evacuated everyone and blew up the empty planes at Dawson Field, thirty miles from Amman, Jordan.

This day opened up a new chapter in Israel's history, although this is easier to see in retrospect than it was at the time. Simply put, from that day on, supporting Israel was no longer free. Israelis had always known the cost of the Arab world's rejection of the Jewish state because they had to pay it on a daily basis, during as well as in between the "official" periods of hostilities, such as the Sinai Campaign or the Six Day War. However, until September 6, 1970, Arab violence had been confined to the region itself. After that day people in every country, especially in the West, had to contend with the potential of paying a price—that is, the potential of being bombed, hijacked, or otherwise caught in the crossfire between Arabs and Israelis.

The public might have faced down the physical hazard, which was not more significant, statistically speaking, than being caught in an earthquake. A more disruptive consequence of the terrorist threat lay in the defensive measures taken against it. Western travellers suddenly faced wartime conditions. Body searches were changing airports into maximum-security prisons. Five-hour trips started taking a full day. The price of oil skyrocketed. The humiliation Westerners felt at having to continually inconvenience themselves for a race in which they had no horse, for an obscure conflict between two alien groups in a desiccated and distant region, did more to influence public opinion against Israel than the threat of physical harm.

Public opinion *against* Israel, it is important to note, far more than against the Palestinians. Air piracy validated a psychological effect known as the Stockholm syndrome, which suggests that captives often end up identifying with the perpetrators of terror rather than with their defenders and rescuers. Beyond posing a deadly threat, terrorists projected a desperation that made them appear the underdog. A world that showed scant interest in Palestinian refugees while the fedayeen attacked only Israelis on Israeli soil suddenly found vast reservoirs of sympathy when the terrorists started blowing up jets belonging to BOAC or TWA.

THE MYTH OF OSLO

The peace process of the 1990s was doomed to failure because it had been based on the premise that both sides sought peace. But, as we have seen, for the Palestinian side peace with Israel means defeat.

Curiously, Israel suffered a setback in the battle for public opinion when people began to understand, or at least intuit, that peace equalled victory for the Jewish state. People perceived that this meant giving up whatever hope existed for a rational settlement in the Middle East. If peace was impossible without a sense of defeat for the Arab/Muslim side, Israel's continued existence had to result in the threat and inconvenience of the jihad spilling over from the Middle East to other parts of the world. Europe and America could no longer expect to contain an irksome, hazardous, and often deadly virus of exported violence through painless and inexpensive remedies, such as an Oslo-type peace process. People, especially Europeans, sensed that changing the name of the process would be no remedy, and neither would changing the cast of characters on either side.

Whether called "Oslo" or "Road Map"—as the Bush administration's successor plan was named in 2003—and whether negotiated with a "militant" Yasser Arafat or with his successor, the "moderate" Mahmoud Abbas, the process would end in the same impasse. Support for Israel meant putting up with the risk and vexation of the Arab/Muslim world's collective sense of insult and injury. This seemed too high a price to pay at a time when the Jews seemed in no particular danger in the Diaspora, and Israel no longer appeared critical or indispensable. Coupled with latent Western, especially European, anti-Semitism, public opinion eventually concluded that the Jewish state—"that shitty little country," as the French ambassador to Britain, Daniel Bernard, referred to Israel in 2001—was simply not worth the bother.[10]

ANTI-SEMITISM

Anti-Semitism used to go hand in glove with right-wing politics throughout the nineteenth and the first half of the twentieth century. Then events took a different turn. As a side effect of the geopolitical split during the Cold War, many countries in the Arab/Muslim world became clients of the Soviet Union. This, along with various other factors—such as the left's growing anti-white racism (disguised as "anti-colonialism") and its association of Jews with "whites"—brought about a gradual shift in the placement of anti-Semitic attitudes on the political spectrum. The same anti-Semitism that used to be an exclusive property of the right prior to the creation of the Jewish state, after around 1950 became, at first slowly, then with increasing rapidity, a property of the left. In the beginning it was disguised as anti-Zionism to save left-liberal sensibilities, but eventually it became common enough for it to appear without disguise.

When anti-Semitism shifted from being a property of the right to being a property of the left, it received a new lease of life, primarily due to the left's influence in media and academic circles in the Western world. Leftish shibboleths have had a way of becoming part of the curricula in public schools and universities very nearly as a matter of course. They have constituted the gold standard in news coverage as well as editorial analysis, and have been dominant in popular entertainment: slightly less in books perhaps, but over-whelmingly in movies and television shows. The media were prevalently left-wing. When anti-Semitism changed its address from the right to left side of the street, it was automatic for Israel's bad press to follow.

We should note one more thing. In the period between the late eighteenth century and the advent of Hitler, ideals of emancipation and liberalism, including the heady notions of liberty, equality, and fraternity, appeared to make assimilation both possible and desirable. This prompted many Jews, mainly in Germany, France, Austria-Hungary, England, and eventually in America, to become strongly opposed to Zionism. They felt that Theodor Herzl's movement arose just at the moment when it was no longer needed, and when, despite such aberrations as the Dreyfus affair, assimilation into civil society offered more safety and better opportunities for Jews.

To many, Zionism seemed to point the way back to a ghetto—an exile, really—from which Jewry was just emerging. The American historian Barbara W. Tuchman recalled her grandfather, the former envoy Henry Morgenthau, proclaiming his opposition to Zionism in an article she described as "exceedingly combative." President Woodrow Wilson's ambassador to Turkey evidently felt that Zionism was bound to rekindle anti-Semitism, raising the spectre of double loyalties for Jews in the Diaspora just at the time when they were gaining full citizenship and social acceptance. In a 1921 article, Morgenthau called Zionism "an Eastern European proposal... which if it were to succeed would cost the Jews of America most of what they have gained in liberty, equality, and fraternity."

Tuchman commented that her grandfather "in his eighties, in the shadow of the Holocaust... privately acknowledged that he had read history wrong."[11] But the interesting thing is that he may not have, even though that is how it appeared to him as well as to Tuchman. When she spoke about her grandfather in an address to the American Historical Association in 1976, Israel's star, though past its zenith, was still shining brightly enough. From the perspective of our own times, however, Morgenthau's initial insight appears more justified. Zionism has undoubtedly helped rekindle anti-Semitism—sometimes disguised as anti-

Zionism—in America as well as in the rest of the world. This was masked for a while by the unexpected success of Israel. Success has a momentum, at least initially, making people reluctant to quarrel with it. But failure, whether real or apparent, has a momentum, too. The only thing that would increase anti-Semitism even more than the creation of the Jewish state had would be the Jewish state's defeat.

A bad press has little to do with "the press" as such. The media only reflect the spirit of the times. Westerners resent being endangered and inconvenienced for a Jewish state that neither the West nor many Jews consider vital to their interests any more.

And it is on this last point where both the West and Israel's post-Zionists are mistaken, I believe. The Jewish state continues to be vital to the interests of both. The fate of Israel subsumes the fate of Western civilization. As the American philosopher Eric Hoffer put it thirty-four years ago, "I have a premonition that will not leave me; as it goes with Israel so will it go with all of us. Should Israel perish, the next Holocaust will be upon us."[12]

59

SNAPSHOTS FROM THE HOLY LAND

POST-ZIONISTS

IN ISRAEL EVERYONE HITCHHIKES. The two girls I picked up just east of Tel Aviv wanted to go to Jerusalem.

"Good, you can show me the way," I said.

"What way? You just drive straight ahead until you get there."

This was the sabra speaking, the native-born Israeli girl. Her friend, also a student at the Hebrew University of Jerusalem, came from Montreal.

They were both going back to the campus at Mount Scopus after a weekend in Tel Aviv.

"So you have never been to Jerusalem?" the sabra asked. "Hire us as your tour guides. We'll show you everything."

"What do you charge?"

"Lunch. Is it a deal?"

It was a deal. The girl from Montreal, as it turned out, knew the Old City inside out. She could discuss landmarks from the Antonia Fortress to the Via Dolorosa to the Wailing Wall. She had been living in Jerusalem for only two years, but seemed to know the history of every stone.

The sabra knew nothing and cared less. "This?" she would say. "It's an old building. It has always been an old building. Okay? Now let me ask you something: how does one become a stewardess for Sabina?"

The girl from Montreal was enthusiastic about Jerusalem, about its past, about its future. She was looking forward to living in Israel. After nursing school she hoped to join the medical corps of the IDF, the Israeli Defence Force.

The sabra listened to her with an ironic smile. She was not only native-born: she came from an old Palestinian family. Her Jewish community of about fifty thousand predated Zionism by centuries. They had lived in the Holy Land for generations before the first *aliya*, the first Zionist emigration, set out from Europe in 1882.

For this girl, they had lived there for much too long.

"They kicked me out of the army," she explained. "I behaved so they would kick me out. I wish they would kick me out of the country, but they won't."

"Why do you want to get out so badly?"

"Are you kidding?" she asked. "Everything interesting in the world, everything beautiful, is somewhere else. This is a place for crazies.

"You think I want to spend the rest of my life watching old Jews swaying back and forth before a wall? Or listening to a bunch of kibbutzniks, in running shoes, sing about how great they are? Or looking at Muslims who spit in the street when they see me, then go stick their bums in the air, five times a day, like big white insects?

"Only fanatics live here: fanatic religious Jews, fanatic Zionist Jews, fanatic Palestinian *mechablim* [terrorists], fanatic mullahs.

"When I was on leave from the army I met this stewardess from Sabina. We chatted for hours. Now I want to live in Belgium, like a normal person."

PRE-ZIONISTS

The sabra of Jerusalem was a post-Zionist, but I also encountered a pre-Zionist the same day. He was an orthodox Jew, sitting on the stone steps near the crowded Wailing Wall. He was with a whole group of orthodox Jews, waiting for their turn to *daven*. They were dressed in traditional garb, including wide-brimmed hats decorated with rabbit fur. The younger ones had long *peyes* (sidecurls); the older ones wore beards.

As I sat beside them, an Israeli soldier approached the Jew next to me with a question. He spoke in Hebrew. I did not understand what he said, but the Jew obviously did. Instead of replying to the soldier, however, he turned to his co-religionist sitting on his other side.

"Wus zugt der Goy?" he asked disdainfully, speaking in Yiddish, a language I did understand. "What does the Gentile want?"

The question made perfect sense. For this Jew and for his rabbit-furred companions an Israeli soldier speaking in Hebrew was a Gentile. An offensive Gentile, in fact, who represented a double sacrilege. First, because he wore the uniform of a nation that had the presumption to consider itself a Jewish state *before* the arrival of the Messiah. Second, because he asked an everyday question in Hebrew, the language reserved by the faithful for communicating with G-d.

ANTI-ZIONISTS

Israel has excellent leather. I needed a bag to carry some books I bought in Jerusalem, and caught a glimpse of what looked like a fine leather bag in a shop window.

"How much?" I asked the Arab owner.

"Thirty dollars."

The price sounded reasonable. A bag of similar size and quality would have cost at least seventy dollars in New York. I handed the shopkeeper three ten-dollar bills.

The Arab was flabbergasted. The idea that someone would pay his first asking price had never crossed his mind. He was mentally prepared for every contingency but this. Getting more than he expected for his merchandise did not make him happy. On the contrary, it made him feel cheated and depressed. He muttered something and turned away, leaving it to an underling to finish serving me.

As I left the shop with the bag, I could see my mistake. The word about a mad foreigner was spreading in the streets of Jerusalem. My thoughtless act was threatening to cause a riot. Children were running after me in the narrow streets, screeching with excitement. One picked up a rust-coloured cat and held it up to me.

"Mister! Buy a cat."

60

BY THE WAY

GEOGRAPHY DEFINES, but not exclusively. At its most harmonious, it coincides with culture. Israel has been incongruous precisely because it has been a European country situated outside Europe. If in future it becomes a Middle Eastern country, it will probably become a worse place by most socio-economic measures, but it will be less incongruous.

61

ON TERRORISM

*Since an intelligence common to us all makes
things known to us and formulates them in our minds,
honourable actions are ascribed by us to virtue, and dishonourable
actions to vice; and only a madman would conclude that
these judgements are matters of opinion,
and not fixed by nature.*

—CICERO

Terrorism is by no means a recent invention, but in some historic periods it has been more fashionable than in others. One such period began in the mid-1960s and continues to this day.

It was perhaps predictable that terrorism, both in its domestic and international variety, should increase as the disparity of power increased between nations as well as between the state and its citizens. One need not have a soft spot for terrorism to note that it is a perfectly logical way in which relatively powerless individuals, groups, or countries can sway the actions (and sometimes even the ideas) of overwhelmingly powerful individuals, groups, or governments. This does not make terrorism virtuous or attractive, but it does explain its appeal to the weak.

When adversaries are evenly matched, the outcome of a contest is always in some doubt. This allows the contestants to observe some agreed-upon rules and to act with a measure of restraint. They can do so without having to give up all hope at the outset of attaining their goals. But in unequal contests—say, between an underdeveloped nation and a super-power—the outcome is never in doubt, unless the rules go by the wayside. Voilà, terrorism.

Domestically, as the state's machinery becomes more and more pervasive and powerful, dissenting groups and individuals have less and less

325

room to manoeuvre. This, too, makes the terrorist option increasingly seductive.

Terrorists like to claim that their way is the only way for the weak to exert influence upon the strong. This is a half-truth. Domestic and international powers may yield to persuasion or popular sentiment. Liberal democracies are susceptible to changes in the *Zeitgeist*. The spirit of the times can even influence tyrannies over long periods. Tribunals of domestic or international law may also balance disparities, since powerful entities can have various pragmatic reasons to subject themselves to outside judgements. Finally there are systems of alliances. They provide the most reliable support for the weak, especially in the international arena. In 1990, for example, Iraq would undoubtedly have succeeded in annexing Kuwait if Kuwait had not been protected by a U.S.-led alliance.

Still, when persuasion, *Zeitgeist*, laws, or alliances prove to be insufficient, the weak are at the mercy of the strong, today as much as in prehistoric times. In such cases terror becomes an alternative to submission—sometimes the only alternative. This does not justify or excuse terror, either morally or aesthetically, but it is a fact. When people are reduced to a choice between giving up things or blowing up things, some will embrace the more explosive option. Blowing up things may not bring about the desired result, of course, but then nothing—not war, not diplomacy, not persuasion, not prayer—guarantees the desired result. Terror may be futile, but other choices may be just as futile, and as an alternative to surrender, terror has a certain appeal. A random assault on non-combatants is a gruesome foul, but survival is not a sporting affair.

Terrorists excuse themselves by saying that their ends justify their means, but in practice the reverse is more usual: it is the terrorists' means that come to define their ends. Militants who think that their means will not sully their goals delude themselves. Regimes or states established or preserved by terror usually end up becoming terrorist regimes or states.

People at the extremes, left or right, are sympathetic to terrorism, so they deny its existence. The hoariest cliché holds that "one man's terrorist is another man's freedom fighter." Noam Chomsky views it as an analytical error to describe terrorism as "a weapon of the weak" because terrorism is always the force that is applied by *them* against *us,* regardless of who us and them may be (and regardless, presumably, also of the nature of the force). Chomsky calls it a "given" that since history is written by the mighty, it will always be the force applied by the poor against the powerful that is described as terrorism.[13] This invites the question of why history records a chapter of the French Revolution as the Reign of Terror—after all, the Bastille was stormed successfully, Louis XVI and Marie Antoinette lost their heads, and history was written by the heirs of the Revolution—but perhaps it is just as well not to inquire too closely into the logic of those who defend terror.

62

THE WHITE JEWS OF THE WEST

THE INFLUENCE OF THE WEST, first carried by the writings of the Encyclopedists, then by the French Revolution, and eventually by the armies of Napoleon, continued to spread over the East throughout the Victorian and Edwardian eras. The "East" in this sense included Central and Eastern Europe. By the late nineteenth century modern Western ideas were believed to signify the peak of human culture. "Jesus wept; Voltaire smiled. From that divine tear and from that human smile is derived the grace of present civilization," as Victor Hugo put it in 1878, on the occasion of Voltaire's centenary. Westernization was the coming trend from Asia Minor to the Far East; from Turkey to Japan.

In Eastern Europe the carriers of Westernization were often Jewish. There were many reasons for Jews being among the first to absorb the ideas of the Enlightenment, and to represent the French as well as the Industrial Revolution in the lands of the Hohenzollern, Habsburg, and Romanov dynasties. One reason was that Western enlightenment and liberalism added up to a new deal that included (in theory, at least) people of all social status, ethnic background, or religion. Consequently, it included

Jews. For a Jew to be anything but liberal would have made little sense.

What made a lot of sense for Jews was to be Westernizers, considering that following the eighteenth century the winds of liberalism invariably blew from West to East. By 1908 it was logical, for instance, for Hungary's newest literary magazine to be named *West*. It was equally logical for it to be founded by three Jews: the pseudonymous aesthete Ignotus, the writer and critic Ernö Osvát, and the art patron and benefactor Baron Lajos Hatvany.

It was another matter that *West*'s contributors of fine poetry and exquisite short stories were mostly Gentiles. Jews, while overrepresented in the secondary art forms of cinema, musical stage, daily journalism, and the like—and overrepresented also as editors, publishers, directors, instrumentalists, conductors, patrons, or critics among the functionaries and interpreters of the literary, visual, and musical arts—were represented only proportionately among primary creators such as novelists, poets, composers, or painters. The same was true of the higher echelons of medicine, chemistry, and physics. In the first ranks of the traditional creative arts and sciences, Jews tended to be high achievers, but not overachievers.

As carriers of Western influence, Jews were among the first to establish themselves in the newer branches of the professions and arts that spread, first to Eastern Europe, and eventually to the rest of the world. They included such novel academic disciplines as sociology and psychology, as well as novel versions of traditional disciplines like classical philology, such as neurolinguistics. In philosophy, Jews were often drawn to new areas from existentialism to comparative linguistics (and, eventually, to structuralism). In conventional disciplines such as history, medicine, or law, Jews in Eastern Europe were somewhat overrepresented, but not nearly as disproportionately.

Tragically, though hardly surprisingly, Jews came to be resented for their domination of the new professions and disciplines that they helped to spread to all parts of the globe. People left behind by the changing times often blamed Jews as the agents of change. Those for whom Westernization meant various degrees of dislocation faulted "Jewish" ideas for their social, economic, or emotional displacement in the modern world. "Jewish" was also equated with "urban" in manners and mores, giving rise to the myth of new Babylons. Examples included Berlin and Budapest (nicknamed "Judapest") and viewed as "guilty" cities with "Jewish" idioms in art and entertainment.

One such idiom was film. Movies were indeed Jewish in Eastern Europe, in the sense that Jews did flock to the film industry from its earliest days. Barely two years after the brothers Lumière, Louis Jean and Auguste, patented and demonstrated their Cinématographe in 1895, a Jewish entrepreneur, Gyula (Julius) Décsi, founded the first movie theatre in Budapest. Jews were in the forefront of spreading the new invention throughout Eastern Europe. At the turn of the century, ninety percent of the licensed motion picture exhibitors in Hungary were Jewish. Jews were also represented in significant numbers among movie makers and distributors. Hungary's original Pannonia Film Studio was founded by a Jew, József (Joseph) Antal, who later became Budapest director of the great German film company, UFA.[14]

Jewish enthusiasm for motion pictures in Eastern Europe soon doubled back to the West. As the latest instrument of popular culture continued its conquest of the English-speaking world, Jews from Austria-Hungary, Poland, and Romania marched in the celluloid vanguard. They included Hollywood's Warner brothers: Harry, Albert, Jack, and Sam. America's legendary Adolf Cukor and William (20th Century) Fox were among their numbers, as were Britain's Sir Alexander Korda *(Rembrandt, The Private Life of Henry VIII)* and Emeric Pressburger *(The Life and Death of Colonel Blimp, Red Shoes, Stairway to Heaven)*. They included such play- and screenwriters as Franz Molnár *(Carousel, The Guardsman)*, Lengyel Menyhért *(Ninotchka)*, and Lászlo Bús-Fekete *(Heaven Can Wait)*. The popular music associated with early cinema was often derived from Viennese operetta, which also numbered many Jews among its leading composers, from Emmerich Kálmán to Victor Jacobi. (The most famous of the Viennese school of waltz and schmaltz, Franz Lehar, composer of *The Merry Widow*, was Austro-Hungarian, but not Jewish.)[15]

The word "cosmopolitan" was not yet in use to describe Jewish carriers of Western influence. A German word that was often used was *Europeär.* It denoted a cultivated individual, a sophisticated man of the world—a European, in short. *Europeär* was a term of approval, but popular resentment of Western or "European" influence followed a parallel track: it bundled together godless modernism, capitalism, egalitarianism, and Judaism. As people in various parts of the world started questioning Western ideas of statecraft and social philosophy—liberalism, democracy, free enterprise—some started questioning Jews by association. By the end of World War I this chaos culminated in Adolf Hitler's paranoid idea of a Judeo-Bolshevik-plutocratic conspiracy. One factoid in the Nazi madness was that Jews were, indeed, to be found on the leading edge of *all* trends and ideas—political, intellectual, scientific, or artistic—that passed through the consciousness of Europe following the French Revolution, including Marxism. (Karl Marx, of course, came from a Jewish background himself.)

The madness of racial blame did not end with Hitler. During the confusion of the 1960s, Western influence was being questioned once more, this time not by the far right, but by the New Left. Soon the New Left went a big step further: it flatly equated the West with evil. Modern Western civilization—Jesus' tears and Voltaire's smile that Victor Hugo had been waxing lyrical about a hundred years ago—became a malignancy, associated by now not only with Jews, but with all Caucasians. Whites and "white culture" became the enemy. As Susan Sontag (herself a Jew) explained it in her 1966 essay "What's Happening in America": "The truth is that Mozart, Pascal, Boolean algebra, Shakespeare, parliamentary government, baroque churches, Newton, the emancipation of women, Kant, Marx, and Balanchine ballets don't redeem what this particular civilization has wrought upon the world. The white race *is* the cancer of human history."

For Jews there was a special irony in the world heralded by Sontag's outburst. Just when Jews finally achieved inclusion into various Western or European societies after centuries of struggle, they became pariahs again—this time *as* Westerners or Europeans. No sooner had Jews graduated to being "white" than whites had become outsiders, with the rank of cancer among the races of the world. It seemed that Jews simply could not win.

8

IN PRAISE OF
GOOD FENCES

63

THE OUTSPOKEN

RABBI OF VELKE-BITSCHE

*One identifies with one's family, because
it is one's family—not because they are better people than
others. For no other reason one identifies with one's
national group more than with others.*

—ERNEST VAN DEN HAAG

THE AUSTRO-HUNGARIAN (TODAY SLOVAKIAN) town of Velke-Bitsche had a celebrated rabbi who did not mince his words. Once he admonished his congregation: "Don't cheat, but if you must, remember to keep it among yourselves. If Cohen cheats you, you'll say: 'The *ganef* [thief] Cohen cheated me,' but if Cohen cheats a Gentile, the goy will say: 'I've been cheated by a Jew.'"

Nowadays many Jews in the Diaspora would resent such advice. They would be outraged for not being allowed to have the same range and variety of character as dominant majorities, i.e., not being permitted to have flaws as individuals without reflecting badly on their entire group. This lament is not restricted to Jews; other small or powerless groups also feel prejudiced by this in comparison to big or powerful entities. They protest that while a dishonest Frenchman is no reflection on the national character of France, a dishonest Jew (Romanian, Nigerian, etc.) is taken to represent Jews (Romanians, Nigerians) in general.

This is obviously unfair, say minorities and nationals of small countries. If an Englishman can be as common as dirt without risking the standing of Great Britain in the estimation of the world, why should a Jew not be allowed to be grasping or boorish without bringing his entire tribe into disrepute? All people include indolent or vulgar or dull individuals, just as they include diligent or cultivated or dazzling ones. Why do bad apples spoil only some barrels?

But they don't. The fact is, bad apples spoil all barrels. People are disposed to permit the luxury of individual judgement only with respect to members of their *own* groups. It takes an Italian to regard an Italian deserter simply as a coward: non-Italians will view him, at best, as an *Italian* coward, and at worst, as a typical Italian. Vulnerable minorities— say, Jews living in France, or Koreans living in Japan—may imagine that they are singled out for unfair generalization by the dominant culture, but unfair generalizations are universal.

Noting that generalizations are unfair is not the same as saying that generalizations are baseless. Individuals are vastly different, but national characteristics do exist. (So do gender, age, cultural, and class characteristics.) Group characteristics can change over historic time—occasionally they change quite rapidly—and they certainly do not obtain in every individual. Still, characteristics within a group tend to be statistically widespread and constant in a given period. Naturally they include characteristics regarded as "good" (stoicism, endurance) as well as "bad" (venality, imprudence.) Stereotypes may be unimaginative and tedious, but they are not necessarily false. They are useless for assessing individuals, of course, but can be quite helpful in evaluating aggregates.

It would be unreasonable to expect people to tolerate the flaws (real or perceived) of small and powerless groups, when they do not tolerate the flaws of even large and powerful ones. People generally tolerate only the flaws of their own groups.

A Hungarian cheated or annoyed by another Hungarian is unlikely to conclude that Hungary is a nation of annoying cheats; he will simply (and accurately) say that he has been victimized by a bothersome crook. But the same Hungarian, if cheated or annoyed by a Jew, may well resolve that Jews are fraudulent pests. The reason, however, is not only that Jews are a persecuted and powerless minority. A Hungarian cheated or annoyed by a German or a Russian will often come to a similar conclusion about Germans or Russians, though Germans and Russians are numerous and powerful.

One could object that while large and powerful groups may be *tainted* by generalizations as much as small and powerless ones, they are not *harmed* by them nearly as much. This is true, but it shows only that when faced with unfair generalizations, as with other kinds of adversity, it is better to be big and strong than to be small and weak. The outspoken rabbi of Velke-Bitsche understood this perfectly.

64

NATIONAL NARRATIVES

To attempt to be religious without practicing a specific religion is as possible as attempting to speak without a specific language.
—GEORGE SANTAYANA

THE GERMANS LOUDLY ASSERT their superiority ("*Deutschland über alles*"), the English bear it with quiet assurance ("tight little, right little island"), and the French submit to it with awe and humility as to a law of nature. ("It is in the nature of France to be great," explained de Gaulle.) It is worth noting that this sentiment came from the leader of a people who have been consistently defeated in every war since 1870—that is, for five generations. The last Frenchman to serve in a victorious campaign would have been a contemporary Frenchman's great-great-great-great grandfather. (This is not counting the general's own Free French forces, of course, who were on the side of the winners in World War II, though as rescued rather than rescuer.)

Yet de Gaulle's remark is hardly surprising, considering that even third- or fourth-rate nations nurture fond myths of their own superiority, including small nations that can barely or only sporadically hang on to their independence. "If the world were God's hat," says a Hungarian ditty, "Hungary would be its plume."

"Nine and Ninety Ways"

Nationalism, as discussed earlier, does not have to be based on ethnic bonds. Nations can cohere around a variety of organizing principles. As Kipling wrote, *"There are nine and ninety ways/ Of constructing tribal lays/ And every single one of them is right."* Any glue that has the capacity to bind suffices. Many different kinds of glue can bond under some circumstances and for a time; probably no glue can bond under all circumstances and forever.

Nationalism is capable of constructing as well as deconstructing countries. It has united or divided sovereign entities throughout the nineteenth and twentieth centuries. In its tribal/cultural form, nationalism constructed Germany and Italy in the mid-nineteenth century, while it started the process of deconstructing the Austrian (Habsburg) empire, following the revolutions of 1848. The 1867 compromise or *Ausgleich* that created the Dual (Austro-Hungarian) Monarchy looked like an edifice of survival for the Habsburg dynasty, but in fact it became the first landmark of its deconstruction. In the course of constructing Germany and Italy, nationalism deconstructed a number of kingdoms, duchies, principalities, and other dynastic entities. On the whole, the modern process of nation-building—most events since the French Revolution—displayed a gradual expansion of (a) tribal/cultural, (b) ideological, or (c) geographic organizing principles at the expense of dynastic ones. But this is not a law of nature, and the twenty-first century may see this process reversed.

Is Nationalism a Disease?

The presence or absence of ethnic strife within a nation is determined to a large extent by the spirit of the times and the prevailing ideas of the period. But there are other factors. It is logical for ethnic strife to be in inverse proportion to the ethnic principle on which the nation-state is organized. In ethnically based nations, minorities that cannot or will not assimilate for any reason may avoid strife most easily by keeping a low profile. This traditional remedy, however, has become totally unpalatable in multicultural societies. The social philosophy that has given rise to the problem has also become resentful of its consequences.

In 2002, following a spate of German-Muslim attacks on German Jews, a well-meaning German police officer advised Jewish residents to avoid wearing items of clothes that might identify them as Jews, such a skullcaps. His suggestion created an uproar. It was taken to indicate the deep roots and ineradicable nature of German anti-Semitism.

Not even the most liberal person would have taken this view fifty years ago. George Orwell begins his 1945 essay "Antisemitism in Britain" by pointing out that "there is no Jewish 'problem' in England. The Jews are not numerous or powerful enough, and it is only in what are loosely called 'intellectual circles' that they have any noticeable influence."

The rather inescapable corollary of Orwell's formulation is that if Jews were numerous or powerful enough, there *would* be a Jewish problem in Britain. But why should it create a "Jewish problem" in Britain—a liberal person might ask today—if there were many Jews or influential Jews in the country? Would not anti-Semitism in Britain be more accurately described as a "British problem" in that case?

Tempted as one is to say yes, the accurate answer is no. It would not be a British problem.

There cannot be a "British problem" in Britain or a "French problem" in France, unless we no longer recognize a given country as British or French. Once we stop recognizing nation-states, all bets are off: we have entered a brave new multicultural world, and possibly, though not necessarily, a better one. But until we reach such an era of globalism (or whatever we choose to call it) Britain cannot have a "British problem" and France cannot have a "French problem" by definition. For that to happen we must deny legitimacy to every model of nationhood, except multiethnic and multicultural ones, and jettison any country unless it is organized along the principles of New York's Grand Central Station. We can despise xenophobia, scorn illiberal edicts, and abhor crimes against humanity (and we

336

certainly should), but we cannot call a nation's preference for its own ethno-cultural makeup a "problem" unless we are prepared to discard the idea of the nation-state.

In 1945 Orwell seemed prepared to discard the nation-state. He posited that anti-Semitism was part of the larger issue of nationalism, which he regarded as a disease. He considered anti-Semitism just a symptom of this general illness.

Another view might consider nationalism a condition rather than an illness—a condition that is capable of becoming a disease, but only in countries that provide no opportunity for the civic assimilation of different groups, and then exclude or persecute the groups they would not permit to assimilate. In short, in countries that behave like Nazi Germany.

THE SACRED EGOISM OF THE PATRIOT

Patriotism has had a bad press in the twentieth century. Charles de Gaulle, although he suffered in a major way from it himself, referred to patriotism as *égoisme sacré*. (*"Il y autant d'égoismes sacrés,"* he said once, talking of the European Common Market, *"que de membres inscrits."*) George Orwell—also a patriot, even if he arrived at his English patriotism by a somewhat circuitous route—saw nationalism as the root of xenophobia, specifically anti-Semitism.

The "sacred egoism" that de Gaulle felt equalled the number of registered members in the Common Market undoubtedly existed, but it was not a mere foible to be denounced and eradicated. It served a perfectly valid purpose.

Patriotism is the emotional ingredient of a union. It is to nations what love is to a marriages. Patriotism creates a psychological bond for human cooperation, allowing neighbours subscribing to some organizing principle to coalesce around a core. It has performed this function in the past, and continues to perform it today. Patriotism may well be the last refuge of a scoundrel, as Samuel Johnson had it, but it is also the first principle of many a decent person.

"Intellectually I know that America is no better than any other country," said the U.S. novelist Sinclair Lewis in a 1930 interview in Berlin, "[but] emotionally I know she is better than every other country." Precisely: this is what being an American (or Frenchman, Italian, etc.) means. The Romans observed that in the end *vincet amor patriae:* the love of country will prevail. Anyone who would dispense with patriotism must also dispense with the *patria.*

There is always an element of sadness in being above, or beyond, belonging. The true cosmopolitan is a lonely figure. The Nobel Prize–winning Austrian ethologist Konrad Lorenz suggested that "the instinctive need to be the member of a closely knit group fighting for common ideals may grow so strong that it becomes inessential what these ideals are." The British-Indian writer Salman Rushdie found that "exiles or emigrants or expatriates are haunted by some sense of loss, some urge to reclaim, to look back, even at the risk of being mutated into pillars of salt." The British-Canadian-Hungarian writer Stephen Vizinczey put it even more directly. "There is no way you can kill off people's desire to belong to a group which speaks their own language and has the same historic and cultural background," he wrote in a private letter in 2002. "The idea that the Germans and the British are just as much your family as your fellow Frenchmen— and vice versa—can be popular only among talented, young, preferably beautiful multilingual people who can find partners to screw everywhere. And they are in the minority."

Some cultures and some periods reduce patriotism to a beer commercial. A character named "Joe Canadian" made a splash in a TV spot for Molson's brew in 2000. In a beery monologue "Joe" puffed himself up and ranted about being neither a whale-blubber-eating rustic nor, heaven forbid, anything like an American. The spot was a huge success, albeit of a campy kind; most Canadians viewed it with a mixture of enthusiasm and self-mockery. (Within a year the young actor who played "Joe Canadian," Jeff Douglas, went to look for work in Hollywood.)

What often gives rise to this type of faux patriotism is the lack of what fuels genuine patriotism, namely distinction. Groups rarely insist on being a "distinct society" when they are one; it is the absence or paucity of distinction that leads people into local patriotic raves. Local patriotism can be as fervent as it is vacuous: among British football fans it may express itself in bloody battles between Liverpool and Manchester United supporters.

But there is another side to the same coin. It reveals itself when genuinely distinct societies are not permitted to view themselves as distinct, at least not officially or not as authoritatively as they would like to: *vide* Quebec, *inter alia*. This, too, can give rise to a type of huffy hyper-patriotism, which usually appears incongruous, though perhaps not as grotesque as the artificial patriotism of the near-identical.

Americans and English-Canadians happen to be very similar linguistically, culturally, ethnically, historically, politically, and institutionally. Though it is quite easy to list "differences" between the two nations (and some people have made careers, or at least hobbies, of doing so) on examination most of the differences turn out to be minor. They are usually less than the regional differences between, say, north and south, or east and west, *within* Canada or the United States.

This engenders in the less powerful and populous of the two entities, English-Canadians, an identity crisis. People who suffer from it may turn obstreperous (or, as the British call it, "stroppy"). This kind of boorish patriotism is a psychological nuisance, as it flares up and subsides periodically. Luckily, in most cases it can be alleviated by a beer commercial.

THE LOCAL PATRIOT AS VICTIM

The time was the early 1980s, the venue, my Toronto apartment, and the topic, the relationship between Eastern and Western Canada. The tone of the discussion was heated. The poet John Newlove, speaking for Western Canada, was berating the poet Al Purdy (may both of them rest in peace), as a representative of Eastern Canada, for exploiting the western half of the country.

The times were conducive to such displays. The world was split into abusers and victims, and it seemed important to be a ranking member of the hierarchy of the oppressed. Margaret Atwood's 1972 book, *Survival: A Thematic Guide to Canadian Literature,* had staked out Canada's claim to permanent victimhood, alongside the rest of the dispossessed people, species, and genders of the earth. Atwood's study had taken the world of Canadian literary criticism by storm. It was a period when without claiming victimization a local patriot could not feel entitled to any respect.

The two poets did not actually come to blows, but at times they seemed close to it. Another guest, Grace Richardson, a writer of children's novels, was monitoring the argument in astonished silence.

Around three o'clock in the morning, after I persuaded the two men of letters to depart in a taxi, Richardson—herself Swiss-born, but of Canadian parents—spoke for the first time.

"One does get tired sometimes," she said, thoughtfully twisting a strand of her hair, "listening to the whining of blacks, but then one thinks of slavery, of Jim Crow, of segregation, and one feels ashamed.... And yes, one gets tired sometimes listening to the kvetching of the Jews, but then one thinks of Auschwitz, the Holocaust, and one feels ashamed.... But listening to the victimization of Western Canada.... well, you know, it's really scraping the bottom of the barrel."

NATIONAL FLAWS

Flying magazine advertises an aircraft as "built to exacting German standards."[1] We feel free to proclaim the existence of national virtues even in our politically correct times; we only balk at a hint that there may be such things as national flaws.

Yet nations do have flaws. If treachery is a flaw, for instance, it is hard to describe Romania as other than flawed. Since the one-time Turkish principalities of Moldavia and Walachia combined into the kingdom of Romania following the 1878 Congress of Berlin, Romania has betrayed

1. its Bulgarian allies during the First Balkan War of 1912 by abandoning them for the Serbs and Turks in the Second Balkan War of 1913, and taking three thousand square miles from Bulgaria as a reward;
2. its neutrality with its German-Austro-Hungarian neighbours by suddenly attacking Hungary in 1916, after entering a secret treaty with the Triple Entente;
3. its entente allies, after its attack on Hungary on August 27 fell apart (the Central Powers occupied Romania's capital about three months

later, on December 6), by eventually signing a separate peace with the
Central Powers at Bucharest;

4. the peace treaty of Bucharest by invading Hungary after the collapse
   of the Dual Monarchy in 1918, and receiving Transylvania as a reward
   at the Treaty of Versailles;
5. the Western powers by abandoning them as Hitler's star kept rising
   and going over the side of the Axis in 1940, returning Transylvania to
   Hungary in the process; and
6. the Axis by abandoning it for the Allies when it became clear Hitler
   was about to lose the war in 1944, and being rewarded with
   Transylvania again.

Turning coats six times in a mere sixty-six years of existence as an independent country (from 1878 to 1944) adds up to an impressive record: it is about one betrayal per decade. Romania's flaws are at the bottom of the moral scale, but flaws can appear at the upper end as well. If Romania has elevated flip-flop into an Olympic sport, Canada has done the same with fence-sitting.

The one-time British colony has become so lofty that it is attempting to become better than fair—which is like bending over backwards to be straighter than vertical. Since the 1960s, Canada has tried to achieve moral leadership in the world by observing strict neutrality between good and evil.

THE CANCER OF DIVERSITY

Two trends that can wreck nations and turn regions into trouble spots are non-traditional immigration and multiculturalism. Both come in different forms and guises, so they need to be defined case by case. For example, in countries that have no tradition (or need) for immigration, *any* immigration can amount to non-traditional immigration.

The kind of multiculturalism that can wreck nations does *not* mean Finnish saunas in Germany or Vietnamese restaurants in France. It does not mean mosques in Munich, or Albanian folk dances in Florence, or private Spanish-language schools in Tampa, Florida. It does not mean urbane expressions of cultural cosmopolitanism that make Paris or London or other great cities of the world civilized or sophisticated. What it does mean is encouraging (or worse, entrenching in law) the retention of undigested, unassimilated foreign communities within a nation, ultimately leading to the idea that there *is* no nation under the country's flag with a common (or "dominant") culture or identity, only diverse communities within the body politic jostling for advantages or looking to redress grievances, real or imagined.

In 1965 the scholar Ernest van den Haag wrote an article in the *National Review* in which the following lines appeared:

"The time has come for the United States to consider itself settled territory—just like Germany, or Italy or Ireland—and to stop encouraging immigration altogether. . . . I see no more reason for us to encourage immigration or invite it than there is for the Italians, the Irish, or the Germans to do so."[2]

The amusing thing when one reads this passage today is that Germany and Italy started altering their own immigration policies and practices in the 1960s just as Professor van den Haag was writing these lines. During the last forty years, far from America following the examples of Germany and Italy, it was Germany and Italy, along with France, Holland, and other European countries, that followed the example of America. By doing so, they naturally encountered some of the same problems as America—in worse ways, actually, as most European societies had evolved with no contemplation of, and little tolerance for, "multiculturalism" and "diversity."[3]

Since the 1960s, the opinion-making elites across the political spectrum from the left to the centre-right in Europe have endorsed and promoted the idea of immigration. They regarded the matter as settled and no longer capable of being debated in good faith. Cautionary voices, such as Britain's Enoch Powell's, were silenced or vilified. This abandoned the field (at least temporarily) to genuinely racist voices from the far right. Inevitably, voters who could expect no hearing on the topic from anyone else were eventually pushed to National Front–type parties in increasing numbers.

This need not have happened. As van der Haag pointed out nearly four decades ago, "Patriotism is not racism. The wish to preserve one's identity and the identity of one's nation requires no justification any more than the wish to have one's own children." By now the inevitable conflict between native populations and unassimilated blocs of immigrants has given rise to ultra-nationalist parties or movements—and sometimes riots and atrocities—in many countries of the European Union. The conflict has also had the incidental effect of splitting the conservative vote worldwide. The rapid rise of the Reform Party (later Canadian Alliance) in Canada, the Progress Party in Denmark, Pim Fortuyn's List in Holland, the National Front in France, the New Zealand First party in New Zealand, the One Nation party in Australia, the Freedom Party in Austria, or the National Alliance in Italy has been at least partially due to traditional conservative parties surrendering to multiculturalist forces. Immigration rivals abortion in its ability to split voters on the right. Needless to say, whenever the political right chooses to fragment itself over any issue, it reduces its electoral chances against the political left.[4]

THE BRIDGE-BUILDING FALLACY

There are constant attempts to cure the ills of diversity by "building bridges." The fallacy that ethnic-religious conflicts are based on cultural ignorance and can be alleviated by fostering communications or "interactions" between diverse groups is deeply ingrained in the liberal ethos. At the benign end this illusion expresses itself in ceremonial gestures as well-meaning Christians, Jews, Muslims, and Buddhists "dialogue" and visit each other's places of worship. At the malignant end come measures of "human rights" legislation, including racial, religious, and gender quotas; compulsory "sensitivity training"; censorship of language or ideas deemed "politically incorrect," and similar outrages by the sub-tolerant organs of the super-tolerant state.

Harmony is expected to flow from scientific liberalism placing the country under the watchful eye of its love police. This hope is based on

Professor Frankenstein's faith in human and social engineering, as outlined in an earlier chapter. The outcome of Frankensteinism may vary depending on the time and the place, but once implemented it is likely to aggravate rather than alleviate ethnic and religious resentments, even while temporarily suppressing them. The result is group hatreds exploding in the bloodiest way at the first historic opportunity, as they did in the former Soviet Union or in the former Yugoslavia.

Friction between groups exists for a variety of reasons and is not the result of isolation and inexperience. On the contrary: groups require continuing contact to disdain or resent each other. Promoting separation between diverse groups—though not without its dangers—is likely to result in more harmony than promoting dialogue. Contact leads to shared experiences, and while experiences can be good or bad, bad experiences have greater specific weight. Clashes always form at points of contact. Nations, like people, tend to fight with their closest neighbours. The Nazi ideologue Alfred Rosenberg studied Judaism; he knew more about it than many a Jew. Organizing visits to synagogues can trigger budding Rosenbergs among Gentile schoolchildren as easily as paragons of tolerance.

One is tempted to reverse all liberal maxims and say that "dialogue distances people" or that "experience narrows the mind." Such reversals are not strictly true either, but they are closer to observed realities than liberal dogmas about dialogue bringing human beings together. Unfortunately for tolerant and inquisitive people who like exchanging ideas, liberalism put into practice often compels a re-evaluation of their own habits of mind.

65

IN DEFENCE OF ETHNIC CLEANSING

"The history of political ideas begins . . . with
the assumption that kinship in blood is the sole possible ground
of community in political functions."
—HENRY SUMNER MAINE *Ancient Law*

CAN ETHNIC PERSECUTION EVER BE JUSTIFIED?

LET ME BEGIN WITH A SERIES of statements that are, or ought to be, self-evident and as such unnecessary. If I feel obliged to start with them, it is to deter unwanted supporters—i.e., ethnic nationalists who may be mistakenly attracted by the title of this chapter.

I consider nothing as despicable as a group of people marking some of their neighbours—in the next house, next street, next village, or next region—as aliens belonging to a different order of humanity. The wretched practice of social discrimination or exclusion, to say nothing of the forcible expulsion, persecution, robbery, or murder of people identified as "others" solely because of their ancestry, race, religion, or cultural-linguistic heritage, is beyond contempt.

The banishment, expropriation, and killing of people because of their ethnicity are crimes. All such acts are the same in kind, whether or not they are the same in degree.

Some acts of ethnic or religious persecution are so unconnected with any rational consideration as to appear insane. At other times they may have some tenuous connection with reality. But even the exigencies of war or other conditions of acute social distress cannot justify measures directed against the person or property of those identified as "outsiders" on the sole basis of their ancestry or faith. Whether committed by French against their Huguenot, Serbs against their Muslim, Hutus against their Tutsi, Turks against their Armenian, Germans against their Jewish, Canadians against their Japanese, or Catholics against their Protestant neighbours, the expropriation, expulsion, confinement, and assassination of people for their ethnicity or religion are criminal acts.

Nothing in the analysis that follows is an attempt to justify such practices.

WHAT ARE THE REASONS FOR ETHNIC OR RELIGIOUS CONFLICT?

Condemning despicable acts is insufficient. One must also ask why they are repeatedly committed, not only in savage times and places, but also in highly developed countries and periods. In the preceding century, as well as in our own, various societies committed acts that not only contravened abstract ideals of decency and morality, but also the actual norms that governed the very societies that committed them. Though some of these acts were perpetrated by criminals, some also involved individuals for whom the commission of such crimes entailed a departure from standards that they otherwise regularly observed in their daily lives.

To understand the dynamics that lead to such departures from accepted norms, it is necessary to look at how human societies are organized.

WHAT CONSTITUTES A NATIONAL SOCIETY?

Societies strive for a sufficient measure of internal cohesion and a sufficient degree of security from external threats. Those are probably the fundamental purposes for which groups unite. National societies come into being when groups within the boundaries of a region achieve a sense of belonging and common identity.

A national society, or even a larger entity, such as an empire, once established, must maintain cohesion. If it cannot, it becomes dysfunctional, and ultimately ceases to exist.

As discussed already, groups become nations by coalescing around some organizing principle. There are a number of different principles available. The very first—family—is self-evident and need not be discussed here.

Human groupings did not go beyond the immediate (or rather somewhat extended) family for the first and longest period of the history of our species. As outlined in Chapter 24, the five other principles that have come into play—sometimes singly, but more often in combination—may be identified as 1. tribal, 2. cultural-linguistic, 3. dynastic, 4. ideological, and 5. geographic.

Tribe

After the familial, the oldest and most straightforward combination is tribal. This is usually, though not always, a cultural-linguistic-geographic combination, i.e., it is a group identified by common descent and common cultural-linguistic tradition living within the boundaries of a given ancestral area. Although such groups are hardly ever "pure" in direct familial relationship or bloodlines—few if any of their individual members can trace their descent from one initial group of ancestral families—they are still predominantly linked by a familial relationship, diluted only secondarily by the influx of migrations, conquests, intermarriages, etc., such as most tribes experience through lengthy historic periods. Importantly, though the origin of a relationship may be adaptive, as in the case of alliances or migration, the legal fiction takes the familial form. A stranger is adopted into the tribe as a "son" or "daughter."

Even in such a group cohesion cannot be taken for granted. If the tribe's geographic area is large, linguistic-cultural differences may arise over time between descendants of the same initial group. The economic development of regions may become dissimilar because of differences in climate, natural resources, and so on. Later descendants may define themselves by their newer regional interests and cultural-linguistic variations more than by a sense of kinship or blood relationship with the ancestral tribe. "Local contiguity," to use Henry Sumner Maine's expression, may replace kinship as a ground for community in political functions. Regions may secede and set up separate political entities in spite of a common blood- and cultural-linguistic heritage linking them to the ancestral tribe— as America seceded from the "mother country."

DYNASTY

Another organizing principle borrows from the familial model by imbuing an actual family with a symbolic kinship, which ties various tribes together in an empire or nation-state. Such a national society defines itself by a dynastic link, where individuals and groups become members of the same family through a dynastic ruler, thinking of themselves as "children" of the same "father" or "mother" in spite of the obvious absence of any tribal or linguistic-cultural relationship. The dynastic king or queen may be described in parental terms (such as "Great White Mother") attesting to this symbolic process.

This organizing principle is more flexible—in a sense, more "modern"—because it enables different groups to achieve cohesion without a need for any familial relationship or legal fiction of adoption. The older tribal organizing principle requires either actual shared descent, or that strangers be "adopted" into the tribe, because political functions cannot be exercised in common outside the family.[5] New members must not only acquire the manners, language, and customs of the tribal group, but assume the fiction of a shared descent. The dynastic organizing principle, however, can accommodate groups of different language, custom, race, and so on into the symbolic "family" of the ruling house.

The historic success of the dynastic principle in many different regions of the world confirms its adequacy for cementing nations, at least as long as it coincides with the spirit of the times and remains psychologically acceptable to people who choose to be governed by it.

IDEOLOGY

The organizing principle of an ideology, meaning a religion or a philosophy, may be adequate even when it stands alone, though it is generally used by people in combination with tribal, dynastic, and geographic modes of social organization. In the sense used here, "ideology" includes any system of beliefs that are sufficiently distinct, exclusive, and strongly held to amount to a cohesive world view, and thus serve the purpose of identity and unity. It is unnecessary to distinguish between secular and religious ideologies. Though religion is usually taken to mean a system of non-rational belief with a metaphysical basis, for achieving identity and unity both religious and secular systems of belief may function in similar ways.

In our times Communism still serves as an example of the secular model. For a while it enabled different national groups to coalesce into a superseding national entity, called the Soviet Union. If Communism had not collapsed for other reasons, it is possible that it would have had enough cohesive force as a quasi-religion for the maintenance of a national entity over a large geographic area, inhabited by distinct groups, many of which were not connected by ethnic, linguistic, or religious ties of any kind, as indeed the USSR had done for the better (or, at least, longer) part of a century.

Compared to tribal and dynastic principles, religion and ideology appear to be less stable. Transcendental systems such as "Christendom" or "Islam" (or "Communism"), even when presenting a united façade against outsiders, are more vulnerable to schisms than other great organizing principles. They are less likely to stand without the reinforcement of tribal-cultural-geographic-dynastic ties, such as Communist ideology draws on for assistance in North Korea or in China. It may be suggested that religion acts more reliably as a divisive force than a cohesive one and is more likely to separate entities into factions than to unite factions into entities. Still, historical examples of religion often show it as a unifying force, especially when used in conjunction with other unifying forces of tribe, dynasty, and geography. For this reason it is not entirely baseless for someone like Osama bin Laden to speak in the name of a "Muslim nation."

Still, ideology—or more generally "culture," comprising stages of religious and philosophical thought, as well as technological and social development, over a historic period—is more likely to create larger but less well-defined entities than nations. Ideology and culture tend to create *civilizations*. Civilizations have traits and tempers; they are recognizable and unique, though they are obviously more diverse and multi-faceted than nations. They may be temporal or geographical, or both. It is possible to think of "Europe" or the "Orient" as civilizations, as it is of antiquity and the modern era, always keeping in mind that civilizations comprise several nations, often at odds with one another. It is not unusual for a nation belonging to one civilization to form an alliance with a nation belonging to another civilization against a third nation within its own civilization. Examples abound, but for illustration it is sufficient to recall the English forming alliances with various Native tribes against the French in North America (and vice versa). In 1609, for instance, when the Huron entered into an alliance with the French against the Iroquois, it was a case of a paleolithic civilization forming an alliance with a neolithic civilization against another paleolithic tribe. No one raised an eyebrow at such civilizational miscegenation. A modern version of it occurred during the 1980s when the United States supported Afghani rebels against the Soviet Union.

Ideological organizing principles can sometimes survive profound changes in the ideology itself. For instance, Zionism remained a core organizing principle for Israel (along with tribal ties, of course) even after the pseudo-socialist ideals that used to fuel it faded. But while remaining at Israel's core, Zionism had undergone a metamorphosis. This change resulted in secular Zionism, energized by populist-collectivist and quasi-Marxist ideals, gradually giving way to religious Zionism, energized by Judaistic, or mystical-historical, notions. The predominantly Western-born settlers who largely replaced the East European–born kibbutzniks as the elite cadres of Zionism in Israel by the 1980s were not inspired by David Ben-Gurion and Poale Zion (the Hebrew Social Democratic Party) but by militant Brooklyn rabbis and the Torah. Settlers were only a small minority, of course, but that made no difference; kibbutzniks had been a minority as well. It is not necessary for tone-setters to form a majority within a society. That is why, if a successful peace agreement between Israel and a future Palestinian state resulted in the abandonment of Jewish settlements in the disputed territories of Judea and Samaria (as it almost certainly would), it would cut to the new core of Zionism, whose tone-setters are inspired by history and destiny rather than by populism and pragmatism. What effect such a blow might have on Zionism as an organizing principle is hard to pre-dict. Adversity may enervate or energize ideologies.

Geography

Examples of unity achieved primarily through "local contiguity" or geogra-phy range from Switzerland to the United States of America, though in both examples religion, in the traditional sense as well as in the sense of ideology, would have to be included as a unifying factor. What makes the concept of a geographic organizing principle somewhat elusive is that ultimately all enti-ties must have geographic unity by definition—otherwise they would not be recognized as entities—and consequently it becomes a matter of interpreta-tion whether the geography of such nations is a cause or a result.

In the case of nations such as Switzerland or, especially, the United States, although their predominantly Christian religions and democratic ideologies have contributed greatly to their cohesion and self-definition, it is possible to conclude that they are organized to a significant extent around the principle of their distinct geographies as well.

What Are the Causes of Internal Strife?

When internal conflict ensues within a nation, in the absence of threats by external enemies (or, less often, by epidemics, famines, or similar disas-ters), the likely cause will be the breakdown of one or more of the country's organizing principles.

Not all civil wars signal a breakdown of organizing principles. If, for instance, a rival dynasty arises in a nation organized along dynastic princi-ples, it may result in a "wars of the roses" type of turmoil. The conflict between the Houses of York and Lancaster, lasting for over a generation, became a defining feature of fifteenth-century England. Nevertheless, it was a low-grade conflict, mainly because it did not bring into question the organizing principle itself. In contrast, the conflict between Parliament and the King during the Cromwell period two hundred years later was not merely a struggle for power between the royalist Cavaliers of Charles I and

the Roundheads of Parliament, but a fight for the replacement of one ideological organizing principle with another, namely absolute (or
near-absolute) monarchy with a puritanical theocracy.

If the primary organizing principle of a country suffers a breakdown,
the tendency of its constituent parts will be to reorganize themselves along
other organizing principles. This sounds self-evident, but it needs to be
stated, because the breakdown of an organizing principle could theoreti-
cally be followed by a tendency to chaos. In general, however, it is not.
What happens instead is that the cohesive force of a rival organizing principle—geography, for instance—becomes the fault line of the earlier
organizing principle that has decayed. A country that is becoming dysfunctional for any reason may experience trends of regional separatism, even in
the absence of ethnic, linguistic, or religious differences in the devolving
regions. Embryonic notions of Albertan separatism in Canada illustrate the
point. It is more common, of course, for a region seeking devolution or
secession not to be merely geographically distinct, like the provinces of
Alberta or Newfoundland, but also ethnically and linguistically distinct, as
the province of Quebec. But, while ethnic distinctiveness hastens and
strengthens devolutionary tendencies, such distinctiveness is not a *sine qua
non*, for the simple reason that ethnic separatism is usually the effect rather
than the cause of a country's (or empire's) dissolution. The *cause* is the
decay of the country's previous organizing principle.

The most common examples of organizing principles breaking down in
the twentieth century have been of the dynastic and ideological type. The
two often worked in combination, as in the case of the Hohenzollern,
Habsburg, and Ottoman empires, where the decline of one dynasty did not
simply result in its replacement by another dynasty, but in the replacement
of the monarchical principle itself, either with attempts at Western-style
democracy, as in Germany and Austria, or an old-fashioned authoritarian
regency, as in Admiral Miklós (Nicholas) Horthy's Hungary, or a kind of
modern proto-fascist authoritarianism, as in Kemal Atatürk's Turkey.

In the case of the Austro-Hungarian monarchy, the demise of the
dynastic principle immediately split the domain of the last Habsburg
emperor, Karl I, along its ethnic-linguistic fault lines into the distinct

nations of Austria and Hungary, with other segments of the empire joining Italy or the newly created entities of Czechoslovakia and Yugoslavia (both of which were to succumb later to their own ethnic fault lines after their ideological organizing principles decayed).[6] Although Austria-Hungary's split was partly due to the victorious Entente powers redrawing the map of Europe at Versailles and Trianon following World War I, the reversion to nation-states organized on the basis of ethno-linguistic principles was a natural consequence, not just of the Central Powers' military defeat, but of the fatal enfeeblement of the monarchical-dynastic principle. After the collapse of the Soviet empire some sixty years later, the decay of the ideological organizing principle of Communism resulted in a similar breakup of Mikhail Gorbachev's realm along its ethno-linguistic fault lines, even without any attempt on anyone's part to redraw the map of Asiatic Russia or Eastern Europe.

An organizing principle need not be benign to do its job, only vigorous. Unattractive as Communism and Saddam Hussein's Baath Party–type Arab national-socialism were, as organizing principles they could maintain for quite a while the political coherence of entities such as Iraq or Yugoslavia that would have split into various distinct parts (or into a state of civil war) without them. Acknowledging this is not to commend Communism or Baathism, only to note a fact. At the same time one should also note a parallel fact, namely that the survival of entities that require unattractive or repressive organizing principles to stay alive is rarely beneficial. As a country, Yugoslavia may have been a more significant entity than the various rump states that succeeded it; however, even if possible, it would hardly have been desirable to maintain Yugoslavia as a country at the price of totalitarian repression or murderous civil war.

All organizing principles are at their furious and repressive worst when they are challenged, which usually happens twice: when they are being created and when they go into decline. "The whole history of civilisation is strewn with creeds and institutions which were invaluable at first, and deadly afterwards," wrote Walter Bagehot in his 1872 book *Physics and Politics*.[7]

Which brings us to ethnic cleansing.

WHEN IS ETHNIC CLEANSING DEFENSIBLE?

Before addressing this question, it is useful to see if one can identify the circumstances under which examples of ethnic cleansing have historically occurred. When such examples emerge as expressions of mass hysteria—pogroms, St. Bartholomew's Day massacres—they cannot be analyzed, except perhaps in medical terms; they can only be condemned and resisted. Irrational manifestations of xenophobia; the misidentification of a group within a nation as a source of economic or social ills or military setbacks; the transference of guilt on some minority for superstitious reasons (or because of deliberate scapegoating by those actually responsible for the problem), along with a host of similar causes and motives, cannot be excused, only repudiated. Whether directed against the Hutus or the Huguenots, ethnic cleansing of this type is indefensible.

But ethnic cleansing—that is to say, the conclusion that two groups of different ethnicity, culture, and sometimes religion cannot inhabit the same geographic region and must be separated—need not always be irrational. Even when the idea is irrational in the abstract, it may be rational in a given moment of history. There are situations in which—whether because of a shift in organizing principles, aggravated by recent or ancient conflicts, economic development, the emergence of demagogic personalities, or for any other reason—two groups lose the ability to share the same space. In such cases the question arises in terms of how best to reduce bloodshed and human suffering—and the answer may present itself in terms of ethnic cleansing.

Needless to say, for ethnic cleansing to be an answer of any kind, it has to be conducted within strict parameters of decency and fairness. There have been examples of secessions and population exchanges—both types of "ethnic cleansing"—that were carried out with a measure of decorum and lawfulness. They include the 1905 separation of Norway and Sweden as well as the 1993 separation of Slovakia and the Czech Republic (in sharp contrast with the bloody fracture of the South Slav union of Yugoslavia). As always, the devil is in the details and so is the redemption. Guarantees of personal safety and civil rights for ethnic minorities who choose to stay in a given geographic region, along with compensation to those who choose to leave, are two among the fundamental principles to be observed. Certain conditions would have to be judged on a case-by-case basis, and so on. The point is, the realignment of a region's population along ethnic-linguistic-religious lines need not be an intrinsic anathema.

Multicultural societies (to use a current term for nations comprising different ethnic, linguistic, or religious groups) are not lofty ideals in themselves. They are not a kind of spiritual goal to which all societies need to aspire. Multicultural entities may be attractive as well as functional; they may be sophisticated and colourful; they may work well in those places and times in which they coincide with vigorous ideological, geographic, or dynastic organizing principles, but they are not some higher plateau, a moral ideal, a form of social organization which all societies ought to achieve. On the contrary: in the absence of bonds that supersede ethnicity, culture, and language—i.e., in countries whose foundational raison d'être has never been dynastic, ideological, or geographic, or in countries where such principles have lost their strength and appeal—multiethnicity is generally a source of friction. In such places cultural differences are irritants rather than colourful attractions. Attempting to fit such nations into a Procrustean bed of multiculturalism can be achieved only at the cost of the stretched, tortured, or amputated limbs of their inhabitants.

This implies no call for ethnic purity. It is not remotely necessary. Ethnic purity has rarely been required or achieved even in societies organized around ethnic principles. It has usually been possible for ethnocultural minorities to exist, even to prosper, in countries that were organized around the tribal identity of a majority. At various periods in history, most countries in Europe, and many countries elsewhere, were naturally and unapologetically based on the principle of being ethnically French, Danish, Russian, Japanese, etc. These countries, even when they embraced parallel organizing principles—such as dynastic ones, for instance—considered their national languages and institutions official and exclusive. (The United Kingdom's paradigmatic language was the King's *English*—it was not the King's Gaelic, German, or Urdu.) Such nation-states had no trouble coexisting with ethnic minorities, even if not on a perfectly equal footing. Minorities, whether welcomed or resented, would likely be second-class citizens to some extent. This did not necessarily preclude them from being treated lawfully or humanely; it only precluded them from being first-class citizens. Often they were excluded from the inner circles of the majority's national society or allowed only a token presence.

In nation-states of this type, ethnic minorities traditionally had the choice of accepting their second-tier status and being tolerated—or not accepting it and being resented or persecuted. Needless to say, minorities were sometimes persecuted even when they accepted their status, but they could be sure of persecution if they tried to compete for full citizenship— or, conversely, if they tried to secede.

SECESSION AND ETHNIC CLEANSING—A BRIEF DETOUR

Secession is available to minorities only if they are concentrated in a geographically defined region—say, Quebec. When available, secession means a drastic change in the status quo. For this reason, it has usually been resisted, not only by the majority population of the country affected, but also by the international community. Opposition to separatism is often the only policy on which liberal and conservative world opinion agrees. Whether it involves Basques in Spain, Chechens in Russia, or Armenians in Nagorno-Karabakh, international opinion usually opposes the idea of separation per se as a danger to regional stability. This is independent of any abhorrence of the separatists' methods, such as terrorism. In the early 1990s, for instance, the first attempts on the part of Croatia and Slovenia to achieve independence were greeted with a notable lack of sympathy by most world powers on both sides of the Atlantic. It was this initial lack of sympathy that encouraged Serb nationalists to try to hold Yugoslavia together by methods that eventually led some of them to being charged with crimes against humanity. Yugoslav ex-president Slobodan Milosevic might not be facing a war crimes tribunal in The Hague today if he had not assumed himself to be licensed by the world community to preserve Yugoslavia at all costs after the erosion of its organizing principle. Between 1991 and 1993 Milosevic had reason to believe that he was being regarded as the chief guardian of Balkan equilibrium. It was ironic when the United States and the North Atlantic Treaty Organization had to resort to arms, first in Bosnia, then in Kosovo, to enforce a series of secessions they initially tried to discourage.

Secessions rock the boat; population exchanges are costly; ethnic cleansing is inhumane. When countries split up they create refugees, disrupt economies, destabilize regions, and give rise to much human suffering. The ripple effects of such events can be felt for generations. Yet secession and population shifts are recognized to be preferable to mayhem. They are preferable to unending civil wars. They are better than massacres, mass graves, and mutilated bodies floating in rivers. As the lesser of two evils, measures that amount to ethnic cleansing are often embraced by big powers and international institutions. What is rare is for this to be *acknowledged*. Since "ethnic cleansing" is a term of disapproval, the expression is seldom used to describe measures of which world opinion approves.

After World War II, for instance, when 3.5 million ethnic Germans were expelled from their homes in the Sudeten region of Bohemia, no one talked about ethnic cleansing (at least, not until Czechoslovakia's president, Václav Havel, apologized for it in the 1990s). The point here is not that the 1945–1946 expulsion of Sudetenlanders was necessarily unjustified. That is a different and debatable question. What is beyond debate is that the expulsion was an obvious example of ethnic cleansing, accomplished with the endorsement, or at least tacit approval, of the international community. The wartime dispossession and displacement of Japanese-Americans and Japanese-Canadians from the West Coast of the continent—again, regardless of any possible justification—were also clear examples of ethnic cleansing. Yet even when apologies were rendered and compensation paid to the displaced people and their descendants, the phrase "ethnic cleansing" was meticulously avoided.

Yugoslavia is another example. There, the phrase "ethnic cleansing" has been reserved for Serb attempts to expel—or, sometimes, to exterminate—Croatians, Bosnian Muslims, and Albanian Kosovars from Serb-controlled and -populated regions. However, after the changing fortunes of war aided by American and NATO intervention brought about the expulsion of tens of thousands of *Serbs* from mixed-population regions in what became independent Croatia, Bosnia, and the protected region of Kosovo, the words "ethnic cleansing" disappeared from the vocabulary of both Western officials and the media. Unsurprising as this may be, it indicates that we employ the phrase "ethnic cleansing" to describe our judgement of certain acts rather than to describe the acts themselves.

This leads to the further conclusion that ethnic cleansing has a range of values, moral as well as practical. Without first determining where a particular act fits on this scale, we can hardly say whether we endorse it or condemn it.

ETHNIC CLEANSING—A LIBERAL SOLUTION

Nothing indicates this ambivalence better than Palestinian demands, supported by United Nations resolutions, for Israel to dismantle its settlements in the "occupied" territories. (The quotation marks are necessary because for many Palestinians the whole of Israel is occupied territory.) While demanding that the future Palestinian state be ethnically cleansed of Jews, Palestinians also demand a so-called right of return to Israel proper for all Arab refugees of the 1948 War of Independence as well as for their descendants.

The question has many dimensions, but the one that is pertinent to a discussion of ethnic cleansing is this: the Palestinian demands, regardless of their merits, take it for granted that Israel, if it is to exist at all, must be a multicultural state, while the future Palestinian state is to be based on the organizing principle of ethnicity.

Since liberal opinion supports the Palestinian demand, as does the United Nations, liberals must endorse the view that while it would be wrong for Israel to exist as a purely Jewish state in the Middle East, the Palestinian state cannot only be purely Arab but specifically *Judenrein*, to borrow, advisedly, a Nazi expression. Only a group that feels entitled to ethnic exclusivity to the point of being "Jew-free" would insist on settlements being dismantled and Jews expelled before it ever becomes a state. By supporting the demand, liberals evidently support the idea of ethnic cleansing.

It follows that liberals see the merits of ethnic cleansing in selective instances. They see it in the Balkans, as long as it involves Serbs; they see it in the Middle East, as long as it involves Jews. Loath to admit it, of course, they mask it by using the phrase "ethnic cleansing" as a value judgement rather than a description.

If Prime Minister Ariel Sharon ever attempted to expel Israel's Arab citizens in the way that the Palestinians demand the expulsion of Jewish settlers from Judea and Samaria, he would promptly be accused of ethnic cleansing. The accusation would be accurate enough—expelling Israeli Arabs *would* amount to ethnic cleansing—but so is expelling Jews from the West Bank. This does not make it necessarily wrong for world opinion to support Palestinian demands for the dismantling of settlements, but it does make world opinion support something it repudiates in principle, i.e., ethnic cleansing. Liberals support it, much as they hate to admit it, because in certain instances it is the lesser of two evils.

Separating people is not as attractive as uniting them. "*Something there is that doesn't love a wall, / That wants it down*," as Robert Frost put it, before ending his poem by repeating the old and savage truth: "*Good fences make good neighbours*." Dislodging Jewish settlers from the West Bank is no guarantee of peace, but not dislodging them is a guarantee of continuing conflict. Ethnic cleansing, like the surgical removal of a cancerous limb, is sometimes the astronomical price that needs to be paid for life.

9

SHEEP YEARS AND
TIGER DAYS

66.

IGNOBLE

SAVAGES

Ingemisco tamquam reus,
Culpa rubet vultus meus,
Supplicanti parce, Deus.
—Thomas of Celano

WHEN THE NATIVES—the indigenous people Europeans used to describe as "noble savages"—came in touch with Western civilization, it soon diminished their nobility and increased their savagery. A Cree storyteller in British Columbia recounts the difference in spirit between bygone days and his own times this way:

"Old men used to lecture their sons and grandsons. Once I saw my grandfather sticking a knife in the ground before lecturing his son. 'If I should get you angry with what I'm going to tell you, pick this knife up and you can stab me,' he told him. He did this because he knew what he was about to say was true. Today, my people, if I was to do the same thing to my grandchild, he'd probably grab the knife and slice my stomach open."[1]

In a culture of noble savagery a person who tells the truth has nothing to fear, while a person who does not tell the truth deserves to be stabbed. Advanced civilizations consider the first proposition too naïve, and the second too brutal. Presumably if aborigines lost their savagery before their nobility, they would no longer stab their grandfathers under any circumstances. A more usual development, however, has been for aborigines to lose their nobility before their savagery, and slice their grandfathers open for telling them the truth.

Unlike the Cree storyteller, I have little fear of my grandchildren slicing my stomach open for telling them the truth. They, in turn, need to have little fear of hearing the truth from me. We are too civilized for such savage and noble ventures. We slice no stomachs and tell no truths.

Like the Cree, though, I marvel at the discontinuity between myself and my descendants.

I recall making my son happy once. It happened on a summer day in 1979 when I accidentally reversed the nozzle of a spray can. It was a beautiful morning, not a cloud in the sky, and we were approaching a large and shiny motorcycle parked behind a fashionable residential building. My son, fifteen, was living in New York with his mother—he had been three when my first wife and I separated—and he was spending part of his summer holidays with me in Toronto. I was dressed to the hilt that morning, in full leathers. We both had new gloves, boots, and helmets, looking like a pair of space-age peacocks. As we stood by the custom-built machine that was to take us for a ride, I thought I saw a speck of dust on the chromed steering clamp. I whipped out a can of Armor-All, aimed it at the offending spot—and squirted myself squarely in the face.

One minute I was a figure of modish masculinity in an Italian television commercial, the next a clown in a circus, covered to my earlobes in thick white goo. I could not blame my son for doubling over in mirth. I regretted only that this was probably the purest moment of joy I would ever give him.

I had been fascinated by my father's universe. My son grew up to be indifferent to mine. He settled on a suburban planet, almost barren of literature, music, or adventure.

Even as a small child Alex seemed staid and circumspect. Once I tried to coax him to the top of a lighthouse in Cape Cod and had to drag him in the end because, obedient as he normally was, he refused to follow me. To this day I am not sure why.

He was not a difficult teenager. On the contrary. Other fathers envied me for him. Obedient, quiet, never in any kind of trouble. Picked up after himself and washed the dishes he used. No jock but no nerd, popular enough, editor of the school newspaper. Drugs? Brawls? Truancy? In the context of my son the very ideas sounded absurd. I wished he had at least smoked, which of course he did not. Never got drunk; never needed to be picked up from an emergency room or a police station. When he broke his ankle once playing football, it actually made me feel relieved. At his age I was in a cast half the time for one reason or another.

When he turned seventeen I offered to buy him a car if he would go to a driving school and get his licence. He said: "Gee, thanks, Dad," then did nothing. He did not get his driver's licence until he was almost thirty.

At university—he went to Cornell, majoring in government studies— Alex spoke intelligently about current affairs. He also dabbled in photography. He seemed most animated, though, when the conversation turned to grocery shopping and laundromats. He appeared to be a househusband in training. Not in training to be a kept man, but in search of a personal Valhalla. It was hard to say whether the outside world was above his head or beneath his contempt. Either way, he looked for fulfillment in domesticity. He just happened to be doing it at an Ivy League college.

"Perhaps you should have kicked me when I was a boy," he said complacently on one occasion when I remonstrated with him.

"A splendid thought, in retrospect," I agreed. "But as a boy, you gave me no reason."

Alex continued to be low-maintenance as an adult. He was never out of work, and never asked anyone for a penny. Blue jeans and hot dogs satisfied his sartorial and culinary needs. He certainly did not expect to be supported. It was less clear how he expected to support others. He was living from hand to mouth, doing dead-end jobs. He had no interest in post-graduate studies. My father motivated me without even trying. I could not motivate my son, no matter how I tried.

One June he phoned me to announce that he was getting married.

"Congratulations. When is the baby due?"

There was a moment's pause. "In August," he said finally. "How did you know?"

It was an easy guess. Alex's habit was to say nothing about anything until the last possible minute. He could give a snail lessons about how to

keep inside a shell. Nor was it a surprise that he decided to make his
girlfriend pregnant and marry her. A
Freudian might have theorized that,
having missed out on a regular live-in
father, Alex decided to recreate himself as one—to become his own
father, in effect. Except, not having
much experience with fathers, he
recreated himself as a mother. He
seemed intent on being in charge of
diapers and dishes.

I tried to think of my son as
Ulysses thought of his own
Telemachus, the heir of his sceptre

"The big monster is afraid of me."
With son, Alex, in Toronto, circa
1968.

and his isle, in Tennyson's poem. "*He
works his work, I mine.*" And, especially: "*Most blameless is he, centred in
the sphere/ Of common duties, decent not to fail/ In offices of tenderness,
and pay/ Meet adoration to my household gods,/ When I am gone.*" Except,
unlike Ulysses, I had no sceptre and isle to leave my Telemachus, and he
would be hard pressed to pay "meet adoration" to my household gods as
he could scarcely recognize their names.

When my son was about five he gave an indication of how he would
tackle his problems. We were watching a show on television, featuring a
monster. The beast was throwing tantrums on the screen, and I could see
that my son was getting apprehensive. The creature worried him. However,
he came up with an answer.

"Daddy, look," he said, pointing at the TV set. "The big monster is
afraid of me."

It was rather elegant. When one reality seems uncongenial, why not
simulate another? I was proud of Alex at the time. Much later I began to
wonder. My father made music and business deals. I scribbled and raced
motorcycles. My son held down a job and did the dishes. He also liked
playing a computer game called SimCity.

My father's generation tried to explore reality. Mine tried to exploit it. My son's generation preferred to simulate it.

It made sense for Alex to gravitate to computers, as he eventually did. As webmaster for an academic institution, setting up models for international scenarios—in essence, computer games—he found himself a niche in a parallel universe. My grandsons showed early signs of following in his footsteps. The older one cried when I put him on a motorcycle and seemed dejected sitting in a small plane's cockpit. He would play SimCity, though, for hours on end.

I spawned a tribe of virtual people. My ancestors discovered flight; my descendants discovered flight simulation. I wondered what the Cree storyteller would say about my grandchildren. How would virtual savages of virtual nobility react to virtual truths?

The Cree storyteller appeared as I was writing this. He wore an old BOAC uniform with a captain's stripes on his sleeve, as if the British Overseas Airways Corporation had not gone out of business in the 1970s.

"Well, old boy," said the Cree airline captain. "I hear you're complaining about your son."

"Just scribbling," I replied guardedly.

"I hear you're upset because he doesn't fly with you," he continued, "the way you used to fly with your father."

I shrugged.

"But wasn't there an incident," he asked, "that might have upset him? Wasn't there a flight where you were the pilot-in-command and something happened?"

"It always comes down to the pilot-in-command, doesn't it?" I said resentfully. "Kick the PIC. Whatever happens, it's his fault."

"Not necessarily, old boy," said the Cree. "Fault is determined by the Aeronautical Board. The PIC is only expected to appear and answer questions. In your case, the allegation is that you abandoned an aircraft in flight. Your son was a three-year-old passenger. You pushed the ejection button and bailed out. Well?"

"I had my reasons," I said.

"No doubt," he replied. "The Board is looking forward to hearing them."

He pointed at a group of Cree youths sitting in a semi-circle. They wore judicial wigs, their knives stuck in the ground. Two of them resembled my grandchildren. They did not look noble; they looked savage. When I opened my eyes, they vanished.

67

THE END OF HISTORY?

The guiding principle that a policy of freedom for the individual is the only true progressive policy remains as true today as it was in the 19th century.
—FRIEDRICH AUGUST VON HAYEK

1. AMMAR OF ANDALUSIA

After the fall of France, the poet George Faludy escaped to Morocco. He was among the cultural figures in Nazi-occupied Europe that Franklin Delano Roosevelt had been persuaded to invite to America. Faludy waited in Marrakech for the president's invitation to arrive.

While waiting, he met a young Arab named Ammar and accompanied him to the desert, where they spent a few days together. In some ways Ammar reminded Faludy of another Ammar, a glittering figure from a thousand years ago, who held sway in Seville during the high noon of Islam. The figure of ibn Ammar al-Andalusi stayed with the poet, and when he found himself in Spain during the 1970s he felt moved to write three stanzas about him. He wrote his lines in Hungarian, and I translated them into English.[2]

In his poem Faludy describes Ammar's world: the parks, the fountains, the minarets, the olive trees, the library, surrounded by the high walls of

Seville during the period of the Moorish conquest. He talks about Ammar, the admired poet and warrior, with his sword and jet-black horse, worshipped and quoted by all. He mentions the fame of his verse, his conquests, his scented nights of remorseless joy: the idolized Ammar, who likens himself to a golden lizard on a golden disc; Ammar, the wit, the hero, the bisexual, who can slither from the lewd lips of a boy into the eager ear of an odalisque, who at his touch will forsake her master and become Ammar's toy. "Nor will this change," Ammar notes, "after my body lies under my obelisk."

The last stanza deals with the decline of Ammar's world. It describes the arabesque as it loosens and falls from the domes of Spain. It talks about the library burning, Ammar's tunic unravelling, the fabric's colours fading, and the boys who knew his poems by heart lying dead. But Ammar himself remains oblivious. *"Brave and clever, he failed to note the fact,"* Faludy writes, *"that faith's no help, nor wit, courage, or dagger/ that no philosophy will resurrect/ a culture once it collapses forever."*

Faludy was not alone in thinking of Moorish Seville. The memory of Ammar the Andalusian, the fall of the glorious Alhambra, the fateful year of 1492, the Christian reconquest of Spain, were being recalled by an increasing number of people in the Arab world. It preyed on one person's mind in particular. "Let the whole world know that we shall never accept that the tragedy of Andalusia be repeated in Palestine," said Osama bin Laden in a taped cave-side speech following September 11, 2001.

The end of history? Writing in the sixteenth century, not long after Ferdinand and Isabella's conquest had returned Andalusia to Christendom, Francesco Guicciardini might have been tempted to compose a phrase similar to the contemporary historian Francis Fukiyamas' famous dictum. After all, the struggle had ended; expansionary Islam had withdrawn into itself in much the same way as Communism would 499 years later. But Guicciardini arrived at a different conclusion. "Past things shed light on future ones," he wrote in *Storia d'Italia*. "The world was always of a kind; what is and will be was at some other time; the same things come back, but under different names and colours; not everybody recognizes them, but only he who is wise and considers them diligently."

Capitalism *is* magnificent. No wonder Fukiyama and other devotees of contemporary Western social models seem at times reluctant to acknowledge that human life—and not mere life, but high civilization—is possible under a variety of social systems. But the notion that achievements in science, literature, architecture, music, statecraft, or the military arts cannot flourish except under conditions of Western-style liberal democracy is contradicted by the entire history of our species. Democracy as we know it has existed only in a few geographical locations and only for brief moments of histori-

"Ammar, the wit, the hero, the bisexual." Maya Jonas with George Faludy, 92, in Budapest.

cal time. It is neither the measure nor the full extent of human civilization. Other places and periods have also produced art, philosophy, science, faith, and joy, sometimes in abundance.

It is only that, on balance, of all the socio-political systems that mankind has put into practice so far, Western-style free enterprise liberal democracy has been the most conducive to individual liberty—the only true progressive policy, according to the great economist, Friedrich von Hayak—as well as to justice, prosperity, and fulfillment for the largest number of people. Some Utopian models promised to be better, but failed. Some theoretical models might be better, but they have not been tried.

Perhaps the most accurate way to put it is that of all the performance-tested social models Western-style liberal democracy comes closest to its specifications. "It flies near book value," as test pilots would say.

Which is why it is viewed with such resentment in other parts of the world.

2. ERIC OF LATVIA

The story of the poet and the ballet dancer illustrates another way in which history refuses to end.

In 2004 a sixty-six-year-old American died in a faded hotel room in a remote town in India. He had been ill for some time and he died alone. Looking through his meagre possessions—books, mainly—the proprietor came upon an e-mail address in North Carolina. He fired off a note, which was how Eric Johnson's friends learned of the final chapter in a bizarre, romantic, and ultimately tragic love story.

Love stories usually begin when the participants meet, but this was a literary romance and it began four years earlier. In 1962 Andre Deutsch published a book called *My Happy Days in Hell*. It was the autobiography of George Faludy, describing his life in Europe under Hitler and Stalin. It was a bravura performance. "Faludy is the kind of man we'd all like to be, besides being ourselves," commented the British historian Arnold Toynbee.

In New York a ballet dancer named Eric Johnson, then twenty-six, read the American edition. He became obsessed with the idea of meeting the man who wrote it. Johnson was not the only ballet dancer who read books, but may have been the only one ever to suspend his career for one. Deciding that he had to learn Hungarian before meeting the author, he stunned the Communist authorities by arriving on their doorstep in 1964, demanding permission to live and work in Budapest. The officials were so dumbfounded that they actually gave Johnson a job as a sportscaster in the English-language section of the state radio network. He worked there for the better part of a year, then said goodbye to his thoroughly confused hosts, and left Hungary in search of Faludy.

He found him in Malta, where Faludy, by then fifty-six, was living alone following the death of his second wife, Zsuzsa—the ethereal beauty who played such a pivotal role in my coming to Canada. Their only son, Andrew, was in a boarding school. As a sexual being, Faludy was an omnivore. He was attracted to beauty, youth, and intellect; the gender to which these qualities were attached made little difference to him. Johnson was certainly intelligent and in 1966 (I am looking at his photograph while writing this) he was undoubtedly beautiful. It would not be accurate to say that it was love at first sight between the poet and the ballet dancer, because for Johnson, then twenty-eight, love had preceded first sight by nearly two years. His love was an intellectual vinculum, which Faludy lustily proceeded to convert into a physical attachment, via the emotional medium of poetry. The outcome was a group of sonnets, among

"Spent the next thirty-six years together." L. to r., Eric Johnson and George Faludy with the author in Toronto, circa 1970.

the finest in the Hungarian language, equalling if not surpassing the poems Faludy had written for his dying wife. *"Fate has decreed me to be twice your age,"* he wrote in one. *"Next to your body I become weak/ The bone falls out of my arm."*

Faludy and Johnson spent the next thirty-six years together, living in various parts of the world, including Toronto, where they shared a small apartment with a pair of free-flying finches. The tiny birds liked to hitch a ride on the carriage of an old-fashioned typewriter Faludy used for his work. The finches learned to hover like miniature helicopters every time the bell rang at the end of a line, waiting for Faludy to slam the carriage home before settling on it again for the next trip. The birds and Faludy wrote several books together, while Johnson contributed Latin poetry to the Vatican's *Osservatore Romano*—just about the only market left in the world for Latin verse. In 1989 he published a slim volume, *Cantus Cicadarum,* by Ericus Livonius—Eric of Latvia, in acknowledgment of Johnson's Baltic background.[3]

After the collapse of the Soviet empire, the couple moved back to Budapest, where people worshipped Faludy and tolerated Johnson. The post-Communist government assigned a spacious apartment on the east bank of the Danube for their lifetime use—more precisely, for the lifetime use of Hungary's national icon, for Johnson, as the poet's "secretary," had no official status of any kind. Still, it looked as if they might live happily ever after in their opulent (by Budapest standards) abode. "I'll look after George as long as he lives," Johnson told me once. "I have no other plans."

It sounded final. Professor Fukiyama might have called it the end of history.

The last time I spoke with Johnson was in the spring of 2002, just before Hungary's runoff elections. He expressed the hope that the liberal-socialist coalition would win, because a centre-right government was more likely to rescind their lifetime occupancy of the apartment. I had a dim view of liberal-socialists, but could not blame either Johnson (by then sixty-four) or the poet (ninety-two) for not wanting to move.

The liberal-socialists did win, but, as it happened, Johnson's occupancy of the apartment was rescinded all the same. The child-god of love let loose his arrow and hit Faludy straight in the heart. The national icon fell, and fell hard, for a twenty-six-year-old photo model named Fanny Kovacs. Cupid's bull's eye made Johnson possibly the first man in history to be jilted by a ninety-two-year-old lover.

If same-sex marriage had been available to Faludy and Johnson, in thirty-six years of living together they might, at one point, have tied the knot. As it was, by the summer of 2002 it was Faludy and Fanny Kovacs who were getting married, and Johnson was on his way to India. Later Faludy told me that he and Fanny would have been happy for Johnson to stay, but evidently the former ballet dancer was not thrilled by the idea of trading a pas de deux for a ménage à trois.

Would the story have been different if the poet had been obliged to divorce the ballet dancer before marrying the model? Perhaps. Or perhaps not. As a student of the classics and a persistent lover himself, Johnson was probably resigned to the fact that Eros is not to be trifled with—at any age. History never ends. *Omnia vincit amor*.

In India, Johnson joined the Dalai Lama's entourage and he wrote letters to friends saying that he was happier than he had ever been. For all I know—we never talked again—it was true. Still, when he was diagnosed with cancer in the fall of 2004 he did not seek treatment. His diagnosis came a year after Faludy and his new wife had posed for the cover of the Budapest edition of *Penthouse* magazine.

68

NUMBERED DAYS

THE BLUE SALON

DURING A BRIEF VISIT TO BUDAPEST in 1972, I was looking at my father standing next to his armchair in what used to be the blue salon. By then it was neither. The hall that once housed the Bechstein piano was reduced to an oddly shaped nook, guarded incongruously by a bronze chandelier.

Father appeared fragile, leaning on his cane. He seemed to be contemplating his shrunken surroundings, along perhaps with his shrunken self. The latter was a function of his eighty-nine years, while atrophied living spaces in the Hungarian People's Republic were a function of the Communist state. The command economy's answer to housing problems was to subdivide dwellings, starting with those of the haute bourgeoisie.

Father seemed too feeble to move. "Daddy, what would you like?" I asked him. "I'll get it for you."

"Ha!" he said, without missing a beat. "If I knew what I wanted, I'd get it myself."

On this note of self-mockery father exited my life. The next day I boarded a flight for London and never saw him again. My visit was in March; by August he was dead. Mother later described how Father waited in his hospital room for her to return from lunch, then sighed deeply and died as she sat by his bedside cradling his head in her arms. Nothing would shake my mother's belief that my father had been ready to go before noon, only he did not want to leave without saying—or rather sighing—goodbye, so he kept death at bay until she had finished her lunch.

"Can one keep death at bay?" I remember asking my mother. She looked at me and responded with her best Mona Lisa smile. "Well, your father did, didn't he?" she said.

My father died of complications following a broken hip suffered in a fall while crossing the former blue salon—the one in which the Turkish opera singer Fatime had once invited my uncle to press his fist into her abdomen. My father probably set out to cross the salon because he remembered something he wanted. To me it indicated the inherent danger of remembering things. The doctors said it was more likely that Father fell because his hip broke than that he broke his hip falling. Apparently old people do not break their bones in falls as much as they fall because their bones break. That was probably why grandfather fell a few years earlier. He was ninety-two. My mother said that grandfather did not go gently into that good night, but kept reducing his nurses to tears right until the moment he drew his last breath. Since reducing Budapest ward nurses to tears was no easy feat, my mother took secret pride in her father's resolutely mean temper even while she kept apologizing for him and distributing baksheesh among the weeping hospital staff.

Grandfather had survived his wife, my Victorian grandmother, by two years. My mother survived my father by twenty-five years, passing away just a few weeks before her own ninety-second birthday in 1997. Even though she loved her husband deeply, and could never speak of him without tears welling up in her eyes (though not actually rolling down her cheeks, which she would have considered self-indulgent), when I first saw her a year or so after my father's death, I noticed that she looked ten years younger. Caring for old people, no matter how much one loves them, is an immense burden. My father's passing, while it devastated my mother, also gave her a new lease on life. She used it well, and spent the next two decades travelling to places like Vienna, Salzburg, London, Toronto, Miami, and New York. Good genes, and being only sixty-seven when my father died, left her with a supply of energy that often exhausted those nearest to her.

On one occasion her stamina enhanced my cinematic currency. Dead on my feet after being dragged all over London, and knowing that suggestions of a pause for refreshments would be coolly received, I pointed to a marquee as we were passing a movie theatre in Soho. "Mother, I need to see this film," I said. "Business. Do you mind?" In truth, I simply needed to sit down. As it turned out, the show on tap was a German film about a sub in the Atlantic. Called *Das Boot*, it was a hit at the time and deservedly so. Not being drawn to submarine warfare as entertainment, without mother I would have missed it.

In stage routines Jewish mothers are overly proud of their children as well as protective of them. Mother fit the first cliché, but not the second. She frowned on my excuses for slacking off or retreating. After a summer

"If I knew what I wanted, I'd get it myself." Father at 89 in Budapest.

of being dangled from a long pole by an earnest swimming master who was cautiously optimistic about my progress, mother took matters into her own hand and pushed me into the deep end of the pool. "Sink or swim," she advised me. I swam. At the age of six I ran to her complaining that a schoolyard bully had hit me. "You have hands, haven't you?" she said. "Whack him before I whack *you*." Her advice was again impeccable, but it did not create a climate of sympathy. My parents neither sought nor extended undue emotional support. They were not cold; they were not distant or forbidding, but they regarded some reserve, even stoicism, as de rigueur for anyone of character and breeding. Ordinary folk—my mother called them "simple people"—were exempt. Simple people could weep and wail all they wanted. They could raise their voices in public and express opinions about places they had never seen. They were at liberty to confuse fashionable bestsellers with books and popular tunes with music. Simple people had this licence because they were lesser life forms, though my mother would never hold it against them. Holding their simplicity against lesser life forms would also have shown a lack of character and breeding.

During the darkest years, while my father stayed home, cooked meals, and played the piano, my mother went to work at an industrial plant called the Red Star Tractor Factory. She kept the books and continued displaying great patience with the simple people around her. Telephones were openly monitored in those years—Stalin was still alive—and my mother was in the habit of conducting her occasional phone conversations with my father in

German. One day she was summoned to the Communist Party secretary's office. Comrade Lajos, pockmarked and short of stature, used to be my uncle's chauffeur. Though a proper martinet, he was somewhat circumspect with my mother.

"Magda, for heaven's sake," he said, "can't you stop talking German on the phone? You're driving the monitors crazy."

"Not to worry, Lajos," my mother replied with her usual dignity. "We talk in East German."

After my mother turned ninety, she instructed me to move her into a nursing home. The institution we settled on was named for the nineteenth-century thespian, Odry Árpád. Situated in a faded mansion in the embassy district of Budapest, it offered rooms to elderly artists, musicians, performers, writers, and their kin. It had a long waiting list. Mother approved of her new quarters, but about eighteen months later, in the fall of 1997, she started feeling unwell. I telephoned from Toronto to ask if she preferred me to come immediately for a few days, or visit with my wife in December and stay for a month. She unhesitatingly opted for the latter. I suspected this was mainly because she liked my third wife, Maya, who could be counted on to bring her gifts of exactly the right kind. In fact, mother's fondness for Maya went beyond gifts. She always yearned for a daughter (her first child had been a girl who died a day after being born) and she had been persistently looking for a substitute. She even adopted a "sister" for me in the person of a gifted and photogenic English writer, Angela Lambert, whom she met at a British Embassy reception in the late 1970s. Mother tried to recruit my previous wives as daughters, too, but they proved poor substitute-daughter material. Maya, something of a China doll, complete with long black hair, was just right. She could be (and enjoyed being) combed, dressed, and exhibited by mother to elderly Budapest ladies whose own peevish daughters-in-law had sour smiles and varicose veins. These ladies wished that they, too, had a China doll to play with. Maya not only allowed herself to be petted and groomed, but being a traditional Oriental girl in some respects (though hardly in others), she treated mother with the customary deference young wives display to their mothers-in-law in the Far East. It was a winning combination.

I took mother at her word and made arrangements to visit Budapest with Maya in December. Though mother was nearly ninety-two and ailing, I trusted her to keep death at bay at least until we arrived. She would do so, I believed, in the same way as my father had done twenty-five years earlier. I realized that Father needed to hold out only for a few hours, while mother would have to hold out for six weeks, but she seemed stronger and in better health. A friend who saw her around that time concurred. "She wasn't in top form any more," he told me later, "but she was looking for-ward to your visit. I was sure that she'd wait for you."

"A traditional Oriental girl in some respects." At our wedding in Toronto, 1997.

She did not, as it turned out. We spoke on a Saturday, and she died Sunday night—"in her sleep," as her nurse reported it the next day, which is the way nurses report deaths all over the world. It must be the phrase of choice in some nursing manual.

Since mother died alone, I have no way of knowing whether she died sound asleep, wide awake, or anywhere in between. I have no way of knowing whether dying took her seconds or hours. I know only how she felt Sunday evening, a few hours before her death, because she described it to an acquaintance, the last person to see her. "Like a dog stuck in a well," she said to her visitor, speaking in Hungarian. *"Ugy érzem magam, mint kutya a kútban."* I wish she had said it in English because it sounds even worse in Hungarian.

My wife had wanted to wash and dress my mother's body, in accor-dance with Oriental custom, which the Hungarians found bizarre. In Budapest there were specialists for such things. After a brief cultural tussle, the host country won. The next time we saw mother she had been trans-formed by specialists into an urn. The unadorned vessel, said to contain

"She wasn't in top form any more."
With mother in Budapest, about a
year before her death.

her ashes, was to repose in a small crypt alongside the urns of her husband and parents. Maya nicknamed the crypt—a plain cavity in a Spanish-style cemetery wall—"Mother's condo." The funeral was equally plain, with no sacerdotal presence. The Budapest autumn responded appropriately with a swirl of yellow leaves in weak October sunshine, but the sound system in the chapel of the old Kerepesi cemetery was subdued to the point of being inaudible. Gounod's *Funeral March of a Marionette* remained an ethereal presence, felt rather than heard. I said a few words, and so did my "sister," Angela, who had flown in from London. She spoke English, naturally, which few of the mourners understood, but appreciated all the more. They told me later that it raised the tone of the occasion.

Maya was pleased that my mother had been cremated, because she regarded putting people in a hole in the ground as a barbaric custom. Cremation was against Jewish tradition, but my mother had chosen it for my father and my grandparents because it made cemetery visits more convenient for her. Plots were in short supply. To honour Jewish tradition, mother would have had to visit three different gravesites in three different cemeteries.

"Wouldn't they have minded, being cremated?" Maya asked her once.

Mother responded with her Mona Lisa smile. "While they're alive, dear, you do things their way," she said. "When they're dead, they're dead."

BEETHOVEN'S MASK

A framed drawing on my wall is dated 9/11, 1920. It is a death mask of Beethoven. My mother, a fifteen-year-old schoolgirl at the time, drew it as an art class assignment.

Six years earlier Sir Edward Grey, the British foreign secretary, made a famous observation as German troops were marching into Belgium. His oft-quoted remark was, "The lights are going out all over Europe. We will not see them again in our lifetime."

Was Sir Edward wrong? After all, within six years of his dire prediction, European schoolgirls were drawing Beethoven masks in their art classes

"When they're dead, they're dead."
Budapest, Kerepesi cemetery, 1997.

again. True, the darkness persisted. Two world wars, combined with Fascism, Nazism, and Communism, extinguished the lives of some 100 million Europeans between 1914 and 1991 (counting all who died on battlefields, in bombed-out cities, in death or labour camps, and in the cellars of the secret police). Still, ultimately both wars ended in victory for the powers representing the best of Western values. Fascism, Nazism, and Communism collapsed. The lights of Europe, which Sir Edward did not expect to see again in his lifetime, came flickering back about fifty-eight years after his death (he died in 1933).

But then again, Sir Edward may have been right. His Europe was not a place but a civilization. It was the West. It was Christendom. It included Washington and New York. And on this "Europe" the assault of darkness did not diminish.

My mother drew her Beethoven mask on 9/11, 1920. Eighty-one years later, exactly to the day, nineteen Islamic warriors crashed three hijacked airliners into the Pentagon and the World Trade Center.

69

A FLIGHT TO

WINDSOR

ON FRIDAY, JUNE 7, 2002, I firewall the throttle and lift off from Toronto City Centre's four-thousand-foot runway eight. The ninety-three-minute flight is to take me to Windsor, Ontario, on the American border. I have absolutely no business in Windsor. My plan is to fly there, have lunch at the airport restaurant, and fly right back.

A climbing right turn over Lake Ontario puts me on course for my first checkpoint, Burlington Airpark, about twenty-six miles due west. Directly below, the water sparkles in the sunlight, but along the shoreline the shimmering ripples become muted in slight haze.

"City Tower, Kilo Whiskey Quebec, Four Stacks, level at one point five."

"Roger, Kilo Whiskey Quebec. For higher, contact Toronto at one three three decimal four. Good day."

I have no business in the rainy city on the Detroit River, but have an excuse for flying there. Tomorrow I am supposed to pilot my wife to Windsor—the only Canadian city *south* of the United States—along with my wife's cousin, here on a visit from Seoul, Korea. She is broadening her education in geography, and I am attending a judicial cocktail party as a journalist. Not having flown to Windsor since my student pilot days, it is prudent to familiarize myself with the route before taking passengers.

But this is only the excuse for my flight. The reason for it is Saint-Exupéry's. I want to clear my head.

"I fly because it releases my mind from the tyranny of petty things," wrote Antoine de Saint-Exupéry. He was, of course, a better writer than a pilot. He was really a writer who flew airplanes, not a pilot who wrote books. Working pilots fly, not to release their minds from anything, but to get from here to there, preferably for a fee. And the best of pilots fly just to fly.

There are also therapeutic pilots: patients popping flight hours instead of tranquillizers. Physicians, bankers, movie stars, some flying serious equipment, all weird ducks pretending to be eagles. I could see myself becoming one. If I do, shoot me.

Traffic is fierce along the approaches to Toronto's Pearson International, but west of Burlington the sky thins out. I bank left to a compass heading of 240 degrees as Toronto Radar hands me over to the first of a string of en-route controllers.

"Kilo Whiskey Quebec at three thousand, looking for four point five."

"Four thousand five hundred approved."

A hawk resents my intrusion into its airspace. It wheels and soars effortlessly alongside, with its head turned as it watches me through the side window, converting altitude to speed, but losing next to none in the process. Dazzled by this superior airmanship, I look away for a second. By the time I turn back, the hawk is gone. "He blinked," it probably tells its mate back at the nest, referring to me.

Kilo Whiskey Quebec settles in cruise flight at four thousand and five hundred feet. Flawless day, twelve-mile visibility, smooth air, puffy summer clouds scattered below. Nothing to do for the next hour but scan for traffic and occasionally twist a little knob on a dial. Tomorrow the right seat will be occupied by Korean cousin Milim. A chart spread in her lap, she will follow our progress with Oriental earnestness.

That is to come. Today it is all tranquil and solitary aloft.

The four-seat plane has no air conditioning. I adjust the overhead vent but even the stream of air rushing inside the cabin feels muggy. There is no relief at altitude for a metal tube suspended in the humid Ontario summer.

"*Der Sommer war sehr gross.*" The voice in the earphones is my own, so I must have spoken out loud as Rilke's line popped into my head. Yes. It has been a very great summer. But great summers come to an end.

I first read "Autumn Day," Rainer Maria Rilke's much-anthologized poem, when I was a teenager. Eons from my own autumn, I found decline romantic, as young people often do. The poem settled in my mind. It settled in Rilke's language, of course. *Herr: Es ist Zeit. Der Sommer war sehr gross.* Now in the skies over southern Ontario I am overcome with an urge to improvise a translation into English. In case a passing hawk wants to listen.

In his poem Rilke replaces Shelley's optimistic question with a mournful one. "If Winter's here, can Spring be far behind?" the English poet asks in "Ode to the West Wind." "If Summer's here, can Fall be far behind?" counters the German poet in "Herbsttag," albeit in very different words.

> *Lord: It is time. The summer was fair.*
> *Rest your shadow on the sundial's face,*
> *Release the autumn breezes in the air.*

Hail, fair autumn breezes. I am about to turn sixty-seven. Recently a young man made me an offer for my last motorcycle. I am resolved to say no. One needs a motorcycle even in autumn. There was a time when I had six, three for the racetrack, the rest for the street. But that was at high noon, with no shadow falling across the sundial's face.

> *Order the last grapes to ripen on the vine,*
> *Let them have two more southerly days...*

Two more southerly days. Just about.

It has been more than a year since I visited a neurologist friend. It was in the spring of 2001.

"What's the matter with you?"

"I think I suffer from every neurological illness known to man."

Over the next hour he considered my multitude of symptoms, then turned to me with the satisfied smile of a keen diagnostician.

"Well, you don't have all the conditions in the world. However, you did manage to pick up two."

I expected him to say obesity and hypochondria, but what he said was, "Peripheral neuropathy and Parkinsonism."

Then he paused.

"Will you elaborate?" I asked.

"Well, neither is life-threatening, at least in the short run..."

"And the bad news?"

"The same as the good news. Neither is curable. If Canada had private medicine like other decent countries, you'd be one of my meal tickets."

As sunlight shimmers, morning frost delays,
And the seed's sweetness yields a weighty wine.

"Say again, last call?"

Toronto en-route radar sounds mystified. I must have pressed the transmission button while improvising Rilke. Note to self: remember not to do it again. One cannot predict how controllers at Nav Canada might react to an onslaught of poetry.

"Disregard, Toronto."

"Kilo Whiskey Quebec, you're leaving my sector, radar service terminated."

The fellow clearly has no time for German modernists. "Can I have another frequency for flight following?" I query. Radar service is optional under visual flight rules, but I rather like Big Brother watching me in the air. It is Big Brother watching me on the ground that makes me uneasy.

"Contact Cleveland at one two zero decimal zero five."

I am being outsourced to the United States, aeronautically speaking. It probably has nothing to do with poetry. Canada must lack civilian radar coverage west of some point along the north shore of Lake Erie.

"Cleveland, this is Charliefox Kilo Whiskey Quebec."

"Go ahead, Canadian Alphabet." The midwestern voice sounds disdainful. Americans use no letters in their call signs, except November for "N." The rest are numbers.

"Kilo Whiskey Quebec is a Cessna Cardinal about ten miles west of St. Thomas en route to Windsor, request flight following," I tell him.

Not in this lifetime, Canuck, the Yank seems to say under his breath. What he says out loud is this:

"Canadian Cardinal, are you squawking VFR? I'm not painting you."

I glance at my transponder, which is transmitting the proper code for visual flight rules. It is being interrogated, too; the little yellow light is flashing. Before I could say so, Cleveland solves the problem to his own satisfaction.

"You're too low, Canadian Cardinal, that's what. Climb at your discretion, then call me again if you like—goodbye."

He sounds gleeful, leaving me alone and unobserved in the skies. Oh well. In the far distance a shape in the lake begins to look like Pointe aux Pins and Rondeau Provincial Park on the chart. Soon it will be time to turn west.

Who is now homeless, will never build a home.
He'll roam in rooms inside a stranger's house.

"There are many kinds of peripheral neuropathies," my keen diagnostician friend says. "One kind is caused by diabetes, another by environmental poisoning, and so on. Yours is idiopathic."

"Meaning?"

He gives a short laugh. "What do you think?" he asks.

"Meaning you haven't got a clue."

"See, it pays to have taken ancient Greek in school." My friend was also born and raised in Budapest. "Now you know what we don't know."

"What I know is my toes tingle, yet I can't really feel them."

"As time goes by, it will be the least of your worries," he says reassuringly.

My big worry is Parkinsonism, he explains, which also comes in many forms. Whichever variety I will turn out to have, it will share characteristics common to the breed. The mind will command, but the body will gradually cease to obey. Hands will not grip, legs will not move, eyelids will not blink, shoulders will not shrug off jackets. Or they might move unbidden. Or tremble. But all this could take years and years to fully develop ("I guarantee you five," my friend says) and in the meantime some patients go on as before. Fly planes, run countries, do anything.

"Parkinson's is a high-class disease," my friend muses. "Some of the best people have it. There's the Pope, the actor Michael J. Fox, there's former U.S. attorney-general Janet Reno..."

Thanks. And possibly Hitler.

"I wish you had stopped at the Pope," I say to him.

Wake up startled, write long letters, and browse
In brittle books, then in alleys alone,
Watch the curling leaves whirl without a pause.

Over Chatham the compass course changes to 275 degrees. The air becomes thicker and lumpier. The visibility in haze near the south shore of Lake St. Clair drops to about half of what it was near the north shore of Lake Erie. A great morning for flying is becoming a middling day.

For the first time in an hour the pitch of the engine changes as I pull back the throttle for a gradual descent to twenty-five hundred feet. Lower and slower also means warmer and wetter. The cabin becomes stifling. I can feel the shirt sticking to my back.

About twenty-five miles from the airport I call up Detroit Approach. The American controller gives me a transponder code, then clears me to contact the Canadian tower at the Canadian field. It is all very polite and efficient, but it illustrates the relationship between the elephant and the mouse. The reason is traffic, not politics—Detroit's three airports near the border have a far higher volume than Windsor's only field—but a Canadian aircraft still needs U.S. permission to land on Canadian territory.

A petty concern? Maybe. Saint-Exupéry: "I fly because it releases my mind from the tyranny of petty things." Or maybe not.

"Kilo Whiskey Quebec, the active is seven, but twelve is available if you prefer."

"We'll take runway twelve, thanks, KWQ."

The tires squeal a little as they touch down on the asphalt. "Autumn Day" has been translated. Not quite Cyrano de Bergerac—"*À la fin de l'envoi, je touche*"—but still something. "*At the end of my translation, I'll land.*"

After shutting down the engine, I put the poem in the logbook.

Lord: It is time. The summer was fair.
Rest your shadow on the sundial's face,
Release the autumn breezes in the air.

Order the last grapes to ripen on the vine,
Let them have two more southerly days
As sunlight shimmers, morning frost delays,
And the seed's sweetness yields a weighty wine.

Who is now homeless, will never build a home.
He'll roam in rooms inside a stranger's house.
Wake up startled, write long letters, and browse
In brittle books, then in alleys alone,
Watch the curling leaves whirl without a pause.

Over lunch (hamburger $8 + coffee $2 + fuel $90 = $100) I make up my mind to use the two southerly days of my autumn to write a book about my summer. Hoping that the last grapes will yield a drinkable wine. Before the leaves start curling.

If I do, it will be my fourteenth book. Perhaps I will call it *A Flight to Windsor*. But I may call it *Beethoven's Mask*.

70

THE SUFI PRINCESS

A detached comparison with other continents of the way Europe stood up to its past trials, and of its contribution to man's history, leaves one with a new confidence and affection for that small figure riding on the back of the Asian bull.
—ARTHUR KOESTLER

THE SULTAN TIPPU IS SAID TO HAVE remarked that it was better to live like a tiger for two days than to live like a sheep for two hundred years. Tigers were very much on the mind of the last Mogul ruler of Southern India, who stamped, engraved, or embroidered the initial letter of the word "sher"

(Hindi for tiger) on his garments, weapons, and kitchen utensils. Tippu was the son of Haidar Ali Khan, who first usurped the throne of Mysore from its sheepish Hindu rulers and gave the British East India Company as much grief as he could. A devout Muslim and Sufi mystic, "the Tiger of Mysore" carried on his father's fight, trying to circumvent British sea power by allying himself with the French. In the end neither tigers nor the French could save him from Arthur Wellesley, the first Duke of Wellington, who besieged the ferocious sultan in his stronghold of Seringapatam, not far from the city of Mysore. Tippu himself perished in the ensuing battle at the age of fifty. He and his father together managed to annoy the British for thirty-eight years, from 1761 to 1799—significantly longer than the two days Tippu allocated to the tiger, but much shorter than the two hundred years he gave to the sheep.

Time may not heal all wounds, but it produces many ironies. The militant Muslim Sultan who dreamt of putting an end to British influence in India had a great-great-great-granddaughter who became a British war heroine. The Sufi princess Noor-un-nisa Inayat Khan, educated at the Sorbonne, escaped to England after the fall of France in 1940, then volunteered to return to Paris as a clandestine wireless operator. It was an immensely dangerous assignment, for which the brave princess, described as somewhat vague, dreamy, and conspicuous,[4] might not have been particularly suited. All the same, the Sultan Tippu's attractive, olive-skinned descendant managed to live like a tiger for much longer than two days. She was captured by the Germans in the end, imprisoned, and eventually shot, but only about fourteen months after being parachuted into occupied France in the summer of 1943. For the first two or three months she even managed to operate her radio. The British awarded her the George Cross, the civilian equivalent of the Victoria Cross, for gallantry.

In St. Paul's of Knightsbridge, which happens to be the church at which the Duke of Wellington used to worship, there is a plaque commemorating fifty-two women who lost their lives during World War II. One name— listed simply as N. Inyat-Khan G.C.—belongs to the Sufi princess, the great-great-great-granddaughter of the duke's defeated enemy.

In 1799 an eyewitness recounted that Colonel Wellesley (as he then was) considered the slain sultan's countenance so fearsome in death that he went to the trouble of personally checking his pulse to make sure the Tiger of Mysore was no longer alive. Wellington had good instincts, for Sultan Tippu had evidently not given up. As we now know, he dispatched his genes to share commemorative honours with his hated British adversary in the duke's very place of worship.

Which brings us to the next point.

71

CLIO ON A BROOMSTICK: AN EPILOGUE

The walls will not defend the townspeople, if the townspeople
will not defend the walls.
—GEORGE FALUDY

EUROPEANS (TO SAY NOTHING OF AMERICANS) are newcomers in the art of running the world. As recently as in my great-grandfather's day (he was born in 1845) four Turkish dynasties ruled the bulk of Asia from the Bosporus to the Pacific. There were the Ottomans of Constantinople, the Qajars of Tehran, the Manchus (Qing) of Beijing, and the Moguls of Delhi.[5] With the exception of the Manchus, they were all followers of Islam. The Manchus became Buddhist, but were descended from the Jurchen or Nuzhen people, who spoke an Altaic-Tungus language; in other words, not to put too fine a point on it, they were Turks. The Muslim Moguls were in serious decline by the nineteenth century, but were not fully deposed until the Indian Mutiny, which finalized the British Raj. But the Raj lasted a mere blink of an eye, from 1858 until 1947, not even a ripe lifetime of ninety years, much shorter than most dynasties that preceded it. For this reason it is not altogether surprising that what appears to

Europeans an eternal, perhaps even a natural, order, is viewed by Asians in a different light. The supremacy of Christendom does not appear ordained. On the contrary. From the Near to the Far East, from Turkey to China, the dominion of European-American civilization has the appearance of a temporary aberration, the goddess Clio getting up on the wrong side of the bed, a blip, a quirk, a mistake to be put right.

So the Old Witch of history is on her broomstick again. She is circling Manhattan. It is the kind of crystalline day pilots call CAVU: ceiling and visibility unlimited. Wars start on such days; epochs end or begin. One keeps reading about it in memoirs: "September 1, 1939, was a beautiful day at the Polish frontier."[6] Perhaps the Old Witch is not instrument-rated, which is why her broomstick usually appears in visual meteorological conditions, such as September 11, 2001, on the U.S. eastern seaboard, a brilliant day. The broomstick circles and doubles back. Black smoke rises. A fireball blossoms in an improbably blue sky.

NOTES

Part 1: Yesterday's Tomorrow

1. William James, *The Varieties of Religious Experience,* Lecture 1 (1902).

2. *New York Times Book Review,* May 29, 1966.

3. Noted by Conrad Black in his biography of Franklin D. Roosevelt, *A Champion of Freedom.*

4. Czechoslovakia had been created in 1918.

5. Letter, dated April 1, 1935, published in *The Letters of T. E. Lawrence,* ed. by Malcolm Brown (New York: NYU Press, 1988).

6. The Hungarian commissar Béla Kun founded the second Communist government in history, after Lenin's. It lasted from May 1 until August 1, 1919. Kun fled to the Soviet Union, where he was killed in one of Stalin's purges in 1936.

7. Stefan Zweig, *The World of Yesterday,* pp. 364–65.

8. Victor and Georg were cousins of the renowned conductor, Otto Klemperer.

9. "Pali" was the nickname of my Prague cousin. His actual name was Paul Roth, later changed to Paul Rigor. As an artist-designer and occasional document forger, Paul was the competitive brother of the late Stephen Roth, a well-known cartoonist who escaped to London before the war. Cousin Stephen worked for the *Daily Mail,* and his collection of anti-Nazi cartoons, *Divided They Fall,* was published in 1943.

10. A passage from Horthy's own memoirs, published in 1953, may serve as an illustration of his ideals. In the passage Horthy describes laying a wreath on Emperor Franz Joseph's crypt in Vienna's Capuchin Church on his return from an enjoyable state visit to Benito Mussolini's Italy in 1936.

    "His Majesty had been my great teacher, to whom I knew that I owed much," Horthy writes. "How often had I not, in performing my task as Regent, asked myself, 'What would His Majesty Francis Joseph have done in a case like this?' Even after his death, I continued to trust in his wisdom. I have never regretted that I retained so many of his arrangements, tested by centuries of use, in dealing with Hungarian problems."

11. Senator Grafstein was editing an anthology about Holocaust awareness at the time.

12. Mark Mazower, *Dark Continent,* p. 154.

13. She became my first mother-in-law eventually, may she rest in peace.

14. The oft-quoted remark was made by Israel Zangwill in 1901. His actual observation was, "Palestine is a country without a people; the Jews are a people without a country."

15. Guiseppe Mazzini (1805–1872) and Guiseppe Garibaldi (1807–1882) were patron saints of Italy's Risorgimento. Lajos Kossuth (1802–1894) was the leader of the Hungarian revolution of 1848 against the Habsburgs of Austria.

16. Baron Edmond James de Rothschild (1845–1934) was a philanthropist and early supporter of Jewish settlements in Eretz Yisrael in the late nineteenth century.

17. *Historia,* 2000/8, Budapest. Excerpts from Mrs. István Horthy's diary, with notes by Péter Sipos.

18. In Mauthausen, as it turned out.

19. Émile Durkheim, *Suicide*, pt. 2, ch. 6, sec. 1 (New York: The Free Press of Glenco, 1951).

20. Quoted in Gilles Deleuze and Félix Guattari, *Anti-Oedipus,* Preface (New York: Routledge, 1989).

21. Benito Mussolini, *The Political and Social Doctrine of Fascism* (ghost-written for Mussolini by the philosopher Giovanni Gentile and published in 1932).

22. Jean Baudrillard, *Cool Memories*, ch. 1 (London: Verso, 1987).

23. Ignazio Silone, *The School for Dictators,* ch. 4 (New York: Atheneum, 1963).

24. Ilona Bowden, the former Countess Ily, became active in various charities, Islamic studies, and Javanese mystical societies following her second marriage. Her memoirs were eventually published in two volumes under the title of *Becsület és kötelesség* (Honour and Duty) in Budapest (Europai Kiadó, 2000–2001). The book became a bestseller in Hungary.

25. Various tribes from Central-East Asia, such as the Avars or the Huns, wreaked havoc on neighbouring (and even distant) tribes until they themselves had been eliminated in turn. The Gothic wars devastated what we know today as

Italy, but the Ostrogoths as a group disappeared from history after their military defeat at the hands of Justinian I, the Byzantine emperor, in 552 A.D., while their Western brothers, the Visigoths, ceased to exist after 711 A.D. following their defeat by the Moors. Then, within six centuries, these great nomads of North Africa, creators of the impressive Umayyad caliphate in Córdoba, Toledo, Granada, and Seville, vanished themselves as a people and a culture. Their last stronghold, Granada, fell to the Christian monarchs Ferdinand V and Isabella I in 1492, and most Moors were physically driven from Spain after that date. As for more recent events, Europeans had no genocidal designs in the southern Pacific region or in South-Central America, but they nevertheless ended up extinguishing entire cultures. Scholars estimate that in the nineteenth century the Congo's population was reduced by ten million people under the colonial rule of Leopold II of Belgium, whose aim was rubber production, not mass murder.

26. One obvious contemporary example in this century is the large-scale extermination of the Armenians by the Turks. Another is the expulsion of ethnic populations from places as diverse as the Crimea, British Columbia, Kosovo, and the Sudetenland. Such deportations occurred before and during, as well as after, the Nazi era.

27. In his monumental *Hitler and Stalin: Parallel Lives*, Alan Bullock, while conceding that a comparison between the Nazi and Soviet holocausts "is valid," distinguishes the latter by saying that the Stalinist system used mass murder "as an instrument to secure political and social, not biological objectives" (p. 974). This peculiarity, though accurate, is somewhat technical. One doubts if it would have mattered much to the victims. Such distinctions seem designed to sidestep controversy rather than to enlighten.

28. Stefan Zweig, *The World of Yesterday*, p. 315.

29. Bernard Lewis, in a Donner Foundation speech, Toronto, May 31, 2002.

30. Some Nazis came to realize this. Walter Schellenberg, Heinrich Himmler's chief of foreign intelligence for the SS, remarked that while exterminating *all* the Jews would have been fine, since the Germans had only one-third of the world's Jews in hand, killing them was worse than a crime, it was stupid. ("... *schlimmer als ein Verbrechen, es sei eine Dummheit gewesen."*)

31. Quoted by H.R. Trevor-Roper in *The Last Days of Hitler*.

32. Quoted in *Le Monde*, June 4, 1987.

33. Victor Klemperer, *I Shall Bear Witness*, p. 29.

Part 2: Mad Cows, Sacred Cows

1. George Faludy, *Erasmus of Rotterdam.*

2. Magyar Szabadságharcos Szövetség.

3. "Come here, motherfucker!"

4. "Where to, now?"—"Always westward."

Part 3: Twelve Golden Mullets

1. George Faludy, regarded by many as the greatest living Hungarian poet, spent the war years in France, Morocco, and America with his first wife, Vali Ács. He served as a tailgunner with the U.S. Air Force in the Pacific. After their return to Hungary following the war, Vali and Faludy divorced and he married Zsuzsa Szegő. She waited for him from 1949 to 1953 while he was incarcerated by the Communists at the labour camp of Recsk. Their only child, Andrew, was born in 1955. After the 1956 revolution, they settled in London, where Zsuzsa died of cancer in 1965. Faludy moved to Malta, where he was visited by a former American ballet dancer, Eric Johnson, who had read Faludy's autobiography, *My Happy Days in Hell*, and wanted to meet the poet. For the next thirty-six years Eric and Faludy lived together, first in Malta, then in Toronto, and, after the collapse of the Soviet empire, in Budapest. In the summer of 2002, Faludy, by then ninety-two, married a twenty-six-year-old poet and photographic model named Fanny Kovács.

2. On November 6, 1956, Jack Pickersgill, minister for citizenship and immigration in Louis St. Laurent's Liberal government, instructed the Canadian immigration office in Vienna to assign top priority to applications from those Hungarians wishing to emigrate to Canada. Eventually about 38,000 Hungarians did so.

3. The first document generally viewed as the ancestral treaty of the European Union was signed on April 18, 1951. Mentored by French Foreign Minister Robert Schuman, the European Coal and Steel Community (ECSC) came into being that year. It was followed in 1957 by the two Treaties of Rome: the European Economic Community (EEC), better known as the Common Market, and the European nuclear development treaty that created the European Atomic Energy Community, called Euratom.

4. A British civil servant, Sir James Arthur Salter, also played a major role in the early formulation of the European idea. Some historians, notably John Keegan, believe Salter's influence equalled Monnet's in importance.

5. As related in *The God That Failed*, the seminal anthology in which such twentieth-century intellectuals as André Gide, Richard Wright, Ignazio Silone, Stephen Spender, Arthur Koestler, and Louis Fischer describe their journey of disillusionment with Communism. *Time* magazine called it the "Canterbury Tales of the 20th century."

6. Luigi Barzini, *The Europeans*.

7. Author's interview with Henry Kissinger, February 2001.

8. *Siberia* (1930) and *The Firebird* (1932).

9. Hannah Arendt, *Crises of the Republic*, "On Violence," sec. 1 (New York: Harvest/HBJ, 1972). The full quote reads: "The heritage of the American Revolution is forgotten, and the American government, for better and for worse, has entered into the heritage of Europe as though it were its patrimony—unaware, alas, of the fact that Europe's declining power was preceded and accompanied by political bankruptcy, the bankruptcy of the nation-state and its concept of sovereignty."

10. Milan Kundera: Paul, in *Immortality*, pt. 3, "The Brilliant Ally of his own Gravediggers" (New York: HarperCollins Perennial Classics, 1999).

11. Author's interview with Henry Kissinger, February 2001.

12. Fortuyn was assassinated by an animal rights activist in 2002.

13. United Press International, April 30, 2002.

14. United Press International, May 18, 2002.

15. See more on this topic in Chapter 32, "Europe: But Will It Fly?"

16. *Commentary*, September 1947.

17. *The Wisdom of the Sands*, ch. 2 (New York: Harcourt, Brace Jovanovich, 1948).

18. *Sentences et Maximes Morales*, no. 73 (1678). (New York: Penguin, 1983).

19. *Observer* (London), October 7, 1962.

20. Author's interview with Henry Kissinger, February 2001.

21. *Aphorisms*, by G.C. Lichtenberg, compiled between 1765 and 1799; tr. by R.J. Hollingdale (New York: Penguin, 1990).

22. Conversation, October 30, 1917, at Smolny, Petrograd, reported by John Reed in *Ten Days That Shook the World*, ch. 3 (1926).

23. *National Post*, May 20, 2002.

24. *The Times* (London), May 21, 2002.

25. "Blue-Rinsed Lady on the Verge of a Nervous Breakdown," *Prospect Magazine*, 2002.

26. Mark Mazower, *Dark Continent*.

27. This exchange is also reported in Barbara Amiel's 1980 autobiography, *Confessions*.

28. I am describing here David Godfrey's views of thirty years ago; I do not know whether he would stand by them today.

29. W.H. Auden, *The Dyer's Hand*, pt. 3, "Hic et Ille," sec. D (London: Vintage International, 1963).

30. *The New Criterion*, Vol. 15, No. 1, September 1996.

31. Should inquisitive readers insist on knowing, the Hungarian's suggestion was for the open-shirted man to become sexually intimate with his Italian mother.

32. Henry Kissinger, *Years of Upheaval*, p. 686.

33. Ibid.

Part 4: On Being a Martian

1. Initially, Hungary's Communists hoped to model their changes on Wladyslaw Gomulka's "Polish Road to Socialism." Nikita Khrushchev reluctantly permitted Gomulka's 1956 reforms as they did not challenge the essence of the Communist system or Poland's membership in the Warsaw Pact, i.e., the Soviet bloc. Although the expression "reform-Communism" was not yet in vogue—it entered the language only some twelve years later, at the time of the "Prague Spring" of 1968—Gomulka's Hungarian epigons were early reform-Communists.

   Within days, the people of Hungary ran away with the revolution that the Communist functionaries started. At that point some functionaries chose to follow the Hungarian people (notably Prime Minister Imre Nagy, later hanged by the Soviets) and some tried to resist them. Eventual refugees to the West included both types.

2. Come here; give me your watches; hands up; all right, then.

3. The people were real. The names are invented.

4. The program was called *Stories with John Drainie*.

5. The Csiky Gergely Theatre, in the Transdanubian city of Kaposvár, about two hundred kilometres southwest of Budapest.

6. For instance, when asked to recommend a modern play for *Festival*, the CBC's leading anthology drama series at the time, I suggested Jean Anouilh's

Poor Bitos. This illustrated three divisions between the CBC and myself at one stroke. First, Anouilh was a rarity among French playwrights in that he was not a man of the left. Second, *Poor Bitos* was vaguely upmarket: it presumed the audience was not totally unfamiliar with the French Revolution. Third, the play, far from being stodgy, was a black comedy. It was serious without being in the least earnest. Needless to say, the CBC was appalled.

7. Andrew Allan, Michael Anderson, Norman Campbell, David Cronenberg, Ivan Fecan, Sturla Gunnarsson, Arthur Hiller, Norman Jewison, Ted Kotcheff, Esse W. Ljungh, Fletcher Markle, Paddy Sampson, and Eric Till are among the names that pop into my head. All were CBC directors and producers at one time or another, some staff, some freelance. One could undoubtedly name another fifty, especially if one included such comedy actor-producers as the incomparable Johnny Wayne and Frank Shuster. Even among the CBC left's proto-communists or doctrinaire environmentalists there were a few gifted programmers, such as Mark Starowicz, David Suzuki, and some of their comrades.

8. Nothing prevents me, however, from disclosing the names of the keen lawyers who acted for me. They were Peter Israel and Howard Goldblatt—the latter on retainer from my "union," the TV producers association. I also feel at liberty to disclose that the distinguished senior counsel who acted for the CBC, Roy Heenan, still owes me twenty-five cents. This was the amount he bet me, as the proceedings dragged on, that in the end the CBC would *not* have to settle with me.

9. John Hirsch was a Holocaust survivor who ended up in Winnipeg after the war. He became a prominent theatre director and headed CBC-TV's Drama Department between 1974 and 1978. He died of AIDS in 1989.

10. As presenter of a nightly TV newsmagazine called *The Journal*, Barbara Frum had been Canada's most popular television personality from 1982 until her untimely death in 1992. Adrienne Clarkson, another television interviewer, was appointed to the semi-ceremonial function of Governor General, Canada's titular head of state, by Jean Chrétien's Liberal government in 1999.

11. Once I remarked to a reporter, the late Frank Rasky, who interviewed us together, that "Barbara would compete even with a can of beans." Rasky misunderstood and wrote that we were so competitive that Barbara once hit me with a can of beans. For some reason the description amused both of us, and we never bothered to correct Rasky.

12. Not much of a story, actually. My mother had an affair with my father in the 1930s while she was still married to her first husband. Apparently I was the

outcome of this liaison. I am using the word "apparently" because my mother never confirmed it; whenever my father brought up the subject, she just smiled like the Mona Lisa. The man whose name I retained all my life was Gyula (Julius) Jonas, the manager of Braun Liquor Works, a leading distillery in Budapest. As a Jew under the Nuremberg laws, he was taken to a forced labour squad attached to the 2nd Hungarian Army on the Eastern front, and went missing during the 1942 Soviet breakthrough at the Don River. A year later my father moved in with my mother. They eventually got married in 1964, just before visiting me briefly in Canada. By then my father was eighty-one and my mother was fifty-nine.

13. U.S. estimates quoted by Jonathan Sacks.

14. Amiel married Conrad Black, later Lord Black of Crossharbour, and I married a Korean-Canadian girl, the former Maya Cho.

15. *By Persons Unknown: The Strange Death of Christine Demeter,* (Toronto: Macmillan of Canada; New York: Grove Press, 1977).

16. *The Scales of Justice,* CBC Radio 1982–1989 and CBC-TV 1990–1996. The dramatized documentaries, which I developed with Guy Gavriel Kay, recreated important or unusual criminal cases.

17. *Greenspan: The Case for the Defence* (Toronto: Macmillan of Canada, 1987).

18. Chief Justice McLachlin and Justices L'Heureux-Dubé, Gonthier, Bastarache, and LeBel.

19. Justices Iacobucci, Major, Binnie, and Arbour.

20. In *The Globe and Mail.*

21. The extradition of Milosevic was engineered by Zoran Djindjic, prime minister and one-time ally, later bitter opponent, of President Kostunica. Kostunica opposed the surrender of Milosevic as a breach of a constitutional ban on the extradition of Serbian citizens, but the American bribe of $1.2 billion in international aid carried the day. Kostunica stepped down as president in 2003 after the new state of Serbia and Montenegro formally replaced the remnants of Yugoslavia. Djindjic was assassinated on March 12, 2003.

22. The institution was embraced enthusiastically by the European Union. When some major powers, notably America, Russia, and China, discovered that they could neither control nor veto the procedures of the court, they refused to sign on to it. By July 2002, with its forces engaged in Afghanistan, America had to threaten the U.N. to withhold funds from peacekeeping operations unless its soldiers and diplomats were exempted from the

court's jurisdiction, at least temporarily. As a result, America was exempted for one year.

23. As President Bush described Iraq, Iran, and North Korea in a speech in January 2002. The author of the phrase was the Canadian journalist David Frum, then a speech writer in the White House.

24. The books were *Vengeance* (Toronto: Lester & Orpen Dennys; London: Collins, 1984); *Greenspan: The Case for the Defence* (Toronto: Macmillan of Canada, 1987); and *Crocodiles in the Bathtub* (Toronto: Totem; London: Collins, 1987).

25. They included the late real estate wizard Eddy Cogan, who also lent the racing team his splendid daughter, Cary, as manager. There were also lawyers Ted Burnett and Peter Israel, filmmaker Norman Jewison, and a large brewery named Labatt's. Dusty Cohl, co-founder of the Toronto Film Festival, became a general accomplice.

26. *A Passion Observed, The True Story of a Motorcycle Racer* (Toronto: Macmillan of Canada, 1989).

27. It turned out that the Seneca was occupied by three young flight instructors returning to their home base. Chatty and relaxed, they did not bother announcing their presence on the frequency or listening for other planes. They never heard our radio call, or if they did, it did not register with them. They entered the circuit behind us, which would have given them a chance of seeing us, but they did not. When it was time for them to turn base, they turned, cutting right across our bow. Being to my left and slightly higher, the Seneca was exactly in my blind spot. If Frid had not caught a glimpse of a banked wing from the starboard seat, the result might have been five fatalities—probably with none of us ever knowing what happened.

Part 5: The Indisposed Empire

1. *Saturday Night*, September 23, 2000.

2. Le Duc Tho refused his share of the Nobel Prize.

3. Henry Kissinger, *Years of Renewal*, p. 140.

4. For Hungarians, their 1526 battle against the Turks at Mohács field is an example. For Serbs, the example is Kosovo.

5. A young man named Jan Palac set himself on fire in central Prague to protest the Soviet occupation on January 19, 1969. He died two days later. A second young Czech, Jan Zajic, also burned himself to death at the same location.

6. François Furet, *The Passing of an Illusion: The Idea of Communism in the Twentieth Century,* p. 1.

7. Charles Hamilton in the journal *Modern Age,* Winter 1987.

8. "It was Benjamin Huebsch of the Viking Press," Zweig wrote, "who has remained the most reliable friend and adviser and who—all and everything having been crushed under Hitler's hobnailed boots—has conserved a last homeland of expression for me, now that I have lost the old one, the one that was my own, the German, the European." *The World of Yesterday,* p. 321.

9. Edmund Wilson: *Letters on Literature and Politics* (New York: Farrar, Strauss, and Giroux, 1977).

10. *Newsweek,* January 24, 1955.

11. *The Lotus and the Robot,* p. 277.

12. Foreword to Allan Bloom's *The Closing of the American Mind,* p. 15.

13. This is hardly a new discovery. Pope saw it some three hundred years ago when he wrote:
    A little learning is a dangerous thing;
    Drink deep, or taste not the Pierian spring:
    There shallow draughts intoxicate the brain,
    And drinking largely sobers us again.
    Alexander Pope, *Essay on Criticism.* Part ii, line 15.

Part 6: The Shrimp Learns to Whistle

1. Conrad Black, who ran the world's fourth-largest newspaper empire in the 1990s, is a biographer of Franklin Delano Roosevelt and Quebec premier Maurice Duplessis. William F. Buckley, Jr., a grandee of American conservatism, is the publisher of the *National Review,* and Anatoli Shcharansky, now an Israeli cabinet minister, was the Soviet Union's best-known "refusenik" during the years of détente. The four telegrams to Svetlana Gouzenko were sent at the instigation of the British-American journalist John O'Sullivan, a former speech writer for Prime Minister Thatcher and the editor of the *National Review* at the time.

2. During a series of interviews with the author in the late 1990s.

3. Pascal, *Pensées* (1670), tr. by A.J. Krailsheimer (New York: Penguin Classics, 1995).

4. *Observer* (London), September 8, 1991.

5. Kim Philby, *My Silent War,* with an introduction by Graham Greene, p. 9.

6. The numbers come from Anne Applebaum's recent study, *Gulag: A History of the Soviet Camps*. See p. 17.

7. BBC-TV, 11 April, 1989.

8. Manny Drukier, *Carved in Stone: Holocaust Years—A Boy's Tale*, pp. 211–212.

9. Stefan Zweig: *The World of Yesterday*, p. 313.

10. Formidable a role model as Prince Gorchakov was, he made one mistake. He sold Alaska to the United States. In 1867, together with the Grand Duke Konstantin Nikolaevich, the emperor's brother, he orchestrated the deal for US$7.2 million. This was a vast sum for a chunk of inaccessible wasteland, and the Prince as well as the Grand Duke permitted themselves a little sarcasm when they remarked that Alaska's loss "would not be too painful." Today—especially when looking at potential sites of the In-Flight Interceptor Communications System of America's national missile defence—Russia's rulers would have to conclude that their hero was painfully wrong.

11. In 1996 Poland's prime minister, Jozef Olesky, resigned following allegations that he had spied for Moscow. In 1990 Czechoslovak People's Party chairman Josef Bartoncik quit when it was alleged during the parliamentary elections that he had been a Communist informer.

12. *Harper's Magazine*, New York, 1926: repr. in *The Essential Lippman: A Political Philosophy for Liberal Democracy* (ed. Clinton Rossiter and James Lare), pt. 1, sct. 1 (New York: Vintage Books, 1963).

13. Mark Twain, "Some National Stupidities," *Complete Essays,* ed. by Charles Neider (New York: Da Capo Press, 1963).

14. William James, Lecture 1 (1902) *The Varieties of Religious Experience* (New York: Touchstone, 1997).

Part 7: The Jewish Question

1. Oriana Fallaci, *Interview With History*, pp. 130–31.

2. Work sets you free.

3. At one of the prime minister's weekly press conferences in March 1978.

4. Worthington was Moscow correspondent for the *Toronto Telegram*. "Burnt by the Sun" is Nikita Mikhalkov's phrase. It is the title of the Russian filmmaker's brilliant movie about the Stalin era, winner of the Academy Award for Best Foreign Film in 1995.

5. For an account of the entire episode, see Peter Worthington's 1984 book, *Looking for Trouble*.

6. *Final Decree* (Toronto: Macmillan of Canada, 1981). Although the publisher was Macmillan, the editor's role devolved on Anna Porter, then of Seal Books, an imprint of McClelland & Stewart, who were bringing out the first paperback edition. The novel has had six editions to date.

7. Eventually a very experienced editor by the name of Frances McFayden, the owner of a tailless Manx cat, was brought in by Collins to oversee the final draft. The title *Vengeance* came from the British publisher, Christopher MacLehose.

8. "Mickey" Anderson, a British expatriate director of the old school, had been at the helm of such veritable cinematic warhorses as *The Dambusters* and *Around the World in Eighty Days* (for which he won an Academy Award). Robert Lantos, a native of Budapest, is a Canadian edition of Sir Alexander Korda—though the times and personalities are different enough for the comparison to be inexact.

9. Barry Mendel has produced such noted movies as *The Royal Tenenbaums*, while Steven Spielberg (*Schindler's List*, *Saving Private Ryan*) is viewed by many as the leading filmmaker of his period.

10. Ambassador Bernard's remark, "*Ce petit pays merdeux*," was made at the London dinner table of Barbara Amiel. When she mentioned it in a column, the *merde* promptly hit the fan.

11. In *Practicing History*, p. 216.

12. *Los Angeles Times*, May 26, 1968.

13. See Noam Chomsky in *El Pais*, December 12, 2001, *inter alia*.

14. See Ferenc Fejtö in *Historia*, 2000/8, Budapest.

15. A joke suggested that Austro-Hungarians came in two varieties. The more destructive kind—Adolph Zukor, William Fox, Joe Pasternak—created Hollywood; the less destructive kind—Leo Szilard, Edward Teller, Theodor von Kármán, John von Neumann, Eugene Wigner—created the atomic bomb. Budapest alone produced so many (mainly Jewish) scientists and mathematicians in the early twentieth century that Enrico Fermi and Isaac Asimov argued the city must have been colonized by Martians in preparation for taking over the Earth.

Part 8: In Praise of Good Fences

1. August 2002.

2. *National Review,* September 21, 1965.

3. "I am saying that we Italians are not in the same condition as the Americans," wrote the fiery journalist Oriana Fallaci in her 2002 best-selling pamphlet, *The Rage and the Pride.* "We are not their melting pot, their mosaic of diversities glued together by a citizenship. I am saying that just because our cultural identity has been well defined for thousands of years we cannot bear a migratory wave of people who have nothing to do with us." (p. 148.)

4. The mainstream media tended to dismiss all such concerns as belonging to the "xenophobic" or "neo-fascist" fringes, until the surprising first-round victory of Jean-Marie Le Pen in France's presidential elections of 2002, followed by the strong showing of Pim Fortuyn's anti-immigration party in Holland, days after the Dutch politician was assassinated by an animal rights activist. After Le Pen's first-round victory over the socialist prime minister, Lionel Jospin, Martin Sieff of United Press International wrote: "Le Pen's success means that Something Must Be Done About Immigration. France has potentially the most dangerous looming Muslim immigrant problem in Europe." In 2003 President Jacques Chirac felt compelled to outlaw the headscarves worn by French-Muslim schoolgirls. The law was couched in terms of preserving the secular nature of France, and it also prohibited the wearing of Jewish skullcaps and "large" crosses in schools, but popular support for the law was motivated by something entirely different. French people felt that the Muslim community made the girls wear their scarves not for religious reasons, but as a symbol of their resistance to assimilation and a statement of their separate identity.

5. See epigraph.

6. Yugoslavia and Czechoslovakia were themselves products of an ethnic-linguistic-cultural organizing principle asserting itself over earlier dynastic organizing principles. However, after World War II, both Slavic tribal unions were overlaid by the ideological organizing principle of Communism. When that organizing principle withered following the Soviet Union's collapse, even narrower tribal fault lines appeared, splitting the two Slavic unions into their constituent Slovakian and Bohemian (in the case of Czechoslovakia) and Slovenian, Croatian, Bosnian, Serbian, Macedonian, and Montenegrin (in the case of Yugoslavia) parts. Only regions like Albanian-Muslim Kosovo remained attached—tenuously, and probably temporarily—to a nation of a different tribe. Even this took the armed intervention of the North Atlantic

Treaty Organization (NATO) to achieve. Without NATO's bombardment of Serbia, followed by its occupation of Kosovo, the region would either have seceded from Serbia or, more likely, it would have been ethnically cleansed of its Albanian population by the Serbs. Whether such an outcome would have been "better" or "worse" than the de jure maintenance of a union by foreign troops, coupled with the de facto ethnic cleansing of most Serbs from Kosovo, is unnecessary to decide.

7. Water Bagehot, *The English Constitution,* ch. 2 (1867). (Cambridge: Cambridge University Press).

Part 9: Sheep Years and Tiger Days

1. Edward Fox from the Onion Lake Reserve, recorded in the BC Archives [6-015, translation from the Cree].

2. The poem "Ibn Amar the Andalusian 1080 AD" is included in my collection *The East Wind Blows West* (Vancouver: Ronsdale Press, 1993, with a foreword by Barbara Amiel and an afterword by J. Michael Yates).

3. Johnson always told me that he was born in Riga and was adopted by an American couple after the war, but some of his friends believed that he was born in America. The title of his poetry book—Cricket Song—recalled the title of one of Faludy's collection of poems, *Tücsökzene* (Cricket Music).

4. By George F. Will, in a syndicated column, August 26, 2001.

5. 1281–1924; 1794–1925; 1644–1912; 1526–1858, respectively.

6. Newspapers later tagged it "Hitler weather"—dry and sunny, perfect for a blitzkrieg.

Selected Bibliography

Amiel, Barbara. *Confessions*. Toronto: Macmillan of Canada, 1980.

Applebaum, Anne. *Gulag: A History of the Soviet Camps*. London: Allen Lane/ Penguin , 2003.

Barzini, Luigi. *The Italians*. New York: Simon & Schuster, 1964.

———. *The Europeans*. New York: Simon & Schuster, 1983.

Black, Conrad. *Franklin Delano Roosevelt: A Champion of Freedom*. New York: PublicAffairs Books, 2003.

Booth, Clare. *Europe in the Spring*. New York: Alfred A. Knopf, 1940.

Bullock, Alan. *Hitler and Stalin: Parallel Lives*. New York: Alfred A. Knopf, 1991.

Chambers, Whittaker. *Witness*. New York: Random House, 1952.

Charen, Mona. *Useful Idiots: How Liberals Got It Wrong in the Cold War*. Washington, D.C.: Regnery Publishing, 2003.

Drukier, Manny. *Carved in Stone: Holocaust Years—A Boy's Tale*. Toronto: University of Toronto Press, 1996.

Dumitriu, Petru. *Incognito*. London: William Collins Sons & Co., 1964.

Fallaci, Oriana. *Interview With History*. Boston: Houghton Mifflin, 1976.

———. *The Rage and the Pride*. Milan: Rizzoli, 2002.

Faludy, George. *My Happy Days in Hell*. London: Andre Deutsche, 1964.

———. *Erasmus of Rotterdam*. London: Eyre & Spottiswoode, 1970.

Ferguson, Niall. *The Pity of War*. London: Allen Lane/Penguin, 1998.

Fest, Joachim C. *The Face of the Third Reich*. London: Weidenfeld & Nicholson, 1970.

———. *Hitler*. London: Weidenfeld & Nicholson, 1974.

Fisher, H.A.L. *A History of Europe*. London: Edward Arnold & Co., 1936.

Friedman, Thomas L. *The Lexus and the Olive Tree: Understanding Globalization*. New York: Farrar, Straus & Giroux, 1999.

Furet, François. *The Passing of an Illusion: The Idea of Communism in the Twentieth Century*. Chicago: University of Chicago Press, 1999.

Goldhagen, Daniel Jonah. *Hitler's Willing Executioners: Ordinary Germans and the Holocaust*. New York: Alfred A. Knopf, 1996.

Grunwald, Henry. *One Man's America: A Journalist's Search for the Heart of His Country*. New York: Doubleday, 1997.

Haffner, Sebastian. *The Meaning of Hitler*. London: Weidenfeld & Nicholson, 1979.

Harris, Lee. *Civilization and Its Enemies: The Next Stage of History*. New York: Free Press, division of Simon & Schuster, 2004.

Hollander, Paul. *Political Pilgrims: Travels of Western Intellectuals to the Soviet Union, China, and Cuba*. New York: Oxford University Press, 1981.

Hübsch, Dr. Adolph. *Monotheismus ohne Confession: die Religion der Zunkunft* (Non-denominational Monotheism: The Religion of the Future). Csacza: Selbstverlage, 1887.

Judt, Tony. *A Grand Illusion? An Essay on Europe*. New York: Hill and Wang, a division of Farrar, Straus, and Giroux, 1996.

Karafilly, Irena F. *Ashes and Miracles: A Polish Journey*. Toronto: Malcolm Lester Books, 1998.

Karsai, László. *Holokauszt* (Holocaust). Budapest: Pannonia, 2001.

Keegan, John. *The Battle for History*. London: Pimlico (Random House), 1997.

———. *The Iraq War*. Toronto: Key Porter Books, 2004.

Kissinger, Henry. *The White House Years*. Boston: Little, Brown & Co., 1979.

———. *Years of Upheaval*. Boston: Little, Brown & Co., 1982.

———. *Diplomacy*. New York: Simon & Schuster, 1994.

———. *Years of Renewal*. New York: Touchstone Books (Simon & Schuster), 1999.

Klemperer, Victor. *The Diaries of Victor Klemperer, I Shall Bear Witness 1933–41*, and *To The Bitter End 1942–45*. London: Weidenfeld & Nicholson, 1998.

Koestler, Arthur. *The Lotus and the Robot*. London: Hutchinson & Co., 1960.

Kramer, Hilton. *The Twilight of the Intellectuals: Culture and Politics in the Era of the Cold War*. Chicago: Ivan R. Dee, 1999.

Lewis, Bernard. *What Went Wrong? The Clash Between Islam and Modernity in the Middle East*. New York: Oxford University Press, 2002.

Lochery, Neill. *Why Blame Israel? The Facts Behind the Headlines*. Cambridge: Icon Books, 2004.

Lukacs, John. *Budapest 1900: A Historical Portrait of a City and Its Culture*. New York: Weidenfeld & Nicholson, 1988.

————. *A Thread of Years*. New Haven: Yale University Press, 1998.

Lynch, Gerald. *Leacock on Life*. Toronto: University of Toronto Press, 2002.

Maine, Henry Sumner. *Ancient Law*. New York: Holt, 1864. (University of Arizona Press edition, 1986).

Malcolm, Noel. *Kosovo: A Short History*. London: Macmillan, 1998.

Maugham, W. Somerset. *The Summing Up*. New York: International Collectors Library, 1938.

Mazower, Mark. *Dark Continent: Europe's 20th Century*. New York: Alfred A. Knopf, 1998.

Montefiore, Simon Sebag. *Stalin: The Court of the Red Tsar*. London: Weidenfeld & Nicholson, 2003.

Nicolson, Harold. *Diaries and Letters 1930–1964*. London: William Collins Sons & Co., 1966.

Philby, Kim. *My Silent War*. With an introduction by Graham Greene. London: Granada Publishing Limited, 1969.

Pryce-Jones, David. *The War That Never Was: The Fall of the Soviet Empire 1985–1991*. London: Weidenfeld & Nicholson, 1995.

Sacks, Jonathan. *Will We Have Jewish Grandchildren?* London: Vallentine, Mitchell & Co., 1994.

Schmidt, Mária. *Diktaturák Ördögszekerén* (On the Bandwagon of Dictatorships). Budapest: Magvetõ, 1998.

Thatcher, Margaret. *Statecraft: Strategies for a Changing World*. London: HarperCollins, 2002.

Trevor-Roper, H.R. *The Last Days of Hitler*. New York: Macmillan, 1947.

Tuchman, Barbara. *Practicing History*. New York: Alfred A. Knopf, 1981.

Vizinczey, Stephen. *The Rules of Chaos*. London: Macmillan, 1969.

Worthington, Peter. *Looking For Trouble*. Toronto: Key Porter Books, 1984

Zweig, Stefan. *The World of Yesterday (Memoirs of a European)*. New York: Viking Press, 1943.

ACKNOWLEDGMENTS

THE SEEDS OF WHAT BECAME *Beethoven's Mask* were planted in 2001 by Angel Guerra, then an editor of Stoddart Publishing. They were subsequently nurtured by my agent, Linda McKnight.

Four of the seventy-one chapters in the book were inspired by pieces originally commissioned by editors Natasha Hassan, Jonathan Kay, David Warren, and Kenneth Whyte for the *National Post, The Idler,* and *Saturday Night.* They appear here in new and different versions. The rest of the chapters have had no existence in print before.

Former *Time* magazine editor-in-chief Henry Grunwald (since deceased), former U.S. secretary of state Dr. Henry Kissinger, former *National Review* editor John O'Sullivan, and former U.S. assistant secretary for defense Richard Perle generously allowed me to take up their time with some questions.

Hungarian historian Maria Schmidt, Professor Larry Black of the Centre for Research on Canadian-Russian Relations, and Dr. George Fodor of the Heart Institute of Ottawa were kind enough to respond to my queries and call my attention to some literature. Professor Filippo Sabetti of McGill University and Professor Franklin Hugh Adler of Macalester College kindly offered further helpful hints and material. Edward L. Greenspan, Q.C., not only answered my questions about criminal and international law, but told me what questions to ask.

Writers could not function without writer friends. Barbara Amiel read an early version of the manuscript, identified problems, and suggested solutions. Conrad Black, Guy Gavriel Kay, Stephen Vizinczey, and David Warren gave freely of their valuable time to help me with later versions.

Peter Israel and Julian Porter extended the benefit of their legal advice. Maya Jonas, my wife, kept the electronic equipment of printers and computers functioning, in addition to performing many more important offices.

My publisher, Anna Porter, played a pivotal role in shaping the manuscript. Editor Jonathan Webb did his formidable best to save me from myself while he and art director Peter Maher were putting together the final version. Copy editor Wendy Thomas made sure I did not leave too much of a mess. Sheila Wawanash proofread and Belle Wong prepared the index.

Beethoven's Mask is a chronicle, and chronicles are at least partly written by those who appear in them. My co-authors are listed in the text and the footnotes, sometimes anonymously, but usually by name.

I am immensely grateful to them all.

TORONTO, 2005

GJ

INDEX